Oracle9i
Development

BY EXAMPLE

201 West 103rd Street
Indianapolis, Indiana 46290

Dan Hotka

Oracle9i Development by Example

Copyright © 2002 by Que Publishing

International Standard Book Number: 0-7897-2671-8

Library of Congress Catalog Card Number: 20-01098174

Printed in the United States of America

First Printing: December 2001

04 03 02 01   4 3 2 1

Trademarks

Warning and Disclaimer

Associate Publisher
Dean Miller

Executive Editor
Candy Hall

Acquisitions Editor
Michelle Newcomb

Development Editor
Howard Jones

Managing Editor
Thomas Hayes

Project Editor
Tricia Liebig

Copy Editor
Sossity Smith

Indexer
D&G Limited, LLC

Proofreader
D&G Limited, LLC

Technical Editor
Patrick McGrath

Team Coordinator
Cindy Teeters

Media Developer
Michael Hunter

Interior Designer
Karen Ruggles

Cover Designer
Duane Rader

Page Layout
D&G Limited, LLC

Contents at a Glance

Table of Contents

Foreword

Learn from the Experts and Be Humble

Why are DBAs so humble? The answer is that being a DBA is a humbling experience even for the most intelligent perfectionists in the crowd. There are several hundred books on Oracle, but there are few that are written for the beginner. Dan has given the beginner to intermediate Developer or DBA a priceless reference of examples in this new effort.

I remember being the beginner DBA back in 1987. Brad Brown and Joe Trezzo used to play a joke on me back in 1987; they would type the ior i (which was the command to wipe out the entire database) on my computer when I was at lunch. The next statement was "Are you sure Y/N?" to which they would type "Y" and wait for me to return. All I needed to do was press "Enter" and the entire database would be wiped out. Immediately upon getting back from lunch, they would ask me to press "Enter" to start something that they wanted to run on my computer. I would begin to press it, but stopped just in time. After scaring me half-to-death with the almost re-initialization of my database, they would chuckle, insisting that "a good DBA needs be able to assess a situation, act with discipline and react quickly and correctly, we were just testing you." They were right—a good DBA must be able to adapt and overcome like few other professionals. It was my first lesson in becoming a good DBA. Something worth noting is that the ior i would not have actually re-initialized my database. It turned out that Brad and Joe were running a Basic program Brad wrote to replicate the look of Oracle's shutdown process.

My second lesson came from sleep deprivation. We used to have to stay up all night to run certain queries because the system we had could not process everything fast enough. We were running a souped-up 286 PC with the cover off and fans blowing on it to keep the extended memory cards and other boards from melting since we had stacked them on top of each other outside the physical dimensions of the box. It wasn't quite your "off the shelf PC," but it was the closest thing to a mainframe replacement that we could get. We were running several departments that we were converting to Oracle.

Ron Janus, the department leader, was driven to get off the mainframe and into the client server world with Oracle. The only problem was that it didn't exist; not the hardware, not Oracle on client/server and certainly not the architecture that could be replicated from another client. The solution? Hire Brad, Joe, and Rich of Oracle Corporation (in our pre-TUSC days) to invent it—which was exactly what we did. I was the beginner, but I was blazing the trail. Staying up all night was common, and we started to get to a point where we had to find a way to make queries faster, which we finally did by accident one night. I forgot a table in a sub-query join and it turned a four-hour query into four minutes— the correlated sub-query was born! The point is that I would never have discovered this if I weren't a beginner. Being a beginner got me to think out of the box and make some great discoveries, since I had no idea where the box was. That was the good aspect of being the beginner.

The bad aspect of being a beginner was my next lesson. I was loading data one night and some of it got corrupted. I began to delete data and soon became tired of repetitively running similar deletes over and over again, so I decided to write a dynamic delete statement. A mistake in this wonderful statement would deliver more pain to my life than any other IT experience to that point. I could never express how much pain, stress, and disappointment I was feeling as I rebuilt the entire database. It was beyond belief. I wished that I had never started down the DBA track. Few things in all of life felt worse than that night. But once again, those who sow in tears reap in joy. I would end up discovering a new method for recovering corrupted data, one that had never been done before. The benefit of being a beginner once again led to a great discovery.

I eventually became the intermediate-to-advanced DBA, but I was still at the dangerous beginner-to-intermediate level (I knew just enough to be dangerous) on UNIX. I was installing Oracle7 on Data General UNIX. I had convinced a client that they should scrap their plan of a six-month development cycle to port to Oracle7 and instead save all that money by having their DBA and myself migrate to Oracle7 over the weekend. It would be the correct decision, but one that would once again test my tolerance, (and that of the client's excellent DBA, Julie O'Brien) for stress.

The version of Oracle for Data General turned out to be immature (the previous Oracle7's I installed all went well, but were on a different flavor of UNIX). I ended up rebuilding and re-linking the Oracle kernal several times with the help of a top 'C' guru named Jake Van der Vort (now a TUSC VP). I had to repeatedly remove the entire Oracle system every time I tried to re-install. I found a great new UNIX command called rm -r that removed the entire Oracle Home (Oracle's main directory) and all directories underneath. This made it very fast to delete everything and start over.

Somewhere around 3AM, I ended up in the root directory ("/") and ran the `rm -r` thinking that I was in the Oracle directory. When I saw things being removed (like pieces of the operating system), I scrambled to break the command. I was too late. I had deleted the entire operating system. I had to call Data General and in one of the most humbling experiences I've encountered, I had to admit that I had deleted everything, and they would need to reinstall the operating system. After a major scolding, they rebuilt the O/S for me. (I did plead with them to keep this quiet. They later told just about everyone that I knew that I had done this.) I felt like a child approaching my parents just after breaking something they told my not to touch. The experience I gained from this was that I should never make anyone who was a beginner feel as bad as I felt during this experience. Being the beginner (this time on UNIX) was both painful and humbling.

Of course, you want to pretend to be the expert if you don't want people to know that you are a beginner (which is not a very good idea). You can sound like an expert, even if you're a beginner, by using a few of the phrases listed below.

"What's documentation?"

"Do a shutdown abort, restart it and call me if it doesn't work."

"The password is *manager* for a reason."

"I'm not calling support for help, I'm calling to listen to the music while I'm on hold."

Instead of pretending to be the expert, learn to be the expert. Learn from Dan Hotka, so that you don't have to relive the experiences that all DBAs have learned the hard way. The reason that I've shared my experiences is so you'll see the benefits of being the beginner. The frustration and pain that I felt as a beginner were the seeds that helped me grow into an expert. You must grow in both knowledge and experience; one without the other can make you a dangerous DBA.

Read the entire book from expert Dan Hotka! You will increase your knowledge and learn from Dan's experience. This priceless combination is the way to take your knowledge to the next level quickly. Being the beginner DBA is one of the most humbling experiences you will ever have, which is exactly why DBAs are so humble. But, the increase in world productivity over the past decade is, in part, attributable to the tireless hours that these DBAs dedicate to their jobs.

About the Author

Dan Hotka is a Senior Technical Advisor for Quest Software. He has over 23 years in the computer industry and over 18 years experience with Oracle products. He is an acknowledged Oracle expert with Oracle experience dating back to the Oracle V4.0 days. He has authored the popular books *Oracle9i Development by Example* and *Oracle8i from Scratch,* published by Que, co-authored the popular books *Oracle Unleashed, Oracle8 Server Unleashed,* and *Oracle Development Unleashed,* by SAMS, and *Special Edition Using Oracle8 / 8I,* by Que. He is a monthly contributing editor to *Oracle Professional,* a Pinnacle Publication, is frequently published in trade journals, and regularly speaks at Oracle conferences and user groups around the world. Dan can be reached at dhotka@ earthlink.net.

Acknowledgments

I have now been writing about Oracle related topics for over 6 years. What started out as something to help utilize my time while on United Airline, has turned into a rather substantial second job. I again want to thank those who have not only contributed to my work in this book but have made a positive difference in my career and life.

A special thanks goes out to my wife of 23 years, Gail Hackett, and my family. Her patience, love, and understanding have allowed me to take on opportunities such as writing and the travel that comes with my work. I want to thank Elizabeth (Libby), Emily, and Thomas, my children, for giving me the foundation that continues to fuel my success.

I want to make sure to thank the people who help make my writing a success. First and foremost, a thank you very much to Debbie Smith, who ensures my English is correct in all that I write. She is the polish on my writing endeavors. Tim Gorman has to be the most Oracle-knowledgeable person I know. His advice and wisdom has definitely enhanced most every Oracle project I have undertaken. Other technical advice has been gleaned from (not in any particular order): Bradley Brown, Gary Dodge, Daniel Fink, Dave Oldroyd, Guy Harrison, Rich Niemiec, Eyal Aronoff, Swamy Kanathur, Robert Nightengale, Marlene Theriault, Paul Masterson, and D. Scott Wheeler. Thank you for your technical assistance on this project and through the years.

I want to thank those managers who have helped mold my career into the success that I continue to enjoy today: Karl Lenk (Sperry-Rand, Inc.), Gary Dodge (Oracle Corp.), Deb Jenson (Platinum Technology, Inc. and Quest Software, Inc.), and Mike Coffman (Quest Software, Inc.).

Thanks to those editors who trusted me through the years to produce quality manuscript: Michelle Newcomb, Farion Grove, Angela Kozlowski, Heidi Frost, and Rosemarie Graham, as well as their staffs.

I want to thank Mike Swing, Dave Oldroyd, and Jaren Jones of the TruTek company (www.trutek.com) for generating the illustrations for chapters 8, 9, 10, and 11. Their assistance is always appreciated. Dave Oldroyd did an exceptional job in providing the Java, web pages, and XML examples (chapters 10 and 11), an essential part of this book. Jaren Jones created the PL/SQL web examples.

I want to thank Allen Sofley of Quest Software for assisting with material for chapter 16: Using TOAD in the Development Arena.

I want to thank Mark Kieselburg of Quest Software for creating the illustrations for chapter 12: Using Portal v3.0 Web Development Software.

Thank you to all the people listed below, who have made a positive difference in my life and career: Tom Villhauer, Bert Spencer, Bill Schulz, Bob Emly, Bob Kenward, Bradley Brown, Brian Hengen, Buff Emslie, Carol Thompson, Cathy (CW) Fountain, Cathy (CL) Langhurst, Chauncey Kupferschmidt, Cheryl McCarthy, Cindy Swartz, Colette Simpson, Colin Blignault, Conny Vandeweyer, Craig Mullins, Dan Wulfman, Dave Brainard, David Letsch, David Metcalf, David Pearson, David Wagner, Deb Goodnow, Dee Pollock, Derek Ashmore, Don Bishop, Donald Hotka, Don Kerker, Don Schroeder, Dorothy Campbell, Doug Evers, Doug Garn, Doug Tracy, Dwight Miller, Elsie Bishop, Floyd Sturgeon, Gayln Underwood, Gloria Brenneman, Gniadeks, Greg Goodnow, Greg Slaymaker, Haydn Pinnell, Heath Race, Heidi Yocki, Jacqueline Fry, Jane Hambright, Janet Jones, Jay Johnson, Jason Dean, Jeff Sheppard, Jeri McGinnis, Jerry Fox, Jerry Matza, Jerry Meyers, Jerry Wegner, Jim "Toadman" McDaniel, Jim and Mary Sanders, Joe Smith, John Koszarek, John Windchitl, Jon Styre, Julie Nelson, Karen Wicker, Kathie Danielson, Kathleen Morehouse, Kathy Metcalf, Kelsey Thompson, Kevin McGinnis, Kevin Schell, Larry Kleinmeyer, Laurie Nelson, Leyria Walters, Linda Litton, Linda McMahon, Lu Johnson, Lynette Kleinmeyer, Marita Welch, Mark and Ann Sierzant, Mark Harry, Martin N. Greenfield, Martin Rapetti, Mary Bricker, Mary Kenyon, Melvin Morehouse, Michel Clerin, Michelle Campbell, Mike Curtis, Mike Hotz, Mike Metcalf, Mike Nelson, Mike Sanchez, Nancy Taslitz, Neil Bauman, Nicole Tokarski, Ofelia Albrecht, Pat McMahon, Patricia Hemphill, Penny Loupakos, Ramsina Lazari, Randy Spiese, Richard Neimiec, Rick Born, Rick Magnuson, Robert Hotz, Robert Nightingale, Robert Thompson, Robyn Cincinnati, Ron Danielson, Ron Hahn, Ron Innis, Ron Mattia, Ron Smith, Rudy Neimiec, Russ Greene, Sarah Hackett, Scott Bickel, Scott Kane, Sean McGrath, Sharon Reynolds, Sheri Ballard, Shona Freese, Simone Abawat, Steve Albrecht, Steve Black, Steve Healy, Steve Jaschen, Steve Renneer, Svet Bricker, Ted Cohen, Tom Bickel, Troy Amyett, Valda-Jean Robison, Vinny Smith, Walt Bricker, Wass Pogerelov, Wayne Smith, Dean Miller, Candy Hall, Michelly Newcomb, Howard Jones, Tricia Liebig, Sossity Smith, and Patrick McGrath.

And finally, thank you very much to my parents, Philip and Dorothy Hotka; my in-laws, Dean and Marian Hackett; my siblings, Mike Hotka and Janice Hotka; and to my grandmothers, Mamie and Gladys, who will always have a special place in my heart.

Tell Us What You Think!

As the reader of this book, *you* are our most important critic and commentator. We value your opinion and want to know what we're doing right, what we could do better, what areas you'd like to see us publish in, and any other words of wisdom you're willing to pass our way.

As an Associate Publisher for Que, I welcome your comments. You can fax, e-mail, or write me directly to let me know what you did or didn't like about this book—as well as what we can do to make our books stronger.

Please note that I cannot help you with technical problems related to the topic of this book, and that due to the high volume of mail I receive, I might not be able to reply to every message.

When you write, please be sure to include this book's title and author as well as your name and phone or fax number. I will carefully review your comments and share them with the author and editors who worked on the book.

Fax: 317-581-4666

E-mail: feedback@quepublishing.com

Mail: Dean Miller
Que
201 West 103rd Street
Indianapolis, IN 46290 USA

Introduction

How does the *by Example* series make you a better programmer? The *by Example* series teaches programming using the best method possible. After a concept is introduced, you'll see one or more examples of that concept in use. The text acts as a mentor by figuratively looking over your shoulder and showing you new ways to use the concepts you just learned. The examples are numerous. While the material is still fresh, you see example after example demonstrating the way you use the material you just learned. Each chapter also includes a quiz and exercises that allow the reader to review the material in the chapter and use the examples from the chapter to solve the exercises.

The philosophy of the *by Example* series is simple: The best way to teach computer programming is by using multiple examples. Command descriptions, format syntax, and language references are not enough to teach a newcomer a programming language. Only by looking at working examples will the student become productive immediately. This book covers Oracle development around the new Oracle9i (version 9.0) database product, but it is certainly of value with the Oracle8 and 8i releases as well. The examples in this book cover various aspects of developing applications in the Oracle environment with an extensive focus on Web development.

While this book is intended more for the beginner, there are many tips and techniques that even intermediate developers will find of interest, such as how to use the flashback query features, tips, and techniques with the Apache and Oracle9iAS Web servers, and Web-enabling SQL*Plus. The beginner will enjoy the SQL and PL/SQL tutorials, the backbone of the Oracle database product. Knowledge of SQL and PL/SQL will be valuable with the remainder of the book in building forms, reports, Web applications, and Web sites.

This book is ideal for:

- The power-user wanting additional tips and techniques

- IT professionals already familiar with Oracle who want to update their skills

- Developers who want to break into the relational world of Oracle

- Non IT professionals (such as sales or management) that need to know more about the Oracle development environment, its terms, and see examples of how various parts of Oracle work

- Class room instruction with its chapter quizzes and lab exercises

This book is not intended to be an exhaustive repository of Oracle syntax or Web-building techniques. Neither will the book teach you all the nuts and bolts of the Java, XML, and PL/SQL languages. Numerous books are available for that purpose. This book does, however, focus on things such as the following:

- Features of Oracle9i

- How to build Oracle applications

- What referential integrity is and how it is used

- How to design relational database applications with performance in mind

- How to build windows/Web-based/wireless-based applications

- How to use various Oracle tools such as Forms, Reports, SQL*Plus, and Portal

- How to use various new database features such as List Partitioning, Flash-back Queries, and External Tables as well as existing tools such as SQL*Loader, External Tables, Export, and Import

- How to tune SQL

- How to build Web sites using PL/SQL, Java, and XML

- How to enhance HTML Web pages with PSP, JSP, and XML

How This Book Is Organized

This book doesn't make assumptions about your prior Oracle, Windows, or Web development background and therefore gives you the opportunity to learn what you need to know about Oracle and developing application in the Oracle9i database environment. The main focus of this book is to illustrate using key features of the database and development tools with meaningful examples. This book is liberally illustrated with working examples of all the topics.

The chapters are organized as follows:

Chapter 1, "Introducing Oracle9i," discusses the base knowledge of what a relational database is and introduces the key database features and tools that will be used throughout the book.

Chapter 2, "Fundamentals of the SQL Language," is a complete hands-on approach to learning the SQL language, the key ingredient to the Oracle database environment.

Chapter 3, "Fundamentals of PL/SQL," is a good hands-on introduction to PL/SQL, Oracles procedural language. The book then turns its focus to building Oracle9i Based applications with:

Chapter 4, "Building an Oracle9i Database," where relational schema design and database constructs are learned. The Sales Tracking Application Database, the database that many of the books examples will build upon, is introduced and built.

Chapter 5, "Building Oracle Forms," shows you how to build simple and intermediate forms using Oracle Developer v6.0 and v6.i, based in windows but easily converted to the Web.

Chapter 6, "Building Oracle Reports," shows you how to build useful reports with both Oracle Developer v6.0 and v6.i as well as SQL*Plus. This chapter shows techniques to make any of these reports Web based.

Chapter 7, "Using Advanced SQL Techniques and SQL*Plus Reporting Features," is exactly what the title suggests, a more advanced discussion with examples on how to use SQL and SQL*Plus in more creative ways to solve business needs.

Chapter 8, "Building Web Sites with Oracle9i" introduces you to the book example Web site that will be built in the following chapters using a variety of techniques. This Web site is simple but functional, displays pictures and information from the Oracle database, allows control from the user, and accepts input from the Web and updates the database.

Chapter 9, "Using PL/SQL to Build Web Sites," introduces you to the basics of using PL/SQL in the Web arena and then builds the sample Web site discussed in Chapter 8.

Chapter 10, "Using Java to Build Web Sites," introduces you to the basics of Java, how it works, and how it works in the Oracle database environment. This chapter illustrates using Java in the Web arena and then builds the sample Web site discussed in Chapter 8.

Chapter 11, "Using PL/SQL Pages, Java Pages, and XML with Apache/Oracle9iAS" has to be the pinnacle chapter of this development book! There are many tips and techniques for the Apache and Oracle9iAS Web server, mainly setup issues and user access issues. This chapter illustrates how to take existing Web sites and Web pages (developed from any HTML generating type product such as front page, and so on) and make them interactive with the database. This chapter also introduces you to XML and XML style sheets, the vehicle that allows the Oracle database to interface with wireless technologies such as cellular telephones and PDAs.

Chapter 12, "Using Portal v3.0 (WebDB) Web Development Software," wraps up the development part of the book with a discussion about what Portal is and how it can easily be used to create custom Web applications, Web sites, and assist at Oracle database administration and monitoring.

Chapter 13, "Oracle9i Indexing Options," focuses on all the various indexing options available and more important, tips and techniques on how each can be best used by various kinds of applications.

Chapter 14, "Oracle9i Application SQL Tuning," focuses on SQL statement tuning and what is involved in understanding how SQL works with the database. You will learn step by step how to find poorly performing SQL statements and how to correct them. This chapter also contains valuable tips and techniques as well as SQL coding guidelines.

Chapter 15, "Oracle9i Partitioning Features," introduces you to Partitioning and all the Oracle9i partitioning and index partitioning options.

The remainder of this book discusses the various tools and utilities that are useful in the Oracle development arena.

Chapter 16, "Using TOAD in the Development Arena," begins the final section of this book (using Oracle tools) with an excellent tutorial on the TOAD tool, a popular Oracle application development tool. You will learn how to use TOAD and be productive with its various components such as the PL/SQL debugger.

Chapter 17, "Using SQL*Loader, External Tables, and Export/Import," discusses the various data-handling utilities of Oracle9i.

Chapter 18, "Using Log Miner," introduces you to Log Miner and illustrates by example how to examine the Oracle logs, learn practical examples such as UNDO SQL (to reverse a wrong delete or update perhaps), and to see who has been doing what to the database.

Chapter 19, "Putting It All Together: A Sales Tracking Application," discusses how the techniques in this book can be used to build a single application. This chapter builds on Chapter 4 and the Sales Tracking Sample Database, by discussing the application concepts around the database design.

Appendix A contains all the answers to the quizzes found throughout the chapters.

Appendix B is full of listings of all the scripts and program code illustrated throughout the book.

Appendix C contains the Web sites of where to get the source code of the examples in this book and where to get any of the software illustrated in this book.

Glossary contains the definitions of many terms and acronyms used throughout this book.

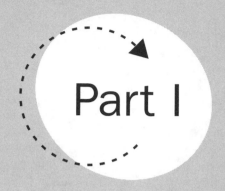

Part I

Learning the Oracle9i Basics

Introducing Oracle9i

Fundamentals of the SQL Language

Fundamentals of PL/SQL

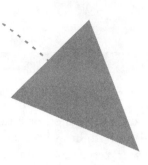

Introduction to Oracle9i

This book will illustrate many of the new Oracle9i database features while proving to be a good learning aid to Oracle Programming. This chapter will focus on some introductory topics such as what is a relational database, what is SQL, the Oracle9i database architecture, and a brief description of the tools that will be used throughout this book. The book is also subdivided into four parts: learning the basics, building applications, tuning issues, and working with tools and utilities. Each of the chapters in these sections will follow these themes.

The reader will learn:

- What is a relational database
- How the SQL language came to be
- Various aspects of the Oracle9i database architecture
- A cursory view of various Oracle related utilities and tools

Oracle—A Relational Database

Relational databases are simply a way of accessing and merging data together where the end user does not need to know how the data will be extracted by the computer. A relational database differs from other kinds of data retrieval methods in that the end user needs only to have an understanding of the data, not an understanding of how to retrieve the data.

Other data retrieval methods include hierarchical and network database systems. Hierarchical data retrieval systems such as ISAM and VSAM are traditionally accessed via COBOL programs in a mainframe environment. Network data retrieval systems such as DMSII (Burroughs), IMS, and IDMS (IBM Mainframe Systems) are also traditionally accessed with a COBOL program utilizing a programmer or a team of programmers that have the knowledge and understand the arrangement of the data. The advantage of these COBOL-based data storage systems is that the access time is traditionally very fast compared to that of relational databases. The huge disadvantage is the complex process for accessing particular data for particular needs. The access to data is very specific and does not lend itself well for today's data warehouse and ad-hoc accesses.

Cobol programming is not for the novice. A simple program can consist of hundreds of lines of code.

What Is a Database?

A hierarchical system stores its data to be later referenced by a particular data or data items known as a key value.

The data is then stored in the order of this key value and can only be accessed by this key value and previous knowledge of what the key value is.

Figure 1.1 depicts how a department and an employee database might be stored in an ISAM hierarchical storage system, or ISAM files. Accessing data in ISAM files is very quick, but the data can only be accessed via its key value. This kind of storage mechanism is very handy for online systems where the data is always accessed via a known number such as a social security number or by last name. Selecting data between ISAM files is handled by the COBOL program by reading the department file first, then reading the employee file, and searching for the particular field. Access can be very fast if the department information is accessed via the employee file. Selecting the data for all employees of department 10 could be a lengthy process. Selecting employees that report to a certain manager could be a lengthy process. Selecting employees by their EmployeeID number is a very quick process. There is no relationship between the department file and the employee file.

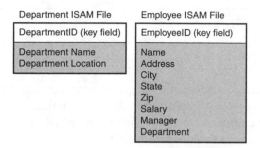

Figure 1.1: *Hierarchical file configuration.*

A network system also stores its data by a key value, but dissimilar data types can be separated into separate storage areas and be reassembled via an access path. For example, in Figure 1.2, accessing data through the department table first would be the only access of the employee data. This storage mechanism is more flexible, as files with single record data such as departments within a company, can easily be related to all the employees that belong to that department.

Once again, access to the data is very quick but the way the data is accessed is always fixed. Selecting data for all employees of department 10 could be a quick process; however, selecting all employees that report to a certain manager could be a very slow process. Note the location of the crow's foot, which indicates that there are employee records associated with each department record. In a network database environment, these employee records can only be retrieved by first reading the department record.

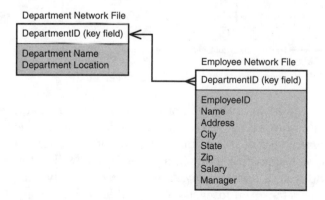

Figure 1.2: *Network file configuration.*

NOTE

Crow's Foot—This data modeling term indicates that there is a one-to-many relationship from this object or file to the one that it points to.

The relational database supports a single, logical structure called a relation, a two-dimensional data structure commonly called a *table* in the database. Attributes or columns contain information about the structure. In Figure 1.3, the employee table contains attributes such as employee name, salary, manager, and so on. The actual data values of a table are called *tuples* or *rows*. A relationship can exist between two or more tables that have no data at all.

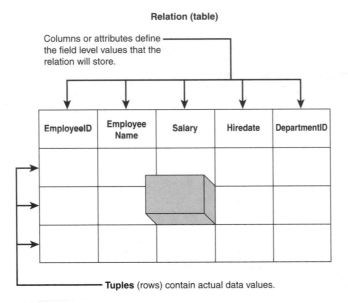

Figure 1.3: Components of Table Employee.

Attributes can be grouped with other attributes based on their relationship with one another and become a composite key or even a composite primary key. A *primary key* is an attribute or group of attributes (composite key) that uniquely identifies a row in a table. Oracle will automatically create a unique index on a primary key. A table can have only one primary key, and when using referential integrity, every table will have one defined. Because primary key values are used as identifiers, they must contain a data item, that is, not be NULL.

NOTE

A composite key is one or more columns, placed at the beginning of the table, in the order of importance, and the group becomes the key value.

You can have additional attributes in a relation with values that you define as unique to the relation. Unlike primary keys, unique keys can contain NULL values. In practice, unique keys are used to prevent duplication in the table rather than to identify rows. Consider a relation that contains the attribute United States Social Security Number (SSN). In some rows, this attribute may be null because not every person has an SSN; however, for a row that contains a non-null value for the SSN attribute, the value must be unique to the relation.

Selecting data from two tables involves a column attribute that is common to both tables. Figure 1.4 shows the relationship between two tables. The relationship between tables can be maintained by the relational database. The primary table or parent table may have one or more related rows in another table or child table. This automatic maintenance and definition is called *Referential Integrity*. Referential integrity rules dictate that foreign key values in one relation reference the primary key values in another relation.

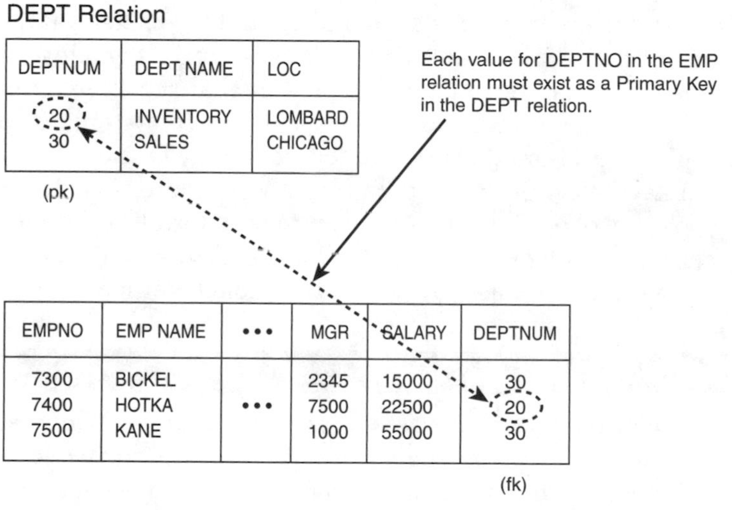

DEPT Relation

DEPTNUM	DEPT NAME	LOC
20	INVENTORY	LOMBARD
30	SALES	CHICAGO

(pk)

Each value for DEPTNO in the EMP relation must exist as a Primary Key in the DEPT relation.

EMPNO	EMP NAME	•••	MGR	SALARY	DEPTNUM
7300	BICKEL	•••	2345	15000	30
7400	HOTKA		7500	22500	20
7500	KANE		1000	55000	30

(fk)

Figure 1.4: *Primary/Foreign key relationships.*

NOTE

Referential integrity is simply SQL code that enforces the relationship between two or more tables based on primary and foreign keys. This really makes the programmer's life easy in our example of employees and departments. With referential integrity defined, the programmer does not need to make sure the department exists in the department table when adding new employees. The Oracle database will check and enforce these rules when defined.

Many tools can take advantage of primary/foreign key relationships and referential integrity rules. You will learn how to use these tools throughout this book. This book will make frequent references to the DEPT and EMP sample tables that install with the Oracle database. These example tables are perfect for learning the SQL syntax. This book will use the EMP and DEPT sample tables through Chapter 4, "Building an Oracle9i Database," then the book will concentrate on the Sales Tracking sample application.

Relational tables have several advantages:

- Tables are easy to create.

- Tables are easy to add to or change.

- Tables are easily related to other tables to present the desired results.

The end user simply needs to understand his or her data, not how to access the data, as depicted in Figure 1.3. Selecting all employees of department 10 is as easy as selecting all employees that report to a certain manager. The user would have the knowledge of the data stored by department and employee and could select data based on any of the columns, not just certain key fields. Selecting data from two or more tables involves a column type (or attribute) that is common to both (or all) tables. One would not relate the Employee Name with the Department ID; however, one could relate the Department ID from each table together.

Introduction to SQL

The relational database uses an industry-standard language called Structured Query Language, or SQL (pronounced *"sequel"*). Dr. E. F. Codd is considered the father of relational databases because of his research in this area. The language, Structured English Query Language (SEQUEL) was initially developed by IBM Corporation, Inc. in 1976, based on Dr. Codd's work. SEQUEL later became SQL (still pronounced *sequel*). Oracle Corp (then Relational Software, Inc.) developed the first commercial relational database using the newly developed SQL language. SQL was adapted in the mid-1980s as the accepted RDBMS standard language.

NOTE

RDBMS stands for Relational Database Management System.

The SQL language easily allows all types of users, including application programmers, database administrators, managers, and end users to access the data. Finally, a relational database management system is the software that manages a relational database. These systems come in several varieties and are available from many different software vendors ranging from single-user desktop systems to full-featured, global, enterprise-wide systems.

The purpose of SQL is to provide an interface to a relational database such as Oracle, and all SQL statements are instructions to the database. In this SQL differs from general-purpose programming languages such as C and BASIC. SQL processes data as groups of records (result sets) rather than as individual records (as in COBOL and other procedural programming languages).

It provides automatic navigation to the data. It uses statements that are complex and powerful individually, and that therefore stand alone. Flow-control statements were not part of SQL originally, but they are found in the recently accepted optional part of SQL, ISO/IEC 9075-5: 1996. Flow-control statements are commonly known as *persistent stored modules* (PSM), and Oracle's PL/SQL extension to SQL is similar to PSM.

Essentially, SQL lets you work with data at the logical level. You need to be concerned with the implementation details only when you want to manipulate the data. For example, to retrieve a set of rows from a table, you define a condition used to filter the rows. All rows satisfying the condition are retrieved in a single step and can be passed as a unit to the user, to another SQL statement, or to an application. You need not deal with the rows one by one, nor do you have to worry about how they are physically stored or retrieved. All SQL statements use the optimizer, a part of Oracle that determines the most efficient means of accessing the specified data. Oracle also provides techniques you can use to make the optimizer perform its job better.

SQL provides a consistent language to control the whole relational database environment. SQL is used to select data from the tables, manipulating data (inserts, updates, and deletes) within the tables, creating/securing/dropping objects, protecting the data and structures (backup and recovery), and sharing data with other relational database environments.

All major relational database management systems support SQL, so the skills you learn in this book can be used with non-Oracle relational database tools.

The academic theory underlying the relational database is somewhat complex, but using and building applications is rather easy. There are three basic components to a relational database: the relational data structures (tables and indexes), the rules that govern the organization of the data structures (constraints), and the creation and manipulation operations that can be performed on the data structures (inserts, updates, and deletes).

Figure 1.5 shows the complexity of traditional programming languages verses the relative ease of using SQL to produce the same results.

```
                    Traditional Procedural Coding method (pseudo code)

raise_date_cutoff := get_delta_date
(get_sysdate(), -6,"month") open/read_write
employee_file
whole not EOF
          read employee_record
          if employee_record(20:2) =: target_department
          then      last_raise := convert_date(employee_rec (43:7))
                    if last_raise > raise_date_cutoff
                    then      salary := decimal_unpack(employee_rec(31:4))
                              salary := salary * 1.06
                              emplyee_rec(31:4) := decimal_pack(salary)
                              rewrite employee
                    end if
          end if
end while
close employee file
```

```
          Nonprocedural Coding Method using SQL

update employee
          set salary = salary * 1.06
          where deptno = :target_department
          and last_raise > add_months(sysdate, -
```

Figure 1.5: *SQL programming versus traditional programming.*

SQL is a nonprocedural language (see Figure 1.6) in that it processes sets of records at a time rather than single records at a time. Oracle uses its optimizer to determine the best method of accessing the data. Oracle has two optimizers: the original rule-based optimizer that makes its decisions based on 19 rules (which include use indexes if they exist, the order of items in the where clause, and so on), and the cost-based optimizer that makes its decisions based on statistics gathered by Oracle's ANALYZE command.

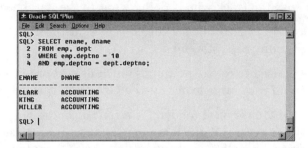

Figure 1.6: *Using SQL to communicate with relational databases.*

SQL provides commands for almost any task, including querying data; inserting, updating, truncating, and deleting rows in a table (data manipulation language or DML); controlling the access to the database and its objects; creating, altering, and dropping of objects (data definition language or DDL); and administrative tasks such as database startup/shutdown, backup and recovery, and so on.

The basic SQL syntax is comprised of the following commands (details of these commands will be covered in various chapters in this book):

- SELECT is used to retrieve information from tables.

- UPDATE makes changes to existing data in tables and indexes.

- INSERT adds data to tables and indexes.

- DELETE removes data from tables and indexes.

- CREATE is used to create almost any object.

- ALTER makes changes to the definition of the objects and/or database settings.

- DROP is used to remove objects from the database.

- COMMIT saves the current pending changes to the database where ROLLBACK removes any uncommitted changes.

- GRANT and REVOKE are used for privilege maintenance on the objects.

Other SQL commands perform specific tasks:

- TRUNCATE quickly removes all the data from a table.

- RENAME allows for objects to be renamed.

- AUDIT is used to track who is doing what to the database.

- EXPLAIN PLAN is used to view the choices that the Oracle optimizer is making for any SQL statement.

- ANALYZE is used to collect statistics (such as sort order, number of rows, size of rows, and so on) for the Oracle cost-based optimizer.

- SET TRANSACTION is used to identify a unit of work. This is useful if there will be several SQL statements that will comprise a unit of work. This transaction mode allows all the SQL statements to be committed or rolled back as a unit of work.

- ROLES are a way of grouping user privileges together and easily assigning these roles to users who have to perform similar tasks.

Chapter 2, "Fundamentals of the SQL Language," covers the basics of the SQL language. The better you understand the SQL language, the better you will understand relational databases.

Oracle9i Features

The Oracle9i family of database products introduced new features such as partitioned tables and indexes (the ability to break each table and index into pieces by a key value and locate across many disk drives). Oracle9i also contains enhancements to previous versions of Oracle such as a new partitioning feature known as *list partitioning*, enhancements to read-consistency known as *Deja-view*, additional buffer pools, multiple block sizes, and major enhancements to Log Miner.

Oracle9i has a new feature called *data pump* that allows for operating-system files to be viewed by Oracle as a relational table. Oracle9i also introduces XML as well as support for Java and SQLJ into the Oracle database environment. Java is one of today's most popular programming languages. Chapter 9, "Using PL/SQL to Build Web Sites" covers using Java to code database functions, procedures, and triggers. Oracle now supports using XML to code these features as well. Chapter 10, "Using Java to Build Web Sites" covers using XML in the database.

Oracle9i continues to support Oracle8's object-oriented features. Oracle9i allows you to define objects and object types (for example, defining data fields such as address, city, state, and ZIP Code as an object and repeatedly using that object)—refer to Listing 1.1. Oracle9 supports the use of nested tables (tables within tables, similar to the network database previously described in this chapter). Where a nested table is similar to the network database is that the rows of the nested table are easily associated with the parent table. Where this configuration differs from the network database is that the nested table can still be accessed as a stand-alone table. Oracle9 also supports arrays, an object type that is similar to a nested table in functionality but is actually part of the row within a table.

Listing 1.1: Creating and Using an Object Type

```
SQL*Plus: Release 9.0.1.0.0 - Production on Sat Aug 11 15:32:14 2001

 Copyright 2001 Oracle Corporation.  All rights reserved.


Connected to:
Oracle9i Enterprise Edition Release 9.0.1.0.0 - Production
With the Partitioning option
JServer Release 9.0.1.0.0 - Production

SQL> CREATE TYPE addr AS OBJECT (
  2       address           varchar2(30),
  3       city              varchar2(20),
  4       state             varchar2(2),
  5       zip_code          varchar2(10)
  6       );

Type Created.

SQL> CREATE TABLE obj_type_test (
  2                           Name      varchar2(30),
  3                           Addr      addr
  4                           );

Table Created.

SQL> INSERT INTO obj_type_test VALUES ('Tom', addr('123 Main Street','
    Any Place','IA','11111'));

1 Row Inserted.

SQL> SELECT name, addr.city
  2  FROM obj_type_test;
```

Listing 1.1:   continued

```
NAME                            ADDR.CITY
--------------------------      ------------------
Tom                             Any Place


SQL>
```

Oracle9i Object-Oriented Programming

Many terms are associated with object-oriented databases or object-oriented programming languages (such as c++ and Java). An *object* consists of both *attributes* (character, number, date, and so on) and *information* (data). Tables and indexes are types of objects.

A *class* is a way of grouping related items together. An Oracle view that combines two or more tables together providing either a subset or a super-set of the combined columns of each table would be one example of a class in the Oracle world.

Encapsulation means that access to the data only happens when the rules are followed. An Oracle9 example of this would be the referential constraints that govern the relationship of data between objects.

Extensibility is the ability to create new objects without affecting other objects. The example in Listing 1.1 describes how an object type can be implemented in Oracle9i.

Inheritance means that a change in one related object type is reflected in all the objects that use the object type. An example of this would be the example in Listing 1.1 where changing the length of the state field would automatically be implemented in all objects that used this `address_type` object. Currently, the Oracle9 database does not implement this level of inheritance.

Polymorphism means that the same object can be given information in different contexts and reacts according to the context of the input. A good example of this in an Oracle9 environment can be visualized using the date data type. Notice in Figure 1.7, the contents of a date field are displayed and the contents of the same field are manipulated by addition. Notice that the field behaved differently based on its point of context, either stand alone or adapting to the addition, even though no other functions were called.

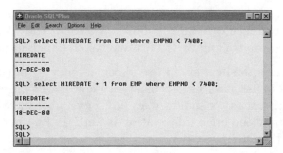

Figure 1.7: *Polymorphism with a DATE object.*

NOTE

An object-oriented database can store the data, information about the data, and methods for accessing the data. Oracle has implemented most of the object-oriented features in Oracle9i.

Oracle9i New Features

Oracle9i has enhanced existing partitioning features to now include longs and lobs. There is also a new partitioning feature called *list partitioning*. Oracle8 introduced range partitioning and handles ranges of numeric and date sequences easily. List partitioning gives Oracle the ability to divide data across partitions based on character data such as the abbreviations for the 50 United States. Listing 1.2 illustrates the list partitioning syntax.

Listing 1.2:   List Partitioning Example

```
CREATE TABLE   emp (
     Empno      number,
     Ename       char(20),
     Eaddress    char(20),
     Estate         char(2),
     Ezip          char(10))
PARTITION BY LIST - (Estate)
(PARTITION Eastern_region VALUES ('VT','NY','CT','MA','ME')
     TABLESPACE TS_Eastern_01,
PARTITION Central_region VALUES ('IA','IL','NE','KS','MN')
     TABLESPACE TS_Central_01,
 .
 .
 .
     );
```

Oracle has always supported a read-consistent view of the database. The redo segments (versions 6, 7, and 8—the before image file before in Oracle versions prior to v6) provided the mechanism to save original information that was being changed, by transaction, in the event that there were SQL queries running prior to any SQL with inserts, updates, or deletes (DML).

Oracle9i has taken the next step in read-consistency by providing the end user the ability to ask for a read-consistent view as of a specific time. This ability to ask for a read-consistent view will have a direct relationship to the amount of time the undo information is kept in the undo tablespace, as determined by the DBA.

This information might be useful for some kinds of reports such as a specific report as of the end of the prior week or month. This information could also be used to undo a change to the database. This would be a much faster solution than using Log Miner. Of course, this kind of undo is only available if the time has not lapsed for the information in the undo tablespace. Log Miner can always be used to undo changes and is not associated at all with the undo tablespace.

Oracle9i now supports multiple block sizes. In Oracle9i, each tablespace can have a different block size. Oracle has added this feature to aid with the transportable-tablespace technology introduced with Oracle v8.

Oracle9i includes features to help make the administration of an Oracle database a bit more automatic such as the automatic addition of tablespace space. Oracle9i will also allow the buffer caches as well as many other features to be adjusted while the database is up and available.

Oracle9i also supports multiple buffer caches. Once again, this will greatly aid the DBA when tuning the database giving the DBA the ability to further separate various types of object access from other types of object access. Objects will be assigned a buffer pool with the new BUFFER_POOL syntax in the storage clause.

Oracle9i supports the concept of resumable SQL. This feature allows for long running SQL statements (such as SQL*Loader, Import, INSERT INTO, SELECT FROM) to suspend themselves if they encounter space related problems. This allows the DBA to fix the problem then resume the process, without interruption to the process.

Oracle has enhanced SQL*Loader to support the direct-path loading of objects. Oracle9i has enhanced the data loading process with external tables. This new feature allows operating-system flat files to be accessed via SQL as if it were already a table in the database. These features are covered in-depth in Chapter 17, "Using SQL*Loader, External Tables and Export/Import." Oracle has also enhanced the Log Miner tool, a useful device to undo erroneous transactions or to perform audit functions external to the Oracle database. Chapter 18, "Using Log Miner," discusses these new features in-depth.

Index-organized tables were introduced in Oracle8 and continue to be supported in Oracle9i. An index-organized table has all the performance features of a standard index on a table but all the data is stored within the index. Index-organized tables are used exactly like tables but with the performance gains of using an index. Oracle9i makes it easier to convert between regular Oracle tables (known as HEAP tables) and these IOT tables.

Oracle Portal V3.0 (WebDB) is an integrated development and monitoring tool for Web-based applications within the Oracle9i Server environment. Oracle Portal enables developers to easily develop Web-based applications. The only software needed to build and deploy Web-based applications is a Web browser. We will cover Oracle Portal in depth in Chapter 11, "Using PL/SWL Pages, Java Pages, and XML with Apache/Oracle9iAS."

Oracle Internet File System (iFS) is a combination of a relational database and a file system. This is a Java application that utilizes the Oracle9i Java environment. The iFS appears to end users and applications as just another file system (like the c:\ drive on your PC). iFS gives access to any file or data stored in the database. Web browsers can display the contents of iFS as normal Web pages. iFS is an easier way of storing various types of files inside the database.

Introduction to Oracle Tools

This book covers the Oracle tools necessary to produce a working Windows and Web-based application. This book will also cover several monitoring and tuning tools used to aid in the maintenance, performance tuning, and problem solving of both the Sales Tracking application environment and the Oracle9i environment.

Oracle development tools have been in the Oracle product set since the version 4 days where forms were called *Fast Forms*, the equivalent of today's wizard that walks the user through building a base form. The reporting tool was a version of today's SQL*Plus, then called *UFI*, or user-friendly interface.

The base-reporting tool was called *RPT* and had some interesting undocumented features. RPT language was the procedural language of Oracle at the time. Oracle v5 brought serious enhancements to the forms and reports-based tools. The forms tool was renamed SQL*Forms v2.0 and a new report writer was added, SQL*ReportWriter v1.0. This version of forms greatly enhanced the programming and capabilities of the online forms. This package of development tools was enhanced through the years, adding a menu package and a graphics development package. Oracle v7 brought some major changes to the database as well as these tools. The tool set was renamed Developer/2000 and was much more Windows-based than the previous character mode development and screens.

The power of the Oracle application-development environment is that these tools are pretty much supported on all environments that the database itself supports. This means that the developer can develop and test an application in a PC environment and deploy it on large UNIX or even main frame computers. This portability of development has been a strength of Oracle since Oracle v4.1.

This book works with Developer v6.0, the latest version of Oracle's application development tools. This environment includes Project Builder, Form Builder, Report Builder, Graphics Builder, Translation Builder, Schema Builder, and Query Builder. This book concentrates on the forms and reports aspects of this tool.

Oracle Developer 6.i (Forms, Reports, and Graphics)

The Project Builder component is what a developer uses to keep all the pieces of the application, such as the various forms and report source code and intermediate code. Project Builder allows the developer to compile single programs or all the programs in the project. Project Builder is a convenient tool used to organize all parts of a particular application-development effort that is using Developer v6.i. Figure 1.8 shows the Project Builder main screen. Note the icons down the left side of the screen; these bring up the Form Builder, Report Builder, Graphics Builder, Procedure Builder, and Query Builder tools.

NOTE

Computers only understand a series of 0s and 1s, machine language. Electronic devices such as a computer only understand a pulse of electricity (a 1) or the lack of a pulse of electricity (a 0). These 1s and 0s are grouped together to create instructions, or commands for the computer to follow. Each 0 or 1 is known as a *bit*. In PCs and Unix, it takes 6 bits to represent a single text character. Imagine the difficulty of programming computers using only a string of 0s and 1s.

NOTE

Source code is the English-like language that a program is coded in by human beings. Intermediate code, or p-code (stands for pseudo code), is what this source language is translated into for a runtime interpreter. This runtime interpreter is another program that translates the p-code on the client computer. Sometimes the interpreter reads the source code and translates this into machine language; however, it is more efficient for the interpreter to translate the p-code.

NOTE

A compiler is a name for the interpreter that converts the program source code into something else, either p-code or machine language.

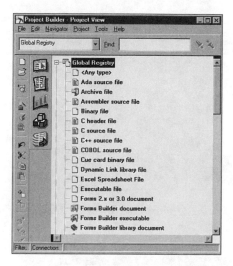

Figure 1.8: *Oracle Project Builder is used to coordinate all the parts of an application.*

Oracle Developer is based on common elements that are used throughout the tool. Once you learn how to use the functionality in one tool, you will understand how to use it throughout the Developer environment.

Oracle Developer contains an Object Navigator that provides a hierarchical structure of all application objects. The Object Navigator provides you with two views: the Ownership view (see Figure 1.9) or the Visual view (see Figure 1.10). The Ownership view displays the objects according to the block representing rows from a table. The Visual view, on the other hand, displays objects according to how they appear on the output screen.

Form Builder is used to build and maintain form-based applications. Programming in Oracle Developer is much different from third-generation languages where the programmer used a text editor and physically wrote the program source code. Applications are built with Oracle Developer by creating onscreen objects that represent the data elements that will be retrieved from the database, visual aspects, program navigation, and so on, see Figure 1.11.

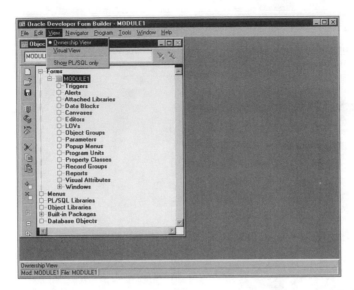

Figure 1.9: *Oracle Navigator Ownership View displays the developed items in navigator form.*

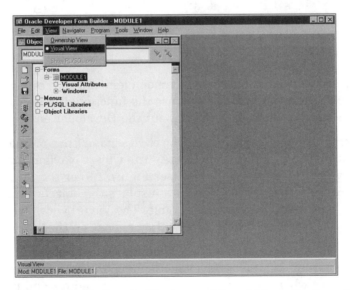

Figure 1.10: *Oracle Navigator Visual View displays the development in a WISIWIG format.*

Selected activities or events are coded in triggers (or program units) that are used whenever the event occurs. Events are like screen navigation, for example, entering a field or exiting a field. A common event to code upon exiting a field would be the data-editing criteria to make sure what was entered in this particular field on the screen was the correct information. This event could be as simple as enforcing a particular date format or ensuring that this data element appears in another table (used as a reference table).

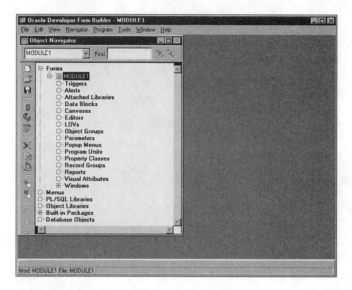

Figure 1.11: *Forms Builder screen.*

NOTE

First-generation language is another term for machine code. The computer only understands a series of 1s and 0s. This makes for very difficult coding. The second-generation languages are languages such as easy-coder and assembler that are a little more English-like but are formatted much like the instructions that the machine is expecting. They are much easier to code in than 1s and 0s but not very English-like either. Third-generation languages such as COBOL made programming much easier. Compilers were then used to read this code and translate it into either the assembly code (p-code per se) or directly into machine language.

NOTE

WYSIWYG (*wizzy-wig*) = What You See Is What You Get.

Report Builder is a wizard-based tool used to create a variety of reports from data from the database (see Figure 1.12). This tool also has a WYSIWYG layout editor. Report Builder has procedural constructs for data formatting, calculating summary information, and so on. This tool could be used to perform database maintenance, but these tasks are better performed by PL/SQL.

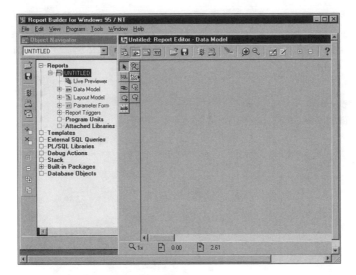

Figure 1.12: *Report Builder screen.*

Graphics Builder is used to generate a variety of types of charts based on data from the database.

SQL*Plus

SQL*Plus (pronounced *sequel plus*) is an interactive character-mode tool for the Oracle9i RDBMS environment. SQL*Plus has a variety of functions in the Oracle environment. You can use SQL*Plus to process SQL statements one at a time or to process SQL statements interactively with end users. SQL*Plus can initiate PL/SQL for the procedural processing of SQL statements as well as to list and print query results. SQL*Plus has powerful character-mode reporting capabilities that can format query results into reports. SQL*Plus is also the character-mode or script processor for administrative functions, and has the ability to accept input from operating-system files or SQL scripts.

NOTE

SQL scripts can contain SQL*Plus report-formatting commands as well as SQL or PL/SQL code. Scripts are commonly used for any repetitive process. SQL*Plus can accept these scripts from the command prompt, and these scripts can also be scheduled to run at predetermined times.

SQL*Plus originated from the beginning of the Oracle RDBMS days as a tool called User Friendly Interface or UFI (pronounced *U-fee*). UFI was used primarily to administer the Oracle database prior to Oracle4. Early administrative tasks included adding users and managing the tablespaces.

Oracle5 brought many enhancements as well as new names for many of the tools. UFI was renamed to SQL*Plus at this time. Some enhancements have been added to SQL*Plus through the years; however, most of the formatting commands and the ease of creating reports are as easy today as they were with the UFI product.

There have been additions to several of the SQL*Plus capabilities, additional ways of starting SQL*Plus, and a changed role for SQL*Plus through the major releases of the Oracle RDBMS kernel. Before Oracle6, for example, using UFI or SQL*Plus was the only way to administer the Oracle database. With Oracle6 came a new tool called SQL*DBA that took over many of the database administrative responsibilities. SQL*DBA had both a graphical mode and a character mode. In Oracle6, additional administrative tasks were added, such as database startup/shutdown and backup/recovery responsibilities. The character mode was still able to run scripts from an operating-system command prompt.

Oracle7 and 8 provide a new interface called *Enterprise Manager* that replaced SQL*DBA as a database-management tool. The character-mode version of SQL*DBA was renamed *Server Manager*. Oracle9i has given these character-mode administrative functions back to SQL*Plus. Future releases of Oracle will not have the Server Manager product. SQL*Plus also exists in the world of client/server and is available with all the major graphical interfaces.

Chapter 2, "Fundamentals of the SQL Language," concentrates on learning SQL and Chapter 6, "Building Oracle Reports," illustrates SQL*Plus formatting commands.

SQL*Loader

Oracle Databases today are ever increasing in complexity and size. Gigabyte-sized databases are common, and data warehouses are often reaching the terabyte-sized range. With the growth of these databases, the need to populate them with external data quickly and efficiently is of paramount importance. To handle this challenge, Oracle provides a tool called SQL*Loader to load data from external data files into an Oracle database.

SQL*Loader has many functions that include the following capabilities:

- Data can be loaded from multiple input datafiles of differing file types.

- Input records can be of fixed and variable lengths.

- Multiple tables can be loaded in the same run. It can also logically load selected records into each respective table.

- SQL functions can be used against input data before loading into tables.

- Multiple physical records can be combined into a single logical record. Likewise, SQL can take a single physical record and load it as multiple logical records.

SQL*Loader can be invoked by typing in sqlload, sqlldr, or sqlldr90 at the command line. The exact command may differ depending on your operating system. Refer to your Oracle operating-system-specific manual for the exact syntax. Please note that all listings and server responses in this chapter may differ from your results based on the operating system that you are using. The sqlldr command accepts numerous command-line parameters. Invoking SQL*Loader without any parameters displays help information on all the valid parameters (see Listing 1.3).

Listing 1.3:   SQL*Loader Help Information

```
Invoking SQL*Loader without parameters:
$ sqlldr
The server responds with help information because SQL*Loader was invoked without
parameters:

SQL*Loader: Release 9.0.1.0.0 - Production on Sun Aug 12 14:36:04 2001

 Copyright 2001 Oracle Corporation.  All rights reserved.


Usage: SQLLOAD keyword=value [,keyword=value,...]

Valid Keywords:

    userid -- ORACLE username/password
   control -- Control file name
       log -- Log file name
       bad -- Bad file name
      data -- Data file name
   discard -- Discard file name
discardmax -- Number of discards to allow        (Default all)
      skip -- Number of logical records to skip  (Default 0)
      load -- Number of logical records to load  (Default all)
    errors -- Number of errors to allow          (Default 50)
      rows -- Number of rows in conventional path bind array or between direct
path data saves
               (Default: Conventional path 64, Direct path all)
  bindsize -- Size of conventional path bind array in bytes  (Default 256000)
    silent -- Suppress messages during run
(header,feedback,errors,discards,partitions)
```

Listing 1.3:   continued

```
    direct -- use direct path                         (Default FALSE)
    parfile -- parameter file: name of file that contains parameter specifications
   parallel -- do parallel load                       (Default FALSE)
       file -- File to allocate extents from
skip_unusable_indexes -- disallow/allow unusable indexes or index partitions
(Default FALSE)
skip_index_maintenance -- do not maintain indexes, mark affected indexes as
unusable  (Default FALSE)
commit_discontinued -- commit loaded rows when load is discontinued  (Default
FALSE)
   readsize -- Size of Read buffer                    (Default 1048576)
external_table -- use external table for load; NOT_USED, GENERATE_ONLY, EXECUTE
(Default NOT_USED)
columnarrayrows -- Number of rows for direct path column array  (Default 5000)
streamsize -- Size of direct path stream buffer in bytes  (Default 256000)
multithreading -- use multithreading in direct path
 resumable -- enable or disable resumable for current session  (Default FALSE)
resumable_name -- text string to help identify resumable statement
resumable_timeout -- wait time (in seconds) for RESUMABLE  (Default 7200)


PLEASE NOTE: Command-line parameters may be specified either by
position or by keywords.  An example of the former case is 'sqlldr
scott/tiger foo'; an example of the latter is 'sqlldr control=foo
userid=scott/tiger'.  One may specify parameters by position before
but not after parameters specified by keywords.  For example,
'sqlldr scott/tiger control=foo logfile=log' is allowed, but
'sqlldr scott/tiger control=foo log' is not, even though the
position of the parameter 'log' is correct.
```

External Tables

External tables is a new facility that makes flat files look like relational tables for the purpose of loading. External tables builds where SQL*Loader leaves off. Because Oracle9i looks at the flat file as a table, data transformation can easily occur via SQL, parallel loading is available, and direct-path loading with index support is possible. This new facility is also completely compatible with SQL*Loader, reading the SQL*Loader control file, making the correct DDL for the new object type. Notice the similarities from the following external table syntax to that you are familiar with in SQL*Loader: both can have field delimiters, record delimiters, identifies bad and log files, and so on.

```
CREATE TABLE emp_load (empno NUMBER, ename VARCHAR(30), ...)
   ORGANIZATION EXTERNAL
   (TYPE ORACLE_LOADER
      DEFAULT DIRECTORY '/Oracle_data_load'
      ACCESS PARAMETERS  -- Specific to the current access driver
```

```
(   fields terminated by ','
    records delimited by newline
    badfile 'bad/bademp_load.dat'
    logfile 'log/logemp_load.dat'
    (empno    integer(4), ename char(10), ...)
    )
    LOCATION ('dat/emp_load111900.dat')
    ...
)
PARALLEL 4
REJECT LIMIT 100;
```

The big difference is that syntax like INSERT INTO EMP SELECT * FROM EMP_LOAD can allow for a single pass of the data when loading Oracle tables. External tables support things a bit more complex like:

```
INSERT INTO EMP
SELECT * FROM EMP_LOAD
WHERE EMP_LOAD.EMPNO NOT IN (
    SELECT EMPNO
    FROM EMP);
```

Of course, you would have the full power of the SQL language such as DECODE to transform the data while it was being loaded. This new feature allows you to do parallel loading from a single file, perform data transformation/conversion, and so on; things that would have necessitated a second pass of a worktable using PL/SQL.

External tables also support an API that is capable of creating DDL and XML for currently defined objects. The new package DBMS_METADATA has two options: GET_DDL and GER_XML. This will facilitate the loading and manipulation of all kinds of objects, not just the traditional relational tables.

Net8

Net8 (called SQL*Net in Oracle 7 and before) is the basis of the Oracle client/server technology. Net8 allows you, the end user, to transparently work with about any version of Oracle on any computer in about any environment without having to program or specifically handle any of the network or connectivity issues. Net8 simplifies Oracle programming because programs (such as Oracle Forms, SQL*Plus, and so on) can be developed and tested on one computer environment and run in a totally different computer environment without any modifications. In the client/server environment (see Figure 1.13), Net8 allows programs to reside and execute on inexpensive PC computers and access data on larger/faster computers. Net8 can also handle thousands of users accessing an Oracle9i environment with the connection manager and multithreaded technology (illustrated in Figure 1.14) component installed.

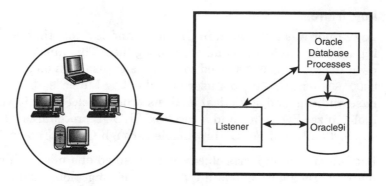

Figure 1.13: *Net8 Client/Server environment.*

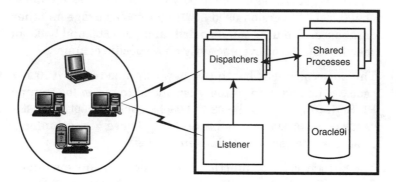

Figure 1.14: *Net8 Client/Server environment using a multi-threaded server.*

An in-depth study of Net8 is beyond the scope of this book. Net8 is a flexible networking protocol that can handle various networking topologies. This allows for Net8 to be able to communicate between the users and the Oracle9i database no matter what the network in place is. Net8 hides the complexities of the network from the programmer and the end user, simplifying the programming of Oracle applications, making Oracle applications very portable, and so on.

NOTE

Network topologies are names given to various network technologies such as the common TCP/IP (the Internet makes big use of this type of network), IPX/SPX (Novell's protocol), and various IBM protocols such as LU6.2 and SNA.

Log Miner

Log Miner was introduced in Oracle8.1 and is a tool that is capable of seeing into the online redo and archive log files. This information can then be used to create REDO SQL used to repeat a transaction on another system and UNDO SQL useful to undo a user mistake. Log Miner is also useful with database auditing and statistical analysis. The Oracle8i and 9i versions of the tool utilizes SQL*Plus and a series of PL/SQL procedures. Oracle9i also supports a Log Miner GUI available through Oracle Enterprise Manager.

Log Miner now supports objects with chained and migrated rows, direct-path inserts additional data types such as longs, lobs, and some object types, including DDL.

The SQL generated by the REDO and UNDO features includes primary keys now (Oracle8i version used ROWID) for easier usage on other target Oracle databases. The user can also drill and get REDO and UNDO for specific users, specific objects, or even activity on a specific column.

This is accomplished with two new columns to the V$LOGMNR_CONTENTS: redo_value and undo_value. Also added to aid in log mining are four new PL/SQL functions to the DBMS_LOGMNR package: COLUMN_PRESENT, MINE_VARCHAR, MINE_NUMBER, and MINE_DATE. These new columns allows the user to access and compare values in the logs.

The column_present function allows the user to view information in the log for specific columns in the SQL. This might make a nice audit facility allowing the DBA to see specific updates to specific columns of specific tables, all without the overhead of the Oracle Audit function.

Log Miner will be covered in depth in Chapter 18.

Export/Import

Export and Import are two character-mode utilities supplied by Oracle Corporation as early as Oracle4. The utilities perform a function that their name implies: export creates operating-system files of data from Oracle tables and import reads these operating-system files and creates the tables and loads the data back into the tables. The two utilities are used together primarily to back up and restore data, move data to other Oracle databases, and migrate data from earlier releases of Oracle to newer releases.

The common utilities Export and Import also have some serious enhancements. Export and Import now support all objects in a particular tablespace as well as wild-card selection when selecting table objects for export.

Export and Import can perform many important tasks in the Oracle9i environment. Export can be used to store data in archives, removing rows that are not being used but can easily be added with Import if the need exists.

Export and Import can be used to create test environments; they have the ability to capture all of a particular user's tables, indexes, and data and re-create in another Oracle instance. Export and Import can also play an important role in database tuning by eliminating certain kinds of fragmentation. Oracle fragmentation and using Export and Import for backup and recovery are beyond the scope of this book.

The operation of the Import and Export utilities is quite straightforward. Export writes the DDL (table definitions, index definitions, privileges, and so on) as well as the data itself. There are many options available to both Export and Import, such as just capturing the DDL information and not the data. Export then saves this information to named operating-system files. The operating-system files that Export creates are known as *dump files*. The dump files, which are in an Oracle proprietary format, are only useful to the Import utility. These dump files can be given specific names (operating-system dependent) or allowed to default to a preassigned name of EXPDAT.DMP.

Listing 1.4 shows the various parameters available for Export, and Listing 1.5 shows the various parameters available for Import.

WARNING

Export creates files that only Import can read and process. Be careful when using Export and Import to move data between different versions of Oracle. Older releases of Import will not necessarily read operating-system files created by newer versions of Export.

Listing 1.4: SQL*Export Help Information

```
Export: Release 9.0.1.0.0 - Production on Sat Aug 11 15:38:22 2001

Copyright 2001 Oracle Corporation.  All rights reserved.



You can let Export prompt you for parameters by entering the EXP
command followed by your username/password:

    Example: EXP SCOTT/TIGER

Or, you can control how Export runs by entering the EXP command followed
by various arguments. To specify parameters, you use keywords:
```

Listing 1.4: continued

```
    Format:  EXP KEYWORD=value or KEYWORD=(value1,value2,...,valueN)
    Example: EXP SCOTT/TIGER GRANTS=Y TABLES=(EMP,DEPT,MGR)
             or TABLES=(T1:P1,T1:P2), if T1 is partitioned table

USERID must be the first parameter on the command line.

Keyword     Description (Default)     Keyword       Description (Default)
-------------------------------------------------------------------------
USERID      username/password         FULL          export entire file (N)
BUFFER      size of data buffer       OWNER         list of owner usernames
FILE        output files (EXPDAT.DMP) TABLES        list of table names
COMPRESS    import into one extent (Y) RECORDLENGTH length of IO record
GRANTS      export grants (Y)         INCTYPE       incremental export type
INDEXES     export indexes (Y)        RECORD        track incr. export (Y)
DIRECT      direct path (N)           TRIGGERS      export triggers (Y)
LOG         log file of screen output STATISTICS    analyze objects (ESTIMATE)
ROWS        export data rows (Y)      PARFILE       parameter filename
CONSISTENT  cross-table consistency   CONSTRAINTS   export constraints (Y)


FEEDBACK              display progress every x rows (0)
FILESIZE              maximum size of each dump file
FLASHBACK_SCN         SCN used to set session snapshot back to
FLASHBACK_TIME        time used to get the SCN closest to the specified time
QUERY                 select clause used to export a subset of a table
RESUMABLE             suspend when a space related error is encountered(N)
RESUMABLE_NAME        text string used to identify resumable statement
RESUMABLE_TIMEOUT     wait time for RESUMABLE
TTS_FULL_CHECK        perform full or partial dependency check for TTS
VOLSIZE               number of bytes to write to each tape volume
TABLESPACES           list of tablespaces to export
TRANSPORT_TABLESPACE export transportable tablespace metadata (N)
TEMPLATE template name which invokes iAS mode export

Export terminated successfully without warnings.
```

Listing 1.5: SQL*Import Help Information

```
Import: Release 9.0.1.0.0 - Production on Sat Aug 11 15:38:44 2001


Copyright 2001 Oracle Corporation.  All rights reserved.
```

Listing 1.5:   continued

You can let Import prompt you for parameters by entering the IMP command followed by your username/password:

    Example: IMP SCOTT/TIGER

Or, you can control how Import runs by entering the IMP command followed by various arguments. To specify parameters, you use keywords:

    Format: IMP KEYWORD=value or KEYWORD=(value1,value2,...,valueN)
    Example: IMP SCOTT/TIGER IGNORE=Y TABLES=(EMP,DEPT) FULL=N
            or TABLES=(T1:P1,T1:P2), if T1 is partitioned table

USERID must be the first parameter on the command line.

Keyword	Description (Default)	Keyword	Description (Default)
USERID	username/password	FULL	import entire file (N)
BUFFER	size of data buffer	FROMUSER	list of owner usernames
FILE	input files (EXPDAT.DMP)	TOUSER	list of usernames
SHOW	just list file contents (N)	TABLES	list of table names
IGNORE	ignore create errors (N)	RECORDLENGTH	length of IO record
GRANTS	import grants (Y)	INCTYPE	incremental import type
INDEXES	import indexes (Y)	COMMIT	commit array insert (N)
ROWS	import data rows (Y)	PARFILE	parameter filename
LOG	log file of screen output	CONSTRAINTS	import constraints (Y)
DESTROY	overwrite tablespace data file (N)		
INDEXFILE	write table/index info to specified file		
SKIP_UNUSABLE_INDEXES	skip maintenance of unusable indexes (N)		
FEEDBACK	display progress every x rows(0)		
TOID_NOVALIDATE	skip validation of specified type ids		
FILESIZE	maximum size of each dump file		
STATISTICS	import precomputed statistics (always)		
RESUMABLE	suspend when a space related error is encountered(N)		
RESUMABLE_NAME	text string used to identify resumable statement		
RESUMABLE_TIMEOUT	wait time for RESUMABLE		
COMPILE	compile procedures, packages, and functions (Y)		
VOLSIZE	number of bytes in file on each volume of a file on tape		

The following keywords only apply to transportable tablespaces
TRANSPORT_TABLESPACE import transportable tablespace metadata (N)

Listing 1.5: continued

```
TABLESPACES tablespaces to be transported into database
DATAFILES datafiles to be transported into database
TTS_OWNERS users that own data in the transportable tablespace set

Import terminated successfully without warnings.
```

There are several database administrative and tuning tasks that are associated with any computer-based application: addition or deletion (when employment is terminated) of users that have access to the system, starting up and shutting down the database, adding additional disk space for the relational tables, monitoring how busy the computer is, and monitoring how well the database is performing.

The first item, DBA Studio (see Figure 1.15), is the main administrative tool that comes with the Oracle9 v9.0.1 software. Quest Software has an easy-to-use tool, Spotlight on Oracle (see Figure 1.16), which helps identify and explain various issues in the Oracle9i database environment. You also learn how to use Quest SQLab/Xpert (see Figure 1.17), a popular tool used to tune SQL statements. The popular PL/SQL development tool TOAD (see Figure 1.18) is covered in Chapter 16, "Using TOAD in the Development Arena," and Figure 1.19 illustrates a new administrative type tool, Quest Central for Oracle. Software availability and trial keys for the Oracle and Quest software are in Appendix B.

NOTE

There are many tools available for Oracle9i to do a variety of functions including monitoring and SQL tuning. I reference and use the Quest Software tools in this book because I am familiar with them and I find them easy to install and learn.

DBA Studio from Oracle Corporation, Figure 1.15, is the tool to use to start/stop the Oracle9i environment, add/modify/delete users, add space to the Oracle9i tablespaces, and make quick changes to the Sales Tracking tables (changes such as adding a column to a table or adding/dropping indexes). You learn how to use this tool in Chapter 6, "Building Oracle Reports."

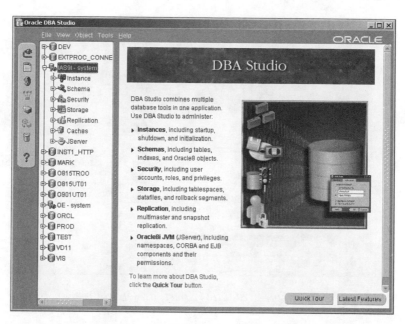

Figure 1.15: *DBA Studio Oracle9i administrative tool.*

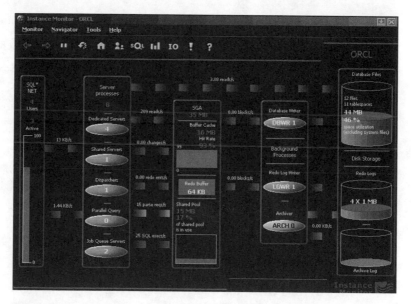

Figure 1.16: *Quest Spotlight on Oracle, an Oracle9i monitor/diagnostics tool.*

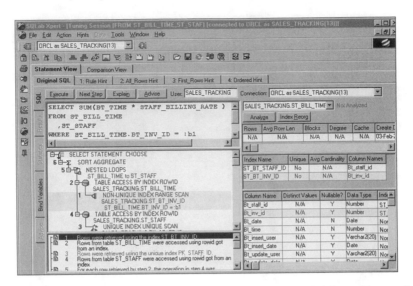

Figure 1.17: *Quest SQLab/Xpert, an Oracle9i SQL tuning tool.*

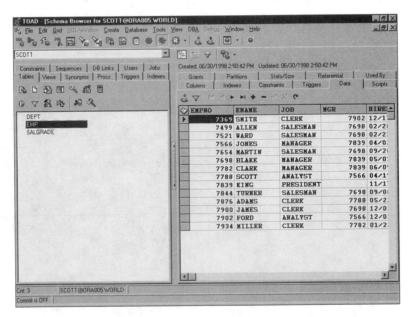

Figure 1.18: *TOAD, an Oracle PL/SQL development tool.*

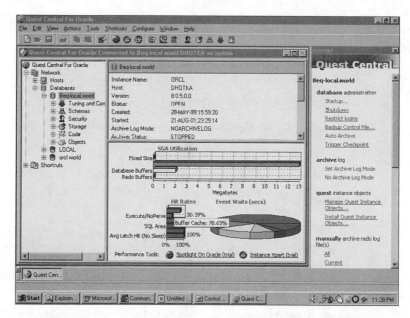

Figure 1.19: *Quest Central for Oracle, an Oracle9i administrative tool.*

Reviewing It

REVIEW

1. What is a relational database?

2. What is the difference between a primary key and a unique key?

3. Who is considered the father of relational databases? What was the first SQL language called? What company produced the first working relational database?

4. The type of SQL used to update data, delete rows, and so on is known as what? The type of SQL used to create objects is known as what?

5. What is Deja-view?

6. List-partitioning is useful for what?

7. How does Data Pump work?

8. What would be a good use of having multiple buffer pools?

9. What is the old name for Net8?

10. Describe the basic role of DBA Studio.

11. Describe Log Miner and what it might be useful for.

CHECK

Checking It

1. Oracle is (mark all that apply)

    a) A hierarchical database

    b) A network database

    c) A relational database

    d) An Object-oriented database

2. ISAM and VSAM are examples of a network database

    True/False

3. Referential integrity is

    a) A relationship enforced at the database level by PL/SQL

    b) A relationship enforced at the database level based on primary and foreign keys

    c) A relationship enforced at the application level by PL/SQL, Java, or XML

    d) A relationship enforced by using concatenated keys

4. Which of the following statements is true:

    a) COBOL works with groups of records

    b) SQL processes data row at a time

    c) SQL lets you work with data at the logical level

    d) It matters to Oracle the order of the data in the database

5. SQL is a procedural language in that it processes sets of records at a time rather than single records at a time.

    True/False

6. Object-oriented support in the Oracle RDBMS was first introduced with which version:

    a) 7.3

    b) 8.0

    c) 8.1

    d) 9.0

7. Resumable SQL allows some Oracle processes/tools to pickup where it left off in the event of space-oriented errors.

   True/False

8. A compiler:

   a) Makes machine language from source code

   b) Makes source code from machine language

   c) Makes runtime interpreters that then read the source code

   d) Makes machine code for runtime interpreters

9. SQL*Plus can:

   a) Process any SQL statement

   b) Handle administrative functions in the database

   c) Can format SQL output into reports

   d) Can take input from a file

   e) All of the above

What's Next?

The objective of this book is to teach you by example how to use Oracle9i to create a complete application, beginning to end.

You will learn:

- How to create GUI Forms-based programs
- How to create GUI and Character-mode reports
- How to use SQL, PL/SQL, and SQL*Plus
- What is necessary to administrate Oracle9i
- How to monitor and tune applications
- How to build Oracle PL/SQL applications
- How to build JAVA applications
- How to build XML applications
- How to create Web-based applications using Oracle developer 6i and Oracle Portal v3.0

In this chapter, you learned the different types of databases present in today's technology environment as well as what a relational database is and where it came from. You also learned some of the new key features of the new Oracle9i database.

The next chapter teaches you the basics of SQL, the basic language that all relational databases share. SQL is used extensively throughout the Oracle database and development tools.

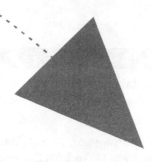

Fundamentals of the SQL Language

This chapter introduces the reader to the SQL language. This chapter is intended for those who are new to the relational database world or perhaps just new to the Oracle database world. For those readers who are new to the relational world, you will find this chapter a great place to start in understanding and working with the SQL language. For those readers new to Oracle, the reader will gain a working knowledge of SQL*Plus; Oracle's main character-mode interface.

The reader will learn

- What is SQL?

- Gain knowledge by using the SQL language

- Understand how to query data, add data, and change data using the SQL language

- Learn basic database creation techniques that will be used in this book and in the real world

SQL Language Basics

Oracle9i is a relational database. All relational databases are based on SQL (Structured Query Language). The better you understand SQL, the more productive you can be in the relational world.

SQL actually has three distinct parts: the query language or SELECT; data manipulation language (DML) that comprises the UPDATE and DELETE commands; and the data definition language (DDL) that has the ALTER, CREATE, RENAME, and DROP commands. There are several various other commands that perform specific functions, such as COMMIT, which tells Oracle that this is desired information and to save it to the database and ROLLBACK, which tells Oracle to discard the changes made by the last SQL statement prior to a COMMIT. There are also a series of commands that control permissions and security such as GRANT, REVOKE, and AUDIT. Other SQL commands include LOCK and VALIDATE.

In this chapter, you learn the basics of SQL as well as useful SQL*Plus SQL formatting commands.

Log In to the Database

Syntax conventions of this book include all-uppercased words indicate SQL syntax in uppercase, user-supplied information, such as variable names, table names, and so on, is lowercase. SQL formatting will always have SELECT, FROM, WHERE, ORDER BY, GROUP BY on separate lines. SQL syntax enclosed with [ ] is optional. Any uppercase SQL syntax that is underlined is the default behavior if no option is specified. User supplied information (such as names) will be in lowercase.

SQL*Plus is the standard SQL character-mode interface to Oracle9i. SQL*Plus is used for ad-hoc queries, character-mode/script reporting, and character-mode/script database administration.

There are several ways to invoke SQL*Plus. The first method discussed is from a command line. The command line can take the following syntax:

```
sqlplus <userid>/<password>@<dblink> <sqlplus file name> <sqlplus
input variables...>
```

The command line can also take any minimal amount of the options, starting from the left of the command. For example, just entering the command SQLPLUS will start SQLPLUS and prompt you for a user id and password. If the SQL*Plus file name option is given with the username and password options, sqlplus is started and the SQL and SQL*Plus syntax in the file (called a sqlplus script) are processed, passing any of the command line options listed as well. If the sqlplus filename option is used and the user-name and password are omitted, the first line in the sqlplus file must be a valid username and password (in the format username/password, a line by itself; see Figure 2.1).

The command prompt method (see Figure 2.1) can be used on any platform that supports Oracle. On the Windows NT environment, open a DOS window (DOS Prompt from the Start Menu) and enter the following command: sqlplus.

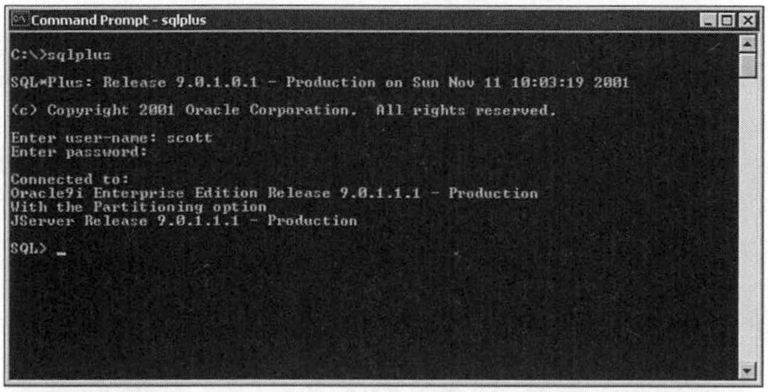

Figure 2.1: *SQL*Plus command line method prompting for user id and password.*

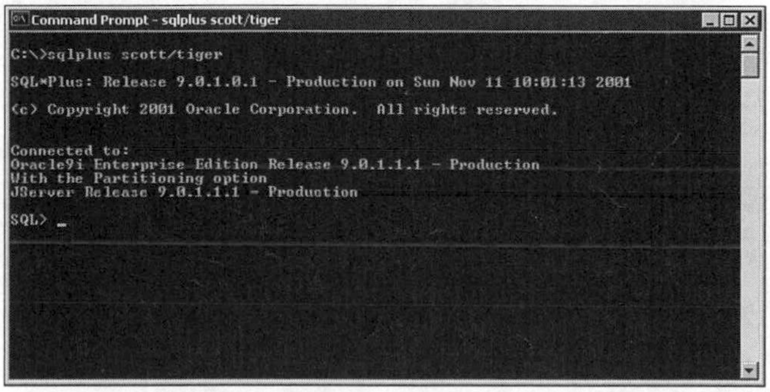

Figure 2.2: *SQL*Plus command line method with user id and password on the command line.*

TIP

Windows and Unix both can record a default sid or Oracle System Identifier that is used when the host string box is left blank. Oracle always needs to know which data-base to log in to. In the case of a single Oracle instance on a single Windows NT work station, you can always leave the host string blank and take the Oracle default that was set at installation time.

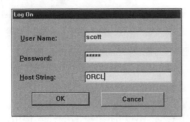

Figure 2.3: SQL*Plus login screen from NT Start menu.

The SQL Editor

The SQL buffer is a work area assigned to the SQL*Plus environment. This buffer only contains SQL or PL/SQL syntax. The contents of this buffer can be loaded, saved, and manipulated with the following commands.

TIP

PL/SQL (pronounced *P - L - S - Q - L*) is an Oracle9i procedural language with SQL imbedded in it. This gives the user the ability to perform various tasks based on row-at-a-time or result set processing of the SQL. PL/SQL is useful for performing looping functions and in-depth calculations based on a variety of variables and other tables.

A or **APPEND** *new text*

Appends text to the end of the current line of the SQL buffer. In Figure 2.4, the L is used to show the current line in the SQL buffer as well as change the current line in the SQL buffer.

```
± Oracle SQL*Plus                                          _□X
 File  Edit  Search  Options  Help
SQL>
SQL> SELECT ename, job
  2  FROM emp
  3
SQL> L
  1  SELECT ename, job
  2* FROM emp
SQL> L 1
  1* SELECT ename, job
SQL> A , sal
  1* SELECT ename, job, sal
SQL> L
  1  SELECT ename, job, sal
  2* FROM emp
SQL> |
```

Figure 2.4: SQL buffer APPEND command.

C or **CHANGE**/target text/new text/

Changes the target text to the new text on the current line in the SQL buffer. Figure 2.5 shows a misspelling of a column name and how L and C are used to quickly correct the problem.

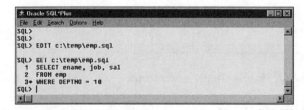

Figure 2.5: SQL buffer CHANGE command.

DEL

Deletes the current line in the SQL buffer.

EDIT *filename*

Utilizes an operating-system-dependent text editor. To edit the SQL buffer with an operating-system dependent text editor (see Figures 2.6 and 2.7), simply leave off the *filename*. The default editor in WindowsNT/95/98 is Notepad; in all Unix environments the default editor is vi. This default editor can be changed in the Windows environments with the regedit command (REGEDIT, HKEY_LOCAL_MACHINE, SOFTWARE, Oracle) or by editing the .profile file on Unix.

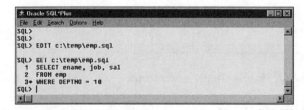

Figure 2.6: SQL buffer EDIT and GET commands.

GET filename

Reads an operating-system-dependent file into the SQL buffer. Figure 2.8 demonstrates how this command can be used in conjunction with the EDIT command (see Figure 2.9) to put the contents of the operating-system file editing back into the SQL Buffer.

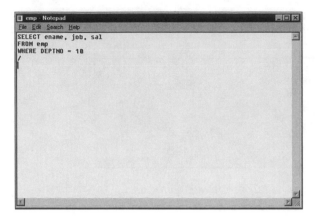

Figure 2.7: *SQL buffer NOTEPAD editing session.*

I or **INPUT** text

Adds the text after the current line in the SQL buffer. Figure 2.8 shows how to use INPUT to insert an additional line to the SQL statement in the SQL buffer.

```
± Oracle SQL*Plus                           _□X
File  Edit  Search  Options  Help
SQL>                                           ▲
SQL> L
  1  SELECT ename, job, sal
  2  FROM emp
  3* WHERE DEPTNO = 10
SQL> I OR DEPTNO = 20
SQL> L
  1  SELECT ename, job, sal
  2  FROM emp
  3  WHERE DEPTNO = 10
  4* OR DEPTNO = 20
SQL> |                                         ▼
◄                                            ►
```

Figure 2.8: *SQL buffer INPUT command.*

L or **LIST** number OR nn nn

Displays the contents of the SQL buffer. When the number syntax is used, LIST will display the line number and make that line the current line in the SQL buffer. The nn nn option will list the range of lines between the two numbers. LIST has been repeatedly demonstrated in this section.

SAVE filename

Saves the contents of the SQL buffer to an operating-system–dependent file with the contents of the SQL buffer.

TIP

When creating SQL*Plus command files, utilize these editing features to arrive at the query results desired: SAVE to the operating system, then edit that file with EDIT to add the formatting and other desired features.

EXAMPLE

START filename param1 param2 … or @filename param1 param2 …

START will execute the contents of the SQL*Plus command file named in *filename* and pass any input parameters to the SQL*Plus command file. The difference between START and GET is that GET reads the contents of an operating-system file and puts the contents in the SQL buffer. START does the same thing but also executes the contents of the SQL buffer. @ has the same functionality as START. Figure 2.9 illustrates the START command use.

TIP

This START feature is utilized when creating the Sales Tracking tablespaces and the Sales Tracking tables and indexes covered in-depth in Chapter 4, "Building an Oracle9i Database." I have used this command to create INSTALL.SQL scripts used to implement application objects.

EXAMPLE

```
± Oracle SQL*Plus                                        _ □ X
File  Edit  Search  Options  Help
SQL>
SQL>
SQL> START c:\temp\emp.sql

ENAME       JOB          SAL
----------  ----------   ----------
CLARK       MANAGER      2450
KING        PRESIDENT    5000
MILLER      CLERK        1300

SQL>
SQL> |
```

Figure 2.9: *SQL buffer* START *command.*

/ (forward slash)

Slash is used to execute whatever is in the SQL buffer. This is a convenient way to execute SQL statements in a SQL script file where START is used to run the whole script. The / will immediately follow the SQL statement on the next line.

Introduction to SQL

The remainder of this chapter is broken up into various sections, each section covering important parts of the SQL language. Each section will build on knowledge gained from the prior section. You will learn how to create SQL queries, create tables/indexes/various database objects, set the correct

SQL permissions, and learn the basics of SQL*Plus reporting. This SQL primer will help you understand the syntax used to create the Sales Tracking application table, index, triggers, and referential integrity.

The DESCRIBE command is very useful for showing the column names and attributes of specific tables. This same information can be viewed by selecting from user_tab_columns. DESCRIBE or DESC for short is easy to remember and gives just the column names and types. These types will be covered in detail later in this chapter when we discuss creating tables.

EXAMPLE

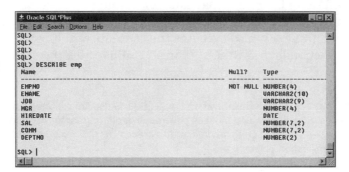

Figure 2.10: *The DESCRIBE command.*

VARCHAR2 (nn) is a variable length character field, where nn is the maximum length. CHAR (nn) is a fixed length character field. NUMBER (nn,dd) is a numeric field where nn is the total length of the field, and if defined, dd is the number of decimal positions. The field types are covered in the section "SQL Creating Objects," later in this chapter.

Tables EMP/DEPT Setup

We will use the Oracle demo tables EMP and DEPT throughout this chapter. These tables are synonymous with the Oracle database; they too have been present since at least the Oracle v4 days. These tables have a minimal amount of data and columns and are perfect for a learning exercise.

Login to SQL*Plus using the user id SCOTT with a password of TIGER. If SQL*Plus complains that this is not a valid user, then log in to SQL*Plus as SYSTEM and star' the script <oracle home>\sqlplus\demo\demobld.sql. If you would like to reset the EMP and DEPT tables back to their original state, run the script demodrop.sql found in the same operating-system directory then run demobld.sql. Figure 2.11 shows a NT directory listing showing these two files and the sqlplus syntax necessary to run them.

NOTE

Scott Bruce was one of the early developers working for Oracle Corp. It is believed that TIGER was his pet cat!

EXAMPLE

```
Command Prompt - sqlplus system/manager@ORCL

 Directory of D:\oracle\ora90\sqlplus\demo

10/09/2001  01:59p    <DIR>          .
10/09/2001  01:59p    <DIR>          ..
05/13/2001  09:01p              3,565 demobld.sql
05/13/2001  09:01p                573 demodrop.sql
               2 File(s)        4,138 bytes
               2 Dir(s)  5,917,851,648 bytes free

D:\oracle\ora90\sqlplus\demo>sqlplus system/manager@ORCL

SQL*Plus: Release 9.0.1.0.1 - Production on Sun Nov 11 10:12:10 2001

(c) Copyright 2001 Oracle Corporation.  All rights reserved.


Connected to:
Oracle9i Enterprise Edition Release 9.0.1.1.1 - Production
With the Partitioning option
JServer Release 9.0.1.1.1 - Production

SQL>
SQL>
SQL> start demobld.sql
```

Figure 2.11: *Creating EMP/DEPT Oracle tutorial tables.*

Learning the Basics

The base syntax of a query would use the SQL key words SELECT, FROM, and WHERE. You will learn additional syntax GROUP BY, HAVING, and ORDER BY used to control how the rows are returned from a table:

SELECT * or column name [alias] [, column name [alias] [,
➥…][function][arithmetic expression]

FROM table name [, table_name [, …] or [sub-query]

➥[WHERE [conditional statement] or [sub-query]]

Let's begin with the simplest SQL query in the book: SELECT * FROM emp; see Figure 2.12.

The basic syntax of a select statement works like this: SELECT all columns (by using an *) or specifically named columns WHERE certain conditions exist or not exist. This WHERE clause can even contain another SQL query.

Single or multiple columns can be selected from a table by specifying the column name after the SELECT clause. Each additional column must be separated by a comma; see Figure 2.13.

The WHERE clause is useful to limit the number of rows returned, or to only return certain rows. Figure 2.13 shows how to select the rows for only those employees that belong to department 10.

EXAMPLE

```
± Oracle SQL*Plus                                        _□×
 File  Edit  Search  Options  Help
SQL>
SQL>
SQL> SELECT * FROM emp;

    EMPNO ENAME      JOB          MGR HIREDATE      SAL      COMM    DEPTNO
    ----- ---------- ---------- ----- --------- -------- -------- --------
     7369 SMITH      CLERK       7902 17-DEC-80      800               20
     7499 ALLEN      SALESMAN    7698 20-FEB-81     1600      300      30
     7521 WARD       SALESMAN    7698 22-FEB-81     1250      500      30
     7566 JONES      MANAGER     7839 02-APR-81     2975               20
     7654 MARTIN     SALESMAN    7698 28-SEP-81     1250     1400      30
     7698 BLAKE      MANAGER     7839 01-MAY-81     2850               30
     7782 CLARK      MANAGER     7839 09-JUN-81     2450               10
     7788 SCOTT      ANALYST     7566 19-APR-87     3000               20
     7839 KING       PRESIDENT        17-NOV-81     5000               10
     7844 TURNER     SALESMAN    7698 08-SEP-81     1500        0      30
     7876 ADAMS      CLERK       7788 23-MAY-87     1100               20
     7900 JAMES      CLERK       7698 03-DEC-81      950               30
     7902 FORD       ANALYST     7566 03-DEC-81     3000               20
     7934 MILLER     CLERK       7782 23-JAN-82     1300               10

14 rows selected.

SQL> |
```

Figure 2.12: *Simplest SQL query.*

EXAMPLE

```
± Oracle SQL*Plus                                        _□×
 File  Edit  Search  Options  Help
SQL>
SQL> SELECT ename, job, sal
  2  FROM emp
  3  WHERE DEPTNO = 10;

ENAME      JOB            SAL
---------- ---------- ---------
CLARK      MANAGER       2450
KING       PRESIDENT     5000
MILLER     CLERK         1300

SQL> |
```

Figure 2.13: *The WHERE clause.*

Because Oracle9i is a relational database, tables are easily related to other tables by using the WHERE clause. Columns with the same data type (or using a function to change the data type discussed in the advanced queries later in this chapter) can easily be related together to select columns from two or more tables that have related data. Figure 2.14 shows how related data is retrieved from both the emp and dept tables. When joined tables have columns with the same name, column references must be qualified to indicate which table columns belong to. Notice line 4 in Figure 2.14 where the emp.deptno and dept.deptno are related together.

SQL Queries

Building on this basic knowledge of the SQL language, you can learn to manipulate the output from queries.

When rows are returned from a SQL statement, they do not have a particular order. They are basically returned in the order that they appear in the underlying Oracle data blocks. There is no guarantee that the rows will be returned in the order that they were inserted.

EXAMPLE

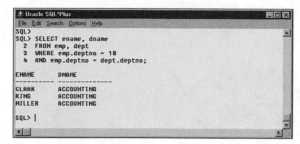

Figure 2.14: *Simple join between two tables.*

The ORDER BY command is used to guarantee a particular order for the rows. Figure 2.15 shows the rows ordered by ename.

EXAMPLE

```
± Oracle SQL*Plus                                    _ □ X
File  Edit  Search  Options  Help
SQL> L
  1   SELECT ename, hiredate, sal
  2   FROM emp
  3*  ORDER BY ename
SQL> /

ENAME      HIREDATE      SAL
---------  ---------   ---------
ADAMS      12-JAN-83      1100
ALLEN      20-FEB-81      1600
BLAKE      01-MAY-81      2850
CLARK      09-JUN-81      2450
FORD       03-DEC-81      3000
JAMES      03-DEC-81       950
JONES      02-APR-81      2975
KING       17-NOV-81      5000
MARTIN     28-SEP-81      1250
MILLER     23-JAN-82      1300
SCOTT      09-DEC-82      3000
SMITH      17-DEC-80       800
TURNER     08-SEP-81      1500
WARD       22-FEB-81      1250

14 rows selected.

SQL> |
```

Figure 2.15: *EMP with ORDER BY ename.*

There are various ways to use ORDER BY. One of the options is either DESCENDING or ASCENDING. The default behavior of ORDER BY is ASCENDING. Figure 2.16 shows the DESCENDING option. In the example, this is handy when the highest number is desired first in the list. Figure 2.16 shows that the order of the columns in the SELECT part of the SQL statement can be used as well on the ORDER BY line. Figure 2.17 shows an ORDER BY clause with the options of 3 DESC, 2, which means order the output by the third column specified in descending order and then by the second column specified in ascending order.

EXAMPLE

```
± Oracle SQL*Plus                    _□×
File  Edit  Search  Options  Help
SQL> l
  1  SELECT ename, hiredate, sal
  2  FROM emp
  3* ORDER BY sal DESC
SQL> /

ENAME      HIREDATE      SAL
---------- ---------- ----------
KING       17-NOV-81    5000
SCOTT      09-DEC-82    3000
FORD       03-DEC-81    3000
JONES      02-APR-81    2975
BLAKE      01-MAY-81    2850
CLARK      09-JUN-81    2450
ALLEN      20-FEB-81    1600
TURNER     08-SEP-81    1500
MILLER     23-JAN-82    1300
WARD       22-FEB-81    1250
MARTIN     28-SEP-81    1250
ADAMS      12-JAN-83    1100
JAMES      03-DEC-81     950
SMITH      17-DEC-80     800

14 rows selected.

SQL> |
```

Figure 2.16: ORDER BY DESCENDING.

```
± Oracle SQL*Plus                    _□×
File  Edit  Search  Options  Help
SQL> L
  1  SELECT ename, hiredate, sal
  2  FROM emp
  3* ORDER BY 3 DESC, 2
SQL> /

ENAME      HIREDATE      SAL
---------- ---------- ----------
KING       17-NOV-81    5000
FORD       03-DEC-81    3000
SCOTT      09-DEC-82    3000
JONES      02-APR-81    2975
BLAKE      01-MAY-81    2850
CLARK      09-JUN-81    2450
ALLEN      20-FEB-81    1600
TURNER     08-SEP-81    1500
MILLER     23-JAN-82    1300
WARD       22-FEB-81    1250
MARTIN     28-SEP-81    1250
ADAMS      12-JAN-83    1100
JAMES      03-DEC-81     950
SMITH      17-DEC-80     800

14 rows selected.

SQL> |
```

Figure 2.17: ORDER BY *additional options.*

There are various ways for selecting specific rows. Previously, we discussed how to use the WHERE clause to limit the rows returned and to join two tables together (refer to Figure 2.14).

Oracle9i supports the whole set of equality and inequality operators:

=	Equal to
!= or <>	Not Equal
>	Greater than
<	Less than

>=	Greater than or equal to
<=	Less than or equal to

Oracle9i also supports the following SQL syntax:

IN (list)	Equal to any item in the list
BETWEEN	Greater than or equal to
AND	Less than or equal to
LIKE %	Matches parts of character strings
IS NULL	Matches on the non-existence of data
NOT (above operators)	Reverses the operation

Some of these options are more efficient for Oracle9i to process than others; this is the topic of discussion in Chapter 7, "Using Advanced SQL Techniques and SQL*Plus Reporting Features." Figure 2.18 shows the BETWEEN operator.

EXAMPLE

Figure 2.18: BETWEEN operator.

Figure 2.19 shows the LIKE command being used to find all names that end in S. Figure 2.20 shows how to find names that have L in the third and forth positions of the name. Notice that % is like a global character in that it will skip any number of characters where _ tells Oracle9i to accept anything in a single position.

EXAMPLE

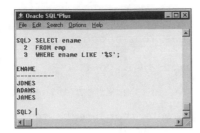

Figure 2.19: *LIKE finding trailing S.*

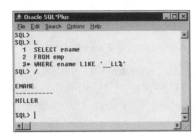

Figure 2.20: *LIKE finding names with LL.*

Fields that do not have a value are *not* blank or zero, they are NULL, or they have no value assigned. You must use the NULL operator to test for the condition of no value in a field. Figure 2.21 shows the Emp table's commission field. Note that there is one row with a 0 commission and several fields where nothing is displaying. Figure 2.22 selects where the commission field is equal to 0; notice that it found the single row with a zero commission field. Figure 2.23 shows that 10 rows are returned when selecting where the commission field is NULL. This proves the previous statement that in regards to numeric fields, zero and null are not the same.

Oracle9i also supports arithmetic operations. These operations are supported in various parts of a SQL statement including the SELECT, WHERE, and ORDER BY clauses. Parentheses ( ) can be used to control the order of evaluation. For example: 4 * SAL + COMM does not produce the same results as 4 * (SAL + COMM).

Figure 2.24 shows various ways to use calculations in a SQL statement. Notice that you can use constants and table columns (SAL * .05) or just table columns against table columns. Later when you learn more about joins, you can perform calculations with data from different tables.

EXAMPLE

```
± Oracle SQL*Plus                          _ □ ×
File  Edit  Search  Options  Help
SQL>                                              ▲
SQL> SELECT ename, sal, comm
  2  FROM emp
  3  /

ENAME            SAL       COMM
---------- --------- ---------
SMITH            800
ALLEN           1600        300
WARD            1250        500
JONES           2975
MARTIN          1250       1400
BLAKE           2850
CLARK           2450
SCOTT           3000
KING            5000
TURNER          1500          0
ADAMS           1100
JAMES            950
FORD            3000
MILLER          1300

14 rows selected.

SQL> |                                           ▼
◄                                            ►
```

Figure 2.21: *SELECT from Emp showing the commissions field.*

EXAMPLE

```
± Oracle SQL*Plus                          _ □ ×
File  Edit  Search  Options  Help
SQL>                                              ▲
SQL> L
  1  SELECT ename, sal, comm
  2  FROM emp
  3* WHERE COMM = 0
SQL> /

ENAME            SAL       COMM
---------- --------- ---------
TURNER          1500          0

SQL> |                                           ▼
◄                                            ►
```

Figure 2.22: *Selecting WHERE COMM = 0.*

EXAMPLE

```
± Oracle SQL*Plus                          _ □ ×
File  Edit  Search  Options  Help
SQL> c/= 0/IS NULL/                              ▲
  3* WHERE COMM IS NULL
SQL> L
  1  SELECT ename, sal, comm
  2  FROM emp
  3* WHERE COMM IS NULL
SQL> /

ENAME            SAL       COMM
---------- --------- ---------
SMITH            800
JONES           2975
BLAKE           2850
CLARK           2450
SCOTT           3000
KING            5000
ADAMS           1100
JAMES            950
FORD            3000
MILLER          1300

10 rows selected.

SQL> |                                           ▼
◄                                            ►
```

Figure 2.23: *Selecting WHERE COMM IS NULL.*

EXAMPLE

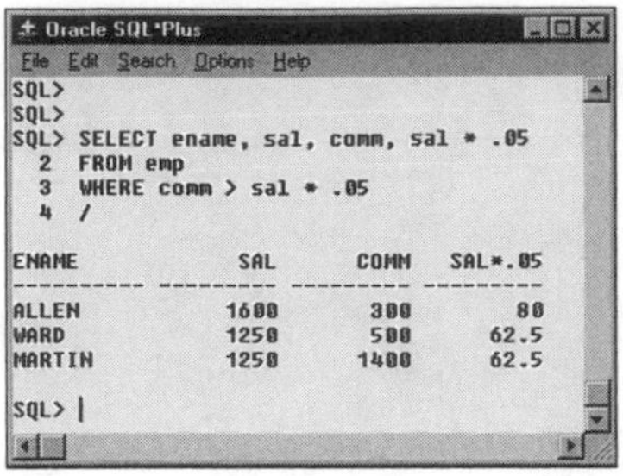

Figure 2.24: *Using calculations in SQL statements.*

In addition, multiple conditions can be specified to satisfy the required results. There are two main operators: AND adds additional selection criteria and OR separates that selection from one condition or another. Figure 2.25 shows an example of using the OR operator.

EXAMPLE

Figure 2.25: *Using the OR operator in a SQL statement.*

Parentheses ( ) can be used to control the order of evaluation. Notice the differences in Figures 2.26 and 2.27. This example wants to choose the managers and salesmen in department 30. Figure 2.26 does not provide the correct results (notice that there is a dept 10 and a dept 20 in the result set) but when parentheses are added in Figure 2.27, the correct results are returned.

SQL Data Manipulation

The SQL language is used to make changes to the data within the tables. This is referred to as *Data Manipulation Language* or DML statements. There are three basic DML statements in the SQL language: INSERT, UPDATE, and DELETE.

EXAMPLE

```
Oracle SQL*Plus
File Edit Search Options Help
SQL> L
  1  SELECT ename, job, deptno
  2  FROM emp
  3  WHERE job = 'MANAGER'
  4  OR job = 'SALESMAN'
  5* AND deptno = 30
SQL> /

ENAME      JOB           DEPTNO
---------- --------- ---------
ALLEN      SALESMAN          30
WARD       SALESMAN          30
JONES      MANAGER           20
MARTIN     SALESMAN          30
BLAKE      MANAGER           30
CLARK      MANAGER           10
TURNER     SALESMAN          30

7 rows selected.

SQL> |
```

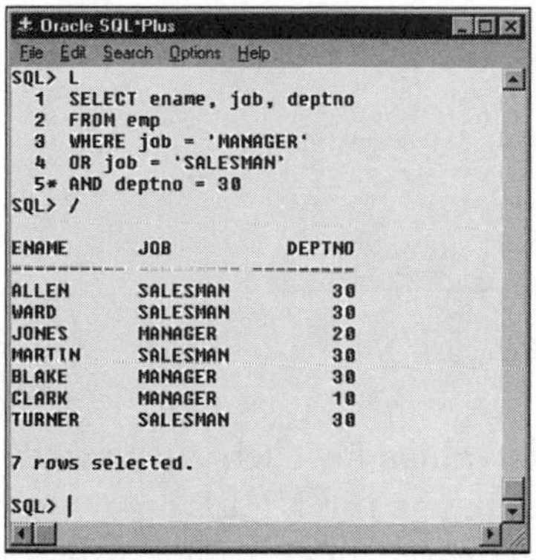

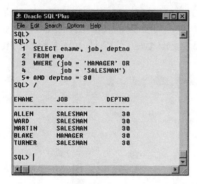

Figure 2.26: *Using AND and OR in a SQL statement.*

```
Oracle SQL*Plus
File Edit Search Options Help
SQL>
SQL> L
  1  SELECT ename, job, deptno
  2  FROM emp
  3  WHERE (job = 'MANAGER' OR
  4         job = 'SALESMAN')
  5* AND deptno = 30
SQL> /

ENAME      JOB           DEPTNO
---------- --------- ---------
ALLEN      SALESMAN          30
WARD       SALESMAN          30
MARTIN     SALESMAN          30
BLAKE      MANAGER           30
TURNER     SALESMAN          30

SQL> |
```

Figure 2.27: *Using AND and OR in a SQL statement with parentheses.*

`INSERT` statements are used to add records to tables. The user must have `UPDATE` privileges to the objects that they will be doing DML against. These privileges are discussed in detail later in this chapter. The `DESCRIBE` command is very useful when adding records to an object.

There are three basic formats of the `INSERT` statement: `INSERT`ing data into all columns of a table; `INSERT`ing just a single column or a subset of the columns; and using a `SELECT` statement to select data from another table.

NOTE

You will learn more about creating tables later in this chapter but for now, please type in the following command to create a table for use in the next series of examples: `create table TEST_CH3 (num_field number(5), char_field char(10), date_field date);`; see Figure 2.28.

EXAMPLE

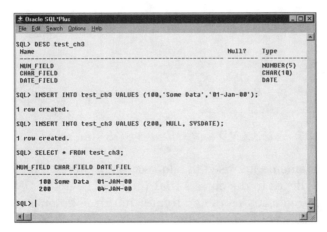

Figure 2.28: *Creating an example table.*

The first INSERT format inserts values for each of the columns of a table. If there is not a value for a column, use the NULL operator to insert a NULL value. Figure 2.29 shows a good series of steps for inserting data. The first step is to do a DESCRIBE of the table to make sure the correct field attributes are used. The first INSERT shows inserting all columns, and the second INSERT shows inserting NULL values and a field called SYSDATE. Insert into the TEST_CH3 table with all the columns; Figure 2.30 shows a similar insert but inserting a NULL value in the CHAR_FIELD column.

EXAMPLE

Figure 2.29: *Inserting data into TEST_CH3.*

TIP

SYSDATE is an Oracle value that always contains the current computer system date and time.

Quotes are needed to tell Oracle9i that the data within is either character data or a date field. Numeric fields do not need quotes. The default date format is DD-MON-YY and can be changed by the DBA. Check with your DBA if you are unsure of the default date format being used at your company.

EXAMPLE

```
± Oracle SQL*Plus                                    _ □ ×
File  Edit  Search  Options  Help
SQL>
SQL> INSERT INTO test_ch3 (num_field, char_field) values (300,'More Data');

1 row created.

SQL> SELECT * FROM test_ch3;

NUM_FIELD CHAR_FIELD DATE_FIEL
--------- ---------- ---------
      100 Some Data  01-JAN-00
      200            04-JAN-00
      300 More Data

SQL> |
```

Figure 2.30: *Inserting data into TEST_CH3 specific columns.*

NOTE

Oracle9i is Y2K compliant. When inserting a date of 01-JAN-00, Oracle9i interprets this as the year 2000, not the year 1900.

SQL*Plus supports the use of substitution variables. You learn more about these later in this chapter when we discuss SQL*Plus Reports. The user is prompted for each field that begins with an &. The && only prompts the user once for a value. Figure 2.31 demonstrates how these substitution variables work when inserting data to the TEST_CH3 table. Notice that if the substitution variable is not enclosed in quotes for character or date fields, they must be provided with the data. This technique of using substitution variables is a quick way to repeatedly add data to a table. The name of the substitution variable can be anything. The more descriptive the name is, the less likely for errors to occur when using this method to enter data.

NOTE

Substitution variables are also very useful in SQL*Plus Reporting, also discussed in this chapter.

The final method for inserting data into a table is by the use of a query to select data from another table. There are many uses for this technique, including moving data from a test environment to a production environment or restoring data from a backup scheme. The SELECT clause must select the same number of columns, in the order listed in the VALUES clause, and be of the same data type as those columns listed in the VALUES clause. Figure 2.32 shows how to populate the TEST_CH3 table with values from the EMP table.

TIP

It is common practice to have one computer environment for the sole purpose of developing applications (test environment) and testing these new applications before deploying them to a production environment, or the computing environment used by the end-users of these computer systems (production environment).

```
± Oracle SQL*Plus                                            _ □ ×
File  Edit  Search  Options  Help
SQL>                                                              ▲
SQL> INSERT INTO test_ch3 VALUES (&Num_Fld,&&Char_Fld,'&Date_Fld');
Enter value for num_fld: 400
Enter value for char_fld: 'Once'
Enter value for date_fld: 10-JAN-00
old   1: INSERT INTO test_ch3 VALUES (&Num_Fld,&&Char_Fld,'&Date_Fld')
new   1: INSERT INTO test_ch3 VALUES (400,'Once','10-JAN-00')

1 row created.

SQL> /
Enter value for num_fld: 500
Enter value for date_fld: 12-JAN-00
old   1: INSERT INTO test_ch3 VALUES (&Num_Fld,&&Char_Fld,'&Date_Fld')
new   1: INSERT INTO test_ch3 VALUES (500,'Once','12-JAN-00')

1 row created.

SQL> SELECT * FROM test_ch3;

NUM_FIELD CHAR_FIELD DATE_FIEL
--------- ---------- ---------
      100 Some Data  01-JAN-00
      200            04-JAN-00
      300 More Data
      400 Once       10-JAN-00
      500 Once       12-JAN-00

SQL>                                                              ▼
```

Figure 2.31: *Inserting data into TEST_CH3 using substitution variables.*

```
± Oracle SQL*Plus                                            _ □ ×
File  Edit  Search  Options  Help
SQL>                                                              ▲
SQL> INSERT INTO test_ch3 (num_field, char_field, date_field)
  2   SELECT empno, ename, hiredate
  3   FROM emp
  4   WHERE deptno = 10;

3 rows created.

SQL> SELECT * FROM test_ch3;

NUM_FIELD CHAR_FIELD DATE_FIEL
--------- ---------- ---------
      100 Some Data  01-JAN-00
      200            04-JAN-00
      300 More Data
      400 Once       10-JAN-00
      500 Once       12-JAN-00
     7782 CLARK      09-JUN-81
     7839 KING       17-NOV-81
     7934 MILLER     23-JAN-82

8 rows selected.

SQL>                                                              ▼
```

Figure 2.32: *Inserting data into TEST_CH3 using a SQL query.*

UPDATE SQL statements are used to change existing data in the tables.
There are two basic formats of the UPDATE command. The basic syntax and
the first format is illustrated in Figure 2.33. Note the format: UPDATE
<table name> SET <col name> = <value or result of a SQL statement>
WHERE <conditional expression>. If the WHERE clause is left off, the UPDATE
will apply the changes to all rows in the table.

EXAMPLE

```
Oracle SQL*Plus                                    _ □ ×
File  Edit  Search  Options  Help
SQL>
SQL>
SQL> UPDATE test_ch3
  2   SET char_field = 'Updated'
  3   WHERE num_field = 200;

1 row updated.

SQL> SELECT * FROM test_ch3;

NUM_FIELD CHAR_FIELD DATE_FIEL
--------- ---------- ---------
      100 Some Data  01-JAN-00
      200 Updated    04-JAN-00
      300 More Data
      400 Once       10-JAN-00
      500 Once       12-JAN-00
     7782 CLARK      09-JUN-81
     7839 KING       17-NOV-81
     7934 MILLER     23-JAN-82

8 rows selected.

SQL> |
```

Figure 2.33: *UPDATE statement on a single column.*

The UPDATE statement in Figure 2.34 shows the second format (updating multiple columns) as well as showing how to update a column with a calculation.

EXAMPLE

```
Oracle SQL*Plus                                    _ □ ×
File  Edit  Search  Options  Help
SQL>
SQL>
SQL> UPDATE test_ch3
  2   SET num_field = num_field + 1, char_field = 'Twice'
  3   WHERE num_field BETWEEN 400 AND 500;

2 rows updated.

SQL> SELECT * FROM test_ch3;

NUM_FIELD CHAR_FIELD DATE_FIEL
--------- ---------- ---------
      100 Some Data  01-JAN-00
      200 Updated    04-JAN-00
      300 More Data
      401 Twice      10-JAN-00
      501 Twice      12-JAN-00
     7782 CLARK      09-JUN-81
     7839 KING       17-NOV-81
     7934 MILLER     23-JAN-82

8 rows selected.

SQL> |
```

Figure 2.34: *UPDATE statement on multiple columns.*

The final DML SQL statement is the DELETE SQL command. Before deleting records from the database, make sure you are deleting the correct records and make sure you can put the records back if necessary. The COUNT(*) function is useful to run with the WHERE clause that is being considered for a DELETE statement.

The other feature that is useful when making changes to the database is COMMIT and ROLLBACK. COMMIT actually writes the requested changes to the Oracle9i database. ROLLBACK allows you to undo any changes made before the COMMIT statement back to the last COMMIT statement. SQL*Plus has a setting called AUTOCOMMIT. By default, autocommit is set on. Figure 2.35 shows a simple scenario that sets autocommit off, deletes from the TEST_ CH3 table, selects to show the empty table, then performs ROLLBACK (without a COMMIT) and again shows the original data.

EXAMPLE

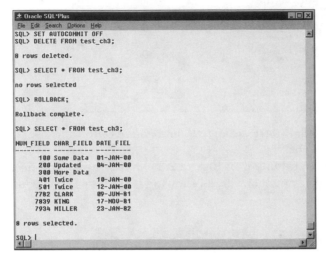

Figure 2.35: COMMIT *and* ROLLBACK *example.*

The DELETE command has only the table being deleted from, and if some selectivity as to what is being deleted is required, a WHERE clause. Figure 2.36 shows the DELETE command with a WHERE clause. Notice how the COUNT(*) function was utilized and showed 4 rows to be deleted when the desired result was to delete only 3 rows. Notice the adjustment made to the WHERE clause of the DELETE statement.

There are two easy ways to delete all the rows from a table. The first is a DELETE command with no WHERE clause and the other is a TRUNCATE command. The differences between the two is beyond the scope of this chapter, but put simply: the DELETE leaves the blocks assigned to the table but just removes the rows; the TRUNCATE command frees all the blocks for use by other objects. This may be desirable if the application calls for varying amounts of data to be temporarily stored in a table, used for reporting, then removed. In this case, it would be better to TRUNCATE the table. When all the rows are being removed from a table, it is invariably better to use the TRUNCATE command.

WARNING

There is no concept of COMMIT or ROLLBACK with TRUNCATE. TRUNCATE overrides these safety features. See Figure 2.37 for an illustration using TRUNCATE with autocommit set off. Notice that all the rows are gone, even after the rollback.

EXAMPLE

```
± Oracle SQL*Plus                                                    _ □ ×
 File  Edit  Search  Options  Help
SQL>
SQL>
SQL> SELECT COUNT(*)
  2   FROM test_ch3
  3   WHERE num_field > 500;

  COUNT(*)
----------
         4

SQL> DELETE FROM test_ch3
  2   WHERE num_field > 501;

3 rows deleted.

Commit complete.
SQL> SELECT * FROM test_ch3;

NUM_FIELD CHAR_FIELD DATE_FIEL
--------- ---------- ---------
      100 Some Data  01-JAN-00
      200 Updated    04-JAN-00
      300 More Data
      401 Twice      10-JAN-00
      501 Twice      12-JAN-00

SQL> |
```

Figure 2.36: *DELETE command.*

EXAMPLE

```
± Oracle SQL*Plus                                                    _ □ ×
 File  Edit  Search  Options  Help
SQL>
SQL> SET AUTOCOMMIT OFF
SQL> TRUNCATE TABLE test_ch3;

Table truncated.

SQL> ROLLBACK
  2   ;

Rollback complete.

SQL> SELECT * FROM test_ch3;

no rows selected

SQL> |
```

Figure 2.37: *TRUNCATE example.*

NOTE

We are done with the TEST_CH3 table. You can remove the TEST_CH3 table with the command DROP TABLE test_ch3 when you are done with the examples in this section, see Figure 2.38.

EXAMPLE

Figure 2.38: *DROP the exercise table.*

SQL Creating Objects

The SQL language is also used to create tables, indexes, and other structures such as database triggers, procedures, and functions. This type of SQL is referred to as Data Definition Language or DDL statements.

NOTE

A database object, in Oracle9i terms, is something that exists within the database that users interact with.

There are several kinds of database objects supported by Oracle9i including

- Tables
- Indexes
- Views
- Sequences
- User-defined data types
- Synonyms
- Clusters
- Constraints
- Tablespaces
- Partitions
- Triggers, Packages, Procedures, Functions

NOTE

While this section provides basic information about creating tables, indexes, views, sequences, user-defined data types, synonyms, constraints, and tablespaces, these topics will be discussed in depth in Chapter 4, "Building an Oracle9i Database," as they pertain to the Sales Tracking application.

Tables are the relational data storage unit in Oracle9i. Indexes allow for quick access to data within tables. Index-organized tables are both a table and an index combined.

Views are a logical table in that they act like tables but are really a SQL query themselves. Views are useful in a number of ways from security (hiding columns/data from certain types of users) to hiding complex SQL access methods from users. A view is accessed with SQL as if it were just a single table.

Sequences are a convenient method of generating sequential numbers. These numbers can be used to ensure uniqueness of rows, or any time an application needs some kind of sequential number.

User-defined data types are definable column attributes, other than the ones that Oracle9i supplies (number, date, character, and so son). These definable data types are convenient for recurring columns such as a series of address fields. They are part of Oracle9i's object-oriented features.

Synonyms provide an easy way to give a table a different or easier name. Synonyms can hide qualification and database links from end users.

NOTE

Qualification in relational terms is stating a table's full name when the same table name might occur in more than one schema. The emp table's fully qualified name is scott.emp.

NOTE

Schema is the term used to describe all database objects created by a particular user. Oracle9i creates a schema automatically when creating a user.

Clusters are a way of physically organizing two or more tables together that have common key fields and are commonly referenced together in the same SQL statement.

Constraints are rules that are applied to the data in tables to ensure the accuracy of the data, the accuracy of the data in relation to other tables, and so on.

Tablespaces is the logical name for the physical operating-system files assigned to Oracle9i. All data-oriented objects (such as tables and indexes) are assigned to a tablespace. You will learn how to direct objects to particular tablespaces for performance and organizational needs in Chapter 4, "Building an Oracle9i Database." Most non-data-oriented objects (such as views, constraints, and so on) are stored in the data dictionary, which is in the SYSTEM tablespace.

Partitions allow data-oriented objects to be split across tablespaces. Remember that physical files are assigned to tablespaces. Partitioning allows for very large tables (tables with millions of rows) to be spread out across several physical disk drives. There are many reasons for doing this, including easier maintenance (backup and recovery), and performance enhancements.

Triggers, packages, procedures, and functions in Oracle9i can either be coded in PL/SQL or Java. You will learn both coding techniques in this book. They are basically code modules that are referenced by SQL or occur because of an event (a post-insert trigger on a table would execute the code assigned to it after a row was inserted into a table).

Figure 2.39 shows the relationship between a table, a tablespace, and the physical operating-system file storage. This example shows the EMP table being created in the C tablespace. The structure of the EMP table is stored in the SYSTEM tablespace in the Oracle9i data dictionary. The data is stored in the extent in tablespace C. It also shows that the EMP tablespace contains one segment or extent that consists of four Oracle9i data blocks.

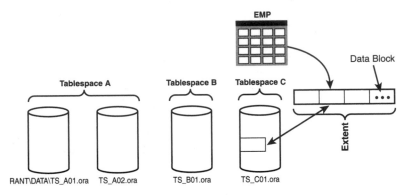

Figure 2.39: *Oracle9i object storage overview.*

NOTE

Chapter 1, "Introducing Oracle9i," covered segments and extents. These terms in Oracle9i are basically synonymous with one another. Oracle9i defines a unit of storage as an extent, and this extent can control one or more data blocks.

TIP

Remember that an extent is a database block or series of contiguous database blocks assigned to the table or index to store rows in.

CREATING TABLES

The CREATE TABLE SQL statement is used to create tables. The basic syntax is

```
CREATE TABLE table_name (column data type [default expression]
[constraint][, …]) [TABLESPACE tablespace name][STORAGE Clause];
```

NOTE

The items between the [ ] are optional.

The table_name must be a unique name for this user. The user must have the CREATE TABLE or CREATE ANY TABLE privilege or the RESOURCE role. These privileges and roles are discussed later in this chapter. The table name must begin with an alpha character, cannot be an Oracle9i reserved word (any SQL syntax, SQL*Plus command, etc, are all reserved words), and can only contain the character set A-Z, a-z, 0-9, _, $, or #.

The standard Oracle9i data types are

- **CHAR (n)**—Fixed-length character field up to 2,000 characters
- **DATE**—Date field—1/1/4712 BC thru 12/31/4712AD
- **NUMBER (n,m)**—Numeric field—up to 38 positions
- **VARCHAR2 (n)**—Variable-length character field—up to 4,000 characters

NOTE

In the previous data types, n = length, m = decimal precision.

The large-object storage data types are

- **LONG**—Variable-length character field up to 2 gigabytes
- **CLOB**—Single-byte character field up to 4 gigabytes
- **NLOB**—Double-byte character field up to 4 gigabytes
- **RAW (& LONG RAW)**—Raw binary field up to 2,000 bytes
- **BLOB**—Binary field up to 4 gigabytes
- **BFILE**—Externally stored binary field up to 4 gigabytes

NOTE

A gigabyte is a trillion bytes. A byte is a single unit of storage that can represent, for example, a character.

NOTE

The Chinese/Japanese languages require double-byte or two bytes of storage to represent a single character.

Figure 2.40 illustrates the CREATE TABLE command. Constraints such as the NOT NULL in Figure 2.40 will be discussed later in this chapter. This table will be created in the USERS tablespace, as this is the default tablespace assigned to the user SCOTT. We could have created the EMP table in a different tablespace by using the TABLESPACE <tablespace name> clause. Notice the NOT NULL constraint and the DEFAULT field value. When rows are inserted into this table, the first field must have a value because of the NOT NULL constraint, and the date field will contain the SYSDATE at the time of the insert if no other value was supplied.

EXAMPLE

```
± Oracle SQL*Plus                                          _ □ X
File  Edit  Search  Options  Help
SQL>
SQL> CREATE TABLE test_emp (empno NUMBER(4) NOT NULL,
  2                          ename VARCHAR(10),
  3                          hiredate DATE DEFAULT SYSDATE);

Table created.

SQL>
SQL> |
```

Figure 2.40: *CREATE TABLE example.*

There are a number of data dictionary views that will display all the information about this particular table.

- **USER_TABLES**—Shows information about the tables owned by the user

- **ALL_TABLES**—Shows information about all the tables the user can access

- **DBA_TABLES**—Only users with the DBA role can see these tables

Figure 2.41 shows a DESCRIBE of the USER_TABLES view. Figure 2.42 shows a SELECT from this view showing the information stored in the Oracle9i data dictionary about our newly created test_emp table. We are only interested in the physical attributes of the test_emp table. Notice that the test_emp table was in fact created in the USERS tablespace and that it also has some storage parameter values. Because we did not supply our test_emp with a storage clause, these values were picked up from the default storage clause of the tablespace. When a storage clause is defined at the CREAT[E?] TABLE statement, it will override the tablespace storage clause.

TIP

The storage clause tells Oracle9i how big to make the extents (how many Oracle data blocks to reserve at a time for data storage), how full to fill the blocks, and so on. The storage clause gives you incredible flexibility in the various data storage requirements for various tables and indexes.

EXAMPLE

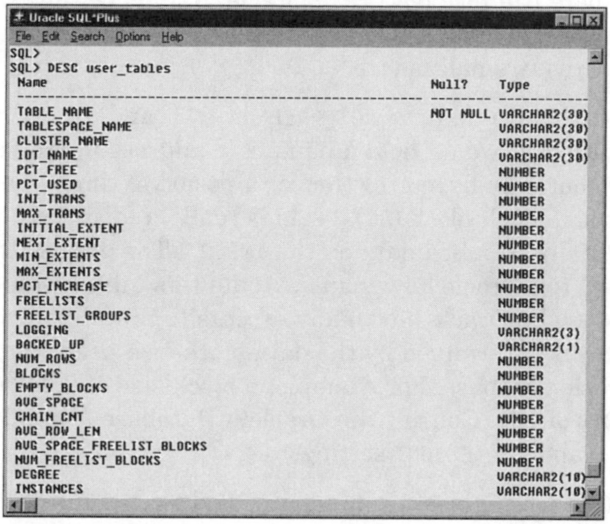


```
SQL>
SQL> DESC user_tables
 Name                                                  Null?    Type
 ----------------------------------------------------- -------- ------------
 TABLE_NAME                                            NOT NULL VARCHAR2(30)
 TABLESPACE_NAME                                                VARCHAR2(30)
 CLUSTER_NAME                                                   VARCHAR2(30)
 IOT_NAME                                                       VARCHAR2(30)
 PCT_FREE                                                       NUMBER
 PCT_USED                                                       NUMBER
 INI_TRANS                                                      NUMBER
 MAX_TRANS                                                      NUMBER
 INITIAL_EXTENT                                                 NUMBER
 NEXT_EXTENT                                                    NUMBER
 MIN_EXTENTS                                                    NUMBER
 MAX_EXTENTS                                                    NUMBER
 PCT_INCREASE                                                   NUMBER
 FREELISTS                                                      NUMBER
 FREELIST_GROUPS                                                NUMBER
 LOGGING                                                        VARCHAR2(3)
 BACKED_UP                                                      VARCHAR2(1)
 NUM_ROWS                                                       NUMBER
 BLOCKS                                                         NUMBER
 EMPTY_BLOCKS                                                   NUMBER
 AVG_SPACE                                                      NUMBER
 CHAIN_CNT                                                      NUMBER
 AVG_ROW_LEN                                                    NUMBER
 AVG_SPACE_FREELIST_BLOCKS                                      NUMBER
 NUM_FREELIST_BLOCKS                                            NUMBER
 DEGREE                                                         VARCHAR2(10)
 INSTANCES                                                      VARCHAR2(10)
```

Figure 2.41: *DESCRIBE of user_tables.*

EXAMPLE

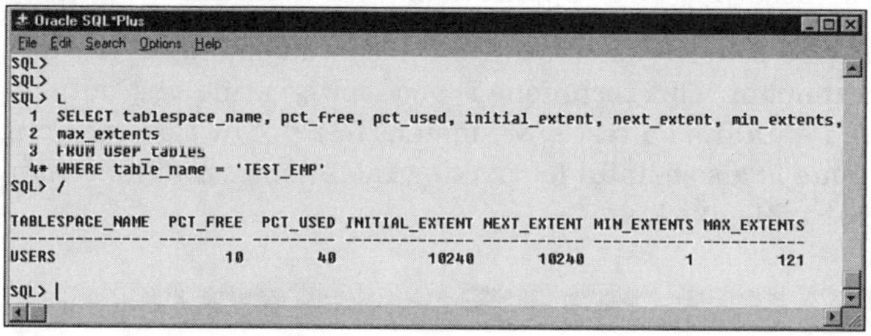


```
SQL>
SQL>
SQL> L
  1  SELECT tablespace_name, pct_free, pct_used, initial_extent, next_extent, min_extents,
  2  max_extents
  3  FROM user_tables
  4* WHERE table_name = 'TEST_EMP'
SQL> /

TABLESPACE_NAME  PCT_FREE  PCT_USED INITIAL_EXTENT NEXT_EXTENT MIN_EXTENTS MAX_EXTENTS
--------------- --------- --------- -------------- ----------- ----------- -----------
USERS                  10        40          10240       10240           1         121

SQL> |
```

Figure 2.42: *SELECT from user_tables.*

Figure 2.42 shows the main storage clause fields: PCT_FREE, PCT_USED, INITIAL_EXTENT, NEXT_EXTENT, MIN_EXTENTS, and MAX_EXTENTS. PCT_FREE and PCT_USED are typically used together to tell Oracle9i how to allocate room in each of the data blocks. When working with these parameters, it is important to understand the nature of the data in the table. PCT_FREE determines the amount of empty space to leave behind in the block for the possibility of accommodating UPDATEs to the rows that might fill NULL fields or add length to existing varchar2 fields. PCT_USED determines when to begin using the block again for UPDATES after this percentage of space exists from DELETE-ing rows. INITIAL_EXTENT tells Oracle9i how many contiguous data blocks to assemble as a unit (EXTENT) and assign to this table.

The INITIAL_EXTENT should be large enough to hold all the initial load of rows as well as about three months of additional rows in the table. The flexibility here is a nice feature of Oracle. Reference tables, such as the abbreviations and names of the 50 states, not only will not change much but are relatively small in size.

A table like this would have PCT_FREE set to 1, and an INITIAL_EXTENT set to 1,000. Tables that would hold a name and address list not only may change frequently, but may have growth over a period of time. The amount of space to leave free in each block (PCT_FREE) is really a factor of how many fields are not initially supplied data on the INSERT. The MIN_EXTENTS and MAX_EXTENTS tell Oracle how many extents this table or index may use. MIN_EXTENTS tells Oracle how many extents to initially allocate to the table. MAX_EXTENTS is determined by the data block size used when initially creating an Oracle database. For example, a block size of 2,048 (2K) has a MAX_EXTENTS of 121. Consult the Oracle9i Database Administrator's Guide for all the valid MAX_EXTENT settings.

A new extent management command called UNLIMITED EXTENTS can replace the MAX_EXTENTS and allow tables and indexes to have as many extents as necessary. This feature can cause adverse performance issues but is useful for those very large applications with thousands of tables and indexes.

Figure 2.43 shows creating a table and populating it with rows with a SQL statement. This technique is good for creating test data or for moving tables and data from a test environment to a production environment. This technique is also helpful for making table copies and its contents to refresh a test table quickly.

EXAMPLE

```
Oracle SQL*Plus
File  Edit  Search  Options  Help
SQL>
SQL>
SQL> CREATE TABLE emp_clerk AS
  2  SELECT ename, hiredate, sal
  3  FROM emp
  4  WHERE job = 'CLERK';

Table created.

SQL> DESC emp_clerk
 Name                                      Null?    Type
 ----------------------------------------- -------- ----------------------------
 ENAME                                              VARCHAR2(10)
 HIREDATE                                           DATE
 SAL                                                NUMBER(7,2)

SQL> |
```

Figure 2.43: CREATE TABLE AS *example.*

SQL allows you to make changes to existing tables. The ALTER TABLE command with the options of ADD, MODIFY, and DROP COLUMN are used for this purpose. The SQL syntax looks like this:

```
ALTER TABLE table name ADD (column datatype [default expression][constraint]
[,column datatype [default expression][constraint]][, …]);
ALTER TABLE table name MODIFY (column datatype [default expression][constraint]
[, column datatype [default expression][constraint]][, …]);
ALTER TABLE table name DROP COLUMN column name;
```

The ADD column command adds a column or columns to the end of the existing table specs. Figure 2.44 builds on the emp_clerk table from Figure 2.48 by adding two fields. The same column specifications that we learned earlier in this section still apply.

EXAMPLE

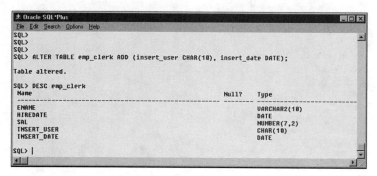

Figure 2.44: ALTER TABLE ADD column example.

The MODIFY column command (see Figure 2.45) changes the column attributes of existing columns. This command can be used to increase the precision of a numeric field or increase the length of a char or varchar2 field. This command can also change a char to a varchar2 or varchar2 to char *if* either the column does not contain any rows or you are not changing the length of the field. You can decrease the size or precision of a field if the table contains no rows and you can change the data type (for example: date to varchar2) if the field contains no data in any of the rows in the table. A change to the default value of a column only applies to new rows added to the table.

The DROP column command is new to Oracle9i. As the syntax implies, only one column can be dropped at a time, and the column being dropped cannot be the last or only column in the table. The column data is immediately deleted and the space is released to the data blocks to accommodate additional INSERTs or UPDATEs. Figure 2.46 shows the DROP column command in use. Another option is to mark the column as UNUSED then DROP the unused columns at a later time. The column data is not physically removed from the data blocks; however, there is no way to undrop a column.

Figure 2.45: ALTER TABLE MODIFY column example.

Figure 2.46: ALTER TABLE DROP column example.

Figure 2.47 shows the SET UNUSED command. Notice the similarities to the DROP COLUMN example, Figure 2.46. Both commands will remove the column from future use. Both commands will allow the same column name to be immediately reused; however, note that this will be a new column and any data associated with the dropped or unused column will no longer be available.

Figure 2.47: ALTER TABLE SET UNUSED example.

The DROP UNUSED COLUMNS command (see Figure 2.48) is used to physically remove the column data from the table's data blocks.

> **TIP**
>
> There is no undrop, a dropped column is unrecoverable. Use Oracle Export to make a backup copy of the table prior to the change in case there would be a need to have the column and its data back.

EXAMPLE

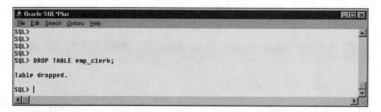

Figure 2.48: ALTER TABLE DROP UNUSED COLUMNS *example.*

We briefly discussed the DROP TABLE <table name> command in the prior section, but it is also quite easy to drop the table and its data. Figure 2.49 shows the DROP TABLE command in use. This command will remove the table and its columns from the data dictionary and return its allocated data blocks back to the tablespace for use with other tables and indexes.

EXAMPLE

```
± Oracle SQL*Plus                                          _ □ X
File  Edit  Search  Options  Help
SQL>
SQL>
SQL>
SQL>
SQL> DROP TABLE emp_clerk;

Table dropped.

SQL> |
```

Figure 2.49: DROP TABLE *example.*

CREATING INDEXES

An index is a sorted list of commonly accessed data based on one or more columns from the associated table. This data is associated with the ROWID, which is a pointer to the block that contains the particular row of data. Maintenance of an index is completely automatic. There is no difference in how the table is accessed or the rows returned if a particular table column has an index or not. Indexes can be created and dropped with no effect on the table.

The main reason for indexes is for faster retrieval of certain rows. Chapter 14, "Oracle9i Application SQL Tuning," discusses exactly why to create indexes, how to control their use, and so on. A table column should have an index if the number of rows returned by placing a WHERE clause on the column is less than 5% of the number of rows in the entire table, the column is frequently used in join conditions with other tables, the column contains a wide variety of values, or the column has a large number of null values. There is a distinct trade-off of table insert and update performance depending on the number of indexes on a particular table. In another words, don't create an index on every column of the table, especially if that table will have frequent inserts.

The basic syntax of the INDEX command is

```
CREATE [UNIQUE] INDEX index name ON TABLE table name (column name
    [, column name][, …]) [TABLESPACE tablespace name][STORAGE parameters] ;
```

An index can be created on one or more columns. When the index contains more than one column, this is called a composite key. Indexes are automatically created when the PRIMARY KEY CONSTRAINT is specified. If the UNIQUE clause is specified, an error will be returned if you try to insert a row where the index column already exists.

Indexes are automatically used when the indexed column is specified in the WHERE clause.

Figure 2.50 illustrates how to create an index on the EMP table.

EXAMPLE

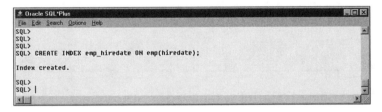

Figure 2.50: *CREATE INDEX example.*

Figure 2.51 shows the information that is available from the USER_INDEXES view about this new index or all indexes.

Figure 2.52 shows information on the indexed columns from USER_IND_COLUMNS.

EXAMPLE

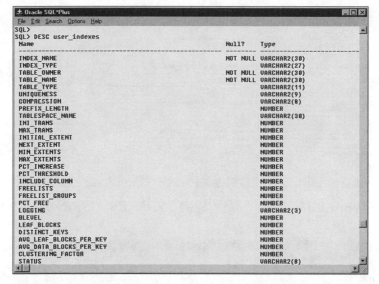

Figure 2.51: *Index information available from USER_INDEXES.*

EXAMPLE

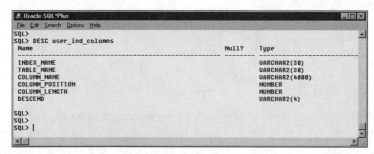

Figure 2.52: *Index information available from USER_IND_COLUMNS.*

Figure 2.53 shows specific information from the USER_INDEXES and USER_IND_COLUMNS views. Notice that the new index was created in the USERS tablespace and that the new index is nonunique. Also notice that the primary key index is a unique index, one of the characteristics of a primary key.

Figure 2.54 shows how to drop an index.

EXAMPLE

```
± Oracle SQL*Plus                                              _□X
 File  Edit  Search  Options  Help
SQL>
SQL> SELECT index_name, uniqueness, tablespace_name
  2  FROM user_indexes
  3  WHERE table_name = 'EMP';

INDEX_NAME                        UNIQUENES TABLESPACE_NAME
--------------------------------- --------- ----------------
EMP_HIREDATE                      NONUNIQUE USERS
PK_EMP                            UNIQUE    USERS

SQL> SELECT index_name,column_name,column_position
  2  FROM user_ind_columns
  3  WHERE table_name = 'EMP';

INDEX_NAME                        COLUMN_NAME    COLUMN_POSITION
--------------------------------- -------------- ---------------
PK_EMP                            EMPNO                        1
EMP_HIREDATE                      HIREDATE                     1

SQL> |
```

Figure 2.53: Select from USER_INDEXES, USER_IND_COLUMNS.

EXAMPLE

```
± Oracle SQL*Plus                                              _□X
 File  Edit  Search  Options  Help
SQL>
SQL>
SQL>
SQL> DROP INDEX emp_hiredate;

Index dropped.

SQL>
SQL>
SQL> |
```

Figure 2.54: DROP INDEX example.

CREATING VIEWS

A view is a selection of one or more columns from one or more tables. A view is a query that acts like a table. Views do not store data so they are not assigned to tablespaces and do not require storage parameters. A view is nothing more than a stored SQL statement in the Oracle9i Data Dictionary.

Views can be useful to hide complex calculations from users (allowing for simple SQL queries to gather complex calculated data), to hide certain columns from some levels of users (a good human resource view would be one that displayed name, address, and hire information but not salary/ bonus information), and so on.

There are two types of views: the simple view that is associated with only one table and has no GROUP BY or functions in the SQL; the complex view is associated with two or more tables, contains functions or GROUP BY clauses. The main difference is that the simple view will allow for DML where the complex view will not.

NOTE

All of the NOT NULL columns must be present in the view to allow for INSERT activity.

TIP

Do all DML through the base table/tables and use views to restrict column access or provide ease of access to rather complex combinations of information.

The syntax for views is as follows:

```
CREATE [OR REPLACE] [FORCE|NOFORCE] VIEW view name AS sql query
   [WITH CHECK OPTION] [WITH READ ONLY]
```

EXAMPLE

The OR REPLACE feature allows for the same name of the view to be used again in a new (or replacement) view. The FORCE|NOFORCE option will allow for a view to be created with or without the underlying tables actually existing. NOFORCE is the default behavior saying that the table must exist before this view can be created. The SQL query can be any valid SQL select statement with alias, and so on. Aliases in views are a convenient way to change the names of the columns. WITH CHECK OPTION allows for only DML commands on rows displayed by the view, and the READ ONLY option is a convenient way to inhibit any DML on this view at all.

Figure 2.55 shows the creation of a view on the EMP table, naming the view EMPLOYEES. Notice how the view acts just like a table. This particular view gives users and applications access to the information that they need but does not allow them access to the sometimes sensitive salary and compensation information that they probably do not need to see.

EXAMPLE

```
+ Oracle SQL*Plus                                                    _ □ X
File Edit Search Options Help
SQL>
SQL>
SQL> CREATE VIEW employees AS
  2  SELECT deptno, ename, job, hiredate
  3  FROM emp;

View created.

SQL> DESC employees
 Name                                      Null?    Type
 ---------------------------------------   -------- --------------------
 DEPTNO                                             NUMBER(2)
 ENAME                                              VARCHAR2(10)
 JOB                                                VARCHAR2(9)
 HIREDATE                                           DATE

SQL> SELECT * FROM employees
  2  WHERE deptno = 10;

 DEPTNO ENAME      JOB       HIREDATE
 ------ ---------- --------- ---------
     10 CLARK      MANAGER   09-JUN-81
     10 KING       PRESIDENT 17-NOV-81
     10 MILLER     CLERK     23-JAN-82

SQL> |
```

Figure 2.55: *VIEW Usage example.*

CREATING SEQUENCES

There are needs in any application that require either a unique number or a nonassigned number. In Oracle9i, primary keys must be unique. Sequences are a database object that is used to create and maintain a sequence of numbers for tables.

Sequences made their first appearance back in the Oracle6 days. Before sequences, developers used a table to maintain a unique number. Each time a new row was inserted, this table needed to be updated, then selected from. This is considerable overhead, but consider when fifty or more users of the same application are all trying to insert records. This single-table approach proved to be quite a performance bottleneck.

Sequences are automatically maintained by Oracle9i. In Listing 2.1, the name, INCREMENT BY, and START WITH are the only required fields. The INCREMENT BY value provides the unit of measure between the numbers and the START WITH is the first number of the sequence. The sequence can also maintain a MINVALUE (for those sequences that decrease in increments) and a MAXVALUE. These values are important when there is either a business rule that dictates the range of values or a field length that might be eventually met. The CACHE option specifies how many sequences will be generated and stored in memory. The default is 20 values. The CYCLE option determines if the sequence will continue to generate values after the MINVALUE or MAXVALUE has been reached. The default behavior is NOCYCLE.

Listing 2.1 Create Sequence Syntax

```
CREATE SEQUENCE sequence name [INCREMENT BY n] [START WITH n] [MINVALUE
n|NOMINVALUE] [MAXVALUE n|NOMAXVALUE] [CACHE n|NOCACHE] [CYCLE|NOCYCLE];
```

EXAMPLE Figure 2.56 shows how to create a sequence for the DEPT table. Remember, the DEPT table currently has four departments: 10, 20, 30, 40. The business rule here is to increment by 10. Figure 2.57 shows how to receive information on the sequence from the data dictionary view USER_SEQUENCES.

EXAMPLE

Figure 2.56: CREATE SEQUENCE generator example.

EXAMPLE

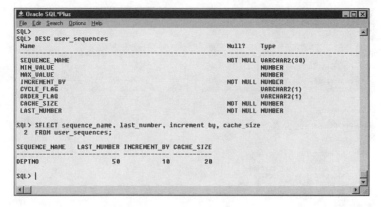

Figure 2.57: USER_SEQUENCES available information.

There are two values associated with sequences: CURRVAL and NEXTVAL. NEXTVAL retrieves the next number from the sequence. CURRVAL contains the last number returned for a particular user session. NEXTVAL returns a new value each time it is referenced. CURRVAL contains the sequence number from NEXTVAL for the particular user session. These two columns always need to be qualified with the name of the sequence. For example: Session A, Session B, and Session C are all individual users using the same sequence generator gen_num that increments by 1 and starts with 10. Session A inserts a record using gen_num.NEXTVAL. Session B inserts a record using gen_num.NEXTVAL. Session C inserts a record using gen_num.NEXTVAL. Session A's gen_num.CURRVAL would equal 10, Session B's gen_num.CURRVAL would equal 11, and Session C's gen_num.CURRVAL would equal 11. The gen_num. CURRVAL will stay constant for this user until this user issues another gen_num.NEXTVAL.

Figure 2.58 illustrates how to use the sequence generator deptno created in Figure 2.56. Figure 2.59 shows the CURRVAL and USER_SEQUENCES view after this usage.

Notice the LAST_NUMBER is 250 but the CURRVAL is 60. Remember that CURRVAL is the current value of the sequence for the current user session. LAST_NUMBER reflects the number of sequence numbers in the sequence cache. By default, sequences cache 20 values. If we had used the NOCACHE option on this sequence, the LAST_NUMBER would be 60.

DROP SEQUENCE sequence name removes the sequence; see Figure 2.60. The sequence must be dropped and re-created to make changes to it. There is no ALTER SEQUENCE command.

```
± Oracle SQL*Plus                                                    _ □ ×
File  Edit  Search  Options  Help
SQL>
SQL> L
  1* INSERT INTO dept VALUES (deptno.NEXTVAL,'Marketing','Des Moines')
SQL> /

1 row created.

SQL> C/Marketing/Speakers/
  1* INSERT INTO dept VALUES (deptno.NEXTVAL,'Speakers','Des Moines')
SQL> /

1 row created.

SQL> SELECT * FROM dept;

   DEPTNO DNAME            LOC
--------- --------------- --------------
       10 ACCOUNTING       NEW YORK
       20 RESEARCH         DALLAS
       30 SALES            CHICAGO
       40 OPERATIONS       BOSTON
       60 Speakers         Des Moines
       50 Marketing        Des Moines

6 rows selected.

SQL>
```

Figure 2.58: *Using the DEPTNO sequence.*

```
± Oracle SQL*Plus                                                    _ □ ×
File  Edit  Search  Options  Help
SQL>
SQL>
SQL> SELECT deptno.CURRVAL FROM sys.dual;

  CURRVAL
---------
       60

SQL> SELECT sequence_name, last_number, increment_by
  2  FROM user_sequences;

SEQUENCE_NAME   LAST_NUMBER INCREMENT_BY
--------------- ----------- ------------
DEPTNO                  250           10

SQL>
```

Figure 2.59: *USER_SEQUENCES available information.*

```
± Oracle SQL*Plus                                                    _ □ ×
File  Edit  Search  Options  Help
SQL>
SQL>
SQL> DROP SEQUENCE deptno;

Sequence dropped.

SQL>
SQL>
SQL>
```

Figure 2.60: *DROP SEQUENCE example.*

Some rules that govern sequences are CURRVAL and NEXTVAL, which can be used in a SELECT, INSERT, or UPDATE command. They may not be used in a view, in a subquery, or in a default value clause of a column.

USER-DEFINED DATA TYPES

One of the object-oriented features of Oracle9i is the ability to create and use data types that are based on a grouping of other data types. These groupings give a name to commonly used fields, and by using them will guarantee that their names and lengths are consistent through an application. User-defined objects can then appear and be used like any other Oracle9i data type.

Figure 2.61 shows how to create a new data type and Figure 2.62 shows how to use this new data type in a CREATE TABLE statement. Figure 2.63 shows how you would access these columns in an insert and a select statement.

```
± Oracle SQL*Plus                                          _ □ ×
File  Edit  Search  Options  Help
SQL>
SQL>
SQL>
SQL> CREATE TYPE name_info AS OBJECT
  2   (ename      VARCHAR2(10),
  3    address    VARCHAR2(10),
  4    city       VARCHAR2(10));
  5   /

Type created.

SQL>
```

Figure 2.61: User-defined data type CREATE example.

```
± Oracle SQL*Plus                                          _ □ ×
File  Edit  Search  Options  Help
SQL>
SQL>
SQL> CREATE TABLE employee
  2   (empid          NUMBER(4),
  3    employee_info  NAME_INFO);

Table created.

SQL>
```

Figure 2.62: User-defined data type usage examples.

```
± Oracle SQL*Plus                                          _ □ ×
File  Edit  Search  Options  Help
SQL> INSERT INTO employee VALUES (100,name_info('Dan Hotka',NULL,'Des Moines'));

1 row created.

SQL> SELECT * FROM employee;

    EMPID
----------
EMPLOYEE_INFO(ENAME, ADDRESS, CITY)
-------------------------------------------------------------------------------
      100
NAME_INFO('Dan Hotka', NULL, 'Des Moines')

SQL>
```

Figure 2.63: User-defined data type usage examples.

To access the individual fields of this new data type requires the use of PL/SQL and REF commands. Refer to the Oracle9i SQL Reference Manual for additional details and example code.

CREATE SYNONYMS

Synonyms are simply different names for a table. They give a simple name to reference a table without having to qualify the table with the schema name or database link name (if the table were located in a different instance of Oracle).

Figure 2.64 shows the SYSTEM account trying to access the EMP table without qualifying the name to SCOTT.EMP. The synonym gives the SCOTT.EMP name a public-accessed name (anyone can access EMP) EMP.

EXAMPLE

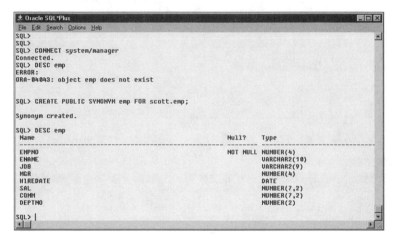

```
 Oracle SQL*Plus
File  Edit  Search  Options  Help
SQL>
SQL>
SQL> CONNECT system/manager
Connected.
SQL> DESC emp
ERROR:
ORA-04043: object emp does not exist


SQL> CREATE PUBLIC SYNONYM emp FOR scott.emp;

Synonym created.

SQL> DESC emp
 Name                                     Null?     Type
 ------------------------------------     --------  --------------
 EMPNO                                    NOT NULL  NUMBER(4)
 ENAME                                              VARCHAR2(10)
 JOB                                                VARCHAR2(9)
 MGR                                                NUMBER(4)
 HIREDATE                                           DATE
 SAL                                                NUMBER(7,2)
 COMM                                               NUMBER(7,2)
 DEPTNO                                             NUMBER(2)

SQL>
```

Figure 2.64: SYNONYM usage example.

CREATE CONSTRAINTS

Constraints are a way of applying business rules at the database level. Constraints ensure that the data entered into tables complies with what is expected in the tables. Constraints can be applied at both the column level or at the table level. They can be applied after the table has been created as well.

There are two main kinds of constraints: data integrity and referential integrity. The data integrity constraints deal with the data that is in the particular column. Constraints such as NOT NULL, UNIQUE, and CHECK deal with the data in a particular column. Referential constraints such as Primary Key/Foreign Key deal with the relationship between tables. The NOT NULL constraint is obvious and frequently used to ensure that the field does in fact contain a value. UNIQUE and PRIMARY KEY constraints are similar in that they ensure that the values in a particular column are unique to all the other values in the column. Oracle will create a unique index for each of these as a means to perform the unique check. A CHECK constraint enables the column to be checked against certain conditions or a list of values.

Figure 2.65 displays several of these constraint types. Notice that the DEPT table has a table level PRIMARY KEY constraint defined on column deptno and that table EMP has a table level FOREIGN KEY constraint on deptno that references the primary key of DEPT. Because there can only be one primary key on a table, it would be redundant to have to name this primary key again in the foreign key constraint reference. This establishes referential integrity between the DEPT and EMP tables. You cannot insert a record into EMP with a deptno that does not already exist in DEPT. There is also a column level CHECK constraint defined in the EMP table as well as several column-level NOT NULL constraints defined. The constraint on the MGR column in the EMP table references the EMPNO column. This will ensure that the MGR number is a valid employee.

EXAMPLE

```
Command Prompt - \bin\vi demobld.sql                               _ □ ×
CREATE TABLE DEPT (
  DEPTNO            NUMBER(2) NOT NULL,
  DNAME             VARCHAR2(14),
  LOC               VARCHAR2(13),
  CONSTRAINT DEPT_PRIMARY_KEY PRIMARY KEY (DEPTNO));

CREATE TABLE EMP (
  EMPNO             NUMBER(4) NOT NULL,
  ENAME             VARCHAR2(10),
  JOB               VARCHAR2(9),
  MGR               NUMBER(4) CONSTRAINT EMP_SELF_KEY REFERENCES EMP (EMPNO),
  HIREDATE          DATE,
  SAL               NUMBER(7,2),
  COMM              NUMBER(7,2),
  CUR_EMPLOYEE      VARCHAR2(1) CHECK (CUR_EMPLOYEE IN ('Y','N')),
  DEPTNO            NUMBER(2) NOT NULL,
  CONSTRAINT EMP_FOREIGN_KEY FOREIGN KEY (DEPTNO) REFERENCES DEPT (DEPTNO),
  CONSTRAINT EMP_PRIMARY_KEY PRIMARY KEY (EMPNO));

CREATE TABLE PRODUCT (
  PRODID            NUMBER (6) CONSTRAINT PRODUCT_PRIMARY_KEY PRIMARY KEY,
  DESCRIP           VARCHAR2 (30));
```

Figure 2.65: *CONSTRAINT examples.*

Figure 2.66 shows valuable information about the constraints in the SCOTT schema. The USER_CONSTRAINTS show a variety of information. The constraint name, type of constraint (P for primary key and R for foreign key), and the table the constraint is on. USER_CONS_COLUMNS shows the actual columns that have constraints on them. The USER_INDEXES view shows the unique indexes created for the primary keys.

Figure 2.67 shows the describe command that displays the NOT NULL column constraints.

EXAMPLE

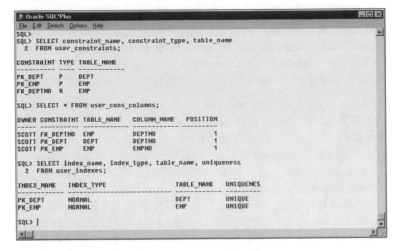

Figure 2.66: *Information on CONSTRAINTS.*

EXAMPLE

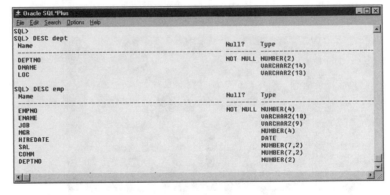

Figure 2.67: *Additional information on CONSTRAINTS.*

Sometimes it can be difficult to load related data into different tables with the constraints defined. The DISABLE and ENABLE CONSTRAINT commands are just for this purpose: to temporarily disable constraints for data loads or data manipulation. The ALTER TABLE table name DISABLE CONSTRAINT constraint name [CASCADE] disables the constraints and any related constraints if the CASCADE option is specified. Likewise, ALTER TABLE table name ENABLE CONSTRAINT constraint name re-establishes the constraint and verifies the data named in the constraint.

Constraints can be added and dropped as well. The ALTER TABLE table name ADD CONSTRAINT constraint name TYPE (column name) adds additional table level constraints and the ALTER TABLE table name DROP CONSTRAINT constraint name removes the constraint from the table.

Another benefit of referential integrity is the ability to remove a parent row and all the children records *or* not allow the parent record to be deleted if there are children records. Figure 2.68 illustrates how referential integrity protects the data in the related columns. The DEPT record was not deleted because there are still child records in the EMP table. There is a constraint option that will allow CASCADE ON DELETE that would also delete these child records in the EMP table.

EXAMPLE

```
Oracle SQL*Plus                                                          _ □ ×
File  Edit  Search  Options  Help
SQL>
SQL>
SQL>
SQL> DELETE FROM dept
  2  WHERE deptno = 10;
DELETE FROM dept
       *
ERROR at line 1:
ORA-02292: integrity constraint (SCOTT.FK_DEPTNO) violated - child record found

SQL> |
```

Figure 2.68: *Attempted* DELETE *from DEPT table.*

TIP

Parent table or parent row refers to the primary key table or row of data in the primary key table. The child row or children records refers to the foreign key table and foreign key data.

CREATE TABLESPACES

The relationship between tables and tablespaces was discussed previously in this chapter at Figure 2.39 (and shown again here in Figure 2.69). Tablespaces are the interface between Oracle9i and the operating-system-level files. The tablespace is also the place where the default storage parameters are stored.

EXAMPLE

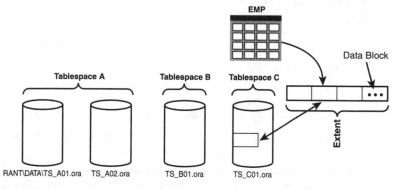

Figure 2.69: *Oracle9i object storage overview.*

This is the base syntax for creating a tablespace:

```
CREATE TABLESPACE tablespace name DATAFILE 'full path operating-system level
    file' SIZE n bytes/K/M DEFAULT STORAGE (INITIAL nK, NEXT nK, MINEXTENTS n,
    MAXEXTENTS n) ONLINE;
```

The single quotes around the operating-system file spec is part of the syntax. The n represents a numeric number. The SIZE can be specified in bytes, number of bytes in K (1024), or number of megabytes (M).

NOTE

I always specify full path for these files. On a single-CPU, desktop configuration of NT, I always put the tablespace files in the same directory as the default database-created tablespace files.

Two data dictionary views are handy for finding information out about the tablespaces. You must be logged in to SQL*Plus as SYSTEM or have the DBA role assigned to see the contents of these two views: DBA_TABLESPACES and DBA_DATA_FILES. Figure 2.70 shows the information available with the DBA_TABLESPACES view. This view shows the tablespaces and the default storage parameters of objects created here that did not have a storage parameter defined.

EXAMPLE

```
Oracle SQL*Plus                                              _ □ ×
File Edit Search Options Help
SQL> CONNECT SYSTEM/MANAGER
Connected.
SQL> DESC dba_tablespaces
 Name                              Null?    Type
 -------------------------------   -------- ----------------
 TABLESPACE_NAME                   NOT NULL VARCHAR2(30)
 INITIAL_EXTENT                             NUMBER
 NEXT_EXTENT                                NUMBER
 MIN_EXTENTS                       NOT NULL NUMBER
 MAX_EXTENTS                       NOT NULL NUMBER
 PCT_INCREASE                               NUMBER
 MIN_EXTLEN                                 NUMBER
 STATUS                                     VARCHAR2(9)
 CONTENTS                                   VARCHAR2(9)
 LOGGING                                    VARCHAR2(9)
 EXTENT_MANAGEMENT                          VARCHAR2(10)
 ALLOCATION_TYPE                            VARCHAR2(9)
 PLUGGED_IN                                 VARCHAR2(3)

SQL> SELECT tablespace_name,initial_extent,next_extent, min_extents, max_extents
  2  FROM dba_tablespaces;

TABLESPACE_NAME        INITIAL_EXTENT NEXT_EXTENT MIN_EXTENTS MAX_EXTENTS
---------------------- -------------- ----------- ----------- -----------
SYSTEM                          10240       10240           1         121
USERS                           10240       10240           1         121
RBS                             10240       10240           1         121
TEMP                            10240       10240           1         121
OEM_REPOSITORY                  10240       10240           1         121
INDX                            10240       10240           1         121

6 rows selected.

SQL> |
```

Figure 2.70: *Information from DBA_TABLESPACES.*

Figure 2.71 shows the names of the tablespaces again, their underlying operating-system files, the size of the files, and their status for use in the Oracle9i database environment.

TIP

Notice that there is a pattern to the naming convention of these files in Figure 2.71, DBA_DATA_FILES view. I recommend naming the physical files that are assigned to the tablespaces in such a manner that one can easily see what physical files belongs to what tablespaces.

EXAMPLE

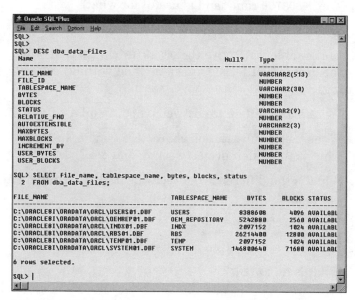

Figure 2.71: *Information from DBA_DATA_FILES.*

Figure 2.72 shows the CREATE TABLESPACE command in use along with the information from DBA_DATA_FILES to show that the tablespace was created with the specifications from the CREATE TABLESPACE command.

EXAMPLE

```
± Oracle SQL*Plus                                                    _ □ ×
File Edit Search Options Help
SQL>
SQL> CREATE TABLESPACE ch3_tablespace
  2  DATAFILE 'c:\oracle8i\oradata\orcl\ch3_tablespace01.dbf' SIZE 10K
  3  DEFAULT STORAGE (INITIAL 1K NEXT 5K MINEXTENTS 1 MAXEXTENTS 100)
  4  ONLINE;

Tablespace created.

SQL> SELECT file_name, tablespace_name, bytes, blocks, status
  2  FROM dba_data_files
  3  WHERE tablespace_name = 'CH3_TABLESPACE';

FILE_NAME                         TABLESPACE_NAME    BYTES   BLOCKS STATUS
--------------------------------- ---------------- -------- ------ --------
C:\ORACLE8I\ORADATA\ORCL\CH3_TABLESPACE0 CH3_TABLESPACE   10240       5 AVAILABL
1.DBF

SQL>
```

Figure 2.72: CREATE TABLESPACE CH3_Tablespace *example.*

Reviewing It

1. What is Oracle's main character-mode interface?

2. What is the syntax of the CHANGE command to change text in the SQL buffer?

3. The DESCRIBE command is useful for what?

4. What will the command SELECT * FROM EMP do?

5. In the table EMP, give the ORDER BY clause that will return the rows in the order of DEPTNO ascending and within DEPTNO, SAL descending.

6. What is the difference between a NULL and a 0 field?

7. When using substitution characters (say in an INSERT statement), what is the difference between & and &&?

8. What is the difference between the DELETE command and the TRUNCATE command?

9. Tablespaces are used for what?

10. Show the syntax to create an index on ename for the table EMP.

11. What is an EXTENT?

CHECK

Checking It

1. SQL*Plus can:

    a) Display data from the Oracle database

    b) Format data into reports

    c) Perform database administrative functions

    d) All of the above

2. In the SQL Buffer, the command I is short for INSERT.

    True/False

3. The default behavior of the ORDER BY clause is ascending.

    True/False

4. Which of the following LIKE commands will return the rows with a name like HOTKA

   a) WHERE ename LIKE '_HOT%'

   b) WHERE ename LIKE 'H_T%'

   c) WHERE ename LIKE '%TKA_'

   d) WHERE ename LIKE '%TOK%'

5. Which is the valid UPDATE statement?

   a) UPDATE emp SET SAL = SAL * 1.05

   b) UPDATE emp WHERE SAL = 20000

   c) UPDATE emp SET ENAME = 1234 WHERE DEPTNO = 10

   d) UPDATE emp WHERE DEPTNO = 10 SET ENAME = 'HOTKA'

6. Which of the following is NOT a valid data type:

   a) BLOB

   b) CHAR

   c) VARCHAR

   d) INTEGER

7. CREATE TABLE <table name> AS SELECT can create a duplicate object.

   True/False

8. You change your mind on a DROP COLUMN command and return the column to the original object.

   True/False

9. Selecting which field causes a SEQUENCE generator to increment?

   a) CURRVAL

   b) NEXTVAL

   c) LASTNUMBER

   d) PREVAL

10. Constraints are useful for:

    a) Ensuring parent/child table relationships

    b) Ensuring only certain kinds of data is in a field

    c) Ensuring uniqueness of column data

    d) All of the above

Applying It

APPLY

Independent Exercise 1:

- Create a Table called people with columns of dept (numeric 4 positions), last_name (character 10 positions), start_date (date field), and salary (numeric 5 positions with 2 decimal positions).

Independent Exercise 2:

- Insert the following data into the table, try out the & substitution character:

    - Dept 10, SMITH, SYSDATE, 10000

    - Dept 10, JONES, SYSDATE, 20000

    - Dept 20, KING, SYSDATE, 15000

    - Dept 20, JONES, SYSDATE, 18000

    - Dept 20, FOUNTAIN, SYSDATE, 12000

Independent Exercise 3:

- Select those rows from Dept 20.

- Select name and start_date with the start_date in the format of MM/DD/YYYY.

- Give everyone in dept 10 a 10% increase in salary.

- Set AUTOCOMMIT off, drop all the rows, and issue a ROLLBACK. Make sure all the rows are put back.

Independent Exercise 4:

- Create a sequence that increments by 10 and begins at 10 over the current DEPT in the PEOPLE table.

    - INSERT <sequence name>.NEXTVAL, GARN, SYSDATE, 5000.

    - Create a primary key constraint on the DEPT column.

- INSERT `<sequence name>.CURRVAL, HACKETT, SYSDATE, 4500.`
- Why did you get this error?

NOTE

The next chapter uses this PEOPLE table for its Exercise examples as well.

What's Next?

In this chapter, you learned the basics of the SQL language and you should now have the minimum requirements to select data from any relational database.

The next chapter teaches you the basics of PL/SQL, Oracle's proprietary procedural language that encompasses and enhances SQL and is used extensively throughout the Oracle database and development tools.

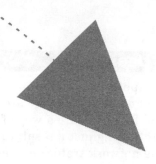

Fundamentals of PL/SQL

PL/SQL, or Procedural Language SQL, is Oracle9i's extension to the SQL language. PL/SQL gives SQL many common programming features such as record processing, various looping syntax, data manipulation/calculation capabilities, and as exception handling. The focus of this chapter is to learn and understand the basic constructs and functionality of PL/SQL.

This chapter teaches you the following:

- What is PL/SQL?

- The basic PL/SQL syntax

- Various programming constructs such as IF/THEN/ELSE and Looping

- PL/SQL handles error conditions

What Is PL/SQL and Why Should I Use It?

PL/SQL is what various features of the Oracle9i application environment is coded in. Stored procedures, stored functions, and database triggers are all coded in PL/SQL or JAVA. Stored procedures and functions are a way of sharing code and doing server-side processing, returning just a result to the application or user at a PC. Figure 3.1 shows the network traffic generated by SQL at an application and the network traffic generated by the use of some server-side code. Notice that the SQL code has to call the rows back to the application (such as Oracle Forms or SQL*Plus) on the PC but the server-side code just sends the result.

NOTE

Record processing is the ability to select one row at a time, manipulate it, and then process the next row. Looping syntax allows you to do repetitive tasks any number of times.

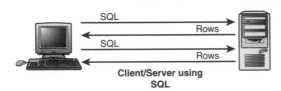

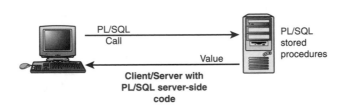

Figure 3.1: *Network Traffic example.*

NOTE

Server-side code is any code that runs where the Oracle9i RDBMS is installed. The database engine actually executes the code and returns just the results such as a few columns or maybe just the output of a calculation.

A *stored procedure* is a code module that does some processing and returns a code stating whether the procedure was successful or not. An example of a stored procedure is to process a group of rows based on a supplied value and to perform DML statements on other tables as a result of processing the rows.

A *function* is the same as a procedure except it does return a value, such as the result of a calculation. Procedures and functions are an excellent way to perform complex calculations or processing that is not easily done with just SQL statements.

Packages are a way of grouping together related procedures and functions, or procedures and functions that may be used frequently by an application. When a procedure or function within a package is referenced, all the functions and procedures in the package are loaded into memory.

Triggers are assigned to tables and provide additional functionality either before or after a DML process. Triggers are useful for maintaining audit trails in the assigned tables, performing additional DML on other tables based on the just-completed DML statement, and so on.

You will learn how to code these same procedures, functions, and triggers in the next two chapters.

These procedures and functions can reside at either the PC or the server (where the Oracle9i database is), but as illustrated by Figure 3.1, the server is usually a much more powerful machine for doing processing, and any time you can cut down on network traffic, the application will perform much better.

PL/SQL can also be coded directly into applications such as SQL*Plus. Figure 3.2 illustrates how this would look, using PL/SQL to manipulate data from SQL*Plus variables.

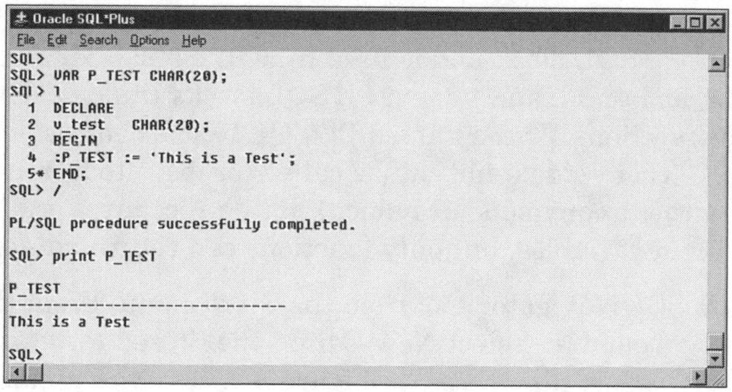

Figure 3.2: *PL/SQL in SQL*Plus example.*

PL/SQL Basic Syntax

All PL/SQL has the same basic format: a DECLARE section where cursors and variables are defined, a BEGIN, and an END where the SQL syntax and

PL/SQL code is put. This is known as a PL/SQL block. *Exception* or *exception handling* is errors or flags in PL/SQL. Exceptions are a way of gracefully handling certain conditions within the PL/SQL block, such as "no records returned from the SQL query" or "last record returned from the SQL query". Other exceptions can be syntax errors in the PL/SQL code itself.

NOTE

Cursors are Oracle's way of processing SQL statements and storing the rows returned from a query, allowing for the PL/SQL block to easily handle individual rows from a query that returns multiple rows. A cursor is a work area in memory for PL/SQL.

TIP

Use the show errors command when working with PL/SQL in SQL*Plus to show any error conditions.

NOTE

This section will use the Quest SQL Navigator tool. SQL Navigator is a good tool for creating and debugging PL/SQL code. Appendix C discusses how to get the tool and provides a trial license key.

NOTE

Log in to SQL Navigator as SCOTT with the TIGER password to work the exercises in this chapter.

There are two types of PL/SQL blocks: the anonymous block is the basic unnamed PL/SQL block and is used in SQL*Plus, 3GL programs such as C or Cobol, and so on; and named PL/SQL blocks can be declared as procedures or functions. These named PL/SQL blocks can reside on the server or at the PC (client side), and can be called (or executed) from other PL/SQL blocks (either anonymous or named). Both procedures and functions can accept input variables, but only functions can return values.

Start the SQL Navigator tool from the Start menu. From the SQL Navigator menu bar, select New Editor, the Stored Program Editor. This will display a box illustrated by Figure 3.3. Give the procedure a name and click OK. This will create a basic PL/SQL block for a procedure, as illustrated in Figure 3.4. Notice the BEGIN, EXCEPTIONS, and END clauses (the END is hidden from view, use the vertical scroll bar on the right side of the edit window to see the remainder of the code) are automatically created.

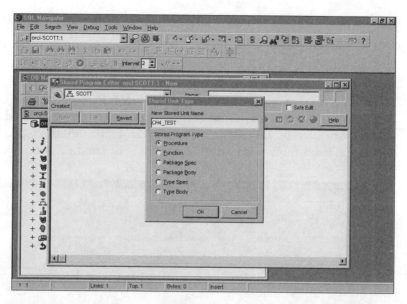

Figure 3.3: *Creating a procedure using SQL Navigator.*

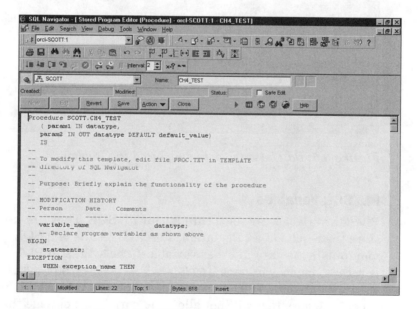

Figure 3.4: *Basic PL / SQL block in SQL Navigator.*

There are also two types of triggers that utilize PL/SQL blocks. Database triggers are defined on a table to perform certain functions at certain times. These triggers execute when certain events occur such as before or after a record is inserted.

Figure 3.5 shows the various database trigger levels supported by Oracle9i. This trigger edit window in SQL Navigator is accessed by clicking on File, then NEW Editor, and then Trigger. Notice the timing box determines whether this database trigger will fire before or after the action determined in box triggering event. The Fire for box determines if the trigger will be executed for each row affected by the DML SQL statement or just once per DML SQL statement. Application triggers are also executed automatically and are used by Developer v6i. Chapter 4, "Building an Oracle9i Database," will discuss their use and illustrate how to create them.

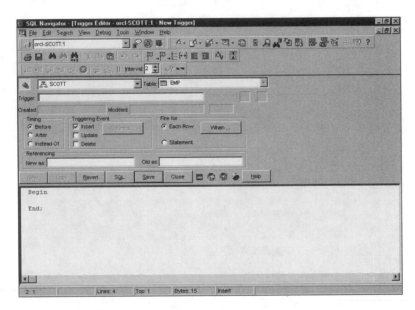

Figure 3.5: *Database triggers supported in Oracle9i.*

PL/SQL Variables

PL/SQL variables are used throughout PL/SQL. They are used to store data, store the results of a calculation, store the results of a SQL query, and manipulate the data in other variables. The syntax in PL/SQL variables is rather simple: `var_name [CONSTANT] datatype [NOT NULL] [:= var/ calc/expression]`. The var name must be unique to the PL/SQL block. The `CONSTANT` option will not allow the variable to change throughout the PL/SQL code execution. This feature would be handy where the PL/SQL block might be subject to somewhat regular code changes.

The datatype follows the SQL standards. The `:=` is the method of assigning a value to the variable. The value can be set equal to a constant, the result of a calculation, or the result of a SQL query. Oracle developers follow some simple guidelines to insure a unique name for variables and give other Oracle developers an idea of the nature of the variable. Table 3.1 shows some common naming conventions used by Oracle developers.

Table 3.1   PL/SQL Common Variable Naming Conventions

Indicator	Type	Example
v_	Standard variable	v_empno
c_	Constant variable	c_sysdate
p_	SQL*Plus variable	p_infield
g_	SQL_Plus global var	g_field_pos

The same variable name can be used inside nested PL/SQL blocks (PL/SQL within PL/SQL) and the name of the variable used by the PL/SQL block will be the locally defined variable, or that variable declared in that PL/SQL block.

For example, Figure 3.6 shows variable v_avar in the outer PL/SQL block and v_bvar in the inner or nested PL/SQL block. Variable v_bvar can reference v_avar but v_avar CANNOT reference v_bvar. The code in the grey box in Figure 3.6 is invalid and will generate an error because the outer PL/SQL block is making reference to a variable defined in the inner PL/SQL block. To save and execute the code block, click on the green triangular box on the bottom tool bar.

TIP

It is advisable to always use unique variable names because referencing variables with the := in inner PL/SQL blocks is a convenient way of passing results to outer PL/SQL blocks when nesting PL/SQL blocks.

TIP

If you put the mouse cursor on the error code returned (PLS-00201 in example 3.6) and double-click, you will get SQL Navigator's Oracle Error Information as illustrated in Figure 3.7.

Figure 3.8 illustrates naming some variables and populating them with values. The %TYPE and %ROWTYPE are special datatypes that will retrieve and use the datatype for a particular column from the database (object-oriented inheritance, discussed in Chapter 1, "Introducing Oracle9i"). %TYPE is useful to guarantee that the datatype and length of the variable matches that of a column in the database. Notice the INTO clause in the SQL statement. This is how data is passed from the tables to the PL/SQL variables.

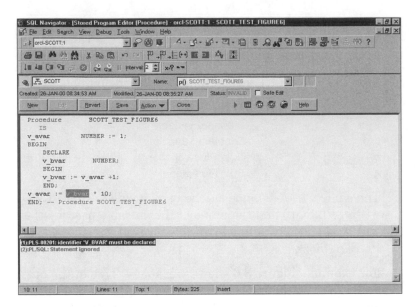

Figure 3.6: *Variable references in nested PL/SQL blocks.*

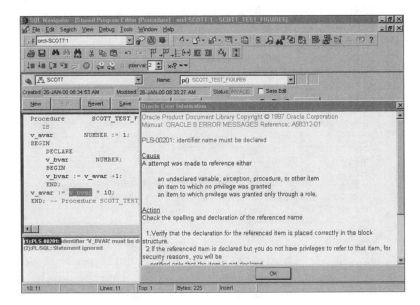

Figure 3.7: *SQL Navigator help with errors.*

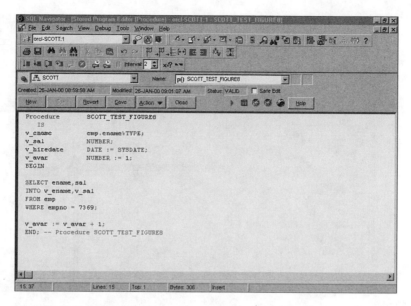

Figure 3.8: *Declaring and populating variables.*

Figure 3.9 shows how to execute the newly developed procedure in DEBUG mode. This will allow you to stop the execution of the code, see the contents of variables, and change the contents of the variables. There are a couple of ways to set a break point: you can left-click the line where you want execution to stop, then press the right mouse button and select Toggle Breakpoint. This will highlight the whole line in yellow; or you can press the Toggle Breakpoint button on the tool bar next to the X=? button. The button with a down arrow (complete left on same line of tool bar) will run the procedure to the first break point. Because this is a procedure, SQL Navigator will start a Calling Code Generation Wizard, just click next and finish, taking the defaults. When SQL Navigator hits the break point, it will stop and display the line of code at the break point.

Now you can move the mouse cursor over a variable and its contents will display monetarily and also display in the status bar at the bottom of the screen, as shown in Figure 3.9. Figure 3.10 shows the Evaluate/Modify variable (by pressing the X=? button with the cursor over the desired variable) that not only shows the contents of the variable but also allows you the opportunity to change the contents.

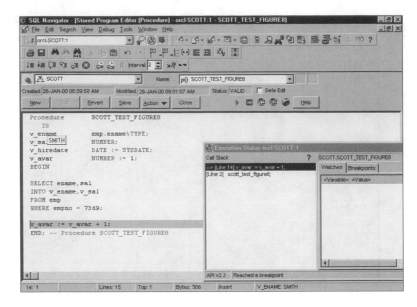

Figure 3.9: *Setting breakpoints in SQL Navigator.*

This breakpoint/debug mode is very useful in visualizing returned rows later when we learn about loops and cursors.

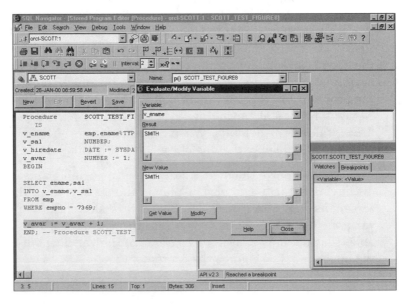

Figure 3.10: *Changing variable contents on the fly....*

Like %TYPE, %ROWTYPE is convenient to use to guarantee the same datatypes are used but also all the columns of a particular table are used. This too is a form of object-oriented inheritance. This feature will guarantee the number of columns and the associated data types always match that of a particular table. Figure 3.11 illustrates a practical use for %ROWTYPE. Notice how v_ename and v_sal are set by qualifying the columns returned from emp with the emp_record prefix.

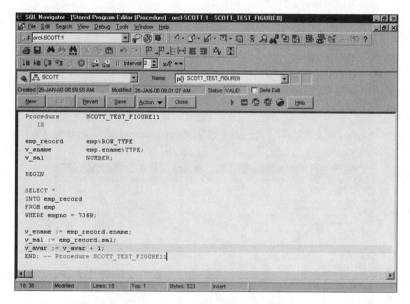

Figure 3.11: *Using the %ROWTYPE Datatype feature.*

Boolean variables are useful for storing the results of a calculation, a comparison, or simply holding a TRUE/FALSE/NULL value.

NOTE

A boolean variable is basically a single computer bit that holds a true or false condition. Booleans are useful for holding the success or failure of a procedure, IF statement, and so on.

Variables can also be passed both to and from the SQL*Plus environment. Notice the :g_dept_sal is populated by the simple query in the PL/SQL block but that %DEPTNO is passed to the PL/SQL block. This is a classic use of bind variables and is an efficient way of coding SQL statements within PL/SQL blocks. Figure 3.12 shows this functionality from within SQL*Plus. Notice the SQL*Plus PRINT command is useful for displaying the contents of a variable. PL/SQL has no such feature as PRINT. Notice that Figure

3.13 shows how to reference SQL*Plus variables and display results with the use of SQL*Plus environment setting SET SERVEROUTPUT ON is set and the PL/SQL feature DBMS_OUTPUT.PRINT_LINE is used.

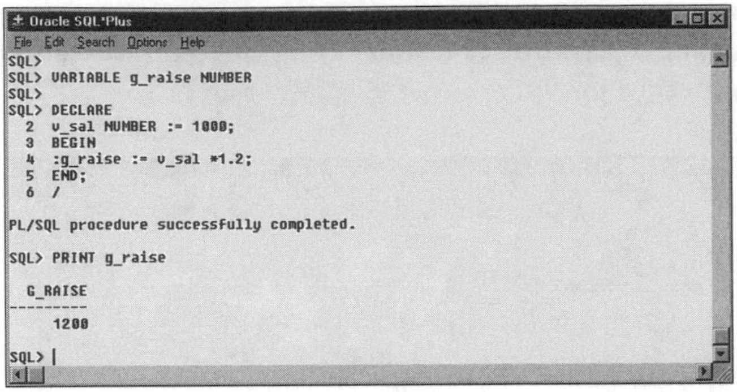

Figure 3.12: *Referencing SQL*Plus variables inside PL/SQL.*

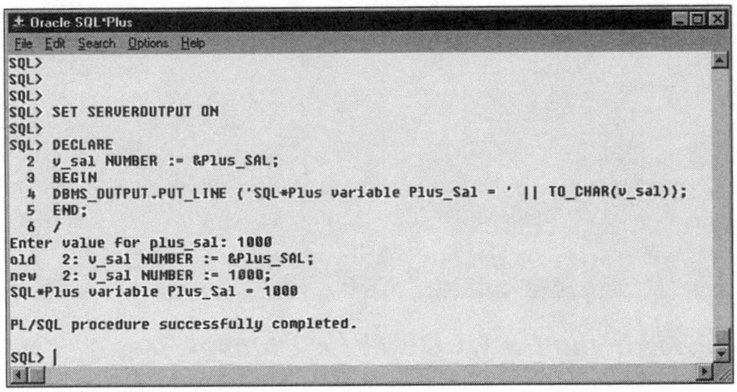

Figure 3.13: *Using PL/SQL Function DBMS_OUTPUT.PRINT_LINE.*

NOTE

PL/SQL supports all DML-type queries and SQL queries; however, PL/SQL does not support the use of DECODE or GROUP BY functions (such as AVG, MIN, MAX, and so on).

PL/SQL Cursors

Cursors are Oracle's way of processing SQL statements, checking their syntax (known as parsing), substituting any bind variables, finding the path to the data (known as the explain plan), and eventually executing and assigning a buffer to hold the row or rows returned.

NOTE

The SQL statement is actually loaded into the Oracle9i buffer known as the library cache. The data buffer is established in the Oracle9i buffer pool. The explain plan is the path that Oracle9i will use to actually get the data, including what indexes will be used.

There are two kinds of cursors in Oracle9i: *implicit cursors* and *explicit cursors*. An implicit cursor is one (illustrated by Figure 3.14) where a SQL statement is defined without any cursor control statements such as use of the CURSOR statement (see Figure 3.15). SQL queries in implicit cursors can only return one row. DML statements can process any number of rows. Explicit cursors are for those SQL queries that return more than one row. These cursors have a command structure so that the PL/SQL block can control the return of data or rows from the database.

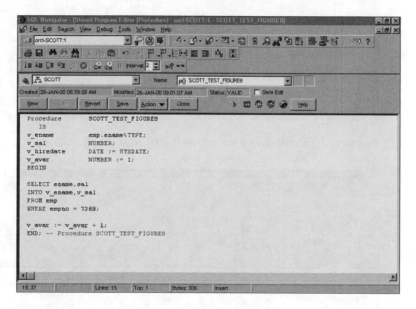

Figure 3.14: *Implicit PL/SQL SQL query.*

SQL Navigator has a code assistant that is useful in defining the basic syntax. This code assistant can be accessed either via the menu bar (Tools (Code Assistant) or by the Code Assistant button on the top tool palette. The code assistant has code syntax layouts for about any programming task desired. Notice Figure 3.15 uses the Syntax & Web Catalog tab. Simply left-click and hold (drag and drop) on the desired code feature and move the mouse pointer (it will pull a shadow object) to the desired part of the

PL/SQL block in the Editor window. This will put the PL/SQL code fragments into the Editor window where you can then change the black type items to the values desired. Figure 3.16 shows the results after modifications.

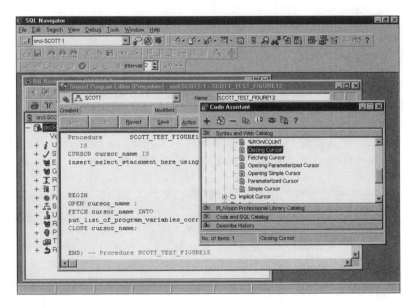

Figure 3.15: *Building an explicit PL/SQL SQL query with SQL Navigator.*

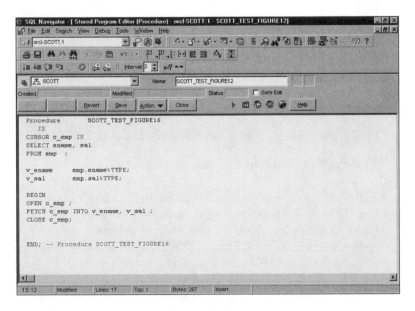

Figure 3.16: *Explicit PL/SQL SQL query.*

Notice that the implicit cursor has the INTO clause in the SELECT statement (refer to Figure 3.14) where the explicit cursor does not. Also notice that the explicit cursor has a name, must be opened, and closed, and puts the INTO clause in the FETCH statement to populate the PL/SQL variables with data. The columns listed in the SELECT clause are in the same order as listed in the FETCH clause.

Implicit and explicit cursors have some attributes that contain information about the cursor function. The following list shows the cursor attributes, and Figure 3.17 shows the logic flow of defining and using explicit cursors. These attributes play a major role of cursor control as we will learn in the next section of this chapter.

- %ISOPEN   Returns a TRUE if the cursor is open.
- %NOTFOUND   Returns a TRUE if row is not returned.
- %FOUND   Returns a TRUE if a roe is returned.
- %ROWCOUNT   Contains number or rows returned so far or number of rows processed by the SQL statement.

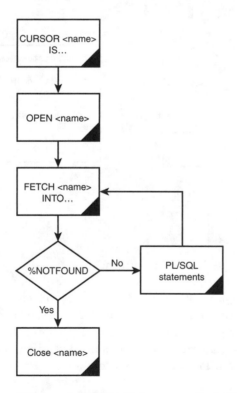

Figure 3.17: *Explicit cursor logic flow.*

PL/SQL Logic Control

There are two ways to control the flow of logic within a PL/SQL block: the IF-THEN-ELSE and LOOPING. These commands can be intermixed, depending on the requirements of the logic needed.

IF-THEN-ELSE

The IF statement allows for the checking of contents of a variable and performing additional instructions based on whether the condition tested TRUE or FALSE. If the condition tested true, the THEN clause is then followed. If the condition tested false, then the ELSIF or ELSE is followed.

The syntax is simple: IF <condition> THEN statement[s]; [ELSIF condition THEN statement[s];] [ELSE statement[s];] END IF; A simple IF statement might not have any ELSE conditions at all. Figure 3.18 illustrates the program logic flow of the IF-THEN-ELSE and Figure 3.19 illustrates a more complex IF-THEN-ELSIF-ELSE program logic.

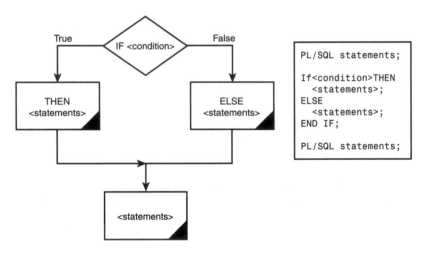

Figure 3.18: *IF-THEN-ELSE logic illustration.*

Listing 3.1 shows a couple of different IF statement usages. Notice the first IF statement simply checks one value. Each IF statement needs an END IF statement. The second IF statement in Listing 3.1 shows the use of the ELSIF statement. Notice that this code is easier to read and easier to code because of the lack of additional END IF statements.

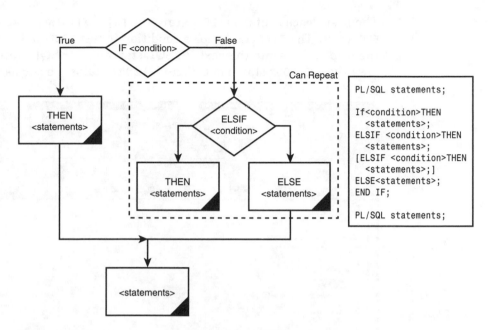

Figure 3.19: *IF-THEN-ELSIF-ELSE logic illustration.*

Listing 3.1: IF Statement Examples

```
...
IF job = 'SALESMAN' THEN
    v_raise := sal * .10;
ELSE
    IF job = 'CLERK' THEN
        v_raise := sal * .15
    END IF;
END IF;


..
IF job = 'SALESMAN' THEN
    v_raise := sal * .10;
ELSIF job = 'CLERK' THEN
    v_raise := sal * .15
ELSE
    v_raise = sal *.20
END IF;
```

LOOPING

PL/SQL provides three types of mechanisms used for repeating processes or looping: the basic loop, the WHILE loop, and the FOR loop. Each loop has some kind of an exit statement or a way to stop looping.

The basic loops syntax is LOOP statement[s]; EXIT [WHEN <condition>]; END LOOP; The EXIT checks for a condition to test TRUE and will then leave the loop and execute the next PL/SQL statement or SQL statement that follows the END LOOP statement. Figure 3.20 contains a basic loop example.

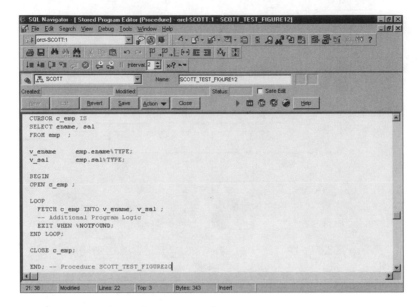

Figure 3.20: *Basic loop example.*

The FOR and WHILE loops handle when to exit in the FOR or WHILE clause. The syntax for the FOR loop is FOR counter IN low-range.high-range LOOP statement[s]; END LOOP;

The WHILE loop loops while some condition tests TRUE. The syntax is WHILE <condition> LOOP statement[s]; END LOOP;

TIP

It is very good practice to NOT make adjustments to the looping counter being used in the EXIT condition from inside the loop.

Figure 3.21 shows the FOR loop in use with explicit cursors. In this example, using the FOR, an implicit open and fetch are performed. An implicit close is performed on the END LOOP. PL/SQL will automatically perform this loop while there are rows in the cursor.

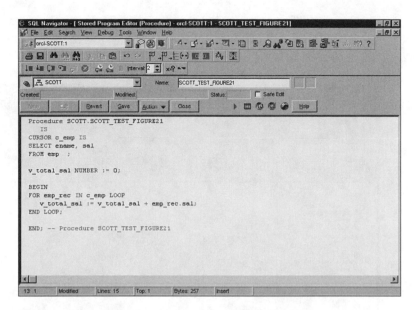

Figure 3.21: *Explicit cursor using the FOR loop.*

Debugging PL/SQL

It is important with any programming language either to be able to follow the code line by line or to be able to stop the code at certain points to check the contents of variables to ensure that the program is functioning as intended. Being able to visually see the code executing is an important ability when debugging or trying to find errors in the code. For example, if the expected result is not returned or the program never ends (a possible runaway loop), it would be nice to be able to step through the code, line by line, and check all the contents of all the variables.

Figure 3.22 uses Quest SQL Navigator to visualize the variables, including the returned values from the SQL statement with each iteration of the loop. Notice that a break point is set (with the mouse cursor on the line and pressing the Toggle Breakpoint button) on the last line of code inside the loop, then press the Run Debugger button and accept the defaults from the Calling Code Generation Wizard.

Each time you press the Run Debugger button, the loop is processed once. Figure 3.22 displays the variable v_total_sal (by pressing the X=? button with the mouse cursor on the variable). This variable is getting sal added to it in the FOR loop (the Run Debugger button was pressed three times). The Run button tells SQL Navigator to proceed to the next step or the next break point. This particular looping example shows the uses of an explicit cursor using the WHILE loop to process the result set of the multirow result set SQL query (the PL/SQL in Figure 3.21).

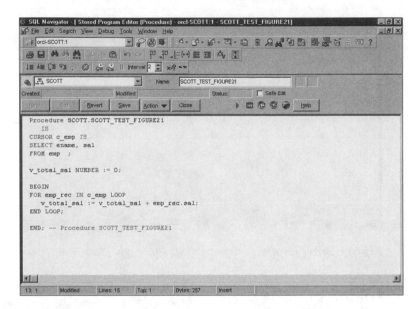

Figure 3.22: *Using SQL Navigator to debug a PL/SQL block.*

Error Handling in PL/SQL

As defined earlier in this chapter, exceptions are errors or flags in PL/SQL. Exceptions are a way of gracefully handling certain conditions within the PL/SQL block, such as "no records returned from the SQL query" or "last record returned from the SQL query." Other exceptions can be syntax errors in the PL/SQL code itself or errors returned from Oracle9i.

The syntax for exception handling, illustrated in Listing 3.2, is optional. If the exception area of the PL/SQL block is not handled, then it is propagated to the calling routine. For example, the SHOW ERRORS command in SQL*Plus is used to show any errors from PL/SQL that were not handled by the PL/SQL block. The exception syntax is

Listing 3.2:   PL/SQL Exception Handling Example Syntax

```
DECLARE
variables
BEGIN
statements;
```

Listing 3.2:   continued

```
EXCEPTION
  WHEN exception [OR exception …] THEN
   Statement[s];
  [WHEN […]]
  [ WHEN OTHERS THEN
   Statement[s];]

END;
```

Notice in Listing 3.2, that there only need be one WHEN clause defined. The WHEN OTHERS clause is good to use so that the PL/SQL block handles the exception rather than having the routine that ran the PL/SQL block have to deal with the error condition. The WHEN OTHERS, if used, must be the last clause. The RAISE_APPLICATION_ERROR procedure will return an error to the application much like an Oracle error would be returned. This is a convenient way to handle errors specific to an application.

There are many predefined exceptions—see Figure 3.23. SQL Navigator contains all the exceptions and are easily accessed through the Code Assistant (from the Tools menu or the Code Assistant button) using the PL/Vision Professional Library Catalog. There are a couple of common exceptions that should always be defined: NO_DATA_FOUND and TOO_MANY_ROWS.

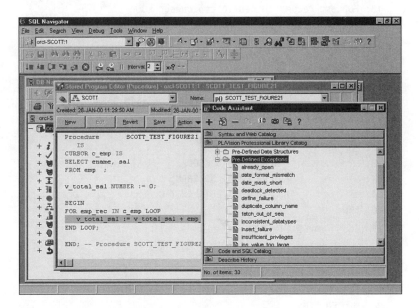

Figure 3.23: *Predefined exception conditions.*

Exceptions can be implicit (Oracle raises the exception) or they can be explicitly raised by the PL/SQL block. There are two PL/SQL functions available when Oracle errors occur: SQLCODE and SQLERRM. SQLCODE will return the Oracle error number and SQLERRM will return the Oracle error message. Notice that these are used in Listing 3.4 in the WHEN OTHERS clause lines 22 through 25. Their values are returned into variables and these variables are then used by the PUT_LINE function. The RAISE command explicitly creates an exception and sets a specially defined variable. Listing 3.4 shows a PL/SQL block that uses both the implicit (line 20 with the NO_DATA_FOUND) and named errors: lines 3, 14, and 18.

Listing 3.4:   IF Statement Examples

```
1:    DECLARE
2:    ...
3:    e_end_rows      EXCEPTION;
4:    v_oraerr       NUMBER;
5:    v_oraerrm                VARCHAR2(255);
6:    v_sal                    NUMBER;
7:    CURSOR dept10_emp_curson IS
8:    SELECT deptno, ename, sal
9:    FROM emp
10: ORDER BY deptno;
11: BEGIN
12: v_sal :=0
13: FOR emp_record IN dept10_emp_cursor LOOP
14:     IF emp_record.deptno > 10 THEN raise v_end_rows;
15:     v_sal := v_sal + sal;
16: END LOOP;
17: EXCEPTION
18:     WHEN e_end_rows THEN
19:             DBMS_OUTPUT.PUT_LINE('Dept 10 Salaries: ' || TO_CHAR(v_sal));
20:     WHEN NO_DATA_FOUND THEN
21:             DBMS_OUTPUT.PUT_LINE('No Employees Found');
22:     WHEN OTHERS THEN
23:             v_oraerr := SQLCODE;
24:             v_oraerrm := SQLERRM;
25:             DBMS_OUTPUT.PUT_LINE('OraErr: ' || v_oraerr || ' ' || v_oraerrm);
26: END;

IF job = 'SALESMAN' THEN
        v_raise := sal * .10;
ELSE
        IF job = 'CLERK' THEN
                v_raise := sal * .15
        END IF;
END IF;
```

Listing 3.4: continued

```
..
IF job = 'SALESMAN' THEN
        v_raise := sal * .10;
ELSIF job = 'CLERK' THEN
        v_raise := sal * .15
ELSE
        v_raise = sal *.20
END IF;
```

Reviewing It

1. What does PL/SQL stand for?

2. What exactly is a stored procedure?

3. What is the difference between a Named PL/SQL block and an Un-named PL/SQL block?

4. What are the three syntax basics of any PL/SQL block?

5. The special datatype %TYPE is useful for what?

6. PL/SQL uses the DBMS_OUTPUT.PRINT_LINE. What needs to be set in SQL*Plus to see this output?

7. What are the three kinds of loops?

8. What are the two variables available to PL/SQL when Oracle errors occur?

Checking It

1. Triggers, Functions, and Procedures can also be coded in JAVA.

   True/False

2. Cursors are

   a) Temporary storage area for PL/SQL

   b) Work area for SQL returning more than 1 row

   c) Work/storage space for PL/SQL

   d) Executable code modules

3. Procedures differ from Functions in that:

   a) Procedures takes no input variables but output variables

   b) Procedures take input variables but Functions cannot

   c) Functions have an output variable where Procedures do not

   d) Functions can have input variables but Procedures cannot

4. The PL/SQL variable name must be unique to the PL/SQL block.

   True/False

5. What is the difference between implicit cursors and explicit cursors?

   a) Explicit processes only 1 row, implicit processes many rows

   b) Explicit cursors are only for DML statements

   c) Implicit cursors are only for DML statements

   d) Implicit cursors can only handle 1 row returned, explicit can handle multiple rows

6. An IF statement really doesn't need an ENDIF.

   True/False

7. If an error condition is not handled by the PL/SQL block:

   a) It is ignored

   b) It is propagated to the calling program

   c) It causes an error inside the PL/SQL

   d) It is handled by PL/SQL default behavior

8. The WHEN_OTHERS error condition can appear *where* in the EXCEPTIONS area:

   a) Must be the first condition

   b) Must be the last condition

   c) Can appear anywhere, order of conditions does not matter

APPLY

Applying It

Independent Exercise 1:

- Create a PL/SQL Procedure that displays the total employee count and the total salary by department.

Independent Exercise 2:

- Create a PL/SQL Procedure that gives the DEPT 10 people a 10% increase in salary and the DEPT 20 people a 20% increase in salary.

Independent Exercise 3:

- Create a Function that outputs the total amount of salary only after the last row has been processed.

- Drop the PEOPLE table.

What's Next?

In this chapter, you learned the basics of the PL/SQL language and you should now have the minimum knowledge needed to code database triggers, functions, and procedures.

In the next chapter, you begin to use the knowledge from the previous two chapters to build a database and then to build applications. Your knowledge of both SQL and PL/SQL will be a good foundation for the remainder of this book.

Part II

Building Oracle9i-Based Applications

Building an Oracle9i Database

Building Oracle Forms

Building Oracle Reports

Using Advanced SQL Techniques and SQL*Plus Reporting Features

Building Web Sites with Oracle9i

Using PL/SQL to build Web Sites

Using Java to Build Web Sites

Using PL/SQL Pages, Java Pages, and XML with Apache/Oracle9iAS

Using Portal v3.0 (WebDB) Web development Software

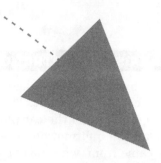

4

Building an Oracle9i Database

This chapter builds a series of tables, indexes, sequence generators, and constraints, a sample database that will be used in examples throughout the remainder of this book. You will learn how to design a relational application, load data into it, and then build the forms and reports that will manipulate and report on the data.

This chapter teaches you the following:

- How to build a relational database based on business requirements

- How to use many of the techniques learned in Chapter 2

- How to build the book sample database used in the remaining chapters

Relational Schema Design and Database Construction

The Auto Sales Tracking application is based on a hypothetical car dealer-ship that repairs used cars and then resells these cars to the public. The sale price of the completed car is based on the original cost of the car plus all the time and repairs. This application tracks all the information neces-sary: where the car came from, where the parts came from, who the car was sold to, plus all the costs associated with each individual car.

I have used a naming convention here so that the relational objects associ-ated with this application can be easily identified when looking at any data-dictionary view, such as DBA_Tables, or even TAB. Because this is a Sales Tracking application, I chose ST to depict the initial prefix to every table, index, or object (tables, indexes, triggers, and so on) that is part of this application. I also like to use part of the table as a prefix to each col-umn name. Having a column name that directly refers to one table or another really assists the programmer or end user when working with the SQL language.

You will notice that I have prefixed all the application objects with ST_; all the column attributes have part or all of the table name in them such as the ST_Inventory table; and all the entities begin with INV_. Your data cen-ter may have its own standards. Please consult your database administra-tor if you need assistance in the naming of application objects and/or programs.

An Overview of Tables and Indexes Including Referential Integrity Constraints

The Sales Tracking database consists of 11 relational tables, 3 sequence generators, and 5 database triggers. Three major tables that track the inventory (used automobiles in this case) support the application: ST_Inventory, ST_Parts, and ST_Bill_Time. Three minor tables are related to the major tables: ST_Vendor, ST_Customer, and ST_Staff. Finally, there are five reference tables that contain consistent data used to ensure that valid data is being stored in the five major and minor tables as well as give descriptions to this same data when displaying information on a screen or in a report. These reference tables are ST_Departments, ST_Job_Code, ST_Model, ST_Make, and ST_Type.

The Entity Relationship Diagram (ERD) in Figure 4.1 shows the major and minor tables of the Sales Tracking application. The central table is the ST_Inventory table. This is the central repository for the main business focus, the inventory of the automobiles that have been purchased, are in various stages of repair, are ready for sale, or have been sold.

The two other major tables are the ST_Parts and the ST_Bill_Tie tables. These tables are used in conjunction with the ST_Inventory to provide such useful information as what the car originally cost, total cost of repairing the car, and the profit/loss of each automobile sold. Notice the many-to-one relationship from ST_Parts to ST_Inventory. This indicates from this picture that there can be one or more parts associated with each car in the ST_Inventory table. A part can be a fender, a tire, or a complete motor. Likewise, with ST_Bill_Time there can be one or more mechanics working on each car, especially through several stages of repairs. There is the welder, who might fix any physical damage, a mechanic, who might have installed a new motor or transmission, and the painter if the car required painting.

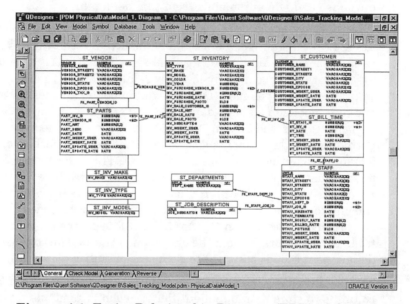

Figure 4.1: *Entity Relationship Diagram (ERD) of the Sales Tracking application Database objects.*

NOTE

A crow's foot depicts that there is a many relationship between the object that the crow-foot is pointing to and the object at the other end. Let's look at ST_Customer and ST_Inventory. There is just one record in the ST_Customer table for just one record in the ST_Inventory table, a one-to-one relationship. This makes sense to the application, as only one person will be purchasing each individual car. The ST_Parts table has a many-to-one relationship to the ST_Inventory table as there can be many parts (ST_Parts) for each car (ST_Inventory) being processed.

Notice that the ST_Inventory and the ST_Parts share a table used for reference, the ST_Vendor table. This table contains information about who is supplying the dealership with both cars and parts. A salvage yard, for example, could be supplying repairable cars as well as fenders and motors.

The ST_Inventory table has three supporting reference (look up/editing) tables associated with it that are not pictured here. These tables are ST_Type, or the type of automobile such as a SUV, sedan, and so on; the ST_Make, or name of the car such as Intrepid, Camry, Corolla, and so on; and the ST_Model, 4-door, hatchback, automatic, and so on. Each of these tables will be used by the forms programs to ensure only valid information is entered into the ST_Inventory table.

The ST_Customer table records the buyers of automobiles. The one-to-one relationship indicates that there is only one record in the ST_Inventory that is associated with a single record in the ST_Customer table. For simplicity's sake, this application will make the assumption that only one person can purchase a single automobile from this dealership.

The ST_Bill_Time table has a many-to-one relationship to the ST_Inventory table. Several staff members could be involved in the various stages of preparation of a single automobile for final sale. The ST_Bill_Time and the ST_Staff table have a many-to-many relationship in that staff members would be working on more than one automobile and possibly even more than one automobile in a single day. The ST_Staff table is supported by ST_Departments and ST_Job_Description. Each staff member is associated with different departments such as collision repair, mechanic, detailing (cleanup), painting, sales, or management. This information could be useful to see what percentage of an automobile is handled by each type of process it required. The ST_Job_Description is a reference table to the ST_Staff (note the one-to-one relationship) to ensure the correct job code is assigned to each staff member recorded in ST_Staff. The ST_Departments is another reference table to the ST_Staff (note the one-to-one relationship) to ensure the correct department code is assigned to each staff member recorded in ST_Staff.

The ST_Inventory table contains the necessary entities (see Figure 4.2) or columns to store a unique identifier for each automobile, in other words, the ST_INV entity. This field is associated with one of the Oracle sequence generators, ST_INV_SEQ. This sequence is used to ensure a unique number is associated with each automobile, no matter how many people may be entering cars into the ST_Inventory table. This field is also the primary key so that referential integrity constraints can be established, enforcing the relationships between the tables as pictured in Figure 4.1. There are a couple of foreign keys, or fields that will have relationships to other tables as well. These fields include Inv_Purchase_Vendor_Id and Inv_Sale_Customer_Id. These fields are respectively related to ST_Vendor and ST_Customer. The referential integrity rule will ensure that there is a valid record in ST_Vendor and ST_Customer before the ST_Inv record will be recorded (or committed in relational terms) to the database. The Inv_Model, Inv_Type, and Inv_Make are enforced by the ST_MAIN program that will be used to maintain the ST_Inv table. The remainder of the fields are used to store pertinent information that relates to a particular car.

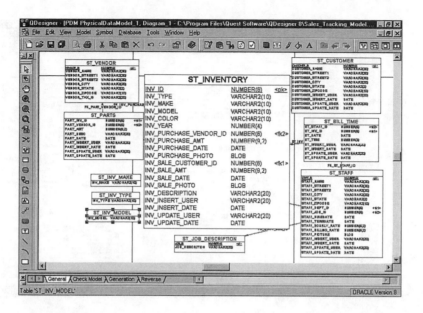

Figure 4.2: *Sales Tracking application ERD diagram focusing on the* ST_Inventory *entities.*

NOTE

Entity in relational terms is another name for fields or columns in a table.

The ST_Parts table contains the information necessary to track parts purchased for the cars in ST_Inventory (see Figure 4.3). There is the price of the part, the date it was purchased, a brief description as well as two foreign keys. The first foreign key, PARTS_Inv_Id, is related to ST_Inventory INV_Id to ensure that all parts acquired are associated with a particular automobile. The other foreign key, PARTS_Vendor_Id, ensures that all parts purchased can be traced back to their origin, tracked in the ST_Vendors table.

There are four fields that do not appear in this list. These fields are Inv_Insert_User, Inv_Insert_Date, Inv_Update_User, and Inv_Update_Date. These same fields appear in all the major and minor tables of this application (ST_Parts, ST_Vendor, ST_Bill_Time, and ST_Staff). These four fields track which user inserted the record to the table and which user was the last to update the table. This information could be useful if the wrong information was entered to see who might need additional training on how to use the application. These fields are automatically maintained by database triggers (Figure 4.4 maintains the ST_Inventory maintenance fields), or some code that executes each time a record is inserted or updated in these tables.

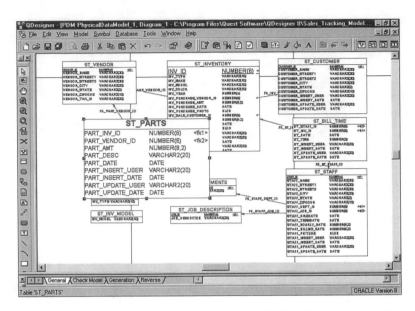

Figure 4.3: *Sales Tracking application ERD diagram focusing on the* ST_Parts *entities.*

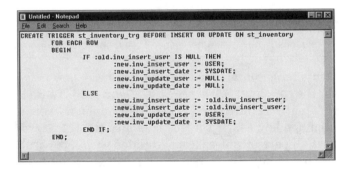

Figure 4.4: ST_Inventory's *database trigger.*

The ST_INVENTORY table is the main table of this application. This table tracks the vehicles: their initial cost, their sales cost, where they were purchased and to whom sold. The INV_ID is identified as a primary key, so Oracle8i will build an index on this column to ensure that its values are always unique and to provide fast access to the data. There are also two foreign keys on the INV_VENDOR_ID and INV_CUSTOMER_ID to guarantee that the related VENDOR_ID and CUSTOMER_ID exist in the ST_VENDOR table and the ST_CUSTOMER table prior to any INVENTORY activity. The business rule that applies here is that one cannot purchase a vehicle from a vendor that is not in the Sales Tracking application, nor can one sell a vehicle to a customer who is not in the Sales Tracking application.

The ST_INVENTORY table also has three reference tables, used by the ST_INVENTORY application to assist the data entry operator in filling in columns with valid data: INV_TYPE, INV_MAKE, and INV_MODEL. These three tables are used to load ST_INVENTORY columns with data or to verify that valid information is entered.

When vehicles require repairs, the software will need to track associated labor costs and required parts costs to correctly arrive at a cost of each vehicle. This information will help determine a sale price for the vehicle to ensure that there is a profit made on each vehicle. The ST_PARTS table is used to track parts used on the vehicles. The business rule that applies here is that parts must be associated with an individual vehicle, so there is a foreign key constraint linking this table to the ST_INVENTORY table. Another business rule that applies to ST_PARTS is that they must be purchased from a valid vendor in the ST_VENDOR table, so there is also a foreign key constraint linking this table to the ST_VENDOR table.

The other table used to track the total cost of a vehicle is the ST_BILL_TIME table, used to track labor costs associated with each vehicle. There are two business rules that govern this table: that time must be recorded against valid inventory items and that the person doing the work is a valid staff member. There is a foreign key between this table and the inventory table to ensure that valid vehicles are being worked on. The ST_STAFF table contains information about the employee, including a picture, billing rate, hourly rate, and contact information. In our example, the billing rate and hourly rate will be the same. There is a foreign key linking the ST_BILL_ TIME table with the ST_STAFF table to ensure that only valid employees are performing the work on the vehicles.

The ST_STAFF table has two reference type tables: ST_DEPARTMENTS and ST_ JOB_DESCRIPTIONS. The business rule that applies here is that each employee must be associated with a valid department and that each employee be associated with a valid job description. There are foreign key constraints between the ST_STAFF and ST_DEPARTMENTS/ST_JOB_DESCRIPTIONS to ensure that each employee contains correct department and job description.

The ST_STAFF department/job description will be handled with foreign key constraints. This ensures proper data in the ST_STAFF fields. This concept differs from that of the ST_INVENTORY model/make/type where the Oracle Form-based application will perform the integrity check. There are two reasons for the differences: first, to introduce you to a variety of ways of performing similar tasks; and second, because the data in the model/make/type might be subject to ad-hoc entries where the fields of ST_STAFF are not.

Building the Sample Application Database

Chapter 1, "Introducing Oracle9i," discussed the Oracle9i architecture—the relationship of physical computer files being created and assigned to Oracle9i tablespaces. Chapter 2, "Fundamentals of the SQL Language," illustrated how to create these tablespaces and assign a computer file to them.

The tablespaces of an Oracle database are much like the folders or directories found on a PC in that they are storage areas for information. These tablespaces, folders, and directories are designed to help locate information or to locate information on different parts of the computer. For example, the 'bin' folder on a computer is typically used to store programs. Folders or directories such as data would be for information files. The Oracle tablespace is similar in that different database objects such as tables and indexes can be assigned to various tablespaces for both convenience (allows the users and administrators to relate a tablespace name easily with a particular application or parts of an application) and performance.

Tablespace Layout

Chapter 13, "Oracle9i Indexing Options," utilizes the tablespace arrangement built in this chapter to adequately separate the Sales Tracking database objects by their disk-related activity. Figure 4.5 shows all the tablespaces assigned to the ORCL Oracle9i database. Notice all the tablespaces that begin with an ST_ belong to the Sales Tracking application and were created with the script in Listing 4.1.

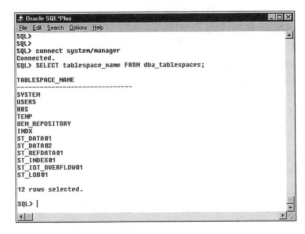

Figure 4.5: *Tablespaces assigned to Oracle9i Database ORCL.*

NOTE

Each tablespace has its own computer file or files, and these files are not shared by other tablespaces. This method of creating files on the computer system is a great way to physically separate database objects. On larger computer systems with many disk drives, these tablespace files would be created on separate physical disk drives to help with data retrieval performance. The author's single disk drive Windows NT 4.0 system will still create multiple tablespaces. This technique would greatly aid the administrator who had to move this application from a smaller computer to a larger one. The database administrator would only have to adjust the filenames on the DATAFILE lines in Listing 4.1 to accommodate most any computer system.

EXAMPLE

Listing 4.1: Install Sales Tracking Database

```
rem
rem      Sales Tracking Application Oracle8i Initial Database Setup
rem         Oracle9i By Example
rem            by Dan Hotka
rem         Que Publications May 2001
rem         All Rights Reserved
rem
spool INSTALL_sales_tracking_database.log

DROP TABLESPACE st_data01          INCLUDING CONTENTS CASCADE CONSTRAINTS;
DROP TABLESPACE st_data02          INCLUDING CONTENTS CASCADE CONSTRAINTS;
DROP TABLESPACE st_index01         INCLUDING CONTENTS CASCADE CONSTRAINTS;
DROP TABLESPACE st_refdata01       INCLUDING CONTENTS CASCADE CONSTRAINTS;
DROP TABLESPACE st_iot_overflow01  INCLUDING CONTENTS CASCADE CONSTRAINTS;
DROP TABLESPACE st_lob01           INCLUDING CONTENTS CASCADE CONSTRAINTS;

CREATE TABLESPACE st_data01
       DATAFILE 'd:\Oracle\Oradata\ORCL\st_data01.dbf' SIZE 10M REUSE
       DEFAULT STORAGE (INITIAL 10K
                        NEXT 10K
                        MINEXTENTS 5
                        MAXEXTENTS 100
                        )
       ONLINE;

CREATE TABLESPACE st_data02
       DATAFILE 'd:\Oracle\Oradata\ORCL\st_data02.dbf' SIZE 10M REUSE
       DEFAULT STORAGE (INITIAL 5K
                        NEXT 5K
                        MINEXTENTS 5
                        MAXEXTENTS 100
                        )
       ONLINE;
```

Listing 4.1: continued

```
CREATE TABLESPACE st_refdata01
        DATAFILE 'd:\Oracle\Oradata\ORCL\st_refdata01.dbf' SIZE 1M REUSE
        DEFAULT STORAGE (INITIAL 1K
                    NEXT 1K
                    MINEXTENTS 1
                    MAXEXTENTS 100
                    )
        ONLINE;


CREATE TABLESPACE st_index01
        DATAFILE 'd:\Oracle\Oradata\ORCL\st_index01.dbf' SIZE 5M REUSE
        DEFAULT STORAGE (INITIAL 5K
                    NEXT 5K
                    MINEXTENTS 5
                    MAXEXTENTS 100
                    )
        ONLINE;


CREATE TABLESPACE st_iot_overflow01
        DATAFILE 'd:\Oracle\Oradata\ORCL\st_iot_overflow01.dbf' SIZE 10M REUSE
        DEFAULT STORAGE (INITIAL 5K
                    NEXT 5K
                    MINEXTENTS 5
                    MAXEXTENTS 100
                    )
        ONLINE;


CREATE TABLESPACE st_lob01
        DATAFILE 'd:\Oracle\Oradata\ORCL\st_lob01.dbf' SIZE 10M REUSE
        DEFAULT STORAGE (INITIAL 10K
                    NEXT 10K
                    MINEXTENTS 1
                    MAXEXTENTS 100
                    )
        ONLINE;



CREATE USER sales_tracking
        IDENTIFIED BY sales_tracking
        DEFAULT TABLESPACE st_data01
        TEMPORARY TABLESPACE temp;

GRANT CONNECT, DBA TO sales_tracking;

spool off
exit
```

Listing 4.1 is designed to be run from SQL*Plus, and the SYSTEM password must be used. The author's Windows NT system has one physical hard drive with four logical partitions: C:, D:, E:, and G:. The Oracle9i ORCL database is installed on the D. Notice the file path in the DATAFILE lines in Listing 4.1 corresponds to the directory path of the Oracle8i ORCL installation on the D: partition.

WARNING

Make sure to adjust the operating-system directory path to that of your computer prior to running this script.

WARNING

Notice the DROP TABLESPACE commands at the beginning of Listing 4.1. This script should only be used for initial installation on a computer.

Each tablespace has its own assigned default storage parameters. These parameters will become the default for any object being created in this tablespace that does not have its own storage clause. It is more efficient for Oracle8i if all the extents (or units of storage) are the same size. This will be discussed more in detail in Chapter 7, "Using Advanced SQL Techniques and SQL*Plus Reporting Features."

This script also creates the Sales Tracking DBA account. All the objects will be created by a single user: sales_tracking. This greatly aids administration, backup, and recovery.

Figure 4.6 shows the newly created tablespaces.

Figure 4.6: *Oracle9i ORCL tablespaces.*

Creating the Database (Tables, Indexes, and Constraints)

The Sales Tracking database objects have many relationships. Many times, these relationships or constraints cannot be created until all the objects or tables have first been created. Oracle9i would not allow for a constraint or relationship to be created on an object that did not exist. Listing 4.2 is only a partial listing of the INSTALL_sales_tracking_database_objects.sql; Appendix C, "Web Sites and Product Codes," contains the whole listing. This script is also intended to be run only once per computer system. Listing 4.2 begins with creating a log file to capture the status of each drop and create statement of the script. Notice the DROP commands to clean up any database objects and prevent Object already exists errors in the event that this script has to be run more than once on a particular computer system.

NOTE

The SQL*Plus spool command in Listing 4.2 shows a way to capture all the competed and error messages that might have been displayed. These longer scripts more than fill a computer screen. Using a log file to capture all the messages is not only a good idea but a necessity to see if there were any problems, and of so, what the problem was.

Notice the CREATE TABLE st_inventory statement. The primary key constraint is defined inline and the index that will be created is also assigned to its own tablespace. Notice that all the objects in this script have their own storage parameters and tablespace assignments. This st_inventory object contains two LOBs (large objects such as pictures, video, sound files, and so on), both being pictures, and both will be stored in the tablespace ST_LOB01 as noted by the syntax in the storage clause. The st_inv_seq sequence is then created. This will be used by the ST_Inventory form to always create a unique number for the primary key st_inv_id. The next object to be created is the st_vendor table. Notice the out-of-line constraint in the ALTER TABLE command near the end of this listing. The foreign key constraint (that will ensure that any vendor_id being inserted in the st_inventory table first exists in the st_vendor table) could not be created until after the st_vendor table was created. Review the entire listing in Appendix C. Figure 4.10 illustrates the sqlplus syntax needed to run this script.

NOTE

An inline constraint is one that is defined where the field that it applies to is defined. An out-of-line constraint is one that is added with separate syntax at a later time. In Listing 4.2, the INV_ID column in the ST_INVENTORY table has an inline constraint. The primary key constraint is defined at the same time as the INV_ID column. The last command in Listing 4.2 is an out-of-line constraint where the ALTER TABLE syntax is adding a foreign key constraint.

NOTE

There is no reason that these objects could not be created in SQL*Plus as shown in Chapter 2 or by tools such as SQL*Navigator. The author finds it convenient to use INSTALL_xxx.sql files in this method to ensure that all objects are initially created in the correct order and without error.

EXAMPLE

Listing 4.2: Install Sales Tracking Database Objects (Partial Listing)

```
rem
rem       Sales Tracking Application Oracle9i Objects
rem         Oracle9i By Example
rem            by Dan Hotka
rem         Que Publications May 2001
rem          All Rights Reserved
rem
spool INSTALL_sales_tracking_objects.log

DROP TABLE st_inventory CASCADE CONSTRAINTS;
DROP SEQUENCE st_inv_seq;
DROP OBJECT address_field;
DROP TABLE st_parts CASCADE CONSTRAINTS;
DROP TABLE st_inv_type CASCADE CONSTRAINTS;
.
.
.
DROP TRIGGER st_bill_time_trg;

CREATE TABLE st_inventory
      (inv_id                  NUMBER(6)      CONSTRAINT pk_inv_id PRIMARY KEY
                                              USING INDEX TABLESPACE st_index01,
        inv_type              VARCHAR2(10),
        inv_make              VARCHAR2(10),
        inv model             VARCHAR2(10),
        inv_color             VARCHAR(10),
        inv_year              NUMBER(4),
        inv_purchase_vendor_id  NUMBER(6),
        inv_purchase_amt      NUMBER(9,2) NOT NULL,
        inv_purchase_date     DATE NOT NULL,
        inv_purchase_photo    BLOB,
        inv_sale_customer_id  NUMBER(6),
        inv_sale_amt          NUMBER(9,2),
        inv_sale_date         DATE,
        inv_sale_photo          BLOB,
        inv_description       VARCHAR2(20),
        inv_insert_user       VARCHAR2(20),
```

Listing 4.2: continued

```
         inv_insert_date          DATE,
         inv_update_user          VARCHAR2(20),
         inv_update_date          DATE)
         TABLESPACE st_data01
         PCTFREE 30
         PCTUSED              50
         STORAGE (INITIAL 10K
                 NEXT 10K
                 MINEXTENTS 5
                 MAXEXTENTS 10)
         LOB (inv_purchase_photo, inv_sale_photo) STORE AS
                 (TABLESPACE st_lob01
                  STORAGE (INITIAL 10K
                          NEXT 10K
                          MINEXTENTS 5
                          MAXEXTENTS 100)
                  CHUNK 500
                  NOCACHE
                  NOLOGGING);


CREATE SEQUENCE st_inv_seq
        START WITH 1
        INCREMENT BY 1
        CACHE 10;


        .
        .
        .




CREATE TABLE st_vendor
        (vendor_id             NUMBER(6)      PRIMARY KEY,
         vendor_name           VARCHAR2(30)    NOT NULL,
        .
        .
        .
        .


ALTER TABLE st_inventory      ADD CONSTRAINT fk_inv_purchase_vendor_id FOREIGN
KEY (inv_purchase_vendor_id)

                              REFERENCES sales_tracking.st_vendor(vendor_id);
        .
        .
```

Listing 4.2:   continued

```
.
.
/

spool off
exit
```

Creating Database Triggers

Notice the final four fields of the ST_INVENTORY table (inv_insert_user, inv_insert_date, inv_update_user, and inv_update_date). These are fields that track who inserted the record into the table and who made the last change to the table. SYSDATE is used for each of the date fields. These fields are important for applications that contain data critical to the needs of the business. This is a method of tracking who did what and when to the database. If erroneous data appears in the tables, this gives the database administrator an idea of where to begin to look for problems in programs or with any training issues with end users.

A database trigger is a piece of PL/SQL code that is run by the Oracle9i database based on certain types of DML activity on any table the trigger is created for. Listing 4.3 illustrates a database trigger that will execute before an insert or update to the st_inventory table, assigning the correct values to the four audit fields. A database trigger is useful in this instance to ensure that these fields are maintained, no matter what program was used to perform the DML (such as Oracle Forms, SQL*Plus, or a third-party program).

Notice the new. and old. prefixes on the fields. In database triggers, the prior value and the new value of any field are accessible with these two prefixes. The use of these prefixes to reset any of the values ensures that these fields accurately reflect the activity of the users.

Listing 4.3:   Sales Tracking Database Triggers (Partial Listing)

EXAMPLE

```
rem
rem      Sales Tracking Application Oracle8i Objects
rem         Oracle9i By Example
rem            by Dan Hotka
rem         Que Publications May 2001
rem         All Rights Reserved
rem
spool INSTALL_sales_tracking_objects.log
```

Listing 4.3: continued

```
.
.
.

CREATE TABLE st_inventory
        (.
.
.
.
.

CREATE TRIGGER st_inventory_trg BEFORE INSERT OR UPDATE ON st_inventory
        FOR EACH ROW
        BEGIN
                IF :old.inv_insert_user IS NULL THEN
                        :new.inv_insert_user := USER;
                        :new.inv_insert_date := SYSDATE;
                        :new.inv_update_user := NULL;
                        :new.inv_update_date := NULL;
        ELSE
                        :new.inv_insert_user := :old.inv_insert_user;
                        :new.inv_insert_date := :old.inv_insert_date;
                        :new.inv_update_user := USER;
                        :new.inv_update_date := SYSDATE;
                END IF;
        END;
/

.
.
.
/

spool off
exit
```

Summary

In this chapter, you installed the sample database and learned how Oracle9i maintains the relationships between these objects.

Reviewing It

1. Why does the author recommend using a prefix on all the application database objects?

2. Why does the author use a database trigger to maintain the data in the INSERT_USER, INSERT_DATE, UPDATE_USER, and UPDATE_DATE?

3. Why does the author spool a .log file out of the INSTALL scripts?

4. What is the ST_INV_SEQ useful for?

5. What is the difference between an inline and an out-of-line constraint.

CHECK

Checking It

1. An ERD crows foot pointing towards an object means:

   a) The table with the crows foot is a subset of the table at the other end

   b) The table with the crows foot has a 1-to-many relationship with the other object

   c) The table with the crows foot has more rows than the other object

2. A straight line in an ERD diagram indicates a one-to-one row relationship between the two objects.

   True/False

3. Creating multiple tablespaces is useful for:

   a) Tuning the application via distribution

   b) Aid in moving the application to larger computer systems

   c) Allows for different storage parameter defaults

   d) All of the above

4. Is SQL*Plus the only tool useful in creating database objects?

   True/False

5. What is the purpose of :new.inv_insert_user := :old.inv_insert_user; in the Listing 4.3.

   a) To insure the contents of the INV_INSERT_FIELD does not change

   b) To force the INV_INSERT_FIELD to a new value

   c) To allow for other processes to change the INV_INSERT_FIELD

Applying It

Independent Exercise 1:

- Download both INSTALL scripts from www.quepublishing.com.

- Review the Oracle9i directory structure on your computer.

- Edit INSTALL_Sales_Tracking_Database.sql and validate/change the file locations on the various CREATE TABLESPACE statements

- Execute the edited INSTALL_Sales_Tracking_Database.sql to create the book example Tablespaces.

- Review the LOG file for any errors.

Independent Exercise 2:

- Review the INSTALL_Sales_Trackng_Objects.sql.

- Execute the INSTALL_Sales_Tracking_Object.sql to create the book example objects.

- Review the LOG file for any errors.

Independent Exercise 3:

- Download the EXPORT_Sales_Tracking.dmp file from www.quepublishing.com.

- IMPORT the EXPORT_Sales_Tracking.dmp file.

What's Next?

These objects will be used in examples throughout the remainder of this book. The next chapter shows you how to build Windows- and Web-based Forms (useful for data entry and data query) using Oracle Developer 6i.

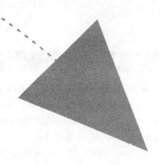

Building Oracle Forms

This chapter will build two forms, a simple form and a more advanced form using a PL/SQL function. Both of these forms will be based on objects created in Chapter 4, "Building an Oracle9i Database." You will then learn how to convert these forms to HTML and discover some techniques necessary to be successful with Oracle Forms in the HTML environment.

This chapter teaches you the following:

- Building forms usng Developer 6.0 or 6i
- Converting forms to HTML

Building Forms Using Developer 6.0 or 6.i

The next section begins with a simple form, describing in detail the terms associated with Oracle Developer and illustrating common techniques for building forms-based applications. Each forms-based program built draws upon the knowledge gained with the previous program. Chapter 19, "Putting It All Together: A Sales Tracking Application," will discuss how these forms fit into the Sales Tracking application.

Oracle Developer for Forms

The program units within Oracle Form Builder are called *modules*. Four kinds of modules exist: form modules, menu modules, object library modules, and PL/SQL library modules. This section concentrates on the form modules. You will learn how to build various types of forms, share code between programs, and discover the power of Oracle Forms.

The first application or program you will build is the ST_VENDOR application. This is a rather simple forms-based application based on a single database object: ST_VENDOR. Begin by starting the Form Builder program by double-clicking its icon or by selecting Start, Oracle Developer 6.0 (or 6i), Form Builder. This starts the Where to Start Wizard (see Figure 5.1). Four main options are available:

- Use the Data Block Wizard
- Open an Existing Form
- Build a New Form Manually
- Build a form based on a template

In addition, two learning selections are available:

- Run the Quick Tour (concepts)
- Explore the Cue Cards (tasks)

These two learning sections make excellent review.

TIP

Radio group—The selections on the wizard shown in Figure 5.1. Notice that single-clicking each option places a black dot in that option and removes the black dot from the previously selected item. This is similar to car radios, where only one button can be pressed at a time, making the selection.

Figure 5.1: *The Form Builder Where to Start Wizard.*

Select the Use the Data Block Wizard option. This brings up the Welcome to the Data Block Wizard screen. Click Next and the next screen displays the first choice (see Figure 5.2). Forms can be based on tables, views, or stored procedures. This section builds applications that are always based on tables or views. Make sure the radio button next to Table or View is selected, and click the Next button.

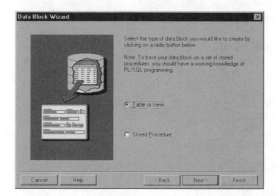

Figure 5.2: *Tables, views, or stored procedure options.*

The next screen asks for the table or view on which to base the application. Click the Browse button (see Figure 5.3). This causes Form Builder to access the database. Figure 5.4 shows one way of logging in to the database. Another method is to select Connect from the File at the top of the Form Builder menu bar (upper-left corner of the screen). The example database uses the user ID sales_tracking, and the password is the same: sales_tracking. The database is ORCL, as per the installation we performed in Chapter 4. After you're successfully logged in, a selection box will appear with all the tables and views available to this particular login (see Figure 5.5). The sales_tracking user ID was used to build all these objects.

NOTE

Our application uses the sales_tracking user ID (the password is the same) and the ORCL database name (tnsnames entry) was created during the Oracle9i database installation. Check with your database administrator if you did not perform the Oracle9i database software installation for the database name (tnsnames entry). Your installation might have required a different user ID and password and even a different database name.

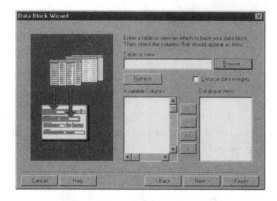

Figure 5.3: *Data Block Wizard—table or view entry.*

Figure 5.4: *Data Block Wizard—connect to database.*

Figure 5.5: *Data Block Wizard—table/view selection.*

Select ST_VENDOR from this list. All the ST_VENDOR columns to which the user has access are now displayed in the lower-left pane. You can select each column you want to have in the form individually by clicking the column (to highlight it) and then the > button, or you can select all the columns by clicking the >> button (see Figure 5.6). Sometimes it is easier to select all the columns and then deselect the few that are not desired by clicking to highlight them and clicking the < button. The << button will deselect all the columns.

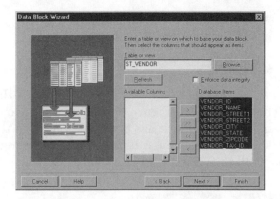

Figure 5.6: *Data Block Wizard—column selection.*

Click the >> button to select all the columns and then click Next. The final screen in the Data Block Wizard will appear. Select the default option Create the Data Block, then call the Layout Wizard, and click Finish. When the Welcome to the Layout Wizard screen appears, click Next. Figure 5.7 shows some options on the next screen: Content, Stacked, Vertical Toolbar, Horizontal Toolbar, and Tab. A *canvas* is the visual part of the application. A *content canvas* is the canvas that appears when the application first starts up. Each form must have a content canvas. A *stacked canvas*, on the other hand, has the capability to overlay or appear on top of other canvases to hide information or to show parts of information when other information is being accessed. A *toolbar* automatically appears in all forms, and, finally, *tab* canvases, like stacked canvases, automatically overlay one another. Tab canvases differ in that a tab remains visible along the top of the canvas, and when clicked, it brings the associated tab canvas to the top. You will learn how to use both the content canvases and tab canvases in this section.

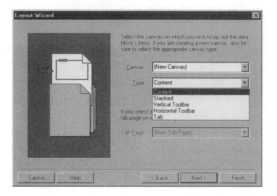

Figure 5.7: *The Layout Wizard canvas selection.*

Select Content in the second box, leaving (New Canvas) as the only option in the first box. Then, click Next. Figure 5.8 shows the Layout Wizard Data Block layout screen. Only one block has been selected from the Data Block Wizard; select this and select all the columns in the same manner as you learned in the Data Block Wizard, and then click Next.

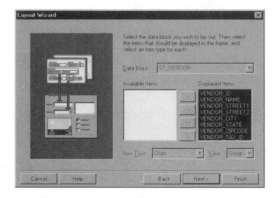

Figure 5.8: *Layout Wizard Data Block / Column selection.*

The next screen is illustrated in Figure 5.9. This Layout Wizard screen is a convenient place to change the prompts that will appear onscreen and the size of the fields onscreen. Several ways are available to make these kinds of changes; for now, accept the defaults on this screen and click the Next button.

The next screen is where you can make the selection of a form (single row per screen) or tabular (multiple rows per screen) layout. A *frame* is directly related to a block, and of course, the block has a direct reference to a table or view. Keep in mind that more than one frame can exist per canvas. Our ST_VENDOR application will display only one record at a time, so be sure the Form radio button is selected and click Next.

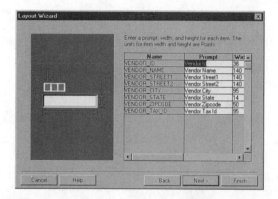

Figure 5.9: *Layout Wizard prompt and field size screen.*

The next screen gives the frame a name (see Figure 5.10). No set standard for names exists, but using some kind of naming convention that includes what the form relates to is advisable. A naming convention will make the objects easier to find and relate to their function in the Object Navigator of Form Builder. Use a similar naming convention for the blocks as well. Type a name in the Frame Title and let the other fields default to one record displayed and no other selections made. Click the Next button.

NOTE

I display only one record on a forms-based application and as many as 15 records on tabular-type forms. I also always use a scrollbar on the tabular-type forms.

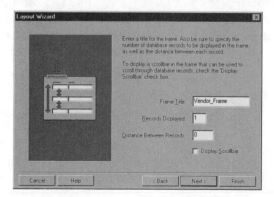

Figure 5.10: *Layout Wizard form name and record count selection.*

This will complete the Layout Wizard. Click the Finish button and the Object Navigator will appear, as well as the canvas layout (see Figure 5.11).

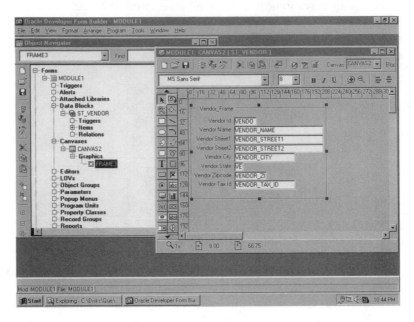

Figure 5.11: *Object Navigator and Canvas Layout windows.*

The fields and labels can be easily moved around onscreen by first single-clicking the item to be moved and then clicking and holding down (this will pick up the object) while moving the mouse and moving the object to the place desired on the canvas. Labels can be double-clicked to highlight them, enabling the text within to be changed. These fields can easily be moved by single-clicking and then clicking and holding to move to a new location as well. Make sure you notice the Object Navigator. You can now see the data block, the name you gave the data block, the canvas, the name you gave the canvas, and the frame with the name you gave the frame. Canvases are the physical screen layout, and all the triggers and the data block area control data access.

All the Oracle manuals are available by clicking the Help button at the right end of the toolbar. Figure 5.12 shows the main help screen. Each of these manuals is accessed by double-clicking the desired selection. Each manual has a hyperlinked index, which means that any item can be instantly referenced in the index by simply clicking the phrase or term.

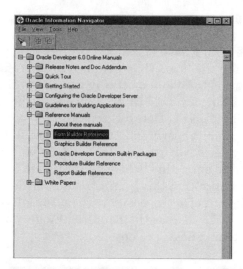

Figure 5.12: *Oracle online help manuals.*

Just about every item, canvas, block, frame, and so on has a *property palette* that contains all the information about the particular item. This palette can be accessed with a variety of methods. You can either double-click the item or canvas or double-click the item, block, or canvas in the Object Navigator. In addition, you can right-click these same items and then select Property Palette from the pop-up menu. Notice that the items are now displayed in the Object Navigator. This was easily accomplished by clicking the + next to the Items entry in the Object Navigator under the data blocks (see Figure 5.13). You should notice that as you click items on the canvas, the associated item automatically highlights in the Object Navigator. The ST_VENDOR Block Property Palette is displayed in Figures 5.13 and 5.14. Review all the items available in the Block Property Palette. For instance, you can see that the block name can be changed, the database tables being referenced are named, and so on.

Many of the forms features are controlled by the Item Property Palette. This palette controls all the aspects of each item, including its visual attributes, how text is entered, and whether the field is even enterable, as well as its associated help text and its list-of-values (LOVs). Take a moment to look at the Item Property Palette. It is important to understand most of the options on this palette to be able to better control how the form appears and interacts with users. For instance, the General area gives the item a specific name, typically the same name the item receives if assigned to a database field. The next item is the item type. This item could be a picture, sound, radio button, or text item. Later, we will see how to control the attributes of the text items (such as numbers, dates, and so on). The Functional area of the Item Property Palette controls how the computer cursor will work when in the field. This area also controls how the text will be entered, if the cursor is to be automatically moved to the next enterable field upon completely filling the field (Auto Skip), and whether the data will be displayed in the field (Conceal Data). Next, take a look at the Navigation and Data parts of the Item Property Palette. The important field in the Navigation part is Keyboard Navigable, which indicates whether the computer cursor is allowed to enter this field. The Data part of the palette controls the type of item; notice that this item is a number field with a maximum enterable length of seven positions. The Initial Value is useful to display any default values, whereas the Required Field is useful to ensure that all NOT NULL defined fields are entered.

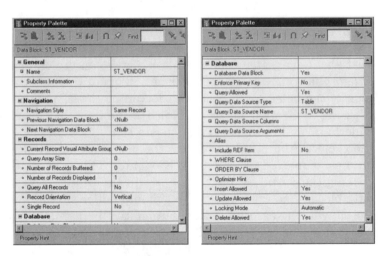

Figure 5.13: *The Data Block Property Palette.*

The Data Block Wizard picks up the type, length, and required field information from the database table. Copy Item From (Item Property Palette) is useful in multi-tab– or multi-canvas–type applications so that users need to input data only once for use throughout the application. The Synchronize With Item will push this value to other items in the same form application. Important fields in the database part of the Item Property Palette include whether this item is assigned to a database table/column (Database Item) and the name of that database column if the answer is yes (Column Name). Other fields in this area help control how this particular item will interact with the Oracle9i database—namely, whether it can be queried, updated, and so on. You also should take a look at the List of Values (LOV), Editor, and Physical parts of the Item Property Palette. The List of Values part indicates whether an LOV is assigned to this particular item. This is simply a pointer to the actual LOV. (LOVs are covered in detail later in this section.) The Physical part of this Item Property Palette indicates with which canvas (Canvas) this item is associated and whether it is displayed (Visible). The other item of interest in the Physical section of the palette is the scrollbar setting. Remember, for our form, we asked that the scrollbar not be displayed from the Layout Wizard.

TIP

Oracle6/6i Forms allows you to specify a one-time where clause that lets you change the WHERE clause on a block for the next operations only.

Other items of interest in the Item Property Palette are physical attributes of the item, such as its font, colors, and so on. You also have the option of configuring the same type of attributes for the prompt. The Hint and Display Hint Automatically attributes are the highlights of the Help part of this property palette. Any hint text defined will appear at the bottom of the form, and it will appear automatically when the field is entered if the Display Hint Automatically is set to Yes.

TIP

List of values—A forms feature that opens up an additional window with data from another database table so the user can easily make entry selections from this list.

When you look at the Data Block Property Palette on your system, you'll see that it has just a few key areas of interest. Most of these areas were already set up during the Data Block Wizard, and little reason should exist to make changes. When you open the Item Property Palette, it displays the General, Navigation, and Records settings. The General area contains the block name, and the Navigation area controls the relationship of this block to other blocks that might be defined in the application. This application has only the single block that references the ST_VENDOR table, so the previous and next blocks are automatically set to null. The Database part of the palette shows that this data block is assigned to a database table, the name of that table, and any default forms behaviors that are desired for this application.

The highlights of the Frame Property Palette are the physical attributes, such as the Color section that controls the foreground, background, edges, fill patterns, and so on. Figure 5.14 displays this part of the Frame Property Palette and shows where the frame itself (Edge Pattern) is set to transparent. This removes the box that appears around the items by default.

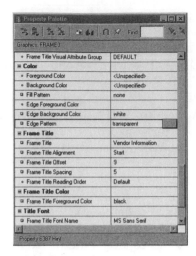

Figure 5.14: *The Frame section of the Item Property Palette.*

TIP

It is a good idea to save your work from time to time. I recommend creating a directory and keeping all the application programs together in the same directory or folder. Save your form as ST_VENDOR in the folder named Sales_Tracking_Pgms. When the form is saved, this name then replaces the default MODULE1 name with the new name of the form.

Figure 5.15 displays the frame after rearranging the items and prompts and making the Edge Pattern transparent. To make navigation between the fields flow nicely when using the Tab key, the items in the Object Navigator (left side of Figure 5.15) should be in the same order as they appear on the Canvas layout (right side of the figure). This is easily accomplished by clicking the item to be moved in the Object Navigator, clicking and holding, and then moving the mouse up or down; as the item moves, a line will appear between the other items. Release the button when the line is between the items, placing the moved item in the correct sequence with the items on the canvas.

The ST_VENDOR database table has an associated sequence—ST_VENDOR_SEQ—that is used to ensure a unique VENDOR_ID (which happens to be a primary key). A sequence is used so that no matter how many users are entering vendor information with this form, a unique vendor identification will always be generated. Several *triggers* are associated with a form-level data block, and many more types of triggers can be used to control keystrokes, change the functionality of pre-assigned forms keys, and so on. The desired function is to retrieve and display the next available sequence number in the VENDOR_ID item prior to the record being inserted into the database. This functionality is implemented with a block-level Pre-Insert trigger. This trigger will run the assigned PL/SQL code just prior to inserting the record in the database. When you right-click the data block ST_VENDOR, a pop-up menu appears and you can select the PL/SQL editor.

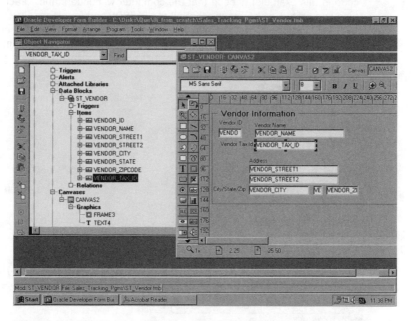

Figure 5.15: *Canvas layout of the ST_VENDOR form.*

NOTE

Trigger—Some code that executes on an event, such as a keystroke or before or after a record is inserted, updated, or deleted. The Forms Development Guide (from the Help menu) lists all the types of triggers supported in Oracle Developer V6.0. (Chapter 3, "Fundamentals of PL/SQL," covers how to create and use PL/SQL.)

The PL/SQL Editor immediately prompts you for the type of trigger desired (see Figure 5.16; this is actually an LOV!). Select PRE-INSERT, which causes a PL/SQL editing window to appear (see Figure 5.17). Click the Compile button when you're finished entering the code. If any errors occur, a box will appear at the bottom of this window with the line number and problem discovered. However, if no problems exist, the Compiled Successfully message will appear in the lower-right part of the screen. Notice the :ST_VENDOR.VENDOR_ID in the INTO clause. The : tells Oracle

Forms that this is an item within the form. ST_VENDOR is the name of the data block, and VENDOR_ID is the name of the item. Notice that this SQL statement is referring to the form item and not the database item.

NOTE

Compiling—A computer term that refers to the conversion of the source code (PL/SQL code in this example) to code that the computer will understand. Oracle Forms are *run-time interpreted*, which means that all the PL/SQL and forms code (from the palettes, and so on) will be converted into some intermediate code, which is then interpreted into instructions the computer will understand by the Oracle Forms Runtime program.

Figure 5.16: Selecting the trigger type.

Figure 5.17: The PL/SQL Editor with ST_VENDOR_SEQ code.

Save your work by selecting File, Save from the upper-left menu bar. Click the traffic light on the Canvas window. This compiles the form and starts the Forms Runtime environment (runs the newly developed form).

NOTE

When a form is saved, it is given a file suffix of .fmb, which stands for forms binary file. When a form is compiled, a file generated with the same name as the save but with a suffix of .fmx. This .fmx file is what the Oracle Developer Forms Runtime program reads and converts to instructions the computer understands. These .fmb and .fmx files are portable across various types of hardware platforms, which makes the Oracle application very portable in the computing environment. Oracle Developer Forms Runtime is coded specifically for these various environments, not the .fmb and .fmx files.

Figure 5.18 shows the newly developed ST_VENDOR form application and puts the cursor in the first enterable field: Vendor ID. The first issue you will discover is that the Vendor ID is a primary key field to the underlying database table ST_VENDOR, so the Layout Wizard made this a mandatory entered field. However, the behavior we want is to enter the other fields and have this field filled in for us from the sequence generator when we click the Save button (the disk icon button on the toolbar). Click the Exit button (the open door on the toolbar) and access the VENDOR_ID Item Property Palette (see Figure 5.19). Find the Required field in the Data section of this palette and change it to No. Because we really do not need to enter this field first, move the item to be the last item in the Item list in the Object Navigator. The field will still appear first onscreen, but the Vendor Name field will now be the field the computer cursor will stop at first. When you return to Runtime by clicking the traffic light, you can enter data, beginning with the Vendor Name field (see Figure 5.20). Notice that the Vendor ID automatically fills in when the Save button is clicked.

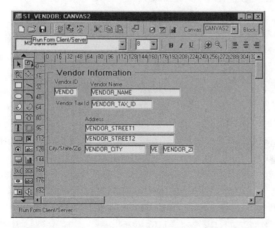

Figure 5.18: Running the ST_Vendor form.

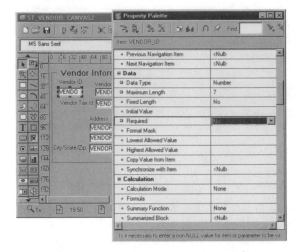

Figure 5.19: *The VENDOR_ID Property Palette.*

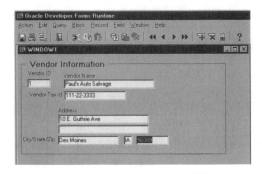

Figure 5.20: *ST_Vendor Runtime with data.*

Oracle Forms Default Behavior

Oracle Forms has many features that do not have to be programmed or set up in the Object Navigator. For example, Oracle Forms can enter data, change data, delete data, and query data without having to add any code in the Object Navigator to perform these tasks. The buttons on the toolbar are quite useful as well (see Figure 5.21). Starting from left to right: The disk button is the Save or Commit Records button. The next one to the right is the Print button, and the button next to it is the Printer Setup button. The open-door button is the Forms Exit button. Then you see the Cut, Copy, and Paste buttons (starting with the scissors). The next three buttons are the Query Mode buttons. The first in the trio is Enter Query Mode, the middle one is Execute Query, and the rightmost button of the three is Exit

Query Mode. The << button navigates the form to the previous block; the < button positions the cursor at the previous record. The > button is the Next Record button (this button and the Previous Record button are very useful with tabular-type displays where multiple records are displayed onscreen), and the >> button navigates the form to the next block. The + button inserts a record, and the X button deletes a record. The padlock button places an Oracle lock on the record the cursor is in (not allowing others to make changes to this row), and the ? button is the Forms Help button.

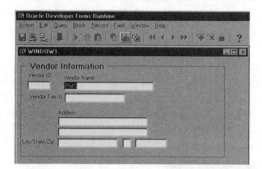

Figure 5.21: *Oracle Forms Query mode.*

Query mode is a powerful feature. When in Query mode, one or more fields can be filled in to search for records. Notice in Figure 5.21 that the pattern searching learned in Chapter 2, "Fundamentals of the SQL Language," works in Query mode as well. When the Enter Query button is clicked, only the Execute Query and Exit Query buttons are highlighted. Figure 5.22 shows the results of the query. If no fields were filled in during the Query mode, Oracle Forms begins returning all the rows from the assigned database table. The < and > buttons are useful for scrolling through the returned rows.

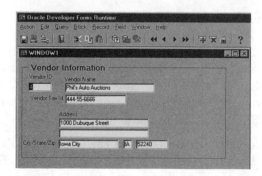

Figure 5.22: *Results of the Query mode.*

Another toolbar exists to the left of the Object Navigator. This toolbar has many of the options in the File menu as well as some useful runtime buttons (see Figure 5.23). The top button on this toolbar, which looks like a white page of paper, is the New Module button. Click this and MODULE2 appears in Object Navigator, as you see in Figure 5.23. The folder button is the Open Existing Form button, and the disk button is the Save button. The next three buttons deal with the Forms Runtime: the traffic light runs the form in Windows mode, the traffic light with the globe behind it runs the form in a Web browser (Web mode), and the button under that one (a yellow bug) is the Forms Runtime in Debug mode. Next are the Cut-Copy-Paste buttons. After those three is a button with a + and white box, which creates a new item in the Object Navigator (the item is based on where the cursor is in the Object Navigator). The next button, -, deletes the item that is currently highlighted. The +, -, and ++ in boxes (the last three buttons) simulate entering or exiting items in the Object Navigator that have a + or X next to them. If an Object Navigator item has a + next to it, more levels of items exist that can be displayed.

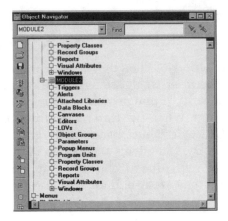

Figure 5.23: *New module in Object Navigator.*

To start the Data Block Wizard, select Data Block Wizard from the Tools menu. Notice that MODULE2 is highlighted in the Object Navigator. This is how Form Builder knows to which form to add a data block. Build a block for the database table ST_CUSTOMER using the same options you learned when creating the ST_VENDOR form.

Scroll up in the Object Navigator (or Open the ST_VENDOR form if it is closed) and access the PRE_INSERT trigger we created in ST_VENDOR. Click the Copy button on the toolbar, scroll down to MODULE2, and click the Paste button. This should copy the trigger from the previous form to this new form. Double-click the new trigger and change it so that this trigger accesses the customer sequence and CUSTOMER_ID items instead of the vendor sequence and the VENDOR_ID item (see Figure 5.24). Save this new form as ST_CUSTOMER and try it out.

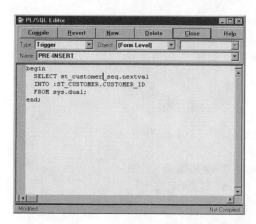

Figure 5.24: *Editing the PL/SQL trigger from ST_VENDOR.*

Let's build a tabular-type form. First, we need to create a new module in the Object Navigator and start the Data Block Wizard. The database table will be ST_DEPARTMENTS (see Figure 5.25). On the screen that follows, be sure to select the Tabular Style radio button this time. Figure 5.26 shows how to configure the number of rows displayed as well as how to select a scrollbar that will provide easy access to additional records not displayed when in Query Mode. Figure 5.27 shows what the default canvas layout looks like. Save this module as ST_DEPARTMENTS.

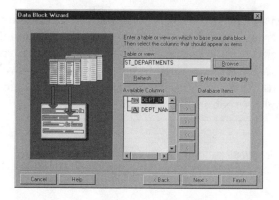

Figure 5.25: *The Data Block Wizard for ST_DEPARTMENTS.*

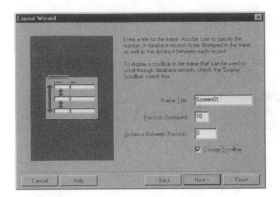

Figure 5.26: *Layout Wizard rows displayed.*

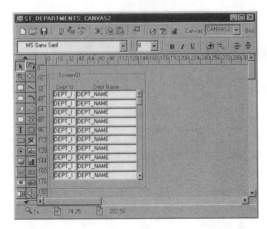

Figure 5.27: *Module ST_DEPARTMENTS canvas layout.*

Be sure you create the PRE-INSERT trigger for the database sequence.
Your Runtime screen with data should look similar to the left screen in
Figure 5.28. The ST_JOBS application has the same features as
ST_DEPARTMENTS; we now need to build this form, as well as access the
ST_JOB_DESCRIPTIONS database table. The completed form should look
similar to the right screen in Figure 5.28.

NOTE

The Que companion Web site for this book at www.quepublishing.com contains all the
examples, installation scripts, and data illustrated in this book.

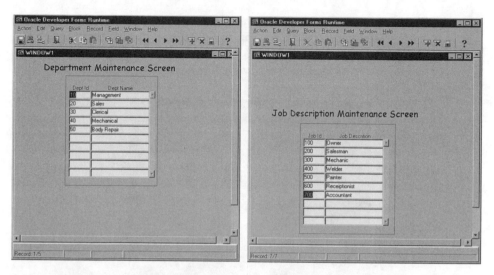

Figure 5.28: *ST_DEPARTMENTS and ST_JOB_DESCRIPTIONS runtime with entered data.*

Build Tab-Type Style Applications

The next application uses a tab-type canvas style. This application, ST_ TYPE_MAKE_MODEL, will be a table-maintenance application that is used just to maintain the records in the following three tables: ST_INV_ TYPE, ST_INV_MAKE, and ST_INV_MODEL. These tables will become LOVs in our final forms-based application example. This application could easily be three separate forms-type programs because each of the tabs will be unrelated to any of the other tabs. This is probably not the best use of a tab-type application, but it works as an example.

Now, let's create a new module in the Object Navigator and run the Data Block Wizard for database table ST_INV_TYPE. In the Layout Wizard, select Tab type canvas in the second window. This will create a default canvas display similar to the one shown in Figure 5.29. Start the Data Block Wizard again for ST_INV_MAKE (see Figure 5.30). Because another table is being added to the same form, the Data Block Wizard is smart enough to know that a relationship might be necessary between this block and the ST_INV_TYPE block just added. However, for this application, no such relationship exists, so you can leave the fields blank.

Once again, the Layout Wizard is smart enough to see that we are building a tab-type application and appropriately takes the correct defaults (see Figure 5.31). Figure 5.32 shows what the canvas now looks like with the two tabs on the canvas. No sequences are involved with these three database tables. Following the process just outlined for the ST_INV_MODEL table, change the tab headings in the property palette or on the canvas, which should cause your application to look similar to Figure 5.33.

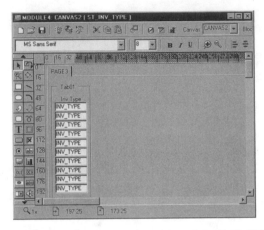

Figure 5.29: *Canvas layout ST_INV_TYPE tab.*

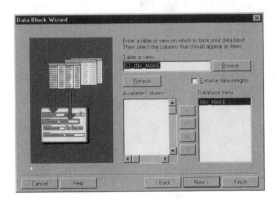

Figure 5.30: *The Data Block Wizard for ST_INV_MAKE.*

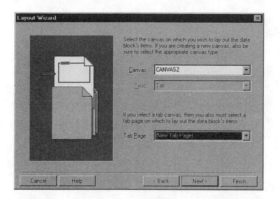

Figure 5.31: *The Data Block Wizard screen to create relationships.*

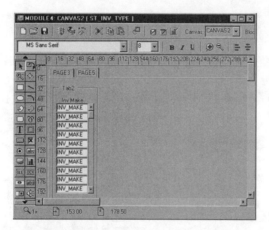

Figure 5.32: *Layout Wizard with new canvas tab.*

Our ST_STAFF application will build on the forms-style application you
have already learned. It will introduce how to set up the LOVs on a particular screen item. To get started, let's create a new module and go through
the Data Block Wizard (for the ST_STAFF database object) and Layout
Wizard (forms-based, single-row-displayed style). Save this new application
with the name ST_STAFF. Your newly created form should look similar to
Figure 5.34. As you can see in Figure 5.34, you can add an LOV when you
select the LOV Wizard from the Tools item on the top menu bar.

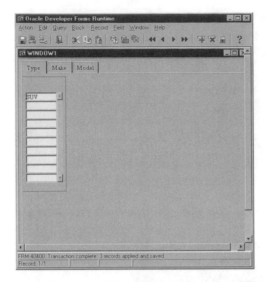

Figure 5.33: ST_TYPE_MAKE_MODEL *runtime with entered data.*

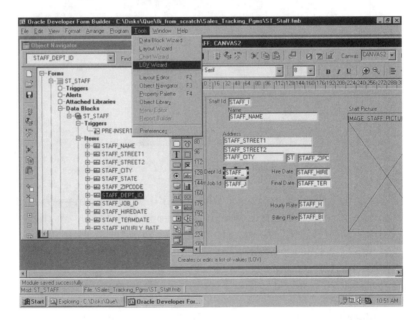

Figure 5.34: LOV Wizard access on ST_STAFF application.

When you work with the LOV Wizard, ensure that the radio button New
Record Group Based on a Query is selected and click Next. Click the Build

SQL Query button. This accesses the Query Builder, prompting you to select a table from a list (see Figure 5.35). Click the Include button, and a check box of items to display will appear (see Figure 5.36). Click both items for this application and then click OK. Figure 5.37 shows how the LOV Wizard is filled in with the newly built query.

Figure 5.35: Select a database table.

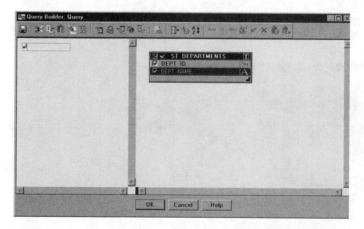

Figure 5.36: The Select Display Items pop-up menu.

As you can see in Figure 5.38, you should select the items for display in the LOV from the assigned query that we just built. Select both columns by clicking the >> button. This will bring up the LOV Wizard Column Properties screen (see Figure 5.39). Be sure you click Look up return item because doing so generates the Items and Parameters box. This selection shows which field from the database table assigned to the LOV will be passed back to the assigned application item. Select the ST_STAFF.STAFF_ DEPT_ID item from this list and click OK, and then click the Next button. This brings up an LOV Wizard screen where you choose how many database rows to display in the LOV (see Figure 5.40). Enter 20 and click Refresh record group data before displaying LOV. This feature reruns the query to ensure the most current values appear onscreen from the LOV. Finally, click Next.

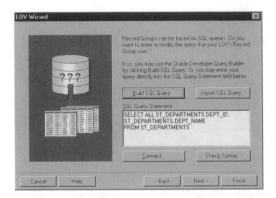

Figure 5.37: The LOV Wizard with a newly built query.

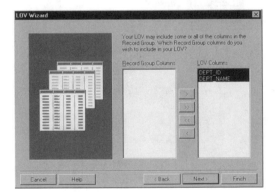

Figure 5.38: LOV Wizard display columns.

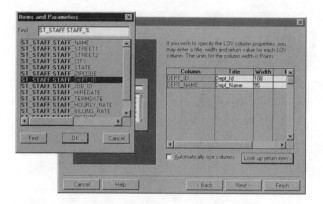

Figure 5.39: LOV Wizard return items.

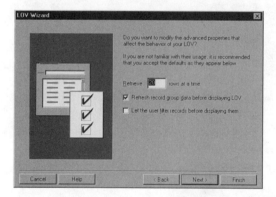

Figure 5.40: LOV Wizard for rows to display.

Figure 5.41 shows the last LOV Wizard screen, which will enable you to
select a screen item for the return value you selected in Figure 5.39. Select
the STAFF_DEPT_ID item from the list with either the > or >> button.
Click Next or Finish because the only screen left is the final LOV Wizard
screen. Figure 5.42 shows how the new LOV appears in the ST_STAFF_ID
Property Palette. To access the LOV from the Oracle Forms Runtime of
ST_STAFF, select Display List from the Runtime Edit menu. Figure 5.41
shows what the LOV looks like.

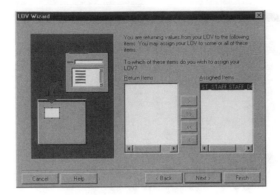

Figure 5.41: LOV Wizard returned value screen item assignment.

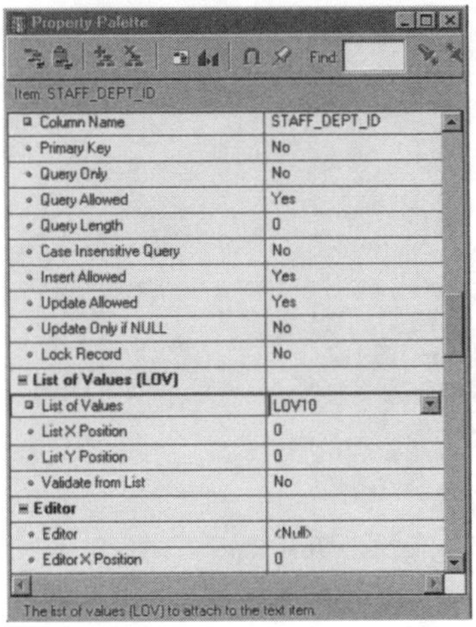

Figure 5.42: STAFF_ID Property Palette showing LOV assignment.

It is much more convenient for the person using the application to activate the LOV when a button is assigned to access the LOV. The presence of this button indicates to the user that more information is available for this field by clicking the button. The Button tool is the rectangular item just under the T (Text Item) on the left toolbar on the canvas layout screen (see Figure 5.44). This button item is automatically assigned a name. In addition, it is always recommended that you change the name of these buttons to reflect the nature of the buttons. Right-click the new button item in the Object Navigator and add a WHEN-MOUSE-CLICK trigger.

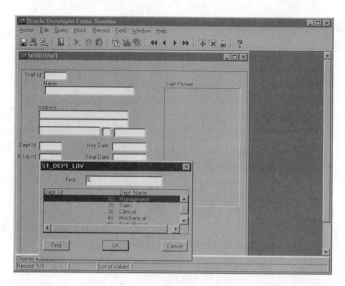

Figure 5.43: *LOV in the forms runtime of ST_STAFF.*

The only text of this trigger is to call the LIST_VALUES key built-in (see Figure 5.45). A built-in function is also available that replicates any key or menu item function in the Forms environment. This particular function runs when the WHEN-MOUSE-CLICK trigger fires and has the same functionality as calling the LOV from the menu bar. Figure 5.45 also shows the ST_DEPT_LOV being displayed after the button is clicked.

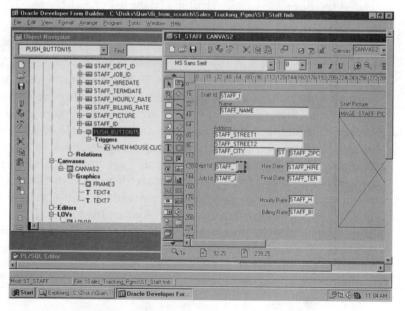

Figure 5.44: *Adding a push button for the LOV.*

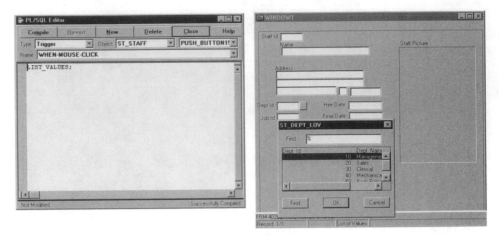

Figure 5.45: *Continuing the process of adding a push button for the LOV.*

In most cases, it is desirable to edit or verify that the data entered into a particular field is valid data. The Item Property Palette is a useful place to ensure that if a field is to contain a number, only numbers can be entered. This again is the default behavior of Forms Runtime, which verifies that information entered into a field matches the assigned attributes of that field. When the data in a field can be checked for particular content (all uppercase, containing a certain range of numbers or dates, and so on) or to ensure that it's a valid entry in a database table, a PL/SQL trigger must be coded to check for the particular attributes or existence of a row.

The WHEN-VALIDATE-ITEM trigger, if defined, runs when the cursor attempts to leave the forms item to which the trigger is assigned. Figure 3.46 shows how to add this trigger, accessing it by right-clicking STAFF_DEPT_ID and selecting the Smart Triggers menu item. The Smart Triggers menu item contains the commonly used triggers for the particular part of the Object Navigator being accessed. For example, a different list of Smart Triggers will be at the block and form levels of a form. Figure 5.47 shows the PL/SQL and SQL code necessary to check to see whether the STAFF_DEPT_ID item exists in the ST_DEPARTMENTS table. Notice several of the PL/SQL techniques that are discussed in Chapter 3, at work here, such as the variable naming convention, the %TYPE, and so on. The RAISE Form-Trigger-Failure returns a failure to the form from this trigger, thus displaying the message in the EXCEPTIONS clause. Notice in Figure 5.47 that an invalid entry of 5000 was entered and indeed the message that was coded in the trigger is the message that appears at the bottom of the screen. The cursor will not be able to move from this field until a valid entry is made.

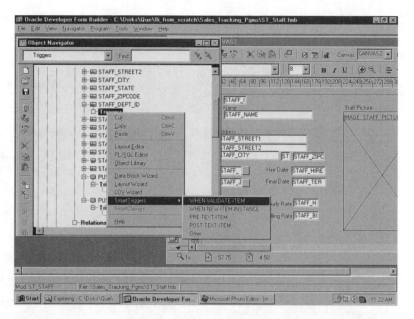

Figure 5.46: *Adding the WHEN-VALIDATE-ITEM trigger.*

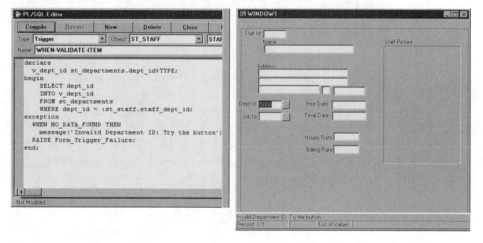

Figure 5.47: *The WHEN-VALIDATE-ITEM trigger code.*

Add a button for the Job ID item to access the LOV for that item. Also add a WHEN-VALIDATE-ITEM trigger to verify the contents of the Job ID item with that of the ST_JOB_DESCRIPTION database table.

As we enter a new area of development in our project, you'll see that the ST_STAFF application makes reference to a picture field. This was defined at the database level as a binary long object (BLOB). The property palette for this particular item contains options to the various types of BLOBs, such as video, sound streams, and so on. To store a picture in the database, we will use the Windows cut/paste edit features to accomplish putting the picture in the application. Access the picture via a Windows program such as Paintbrush or Microsoft Photo Editor (see Figure 5.48).

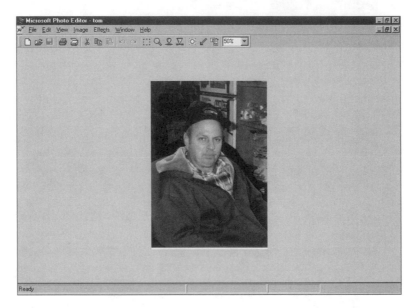

Figure 5.48: *Access the picture via a Windows application.*

Two methods of copying this picture are available: You can either click Edit on the top menu bar and select Copy, or some programs will allow a right-click to access the Edit menu (and then select Copy). This copies the image into a work area in the Windows operating system. In the ST_STAFF application, click the picture object one time (the gray box under Staff Picture in Figure 5.49), click Edit on the top menu bar, and then click Paste. The picture from the Windows program should now appear in the Staff Picture box (see Figure 5.50). Click the Save button to commit this record to the database.

Build the ST_BILL_TIME application based on the ST_BILL_TIME table; do not display the four audit fields (INSERT_USER, INSERT_DATE, UPDATE_USER, and UPDATE_DATE). The fields are maintained via a database trigger as an audit vehicle so the DBA can see who created the record and who last updated the record. Display ten records on the canvas with a scrollbar on the right. Be sure to save your work with Save As from the File menu and name the form ST_BILL_TIME.

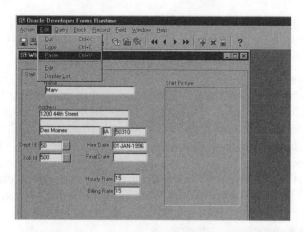

Figure 5.49: *Paste the picture into the ST_STAFF picture item.*

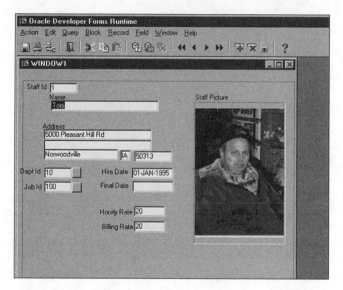

Figure 5.50: *ST_STAFF data with the picture object.*

Sometimes displayed items are not associated with a block, such as totals. In addition, sometimes it's convenient to add buttons to help the application user with tasks such as adding up a column of numbers just entered and saving records to the database. It is good design to give the user a distinct set of buttons to click, thus controlling and limiting the mouse movements within an application.

As you have learned, all form items are associated with a block. And blocks so far have always been associated with a database table. However, a *control* block is a form block that is not based on a database table. This control block is where total fields are placed and is a convenient place for buttons, hidden fields (often used to hold variables), or any item that is not to be associated with a data block.

Add a new block to the ST_BILL_TIME application by first clicking the Data Blocks label in the Object Navigator and then clicking the green + on the toolbar along the left side of the Object Navigator. This will bring up a New Data Block box (see Figure 5.51). Check the Build a New Data Block Manually radio button and click OK. Access the New Blocks Property Palette by double-clicking the block item (or right-click the block item and select Property Palette with a click) and then name the block Control Block, ensuring the Database Data Block item under Database is set to No.

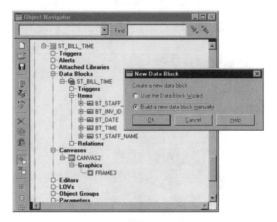

Figure 5.51: *Adding a control block.*

Blocks assigned to a database table have the inherited functionality of Insert, Update, Delete, and Query mode features. Anything that happens to a control block must be specifically set up. The requirement for ST_BILL_TIME is to provide an easy method for the user to ensure the time entered adds up to 40. An item will need to be added to the control block to hold this calculation, as well as a button added for the user to click when this calculation is to occur. It would also be nice to add a Save Records button so the user does not have to move the mouse from the bottom of the form to the top of the form just to save the work performed.

Click the control block in the Object Navigator and then click the Text Item tool (the abc in a white box in the Canvas Tool Palette) and create the text item exactly under the BT_TIME column of the tabular database item (see Figure 5.52). Clicking the control block first will ensure that the new text item gets created in the control block. Use the Button tool to add two buttons, as illustrated in Figure 5.53.

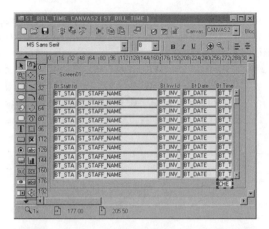

Figure 5.52: *Adding a text item to the control block.*

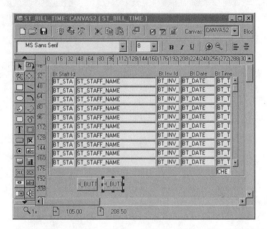

Figure 5.53: *Add two additional buttons to the control block.*

The desired behavior in this example is to access each row of the
ST_BILL_TIME data block, add the contents to a field on the control block
named CHECK_TIME, and perform this task repeatedly for each row that
appears onscreen. This can be accomplished with a series of PRE and
POST item triggers on the ST_BILL_TIME item, or this task can be accomplished by clicking a button and having a trigger loop through the records
and perform the calculations. This method is more accurate and depend-
able because of adding records and deleting records. This method will add
only those records that are currently being displayed.

TIP

Built-in sub-programs exist for all the keystrokes available in Forms (see the built-ins
overview in the online help). You might want to review all the built-ins available for use
within the Forms development environment.

The logic to perform the field additions is illustrated in Figure 5.54. This logic will be assigned to a WHEN-BUTTON-PRESSED trigger to the first button on the Control Panel. Change the label on this button to Check Time. Notice the use of built-ins: GO_BLOCK, FIRST_RECORD, and NEXT_RECORD. GO_BLOCK goes to the named block as if you were using the >> and << keys. The FIRST_RECORD built-in positions the cursor at the first record of the block. Finally, NEXT_RECORD in the loop is similar to clicking the > key. The :system.last_record gets set when the last record of the form has been accessed. The logic now resides all in a single PL/SQL trigger and is easy to follow. The property palette in Figure 5.54 illustrates the CHECK_TIME item on the CONTROL_BLOCK. Also notice in the figure the Data section where Data Type is set to a number and the Maximum Length is set to 4.

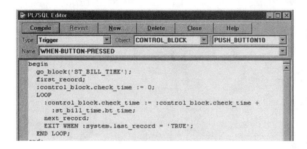
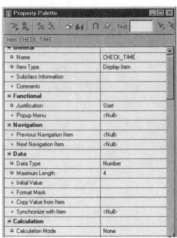

Figure 5.54: *Adding up the BT_TIME field.*

Numerous ways exist to populate display items with information from blocks, default dates or entries, and so on. Figure 5.55 is a version of the WHEN-VALIDATE-ITEM seen previously in Figure 5.47. Notice the difference. Instead of just checking that the displayed item is in a database table, Figure 5.55 populates the ST_STAFF_NAME item when the ST_STAFF_ID is being validated; otherwise, an error message is returned. Figure 5.56 is a way of populating a field with the default date. Notice that the PRE-TEXT-ITEM trigger will fire before the cursor is placed in the field. This puts the default date into the field but enables the application user to change the date if so desired.

Figure 5.55: *BT_STAFF_ID item WHEN-VALIDATE-ITEM trigger.*

Figure 5.56: *BT_DATE item PRE-TEXT-ITEM trigger.*

Figure 5.57 illustrates all the work performed on the ST_BILL_TIME application. The staff member's name automatically fills in, as well as the current date. Notice that the Time does not add correctly; 45 would be the correct answer. To restart the ST_BILL_TIME application in Forms Debug mode, click Program from the menu, choose Run From, and click Debug. This mode enables you to see what variables are set to, as well as watch the trigger activity (see Figure 5.58).

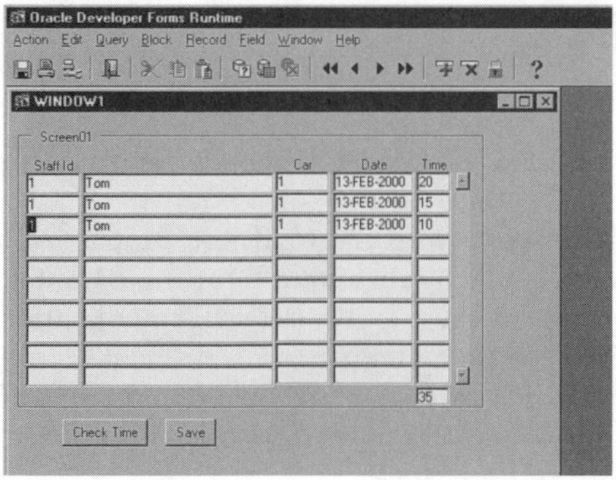

Figure 5.57: *ST_BILL_TIME application with an addition error.*

Figure 5.58: *Debug mode information.*

Notice the code inside the loop in Figure 5.59. The CHECK_TIME field is accumulated at the beginning of the loop, the next record is incremented, and—if this happens to be the last record—the loop is exited. The last record displayed never got added into the CHECK_TIME item. The highlighted code in Figure 5.59 shows how to fix the trigger, and Figure 5.60 shows a perfectly working ST_BILL_TIME application.

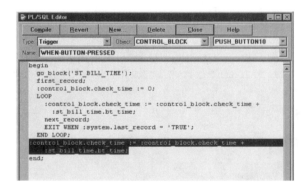

Figure 5.59: *Editing the WHEN-BUTTON-PRESSED trigger.*

So far we have discussed how to create all the supporting applications to the main ST_INVENTORY application. Figures 5.61, 5.62, 5.63, and 5.64 illustrate the four tabs of the ST_INVENTORY application. This tab-type application is still based on a single block but has related information grouped together on each tab page. Figure 5.61 utilizes radio buttons for the automobile color, whereas Figure 5.64 uses a database function to calculate the final profit/loss total.

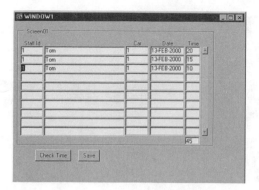

Figure 5.60: *ST_BILL_TIME application working correctly.*

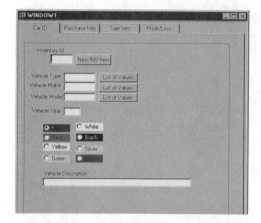

Figure 5.61: *ST_INVENTORY application Car ID tab.*

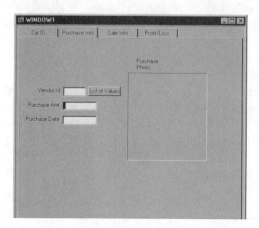

Figure 5.62: *ST_INVENTORY application Purchase Info tab.*

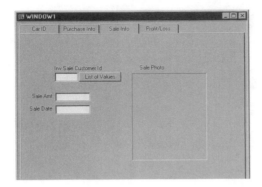

Figure 5.63: *ST_INVENTORY application Sale Info tab.*

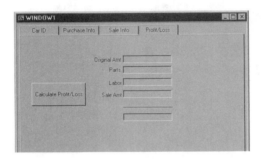

Figure 5.64: *ST_INVENTORY application Profit/Loss tab.*

Begin building the ST_INVENTORY application by creating a tab canvas and placing all the ST_INVENTORY fields on this first tab, except for the four maintenance fields (INV_INSERT_USER, INV_INSERT_DATE, and so on). Use the Layout Wizard to create the other three tabs, but do not assign any fields to them in the Layout Wizard. You can highlight several items at a time by holding down the Shift key while clicking items. Use the Edit and Cut menu items on the top toolbar to remove the items from the first tab canvas and move them to the other canvases. Add the New INV Item button; its WHEN-BUTTON-PRESSED trigger should receive the next sequence number from the ST_INV_SEQUENCE generator. Add LOVs to the following: INV_TYPE (Vehicle Type), INV_MAKE (Vehicle Make), INV_MODEL (Vehicle Model), INV_PURCHASE_VENDOR_ID (Vendor ID, Purchase Info tab), and INV_SALE_CUSTOMER_ID (Inv Sale Customer ID, Sale Info tab).

Figure 5.65 shows how to change the INV_COLOR item from a text item to a radio group (Item Type on the property palette). Notice the Initial Value on this same property palette. Be sure the INV_COLOR item is highlighted in the Object Navigator so that the radio buttons will be created and assigned to this item. On the tab canvas, add eight radio buttons using the radio button on the canvas tool palette, and use Tools, Align Objects (from the top menu bar) to align the radio buttons with one another (see Figure 5.66). Use the Item Property Palette for each radio button to change its name and label to the color, to change its default value to the color, and to change its background color to be the color it is representing.

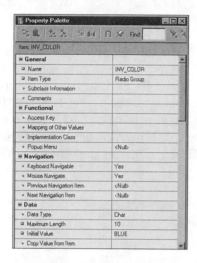

Figure 5.65: INV_COLOR item radio group property palette.

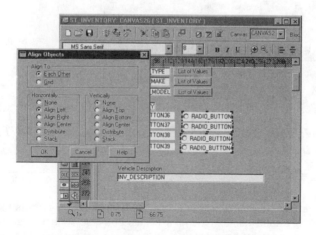

Figure 5.66: Canvas item alignment tool.

Figure 5.64 could easily be a control block because none of these fields are derived from the database. The Original Amt and Sale Amt are copied or synchronized with other items from this same form (INV_PURCHASE_ AMT item and INV_SALE_AMT). This is accomplished by placing the fields with which to synchronize these in the Synchronize with Item window. Then, on each item's property palette, you must name the block item from which to perform the copying. Figure 5.67 illustrates the Calculate Profit/Loss WHEN-BUTTON-PRESSED trigger. Two SQL queries exist to populate the parts cost and the labor cost items; notice the use of the SUM SQL function. The total easily could have been derived with a simple calculation statement (this calculation is commented out in the trigger), but the ST_CALC_PROFIT function will be used instead. This will show how to incorporate a function into a form. Using PL/SQL functions and procedures enables the reuse of code. For example, the ST_CALC_PROFIT function could be used in reports as well. Notice how the PL_TOTAL item is populated with the return value from the function. Also notice that the function calls for an input variable, INVENTORY_ID, and that the INV_ID from the first tab is passed to the function.

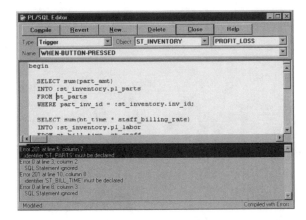

Figure 5.67: *The Calculate Profit/Loss button's WHEN-BUTTON-PRESSED trigger.*

TIP

If you are getting questionable errors from the PL/SQL Editor, such as the PL/SQL Editor thinking a table name in the From clause of a SQL statement should be a variable name, the cause of the problem is that you are not connected to the database. Click File, Connect (see Figure 5.68) and connect to the database.

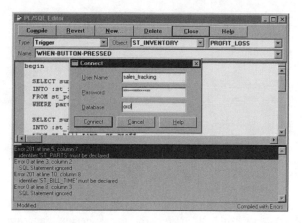

Figure 5.68: PL/SQL Editor with Connect box.

Listing 5.1 illustrates the ST_CALC_FUNCTION that was built using the Quest SQL Navigator tool as shown in Chapter 3. Notice that the part_amt calculation (under the comment — add in parts —) uses a cursor loop and the labor_amt (under the comment — add in labor costs —). No real reason exists that the part_amt could not have been calculated with a similar SQL statement using the SUM function. This function, as well as using the function at all, aids in the learning process by illustrating as many topics as possible. A function always returns a value: Notice how this is accomplished, especially in the Exceptions part of the function.

EXAMPLE

Listing 5.1:   ST_CALC_PROFIT Function

```
CREATE OR REPLACE
Function ST_CALC_PROFIT
  ( v_inv_id IN NUMBER)
  RETURN  NUMBER IS PROFIT_LOSS NUMBER(8,2);
--
-- MODIFICATION HISTORY
-- Person      Date    Comments
-- ---------   ------  -------------------------------------------
-- Hotka       2/13/00 Used to calculate profit or loss from INV_ID
--
    v_purchase_amt    st_inventory.inv_purchase_amt%TYPE;
    v_labor_amt       NUMBER(8,2);
    v_sale_amt        st_inventory.inv_sale_amt%TYPE;
    CURSOR c_inv_parts IS
        SELECT part_amt
        FROM st_parts
        WHERE part_inv_id = v_inv_id;
```

Listing 5.1:   continued

```
BEGIN
-- get purchase amount --
    PROFIT_LOSS := 0;
    SELECT inv_purchase_amt
    INTO v_purchase_amt
    FROM st_inventory
    WHERE inv_id = v_inv_id;

    PROFIT_LOSS := v_purchase_amt;
-- add in parts --

    FOR c_inv_parts_record IN c_inv_parts LOOP
        PROFIT_LOSS := PROFIT_LOSS + c_inv_parts_record.part_amt;
    END LOOP;

-- add in labor costs --

    SELECT sum(bt_time * staff_billing_rate)
    INTO v_labor_amt
    FROM st_bill_time, st_staff
    WHERE st_bill_time.bt_inv_id = v_inv_id
    AND st_bill_time.bt_staff_id = st_staff.staff_id;

    PROFIT_LOSS := PROFIT_LOSS + v_labor_amt;

-- make result negative --

    PROFIT_LOSS := PROFIT_LOSS * -1;

-- add in sold amount (if sold) --

    SELECT NVL(inv_sale_amt,0)
    INTO v_sale_amt
    FROM st_inventory
    WHERE inv_id = v_inv_id;

    PROFIT_LOSS := PROFIT_LOSS + v_sale_amt;

    RETURN PROFIT_LOSS ;
EXCEPTION
    WHEN TOO_MANY_ROWS THEN
        return(0);
```

Listing 5.1: continued

```
    WHEN NO_DATA_FOUND THEN
        return(PROFIT_LOSS);
    WHEN others THEN
        return(PROFIT_LOSS);
END; -- Function ST_CALC_PROFIT
/
```

Converting Forms to HTML

Forms can easily be saved for use by a Web environment. The Run Form Web on the developer tool bar is useful to view what the form would look like in a Web browser (the traffic light with the globe behind it runs the form in a Web browser). It is also a convenient way to code and debug a form that is destine for Web access.

When deployed, the form runtime will actually run on the application server and interact with an applet that will actually display the form on the Web browser. Figure 5.69 illustrates that the applet will be downloaded to the Web browser but that the form runtime will actually run on the Oracle9iAS server.

To run Forms Developer applications on the Web, you must install two components: the Forms Client and the Forms Server from the Forms Developer v6.0 Installation Media.

The Forms Client is a Java applet downloaded to a user's Web browser when a Forms Developer application is being accessed. This applet maintains a login and serves as an interface between Forms Server software installed and the Web browser.

These applications have their own URLs that access the Forms Client applet and begin the interaction with the Forms Server. The Forms Server is imbedded in the Oracle9iAS, see Figure 8.9 in Chapter 8, "Building Web Sites with Oracle9i," and shares connection services with the other parts of Oracle9iAS. Oracle9iAS with the Forms Server installed manages the interaction between end users and the Forms Server. The Forms Client receives bundles of interface commands from the Forms Server and translates them (in sets) into interface objects for the end user. Some interface events handled by the Forms Server Runtime Engine in a client/server implementation, such as typing characters in a text field or moving around a dialog box, occur only on the Forms Client in the Web implementation, with no interaction with the Forms Server Runtime Engine.

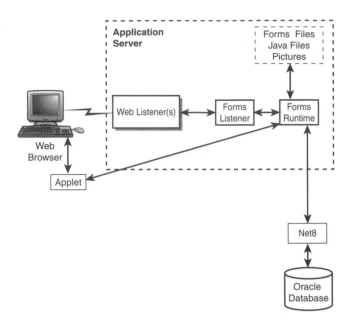

Figure 5.69: *Web Forms runtime environment.*

When the user gives the URL, the HTML pages are downloaded to the Web browser. The forms listener is a Java servlet and the client will download, if necessary, the Java archive file containing the Forms applet. The forms applet is instantiated and the parameters from the HTML page are used to determine the forms application to run. The forms applet then sends a request to the forms listener. The forms listener contacts the forms runtime engine and connects to a forms services runtime process. The forms listener passes any forms command-line parameters (such as database SID, user ID, password, and so on) as well as any user-defined form builder parameters to the forms services runtime process. A connection is established by the forms listener with the forms runtime engine and the connection information is sent to the forms applet. From this point on, the forms applet directly talks to the runtime process. When control goes to the client, the forms runtime creates a timer. The timer value can be set by FORMSxx_ TIMER and it defaults to 15 minutes. If the timer expires, the middle tier process knows that nothing is received from the client for that duration of time and the client no longer exists and can be terminated.

TIP

If using Forms 6i earlier than Patchset4, the default port for Forms server listener is 9000. However, the forms listener servlet—a Java servlet introduced in Forms6i/ patchset4—removes this limitation so that none of the ports need to be exposed at the firewall other than the Web server ports.

Web-Based Forms Tuning Tips

Create a simple form that prompts the user for login information. This form will be small and will initiate all the necessary transactions between the form's runtime and the browser applet. It will also be small in size and will load quickly on the apps server. Then do a new_form from inside this form to start the first form for the user to see. A call_form would take more memory and the original form will stay active but not used. A new_form starts the new form and exits the exiting form.

Make the screen simple, use less graphics, and try to avoid any kind of a timer. This will be covered in greater depth in the following section, however the fewer graphics there are, the faster the form will load into the browser. Also, the use of PL/SQL timers can cause quite a bit of network traffic, something to try to avoid with Web-based applications.

Web-Based Forms Coding Tips

When developing forms the font size will probably be different from that used by the client web browser. Try to use 9-point pitch. Chapter 2 of the forms online documentation discusses acceptable fonts. Use visual attributes to set the button colors as this is also not handled by the client Web browser.

Design your forms to have a Web look about them. Avoid using tool bars. Set up buttons for the various forms states such as next-record, previous-record, block navigation, and Query mode. Avoid using multiple MDI type windows. Try to use tabs instead.

Some triggers will not fire at all and some triggers will create network havoc if used. Be careful with the WHEN-MOUSE-type triggers; they may not work as expected and they may create quite a bit of network traffic. For example, try to avoid using KEY-NEXT-ITEM triggers as they fire as the mouse enters and leaves a field. If you use :SYSTEM.MOUSE_BUTTON_ SHIFT_STATE or :SYSTEM.MOUSE_BUTTON_PRESSED, the values contained in these events will be different from windows based applications to that of the Web. For example, the MOUSE_BUTTON_PRESSED in a windows environment will have a 1 for the left mouse button and a 2 for the right mouse button. In a Web environment, it is either a 1 or nothing at all. Use :SYSTEM.MOUSE_BUTTON_MODIFIERS and check for the values you are looking for such as "Hyper+," "Caps Lock+," "Alt+," and so on.

Remember that the form is actually running on the application server so any HOST command such as to notepad will occur on the application server, not the client machine.

Keymappings will be different from your system and from Web browser to Web browser as well. The forms runtime will use FMRWEB.RES found in <Oracle_Home>\FORMS60 directory by default. You might want to use FMRPCWEB.RES file to give a better key mapping from a PC Web browser environment. This file is found in the same directory. You can copy one to the default name or use a runtime parameter to use the different key-mapping file.

Some helpful forms level parameters to set are

- LookAndFeel=oracle (will use the default Oracle color scheme)
- Usesdi=yes (will turn off the Multiple Document Interface)
- SeparateFrame=false (runs the form in the current browser window)
- SplashScreen=<your logo.gif> (gives the user the appearance that the form is loading immediately)

Summary

This chapter introduced Oracle Developer, where you learned to build various forms with varying levels of complexity. You learned how to format and change the physical screen attributes as well as add specific coding functionality using PL/SQL.

REVIEW

Reviewing It

1. What is the Data Block Wizard useful for?
2. What is the difference between a content canvas and a stacked canvas?
3. Does Oracle Developer come with online help?
4. What is the role of the Item Property Palette?
5. In the following example, explain what this code is doing and explain the column with the ':'

```
begin
select st_vendor_seq.nextval
into :st_vendor.vendor_id
from sys.dual;
end;
```

6. What is a LOV and what is it useful for?

7. How should a LOV be accessed?

8. Describe Query mode and what it is useful for.

9. What is a control block and how does it differ from a data block?

10. In Web-based forms, what triggers may be undesirable?

CHECK

Checking It

1. What are Forms Builder program units called?

   a) Program Units

   b) Modules

   c) .FMB files

   d) .FMX files

2. Data blocks can be based on tables, views, or stored procedures.
   True/False

3. What forms naming standard should be adhered to:

   a) An 8-character name

   b) A name relative to the table being accessed

   c) Ask your database administrator

   d) Forms enforces no naming standards

4. A property palette is associated with:

   a) Items

   b) Data Blocks

   c) Canvases

   d) All of the above

5. How do you change the 'Edge Pattern'?

   a) Frame Property Palette

   b) Item Property Palette

   c) Data Block Property Palette

   d) Canvas Property Palette

6. What block-level trigger should be used for sequence generators:

   a) Post-Update

   b) Pre-Update

   c) Pre-Insert

   d) Pre-Commit

7. The purpose of a tabular form is to display more than 1 row of data at a time.

   True/False

8. By default, LOVs can be accessed in a form via:

   a) Simply navigating to the field

   b) Using the 'Display List' from the menu bar

   c) Right-mouse clicking the item with the assigned LOV

   d) Left-mouse clicking the item with the assigned LOV

9. How are radio-buttons added to a data item:

   a) By the radio-button property palette

   b) By the canvas property palette

   c) By the item property palette

   d) By highlighting the item then adding the radio buttons

10. In a Web-based form: where does the form actually run?

    a) Java code at the Web browser

    b) .FMX file at the Web browser

    c) On the apps server via an applet on the Web browser

    d) .FMB file at the Web browser

Applying It

APPLY

Independent Exercise 1:

- Create a simple form from the SCOT.DEPT table. Display 4 rows and all columns.

- Query just Dept 10.

- Add Enter Query/Execute Query buttons

Independent Exercise 2:

- Create a sequence generator that starts at 60 and increments by 10.

- Add this new sequence to the deptno item in the form created in example 1 when adding rows to the table.

Independent Exercise 3:

- Create a form on the SCOT.EMP table. Display 1 row.

- Add a radio group for job title.

- Add a LOV for deptno.

What's Next?

In the next chapter, we'll show you how to build reports using the gui-mode Oracle Developer interface and the character-mode SQL*Plus interface.

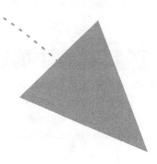

Building Oracle Reports

This chapter will build a series of reports using both Oracle Reports 6.0 and SQL*Plus. These reports are based on objects created in Chapter 4, "Building an Oracle9i Database." You will then learn how to convert these reports to HTML and discover some techniques necessary to be successful with Oracle Reports and SQL*Plus in the HTML environment.

This chapter teaches you the following:

- Building Reports Using Developer 6.0 or 6i
- Building Reports Using Oracle SQL*Plus
- Converting Reports to HTML
- Setting up Windows Icons

Building Reports Using Developer 6.0 or 6i

Reports are easy to create using the Oracle Developer Report Builder. Figure 6.1 shows the first selection box, which is very similar to that of the Form Builder. Run the Quick Tour and Explore the Cue Cards are an excellent way to become familiar with the terminology and capabilities of Oracle Reports.

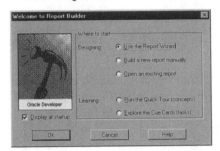

Figure 6.1: *The Welcome to Report Builder window.*

Selecting the Use the Report Wizard radio button opens the Report Builder Object Navigator (which is quite similar to the Form Builder Object Navigator), as shown in Figure 6.2.

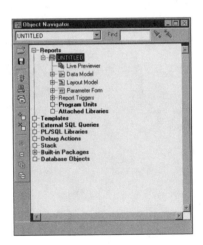

Figure 6.2: *The Report Builder Object Navigator window.*

The Report Wizard supports eight different report styles, as illustrated in Figure 6.3. The Tabular report is the typical style with rows and columns, whereas Form-like can print a row of data per page. This style is useful in the Sales Tracking application to build a sales receipt or a sales document that includes the picture of the vehicle. Mailing Labels are useful for quickly assembling addresses from the database into the correct format (for example, thirty labels per page, three labels in a row, with ten rows per page). Form Letters, on the other hand, incorporate data from a table (such as name, amount, and so on) and embed this information around text in the form of a letter. A form letter is generated for each row returned from the associated SQL query. Group Left and Group Above are useful for situations in which rows will appear on the report. Finally, a Matrix report is a summation-type report in which two related types of data are totaled together in the form of a graph. A relationship in our Sales Tracking application would be sales by month by types of vehicles.

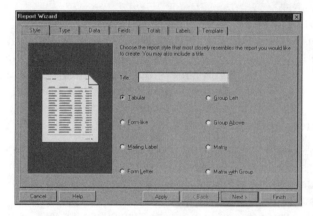

Figure 6.3: Report Builder Report Wizard Style tab.

Enter the title Inventory Status, ensuring that the Tabular radio button is selected, and click Next. Select the default SQL statement on the Type tab and click Next (see Figure 6.4).

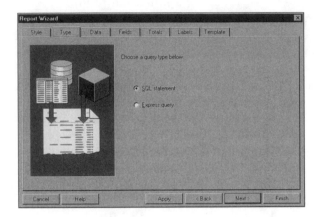

Figure 6.4: *Report Builder Report Wizard Type tab.*

The Report Wizard Data tab prompts you for a connection to the database (see Figure 6.5). Figure 6.6 illustrates the SQL statement used for this report. Notice that you could have used the Query Builder (as discussed in the previous section) to build the query, or you could have accessed a previously built SQL statement stored on the computer's file system. Click the Next button.

Click the >> button to select all the fields from the Data tab for display in the report (see Figure 6.7). The Totals tab shows how to select fields for report totals (see Figure 6.8). Select the INV_PURCHASE_AMT and the INV_SALE_AMT fields for totals. Notice that the INV_SALE_AMT has a null value assignment. Also, remember that the INV_PURCHASE_AMT is a mandatory field, whereas the INV_SALE_AMT is not. Therefore, that field could contain a null, making it unsuitable for display. Calculations without the NVL clause set the column to 0 if null. Finally, click the Next button when you are finished selecting fields for totals.

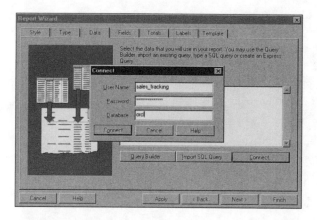

Figure 6.5: *Report Builder Report Wizard Data tab with a database connection.*

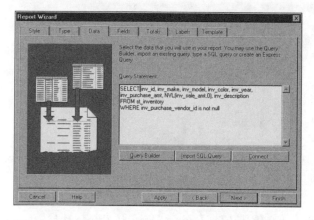

Figure 6.6: *Report Builder Report Wizard Data tab with a SQL statement.*

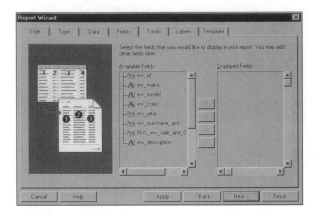

Figure 6.7: *Report Builder Report Wizard Fields tab.*

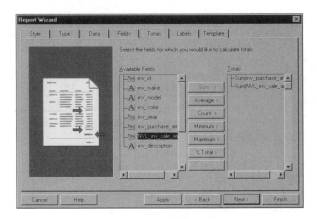

Figure 6.8: *Report Builder Report Wizard Totals tab.*

The Labels tab, as shown in Figure 6.9, enables you to easily change the column labels as they will appear on the report. This is also accomplished from the report layout (similar to the canvas layout of the Form Builder). Make any desired changes in the labels displayed and then click Next. The Template tab displays some default report templates. The Report Builder Online Documentation covers how to build these templates. Select the Confidential Background for this report, as you see in Figure 6.10, and click Finish.

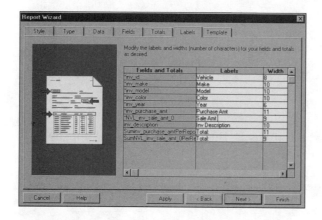

Figure 6.9: *Report Builder Report Wizard Labels tab.*

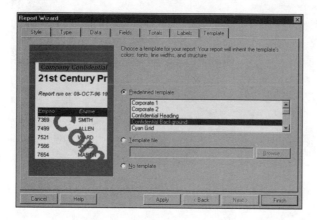

Figure 6.10: *Report Builder Report Wizard Template tab.*

Figure 6.11 shows what the newly developed ST_INVENTORY_STATUS report looks like.

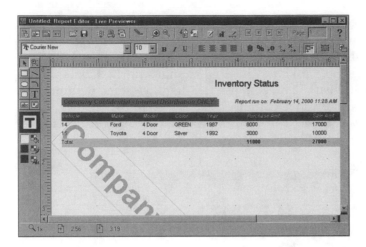

Figure 6.11: *The Report Builder Live Previewer.*

Notice that the items in the Object Navagator appear in the same order in the Live Previewer. (see Figure 6.12).

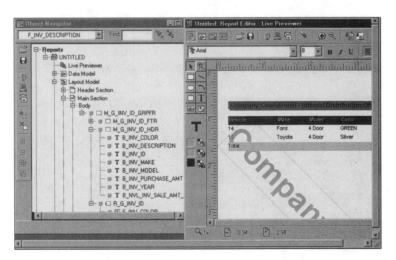

Figure 6.12: *Object Navigator with the Live Previewer.*

Building Reports Using Oracle SQL*Plus

In Chapter 2, "Fundamentals of the SQL Language," you learned how to use SQL*Plus to submit SQL statements to Oracle9i for execution and a result set. We have also discussed how to manipulate SQL statements in the SQL*Plus SQL buffer. Oracle9i also has a SQL buffer where *all* SQL statements are submitted for execution. The Oracle9i SQL buffer accepts only ANSI standard SQL statements, or just SQL—not any of the SQL*Plus buffer commands or formatting commands. Figure 6.13 shows how SQL*Plus and Oracle9i relate together. SQL*Plus (and any other program working with Oracle9i) submits its SQL statements to Oracle9i for processing via Net8. Oracle9i puts this SQL statement in the SQL buffer for execution, where it is parsed (syntax checking), prepared (a plan on how Oracle9i will get the data, possibly using indexes), and executed. Then rows are returned back through Net8 to SQL*Plus. SQL*Plus then applies any of its formatting commands to the result set and displays the results on the end user's terminal or writes them to an operating system file (depending on the options given in the SQL*Plus session).

This section teaches you how to use SQL and SQL*Plus commands to format the output from the queries. The SQL*Plus SQL buffer holds only one command at a time.

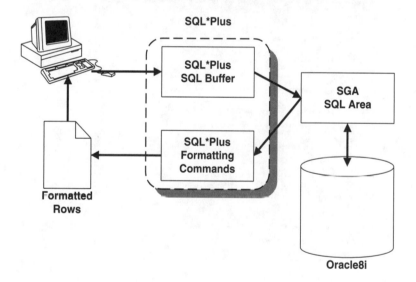

Figure 6.13: *SQL*Plus and Oracle9i SQL statement processing.*

The SQL*Plus COLUMN command (illustrated with SQL Help in Figure 6.14) is useful for giving columns a meaningful format, applying dollar signs ($)

and commas to numeric fields, and providing a better column title. Figure 6.15 shows how to apply this technique to a SQL query. The COLUMN FORMAT command correctly sizes the fields and applies the numeric mask. Also notice the heading fields and the fact that the ENAME column contains a vertical bar (|). Whenever any special character or space appears in the title, it must be enclosed with single quotes. The single vertical bar tells SQL*Plus to put each line of the heading on a separate line.

The SQL language offers an *alias*, which is the ability to give columns more complete names or give a calculated field a name. Figure 6.16 shows how an alias is used in a SQL query. Aliases have many uses. Here they provide a better heading to the SQL statement. Aliases are also useful for giving calculated columns better headings and true names. Figure 6.16 also shows how you can use an alias to give a column a name and then use the SQL*Plus COLUMN command to give some further definition to the output. Notice that the COLUMN FORMAT command and the alias name are the same.

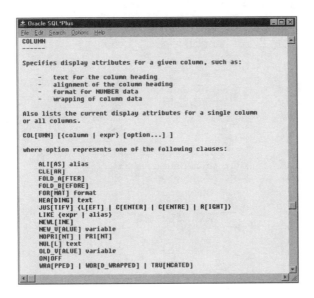

Figure 6.14: *SQL*Plus column help text.*

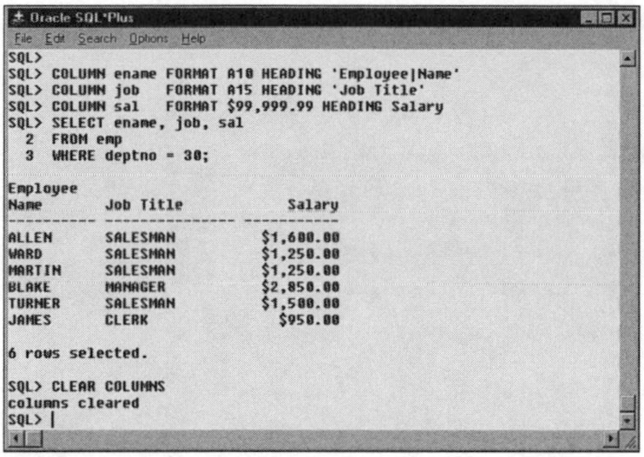

Figure 6.15: SQL*Plus column formatting.

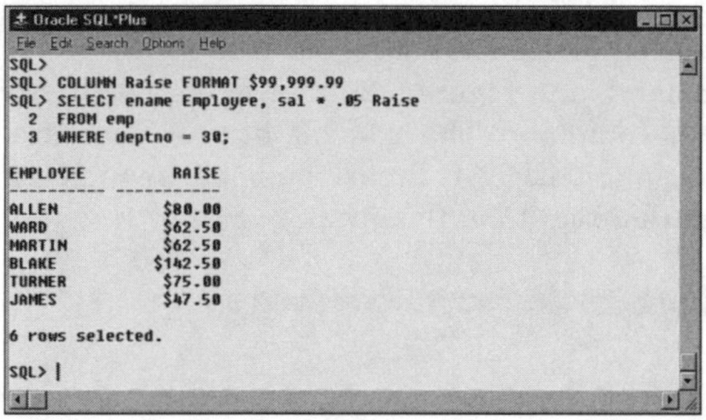

Figure 6.16: Using an alias with column formatting.

SQL statement output also can be ordered together by using the BREAK command (see Figure 6.17). This SQL*Plus command, used in conjunction with the ORDER BY clause, suppresses values on the break column, giving a master/detail appearance, as seen in Figure 6.18. Notice that BREAK and ORDER BY contain the same columns. BREAK also can handle breaks on more than one column, but ORDER BY will need the same columns and in the same order to provide the correct results.

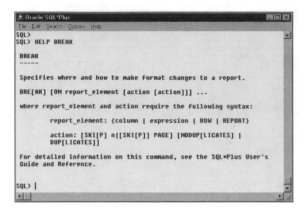

Figure 6.17: *SQL*Plus* BREAK *command syntax.*

The SQL*Plus COMPUTE command is useful for creating subtotals and grand totals with the BREAK command. Figure 6.19 shows the syntax for the COMPUTE command, and Figure 6.20 shows the COMPUTE command in use with the BREAK command. The example has two separate COMPUTE commands: one for the DEPTNO breaks and one for the break on report, which causes the final total to appear.

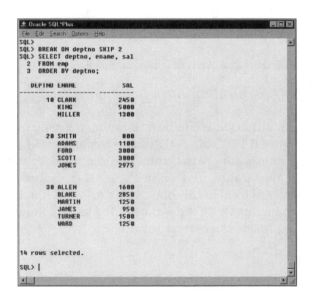

Figure 6.18: *Using the SQL*Plus* BREAK *command.*

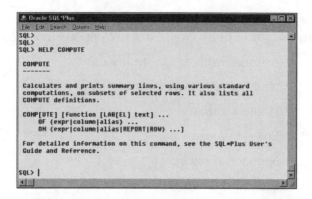

Figure 6.19: SQL*Plus COMPUTE *command syntax.*

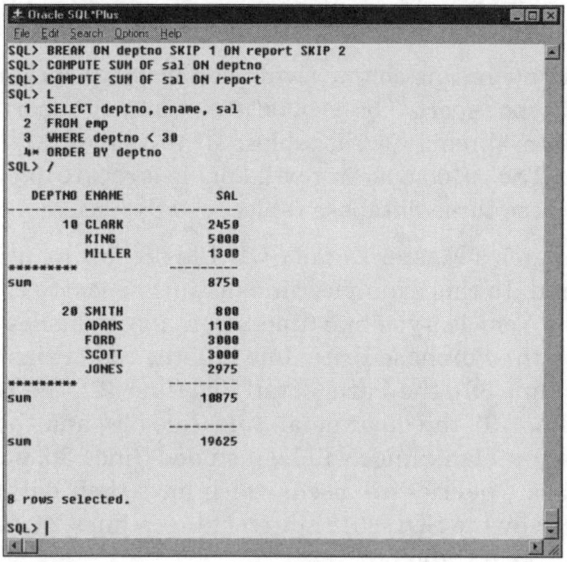

Figure 6.20: *Using the SQL*Plus* BREAK *and* COMPUTE *commands.*

The COMPUTE command can do more than simply add fields (which is accomplished with the SUM option). Other COMPUTE options include the following:

AVG	Average value of non-null values
COUNT	Number of non-null values
MAX	Highest value
MIN	Lowest value
NUMBER	Number of rows
STD	Standard deviation
VAR	Variance

Chapter 7, "Using Advanced SQL Techniques and SQL*Plus Reporting Features," contains additional ways of using SQL*Plus to format reports.

The final example in this chapter will use the UNION operator to create a master/detail type report. The ST_INVENTORY_DETAIL report will contain information from three different tables: ST_INVENTORY, ST_PARTS, and ST_BILL_TIME. The UNION operator will enable a report to easily contain the output from these three database tables.

Listing 6.1 creates a Master/Detail SQL*Plus report by using the SQL UNION command. In this example, nine distinct separate types of lines are to be printed: the Vehicle Type line (line 24), a line of dashes before the final total (line 60), the Purchase Price (line 28), the Sale Price (line 32), the Parts header (line 39), the Parts detail line (line 42), the Labor Used header line (line 49), the labor detail line (line 52), and the total line (63). In addition, a few blank lines will be included (lines 36, 46, and 57). Thirteen separate queries are used, which have their output merged and sorted together by the SQL JOIN statement (see lines 24, 28, 32, 36, 39, 42, 46, 49, 52, 57, 60, 63, and 66).

When using JOIN to merge the output of two or more queries, the output result set *must* have the same number of columns and column types. The headings are turned off (line 17) because regular SQL*Plus column headings are not desired for this type of report. The first column of each query has an alias column name of DUMMY. This DUMMY column is used to sort the order of the six types of lines (denoted by each of the 13 queries). The DUMMY column's only role is to maintain the order of the output lines, so the NOPRINT option is specified in line 21. The final ORDER BY (line 68) actually merges the result set lines to form the report in Listing 6.1. Notice the use of the TO_CHAR function to ensure that the output from this query is indeed character mode for the UNION operator. Also notice that each of the queries returns two columns: DUMMY and a character string. Each SQL query builds one output line. The SQL queries on ST_PARTS and ST_BILL_TIME might return zero or more rows. The DUMMY column will maintain the order of the output lines.

Figure 6.21 shows the output report from Listing 6.1.

TIP

Notice line 63 uses the ST CALC PROFIT introduced in Chapter 5. See listing 5.1 in Chapter 5 for the listing of this function.

EXAMPLE

Listing 6.1: ST_INVENORY_DETAIL.SQL

```
1:  rem
2:  rem     ST_Inventory_Detail.SQL - Demonstrates how to create a Master/Detail
3:  rem                      report using the UNION operator. This technique is
4:  rem                      useful whenever records/text from different tables
5:  rem                      need to appear in the same report.
6:  rem
7:  rem         Oracle9i From Scratch
8:  rem             by Dan Hotka
9:  rem         Que Publications March 2000
10: rem         All Rights Reserved
11: rem
12: ACCEPT INV_ID PROMPT 'Enter Inventory ID --> '
13: SET FEEDBACK OFF
14: SET VERIFY OFF
15: SET LINESIZE 60
16: SET PAGESIZE 24
17: SET HEADING OFF
18:
```

Listing 6.1:   continued

```
19: TTITLE 'Inventory Detail for Inventory_ID &INV_ID'
20:
21: COLUMN DUMMY NOPRINT
22:
23: SPOOL ST_Inventory_Detail.OUT
24: SELECT 1 DUMMY, 'Vehicle: ' || inv_year
    ➥|| ' ' || inv_color || ' ' || inv_make
25: FROM st_inventory
26: WHERE inv_id = &INV_ID
27: UNION
28: SELECT 2 DUMMY, 'Purchase Price:        '
    ➥|| TO_CHAR(inv_purchase_amt,'$999,999')
29: FROM st_inventory
30: WHERE inv_id = &INV_ID
31: UNION
32: SELECT 3 DUMMY, 'Sale Price:           '
    ➥|| TO_CHAR(NVL(inv_sale_amt,0),'$999,999')
33: FROM st_inventory
34: WHERE inv_id = &INV_ID
35: UNION
36: SELECT 4 DUMMY, ' '
37: FROM dual
38: UNION
39: SELECT 5 DUMMY, 'Parts Used:  '
40: FROM dual
41: UNION
42: SELECT 6 DUMMY, RPAD(part_desc,20) || '   ' || TO_CHAR(part_amt,'$999,999')
43: FROM st_parts
44: WHERE part_inv_id = &INV_ID
45: UNION
46: SELECT 7 DUMMY, ' '
47: FROM dual
48: UNION
49: SELECT 8 DUMMY, 'Labor Used: '
50: FROM dual
51: UNION
52: SELECT 9 DUMMY , RPAD(staff_name,10) || '            ' || TO_CHAR(bt_time
    ➥*staff_billing_rate,'$999,999')
53: FROM st_bill_time, st_staff
54: WHERE st_bill_time.bt_inv_id = &INV_ID
55: AND st_bill_time.bt_staff_id = st_staff.staff_id
56: UNION
57: SELECT 10 DUMMY, '    '
58: FROM dual
59: UNION
```

Listing 6.1: continued

```
60: SELECT 11 DUMMY, '                     ------------'
61: FROM dual
62: UNION
63: SELECT 12 DUMMY, 'Profit/Loss            '
      ||  TO_CHAR(st_calc_profit(&INV_ID),'$999,999')
64: FROM dual
65: UNION
66: SELECT 13 DUMMY, '    '
67: FROM dual
68: ORDER BY 1,2
69: /
70: SPOOL OFF
71:
72: ACCEPT anything PROMPT 'Hit Enter when done viewing report'
73: EXIT
```

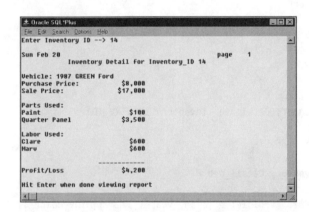

Figure 6.21: SQL*Plus Report ST_INVENTORY_DETAIL.

Converting Reports to HTML

Both Oracle Reports 6.0/6.i and SQL*Plus are capable of creating Web-based reports.

Listing 6.2 enhances the ST_INVENTORY_DETAIL report shown in Listing 6.1 by adding just a couple of lines. Notice the final SET command, SET MARKUP HTML ON. This takes the output report and puts it in HTML format. The only other change to this program over that of Listing 6.1 is the SPOOL command; notice the .htm suffix, this will make the file easily accessible by web browsers. Figure 6.22 illustrates what the output looks like in a Web browser.

Listing 6.2: Web-Based ST_INVENORY_DETAIL.SQL

```
rem
rem     ST_Inventory_Detail.SQL - Demonstrates how to create a Master/Detail
rem                     report in HTML format
rem                     using the UNION operator.  This technique is useful
rem                     when ever records/text from different tables nees
rem                     to appear in the same report.
rem
rem         Oracle9i Development by Example
rem             by Dan Hotka
rem         Que Publications August 2001
rem         All Rights Reserved
rem
ACCEPT INV_ID PROMPT 'Enter Inventory ID --> '
SET FEEDBACK OFF
SET VERIFY OFF
SET TERMOUT OFF
SET LINESIZE 60
SET PAGESIZE 24
SET HEADING OFF
SET MARKUP HTML ON


TTITLE 'Inventory Detail for Inventory_ID &INV_ID'

COLUMN DUMMY NOPRINT

SPOOL ST_Inventory_Detail_Web.HTM

SELECT 1 DUMMY, 'Vehicle: ' || inv_year || ' ' || inv_color || ' ' || inv_make
FROM st_inventory
WHERE inv_id = &INV_ID
UNION
SELECT 2 DUMMY, 'Purchase Price: ' || TO_CHAR(inv_purchase_amt,'$999,999')
FROM st_inventory
WHERE inv_id = &INV_ID
UNION
SELECT 3 DUMMY, 'Sale Price:     ' || TO_CHAR(NVL(inv_sale_amt,0),'$999,999')
FROM st_inventory
WHERE inv_id = &INV_ID
UNION
SELECT 2 DUMMY, ' '
FROM dual
UNION
SELECT 3 DUMMY, 'Parts Used:  '
FROM dual
UNION
```

Listing 6.2:   continued

```
SELECT 4 DUMMY, RPAD(part_desc,20) || '   ' || TO_CHAR(part_amt,'$999,999')
FROM st_parts
WHERE part_inv_id = &INV_ID
UNION
SELECT 5 DUMMY, ' '
FROM dual
UNION
SELECT 6 DUMMY, 'Labor Used: '
FROM dual
UNION
SELECT 7 DUMMY , RPAD(staff_name,10) || '                ' || TO_CHAR(bt_time *
staff_billing_rate,'$999,999')
FROM st_bill_time, st_staff
WHERE st_bill_time.bt_inv_id = &INV_ID
AND st_bill_time.bt_staff_id = st_staff.staff_id
UNION
SELECT 8 DUMMY, '   '
FROM dual
UNION
SELECT 9 DUMMY, '                 ............'
FROM dual
UNION
SELECT 10 DUMMY, 'Profit/Loss            ' || TO_CHAR(st_calc_profit(&INV_ID),
    '$999,999')
FROM dual
UNION
SELECT 11 DUMMY, '   '
FROM dual
ORDER BY 1,2
/
SPOOL OFF


EXIT
```

Oracle Reports 6.0 and 6i are both capable of creating reports for the Web.
HTML format can be specified when running the commands on the command line by setting the DESTFORMAT to HTMLCSS or by choosing File -->
Generate to file --> HTML Style Sheet Menu. The report name will be the
same as the report module name used unless redefined. When this file is
viewed via a Web browser, it looks like Figure 6.23.

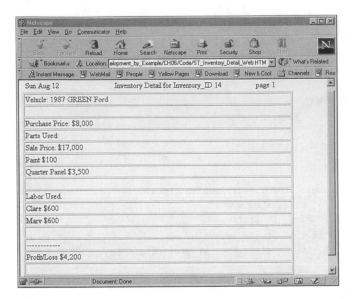

Figure 6.22: SQL*Plus Web Report ST_INVENTORY_DETAIL.

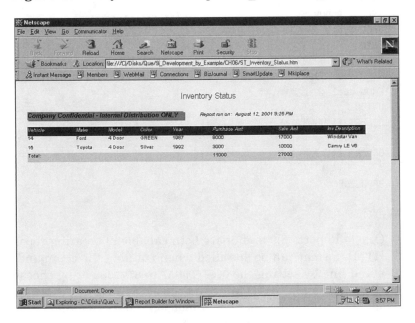

Figure 6.23: Oracle Reports in HTML.

Enhancing Web-Based Reports

In Figure 6.24, notice that the "Hello World" appears at the top. This is easily accomplished by using the SRW packages in conjunction with PL/SQL, or you can even use Java.

The SRW packages enable you to add HTML code by adding these functions via the report triggers. Figure 6.24 shows how to add the "Hello World" text using a BEFORE REPORT trigger (from the property palette or the main report navigator tree).

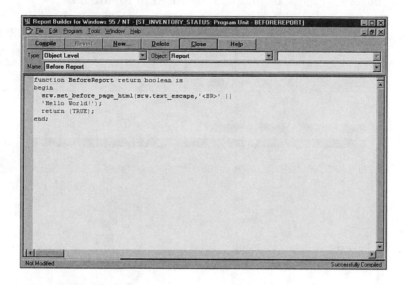

Figure 6.24: Before Report trigger code.

EXAMPLE

Listing 6.3:   Before Report Trigger HTML Code

```
SRW>SET_BEFORE_PAGE_HTML(SRW.TEXT_ESCAPE,'<BR><CENTER>' ||
    'IMG SRC="metro.jpg"></IMG>'|| '</CENTER>');
```

There are six procedures in the SRW package:

SET_AFTER_FORM_HTML	(puts object after all reports)
SET_AFTER_PAGE_HTML	(puts object after each page)
SET_AFTER_REPORT_HTML	(puts object after each report)
SET_BEFORE_FORM_HTML	(puts object before all reports)
SET_BEFORE_PAGE_HTML	(puts object before each page)
SET_BEFORE_REPORT_HTML	(puts object before each report)

The syntax is *srw.set_after_form_html(type,'string');* where type is either file or text. If text is selected, then the string will be an HTML for-matted string, as shown in Figure 6.24. Listing 6.3 illustrates the syntax useful in adding a .jpg file. If file is selected, then the string will be an operating system file.

Java can even be added to the report. To accomplish this, add a new boiler-plate text item in the layout editor. Open the property palette of this new item and change the "Contains HTML tags" property item to "yes." Listing 6.4 will add the "Hello World" text and produce the same reports as the before trigger technique illustrated in Figure 6.25.

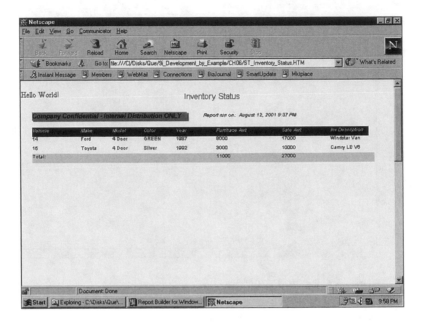

Figure 6.25: *Hello World enhanced HTML report.*

Listing 6.4:   Simple Java Code in Oracle Reports

```
<html>
  <head>
    <script>
       function HelloWorld(){
         "Hello World"
       }
    </script>
  </head>
<body>
  <font size=8>
    <script>
      document.write(HelloWorld())
    </script>
  </font>
</body>
</html>ok pm
```

Setting Up Windows Icons

It is relatively easy to set up icons for the new applications we created. In addition, it is easier to copy an existing icon and change its properties than to set up one from scratch. Figure 6.26 shows the icons that were configured for the Sales Tracking application. Each of these icons was copied from existing icons by right-clicking the desired icon and selecting Create Shortcut. You can right-click the newly created icon and then use the Rename option to give the new icon a descriptive name. Right-click the same icon again and select Properties from the menu. Click the center Shortcut tab, where you will see the actual program name in the Target field. For Oracle Forms, add the full operating system path and name of the .fmx program to be run when this icon is selected after this program name. For Oracle Reports, enter the full path of the .RDF file. In SQL*Plus scripts, add the same information that you would use in a DOS command window. After the program name, enter **userid/passwd@<tnsnames> @<full path & SQL*Plus script>.SQL**. The ST_INVENTORY_DETAIL report has a target line that looks similar to this:

```
C:\ORANT\BIN\PLUS80W.EXE sales_tracking/sales_tracking@orcl
➡@c:\disks\que\9i_development_by_example\sales_tracking_pgms\
➡st_inventory_detail.sql
```

NOTE

The ST_INVENTORY_DETAIL report target line should be typed as all one line. The ➡ symbols are to help the line fit within the character requirements of this page.

Figure 6.26 shows the Oracle Reports icon setup, and Figure 6.27 shows the shortcut properties.

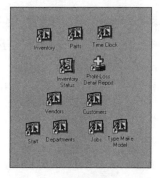

Figure 6.26: *Sales Tracking application icons.*

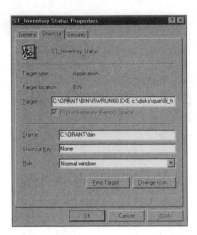

Figure 6.27: ST_INVENTORY_STATUS *report icon property page.*

Summary

In this chapter you learned how to create reports using two different Oracle tools: Oracle Reports and SQL*Plus. You also learned how to add HTML to Web-formatted reports.

REVIEW

Reviewing It

1. What is the difference between a tabular report and a form-like report?

2. Using Oracle Reports, what are the two ways of putting in a SELECT statement for data selection?

3. What is the spool command useful for in SQL*Plus style reports?

4. Where is the best place to put the SRW procedures when enhancing HTML reports?

5. Does Oracle Reports support Java? If so, where does it go?

Checking It

1. How many different report style sheets are there?

   a) 4

   b) 6

   c) 8

   d) 10

2. SQL*Plus is useful for making HTML style reports.

   True/False

3. SQL*Plus Column headings are controlled by:

   a) TTITLE

   b) BREAK

   c) COLUMN

   d) None of these

4. SQL*Plus can make a master/detail report.

   True/False

5. HTML can easily be added to SQL*Plus reports.

   True/False

6. Oracle Reports can easily generate HTML from a command-line command.

   True/False

APPLY

Applying It

Independent Exercise 1:

- Build a master/detail report using Emp and DEPT, showing each department (deptno and dname) followed by an ordered list of employee name, title, and salary, with a subtotal by department on salary and a report total of all salaries.

Independent Exercise 2:

- Build the same report as Exercise 1 using SQL*Plus.

Independent Exercise 3:

- Create HTML output from Exercise 1 and add the Metro Motors Logo to the top of each report, add "Contact us" with an e-mail hyperlink to the bottom of each report.

What's Next?

The next chapter looks more closely at SQL statements such as single and multiple row functions, join conditions, subqueries, views, and some more advanced SQL*Plus reporting techniques.

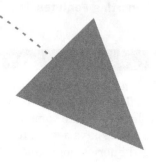

Using Advanced SQL Techniques and SQL*Plus Reporting Features

This chapter extends the knowledge of both Chapters 2, "Fundamentals of the SQL Language," and 6, "Building Oracle Reports," showing the reader more advanced features of the SQL language, then incorporating these advanced features into SQL*Plus reports. This chapter will illustrate many of the new Oracle9i database features and be a good learning aid to Oracle Programming. This chapter will focus on some introductory topics such as what is a relational database, what is SQL, the Oracle9I database architecture, and a brief description of the tools that will be used throughout this book.

This chapter teaches you the following:

- How to use SQL functions

- How to access two or more tables in a single query

- How to build SQL queries based on the results of other SQL queries

- How to incorporate this new knowledge in SQL*Plus reports

Advanced SQL Techniques

This chapter completes the learning process started in Chapter 2, and covers more advanced techniques using the SQL language. The final part of this chapter will apply these new techniques and show how to create some popular types of reports using SQL*Plus. This chapter also covers a variety of topics related to SQL queries including functions, advanced queries (joins and sub-queries), complex views, and read consistency (Oracle9i locking mechanisms).

Functions

SQL functions perform a variety of tasks such as date compares; date formatting; a host of character functions such as string length, substring functions, uppercase/lowercase; as well as several numerical functions such as round, truncate, and arithmetic operations.

SQL functions fall into two categories: single-row functions and multiple-row functions. Single-row functions operate on each row, while multiple-row functions operate on a group of rows.

SINGLE-ROW FUNCTIONS

There are several kinds of single-row functions. Character functions can convert character strings to number or date formats. Number functions manipulate the returning numeric value. Date functions are used to manipulate, compare, and perform calculations between dates.

CHARACTER FUNCTIONS

Character functions convert or change the output of the stored CHAR or VARCHAR2 fields. UPPER, LOWER, and INITCAP are three of the conversion character functions. Figure 7.1 shows examples of UPPER and INITCAP functions.

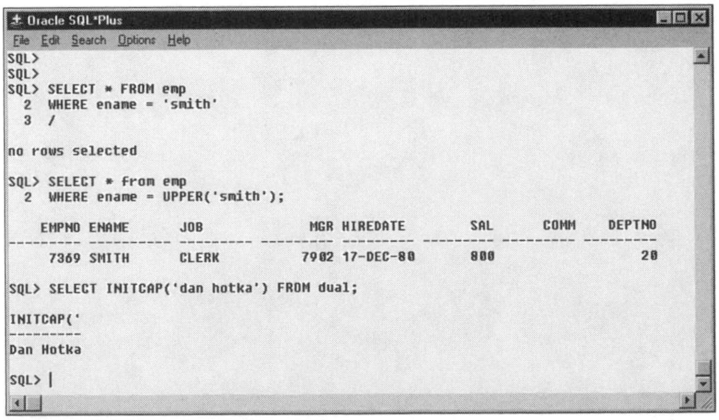

Figure 7.1: UPPER and INITCAP function examples.

NOTE

The DUAL table contains one column and one row and is useful when you're wanting to run a function once. Because the dual table only has one row, whatever function is run in the SELECT statement will run once.

The character manipulation functions are a powerful way to create desired output. Character manipulation functions include: CONCAT, INSTR, LENGTH, LPAD, RPAD, SUBSTR, and TRIM. Figure 7.2 shows some practical uses for some of these functions.

TIP

The '||' in Figure 7.2 also causes concatenation between strings and/or database columns. Notice the handy DROP commands created when combining the SQL syntax for dropping a table with that of the table name from the TAB view. Using the SPOOL command covered in SQL*Plus Reports later in this chapter would create a SQL script that could be used to clean up employees who have left the company.

NOTE

Concatenation is used to merge column data together and/or blend in with additional text to form syntax, as in the figure 7.2. The result of a concatenation is a single new column to the SQL query.

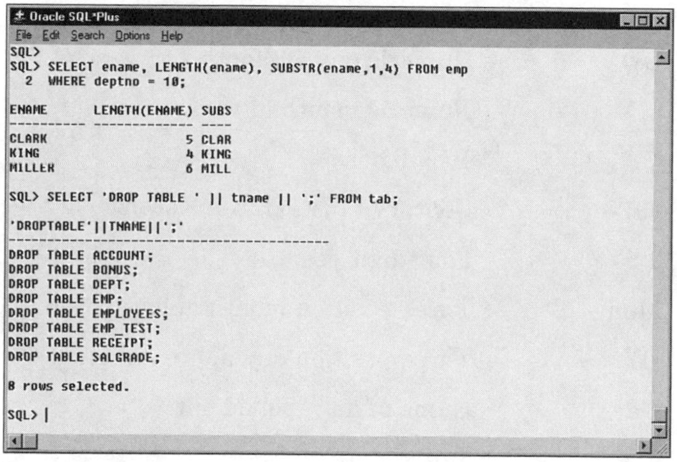

```
Oracle SQL*Plus
File  Edit  Search  Options  Help
SQL>
SQL> SELECT ename, LENGTH(ename), SUBSTR(ename,1,4) FROM emp
  2  WHERE deptno = 10;

ENAME        LENGTH(ENAME) SUBS
----------   ------------- ----
CLARK                    5 CLAR
KING                     4 KING
MILLER                   6 MILL

SQL> SELECT 'DROP TABLE ' || tname || ';' FROM tab;

'DROPTABLE'||TNAME||';'
------------------------------------------------
DROP TABLE ACCOUNT;
DROP TABLE BONUS;
DROP TABLE DEPT;
DROP TABLE EMP;
DROP TABLE EMPLOYEES;
DROP TABLE EMP_TEST;
DROP TABLE RECEIPT;
DROP TABLE SALGRADE;

8 rows selected.

SQL> |
```

Figure 7.2: *Character manipulation function examples.*

The TO_CHAR, TO_NUMBER, and TO_DATE are powerful functions that allow for the conversion of one type of data to another and allows for different types of date formats for both inserting and query purposes. TO_CHAR can be used to format a date into a different date format from the Oracle9i default of DD-MON-YY (see Figure 7.3). Likewise, the TO_DATE is used to convert a valid date in almost any format into the DATE format that Oracle9i understands. TO_NUMBER allows for valid numbers stored in character fields to be used in calculations.

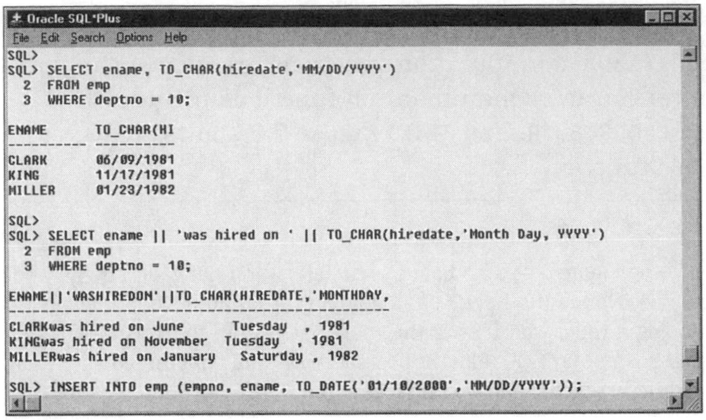

Figure 7.3: TO_CHAR and TO_DATE function examples.

The following are some of the valid date and time formats that can be used with both TO_CHAR and TO_DATE. Consult the Oracle9I SQL Reference Manual for all the combinations of date and time formats.

Partial List of Date Formats:

- DD   Numeric day of month
- MM   Numeric month of year
- YY   Two digit year
- RR   Century function (see Note)
- YYYY   Four digit year
- Mon   Three-position month abbreviation
- DY   Three-position day abbreviation
- Day   Name of day spelled out
- J   Julian date
- MONTH   Month spelled out
- YEAR   Year spelled out

Partial List of Time Formats:

- AM or PM   Time of day indicator
- HH   Hour of day

- HH24   Hour in military time
- MI   Minutes
- SS   Seconds
- SSSS   Seconds since midnight

NOTE

The RR command is used in place of the YY function and assists with century identification on two position years. If the year tested is 00 through 49 and the current year is between 00 and 49, then RR returns the current century. If the year tested is 00 through 49 and the current year is between 50 and 99, then RR returns the previous century. If the year tested is 50 through 99 and the current year is between 00 and 49, then RR returns the next century. If the year tested is 50 through 99 and the current year is between 50 and 99, then RR returns the current century.

Current year=1999, Date=01-SEP-96, RR=1996, YY=1996

Current year=1996, Date=15-JUL-45, RR=2045, YY=1945

Current year=2003, Date=17-MAR-56, RR=1956, YY=2056

DATE FUNCTIONS

There are six date functions that perform various calculations from the number of months between two dates, adding months to a date, getting the next day/previous date, and rounding/truncating dates. Several of these date functions are illustrated in Figure 7.4.

The MONTHS_BETWEEN(date1,date2) function returns the number of months between the two dates. The ADD_MONTHS(date, n) returns a date n months (both future and past) away from the date given. The NEXT_DAY(date, char) where the char is a day of the week will return a date of the day of the week in the char field following the date. LAST_DAY(date) returns the date of the last day in the month of the date. ROUND(date[,'date format'] and TRUNC (date[,'date format']) both perform their function to the nearest date unless a date format is given, then these functions will perform the function to the precision referenced in the 'date format'.

Figure 7.4 shows some practical examples of DATE functions in use.

NUMERIC FUNCTIONS

There are several numeric functions such as ROUND, TRUNC, and MOD. The ROUND (number, precision) function rounds the value of the number to the desired precision. The TRUNC (number, precision) just drops off the characters past the desired precision. The MOD (number, number) calculates the remainder between two columns. Figure 7.5 illustrates how these functions are used.

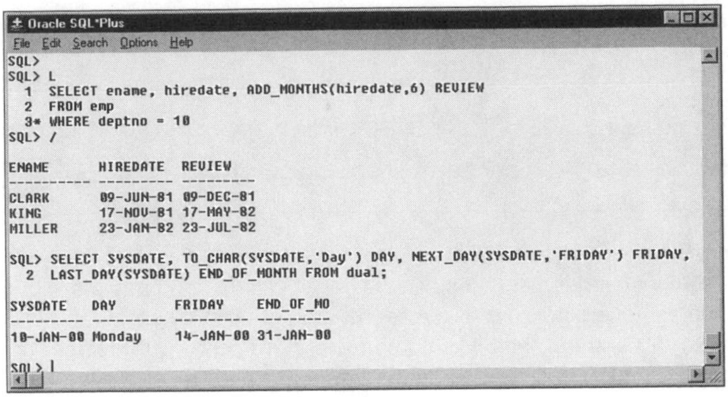

Figure 7.4: DATE *function examples.*

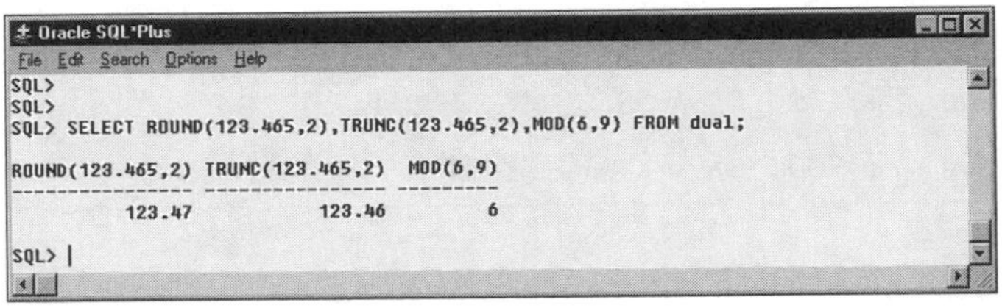

Figure 7.5: Numeric function examples.

OTHER SINGLE-ROW FUNCTIONS

The remaining two functions that do not fit any of the previous categories are NVL and DECODE. NVL stands for *null value* and gives the ability to assign a value to a null field. Figure 7.6 shows adding the SAL and COM fields to illustrate that when something is added to nothing, you get nothing. The NVL function was added to the COMM field—notice the arithmetic then works correctly.

NOTE

Notice in Figure 7.6 that the SQL*Plus buffer editor Change command was used to add the NVL.

The DECODE function is the IF-THEN-ELSE logic to SQL. The syntax looks like this: DECODE (col/variable/expression, string1, result1 [, string2, result2][, ...][, default value]. DECODE works like this: if string 1 =<condition> then return result1 else if string2 = <condition> then return result2 (and so on) else return default value. If there was no default value, then NULL is returned if none of the strings matched the original column/variable/expression. Figure 7.7 shows how to reference a field value and return a character string based on the value.

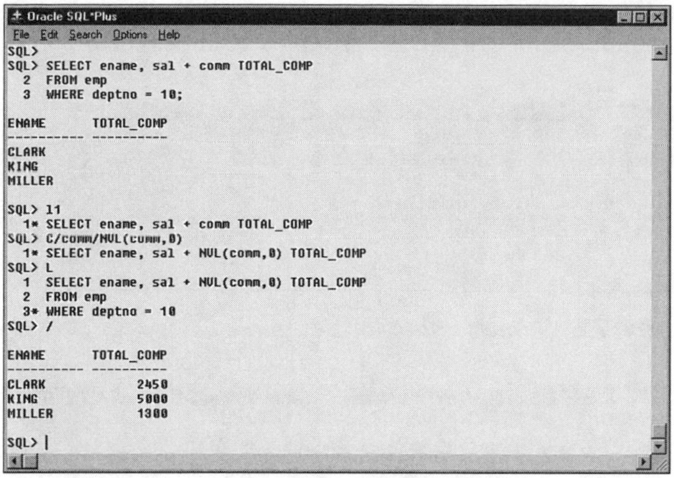

Figure 7.6: NVL *function example.*

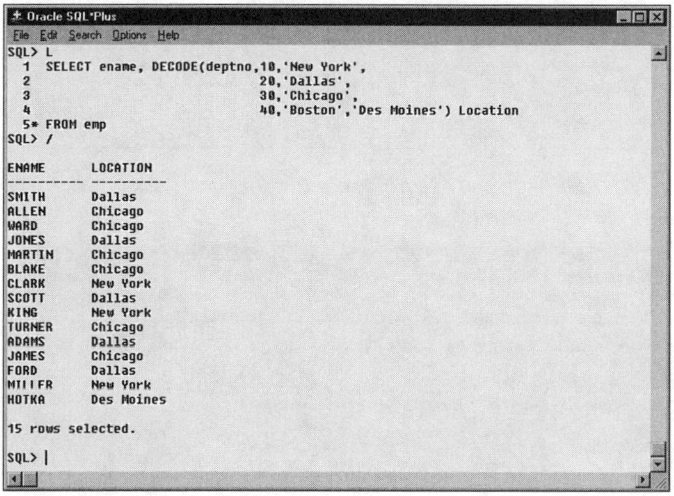

Figure 7.7: DECODE *function example.*

MULTIPLE-ROW FUNCTIONS OR GROUP FUNCTIONS

There several numeric functions such as MIN, MAX, SUM, AVG, STDDEV, DISTINCT, and COUNT. These functions, when used by themselves, will return one row from the query, the output of the function. COUNT is very useful to count the number of rows in a table (or result set). When these functions are used in combination with the GROUP BY clause, the query returns one row for each unique data grouping. Figure 7.8 shows the numeric functions in action, Figure 7.9 shows the same functions with the GROUP BY clause, and Figure 7.10 shows the GROUP BY with the HAVING clause. This HAVING clause allows for only those groups that meet certain criteria.

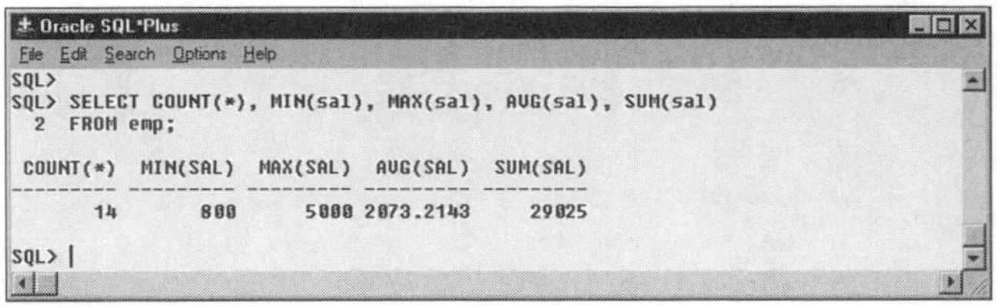

Figure 7.8: Numeric functions example.

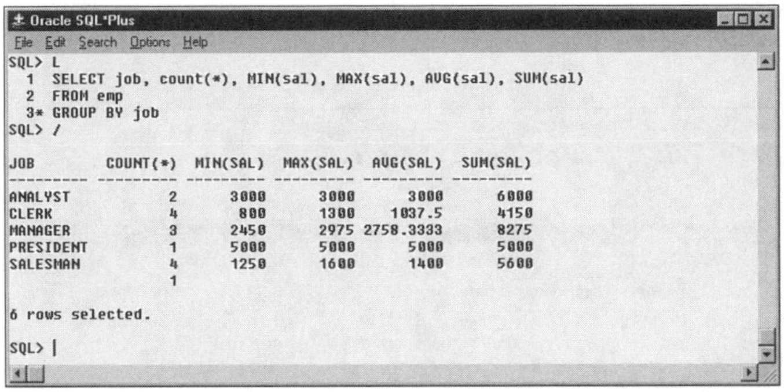

Figure 7.9: GROUP BY function example.

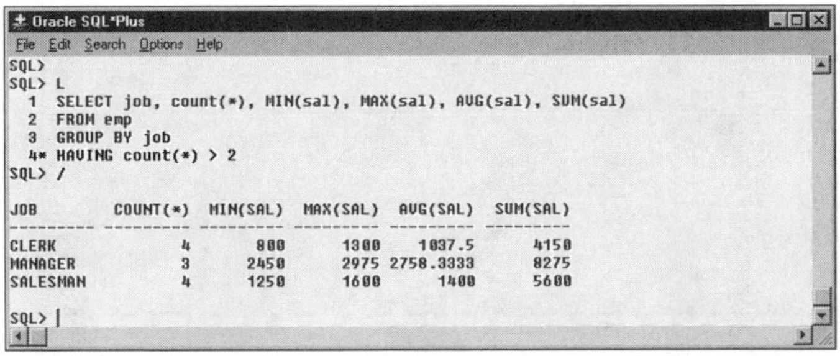

Figure 7.10: GROUP BY with a HAVING clause example.

Figure 7.11 shows how to use the DISTINCT clause in a query. Notice that the first COUNT returns a count for the table but when included with the DISTINCT clause, it returns the number of unique values.

USING MULTIPLE FUNCTIONS

These functions can be nested inside one another to produce the desired result. For example, say the employees are reviewed six months after they are hired but these reviews only happen on Mondays. Figure 7.12 shows a query that would be useful to produce such a list.

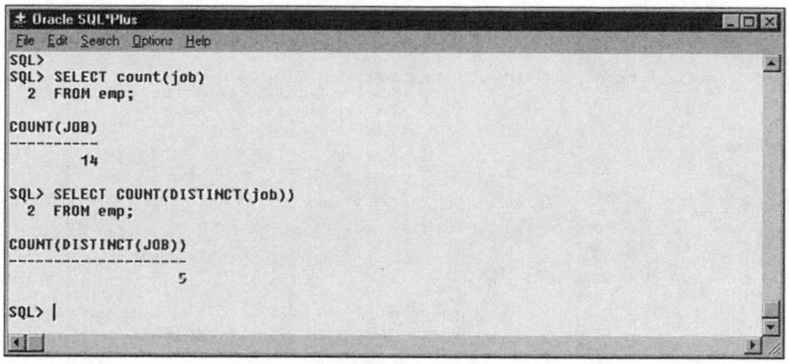

Figure 7.11: DISTINCT *function example.*

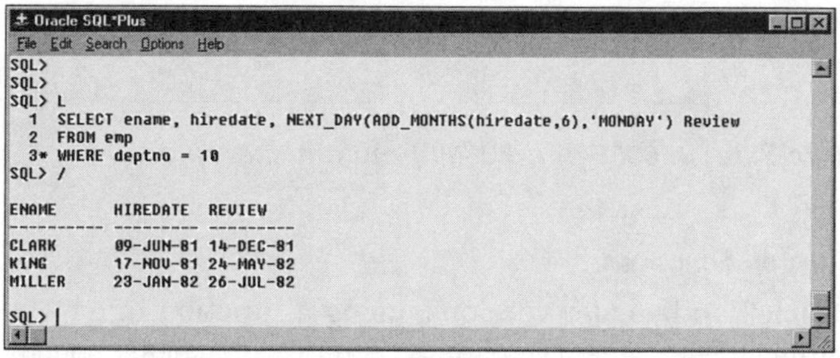

Figure 7.12: Multiple DATE *function example.*

The ROUND function is typically put outside most calculations to correctly size the result. Similarly, the NVL value is included on numeric columns that could contain null values. Figure 7.13 shows a couple of calculations using these two functions.

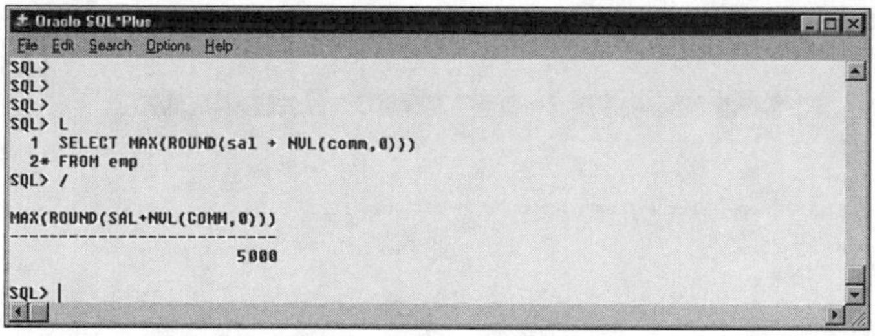

Figure 7.13: ROUND *and* NVL *functions example.*

The final example (see Figure 7.14) shows the DECODE being used with a calculation giving those in department 10 a 10% increase, department 20 a 20% increase, department 30 a 30% increase, and department 40 a 40% increase in salary.

```
± Oracle SQL*Plus                                              _ □ ×
File  Edit  Search  Options  Help
SQL> L
  1   SELECT ename, sal SALARY, DECODE(deptno,10,ROUND(sal * 1.10),
  2                                       20,ROUND(sal * 1.20),
  3                                       30,ROUND(sal * 1.30),
  4                                       40,ROUND(sal * 1.40)) Raise
  5* FROM emp
SQL> /

ENAME         SALARY     RAISE
---------- --------- ---------
SMITH            800       960
ALLEN           1600      2080
WARD            1250      1625
JONES           2975      3570
MARTIN          1250      1625
BLAKE           2850      3705
CLARK           2450      2695
SCOTT           3000      3600
KING            5000      5500
TURNER          1500      1950
ADAMS           1100      1320
JAMES            950      1235
FORD            3000      3600
MILLER          1300      1430

14 rows selected.

SQL> |
```

Figure 7.14: DECODE and ROUND *function example.*

INDEXING ON FUNCTIONS

In Oracle9 and earlier versions, using a function in a WHERE clause (for example: WHERE UPPER(ename) = 'SMITH' or WHERE empno + 10 > 1000) on an indexed column caused Oracle RDBMS not to use the index but to read all the rows in the table to perform the function. The main reason for having an index is for quick results from tables with thousands of rows. Oracle9i solves this problem of not using indexes on columns with functions. Oracle9i allows for indexes to be created and includes the typical function used. This would allow for a quick result when it is necessary to include a function in a WHERE clause. Figure 7.15 illustrates how to create an index on a column with a function.

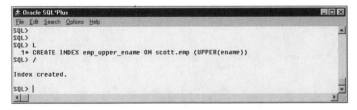

```
± Oracle SQL*Plus                                              _ □ ×
File  Edit  Search  Options  Help
SQL>
SQL>
SQL> L
  1* CREATE INDEX emp_upper_ename ON scott.emp (UPPER(ename))
SQL> /

Index created.

SQL> |
```

Figure 7.15: *Index with a function example.*

Table Join Conditions

This section covers getting data from more than one table at a time (joins). Joins are used to combine columns from two or more tables. Figure 7.16 shows a simple join between EMP and DEPT. Notice that the table name is specified with each duplicate name of columns between the two tables (see the WHERE clause of Figure 7.16). Figure 7.17 shows the same query but using a table name 'alias.' This alias can be used anyplace that further qualification is necessary (columns with the same name in different tables).

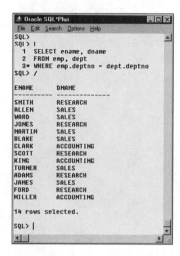

Figure 7.16: *Simple table join example.*

Figure 7.17: *Simple table join with table name qualification example.*

Figure 7.18 shows what happens if you forget the WHERE clause joining a condition between the tables. Oracle9i will return all the rows from one table for each row in the second table. This is known as a *Cartesian Product* and is usually NOT the desired result.

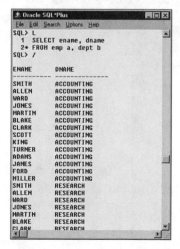

Figure 7.18: *Cartesian product example.*

An outer join is useful to show all possible conditions, even when there are no matches from one of the tables. Figure 7.19 shows the outer join syntax. Notice the '(+) syntax on' in the WHERE clause. This tells Oracle to return rows from the join whether there is a condition match or not.

```
Oracle SQL*Plus
File Edit Search Options Help
SQL>
SQL> SELECT ename, dname
  2  FROM emp, dept
  3  WHERE emp.deptno(+) = dept.deptno;

ENAME      DNAME
---------- --------------
CLARK      ACCOUNTING
KING       ACCOUNTING
MILLER     ACCOUNTING
SMITH      RESEARCH
ADAMS      RESEARCH
FORD       RESEARCH
SCOTT      RESEARCH
JONES      RESEARCH
ALLEN      SALES
BLAKE      SALES
MARTIN     SALES
JAMES      SALES
TURNER     SALES
WARD       SALES
           OPERATIONS
           Des Moines

16 rows selected.

SQL> |
```

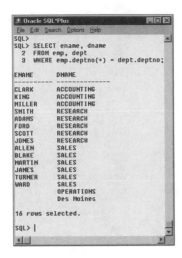

Figure 7.19: *Outer join example.*

Self joins are like a join between two tables except that the conditions are against two different columns of the *same* table. Qualifying the column names would be necessary. The EMP table has an employee id (empno) and a manager (mgr), which is also an empno. Figure 7.20 shows a query that displays the employees and their associated managers. Notice the outer join condition to show that the PRESIDENT does not have a manager.

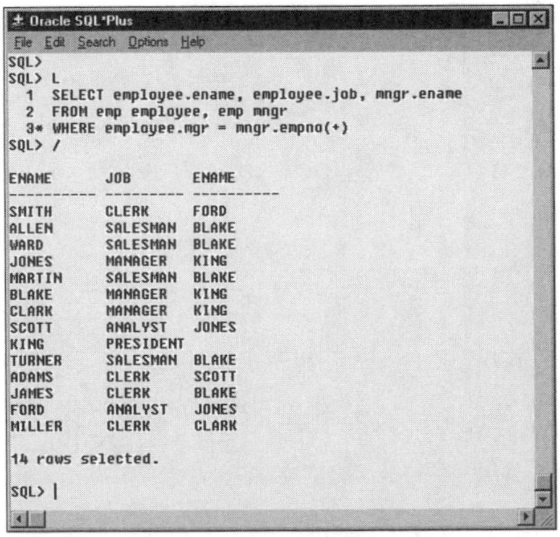

```
Oracle SQL*Plus
File Edit Search Options Help
SQL>
SQL> L
  1  SELECT employee.ename, employee.job, mngr.ename
  2  FROM emp employee, emp mngr
  3* WHERE employee.mgr = mngr.empno(+)
SQL> /

ENAME      JOB       ENAME
---------- --------- ----------
SMITH      CLERK     FORD
ALLEN      SALESMAN  BLAKE
WARD       SALESMAN  BLAKE
JONES      MANAGER   KING
MARTIN     SALESMAN  BLAKE
BLAKE      MANAGER   KING
CLARK      MANAGER   KING
SCOTT      ANALYST   JONES
KING       PRESIDENT
TURNER     SALESMAN  BLAKE
ADAMS      CLERK     SCOTT
JAMES      CLERK     BLAKE
FORD       ANALYST   JONES
MILLER     CLERK     CLARK

14 rows selected.

SQL> |
```

Figure 7.20: *Self join example.*

Whenever there is not an equal condition between two or more tables in a join condition, it is referred to as a *non-equijoin*. Figure 7.21 shows how this works. Notice that there is a condition in the WHERE clause that will return only one row from the SALGRADE table. This relationship is essential or you will get a Cartesian Product. Oracle9i will still return all the rows that match the condition from EMP for each row returned from SALGRADE.

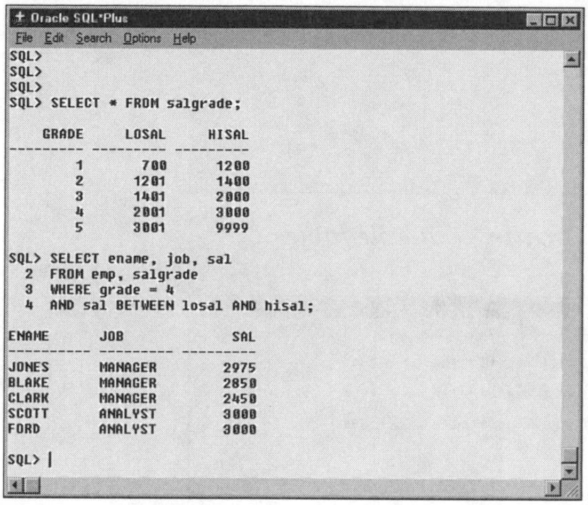

Figure 7.21: NON-Equijoin example.

There is a method of combining the result sets of several queries into one result set. You will learn later in this chapter with SQL*Plus Reporting a few other uses for this feature. The UNION operator combines two or more result sets together and removes any duplicate rows. The INTERSECT operator returns rows that two or more queries have in common, and the MINUS operator returns just the rows between two tables that are not in the other.

To work the examples, you will need to create three new tables (based on the EMP table), as illustrated in Figure 7.22.

The rule for using this technique is that each query MUST return the same number of columns and the same data types for each column. Figure 7.23 illustrates the UNION command. Notice that you can include an ORDER BY clause and that this clause uses the position of the column in the sort order.

The INTERSECT operator will show rows in common between two or more tables. The MINUS operator will show rows that do not appear in two or more tables. Figure 7.24 shows the INTERSECT and MINUS operators in use.

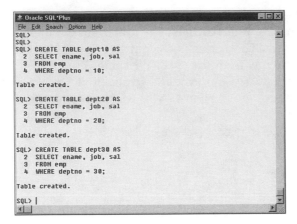

Figure 7.22: Creating example tables.

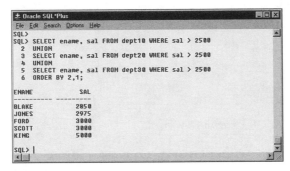

Figure 7.23: UNION operator example.

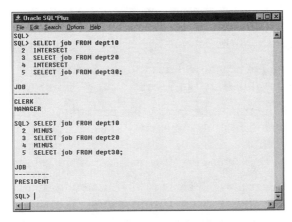

Figure 7.24: INTERSECT and MINUS operator example.

SQL Subqueries

This section discusses getting data based on unknown information (subqueries). Subqueries are useful when the condition of one query is based on information in another table. The syntax is as follows: SELECT column[s] FROM table[s] [(SELECT [column[s] FROM table[s] [WHERE...][GROUP BY ...] WHERE column|constant|expression operator (SELECT [column[s]] FROM table[s] [WHERE ...][GROUP BY ...]). You cannot use an ORDER BY in a subquery. The subquery is supplying row/column information to the outer query so there would be no reason to return rows in any particular order. Notice that you can have a subquery as part of the FROM clause.

Subqueries can be nested, or a subquery can contain a subquery. There is no technical limit to the depth of this type of query.

The subquery or "inner" query executes a single time before the main "outer" query executes. The result set from the inner query is then used by the outer query.

A query can contain multiple subqueries in that each part of a WHERE clause can contain a subquery. The HAVING clause may have a subquery as well.

There are four basic types of subqueries:

- Those that return a single row

- Those that return multiple rows

- Those that return multiple columns in a single row

- Those that return multiple columns in multiple rows

The single-row subquery has a subquery that only returns a single row. The comparison operators that test for the returned result are: = (equal), > (greater than), >= (greater than or equal to), < (less than), <= (less than or equal to), or <> (not equal). The subquery always goes on the right side of the comparison operator and is always enclosed in parentheses. Figure 7.25 shows a query that returns all the employees and their salaries that are above the average salary.

Figure 7.26 shows what happens when a single-row comparison operator is being used on a subquery that returns more than one row.

Subqueries are useful when it is desired to list some columns and use a GROUP BY function. Figure 7.27 shows a query that will find the last employee hired. Notice that the first query failed, but when the WHERE clause is fitted with a subquery, the query returns the desired results.

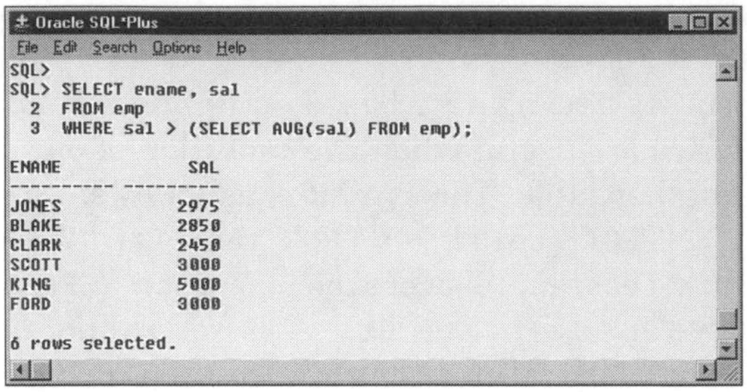

Figure 7.25: *Single-row subquery example.*

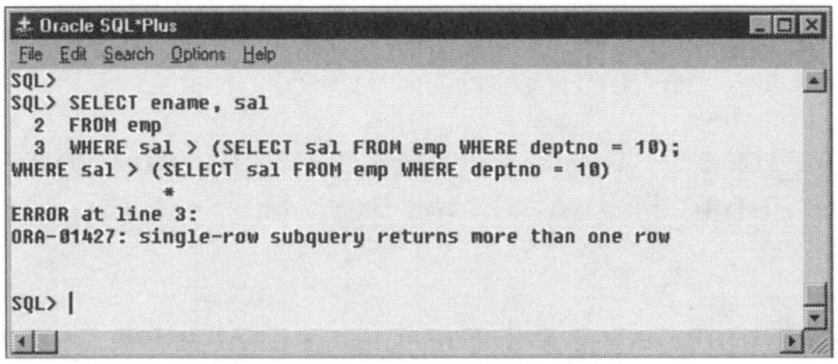

Figure 7.26: *Single-row subquery error example.*

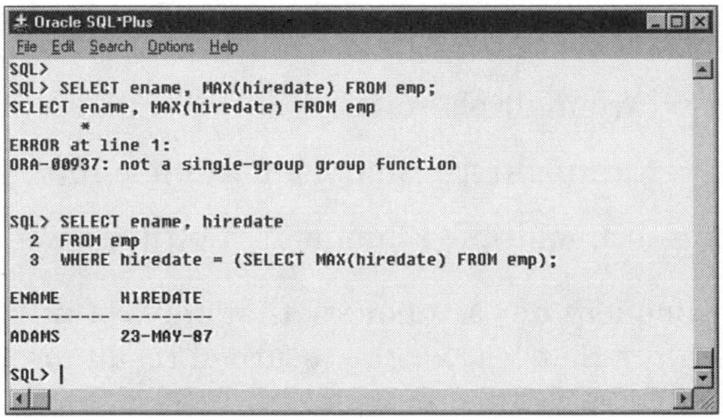

Figure 7.27: *Group function subquery example.*

The multiple-row subquery operators are IN (equal to any value in the result set), ANY (compared to each value returned by the subquery), and ALL (compared to every value returned by the subquery). Multiple-row subqueries can return one or many rows. They are called *multiple-row subqueries* because they have the ability to handle more than one row returned by the subquery. Figure 7.28 shows a SQL statement that will find the highest paid employees of each department (useful for budget cuts). Notice that there are two individuals for DEPT 20. This is because both of these folks make the maximum salary for the department. Also notice that eliminating the job PRESIDENT from the output is in the subquery. Because the

PRESIDENT is the highest paid person in DEPT 10, if this were in the outer query's WHERE clause, we would not have gotten a row for DEPT 10.

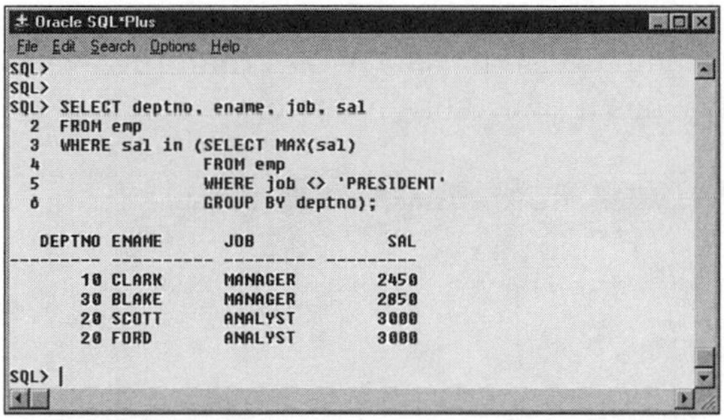


```
SQL>
SQL>
SQL> SELECT deptno, ename, job, sal
  2  FROM emp
  3  WHERE sal in (SELECT MAX(sal)
  4                FROM emp
  5                WHERE job <> 'PRESIDENT'
  6                GROUP BY deptno);

   DEPTNO ENAME      JOB             SAL
--------- ---------- --------- ---------
       10 CLARK      MANAGER        2450
       30 BLAKE      MANAGER        2850
       20 SCOTT      ANALYST        3000
       20 FORD       ANALYST        3000

SQL> |
```

Figure 7.28: *Multiple-row subquery example.*

Sometimes it is necessary to compare more than one column from the results of a subquery. Multiple-column subqueries return more than one column. The rules here are that the same number of columns specified in the WHERE clause must be returned by the subquery. There are two types of multiple-column subqueries: pairwise (where there are two or more columns returned by the same subquery) and nonpairwise where there are multiple subqueries each returning a single row. Figure 7.29 shows both kinds of subqueries in action as well as the different result sets that are produced. The big difference between pairwise and nonpairwise is that pairwise will ensure that the combined columns are from the same row, where the nonpairwise will return the rows that meet the column criteria but not necessarily where the column combination appears in the same row.

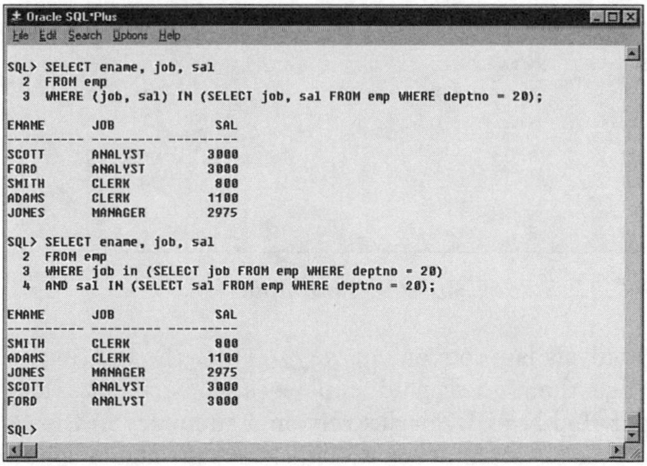


```
SQL> SELECT ename, job, sal
  2  FROM emp
  3  WHERE (job, sal) IN (SELECT job, sal FROM emp WHERE deptno = 20);

ENAME      JOB             SAL
---------- --------- ---------
SCOTT      ANALYST        3000
FORD       ANALYST        3000
SMITH      CLERK           800
ADAMS      CLERK          1100
JONES      MANAGER        2975

SQL> SELECT ename, job, sal
  2  FROM emp
  3  WHERE job in (SELECT job FROM emp WHERE deptno = 20)
  4  AND sal IN (SELECT sal FROM emp WHERE deptno = 20);

ENAME      JOB             SAL
---------- --------- ---------
SMITH      CLERK           800
ADAMS      CLERK          1100
JONES      MANAGER        2975
SCOTT      ANALYST        3000
FORD       ANALYST        3000

SQL>
```

Figure 7.29: *Multi-column subquery examples.*

Oracle9i supports a subquery in the FROM clause. This type of SQL statement is also known as an INLINE View. When this type of a SQL statement is used, the result set from this subquery becomes the data source for that particular SELECT statement. Figure 7.30 illustrates how this might work in looking for those employees that make less than the average salary. Notice how the subquery has a table alias name b.

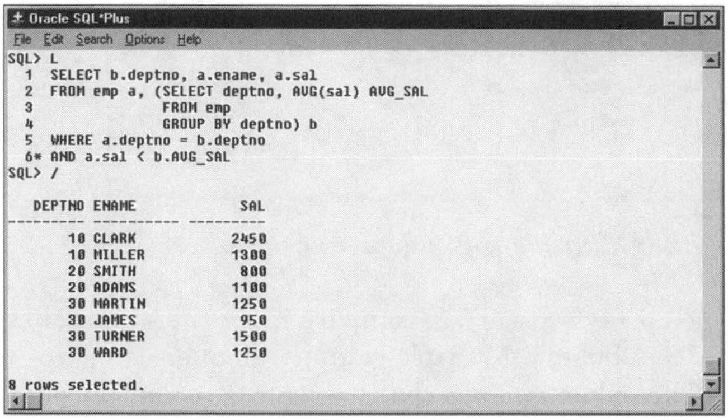

```
± Oracle SQL*Plus                                            _ □ X
File  Edit  Search  Options  Help
SQL> L
  1  SELECT b.deptno, a.ename, a.sal
  2  FROM emp a, (SELECT deptno, AVG(sal) AVG_SAL
  3               FROM emp
  4               GROUP BY deptno) b
  5  WHERE a.deptno = b.deptno
  6* AND a.sal < b.AVG_SAL
SQL> /

  DEPTNO ENAME            SAL
---------- ----------  ---------
      10 CLARK           2450
      10 MILLER          1300
      20 SMITH            800
      20 ADAMS           1100
      30 MARTIN          1250
      30 JAMES            950
      30 TURNER          1500
      30 WARD            1250

8 rows selected.
```

Figure 7.30: *FROM clause subquery example.*

A related subquery is when a field in the inner query is referenced by the outer query. Figure 7.31 shows a related subquery being used to return the same result set as in Figure 7.30. Notice the table alias.

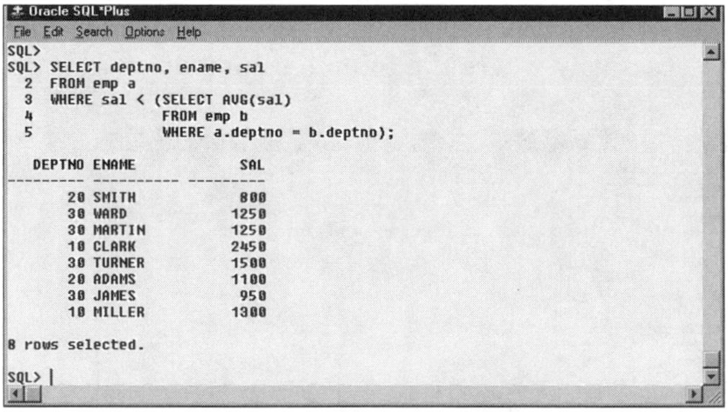

```
± Oracle SQL*Plus                                            _ □ X
File  Edit  Search  Options  Help
SQL>
SQL> SELECT deptno, ename, sal
  2  FROM emp a
  3  WHERE sal < (SELECT AVG(sal)
  4               FROM emp b
  5               WHERE a.deptno = b.deptno);

  DEPTNO ENAME            SAL
---------- ----------  ---------
      20 SMITH            800
      30 WARD            1250
      30 MARTIN          1250
      10 CLARK           2450
      30 TURNER          1500
      20 ADAMS           1100
      30 JAMES            950
      10 MILLER          1300

8 rows selected.

SQL> |
```

Figure 7.31: *Related subquery example.*

Top-N analysis is a convenient way to show the top five selling products, or in our case, the highest paid employees who are not sales people or the president. Top-N SQL queries rely on a subquery in the FROM clause and utilize the pseudo column ROWNUM. This ROWNUM is also a column that could be displayed as part of the SELECT clause, as illustrated in Figure 7.32.

NOTE

A pseudo column is a table column that is not explicitly defined; that is, one comes with each table. ROWNUM is associated with the result set of queries.

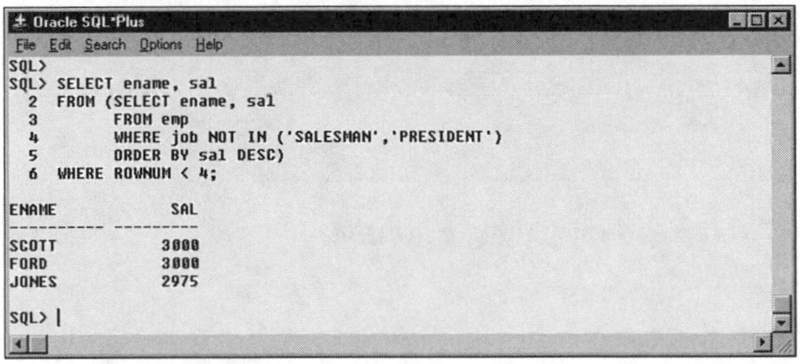

```
Oracle SQL*Plus
File  Edit  Search  Options  Help
SQL>
SQL> SELECT ename, sal
  2  FROM (SELECT ename, sal
  3          FROM emp
  4          WHERE job NOT IN ('SALESMAN','PRESIDENT')
  5          ORDER BY sal DESC)
  6  WHERE ROWNUM < 4;

ENAME         SAL
--------- ---------
SCOTT        3000
FORD         3000
JONES        2975

SQL> |
```

Figure 7.32: Top-N analysis query example.

Complex Views

Now that we understand subqueries, GROUP BY functions, and so on, the SELECT clause used to create the view can contain these features as well. Figure 7.33 illustrates creating and then selecting from a view that makes use of the GROUP BY functions.

NOTE

This kind of view cannot accept DML SQL statements.

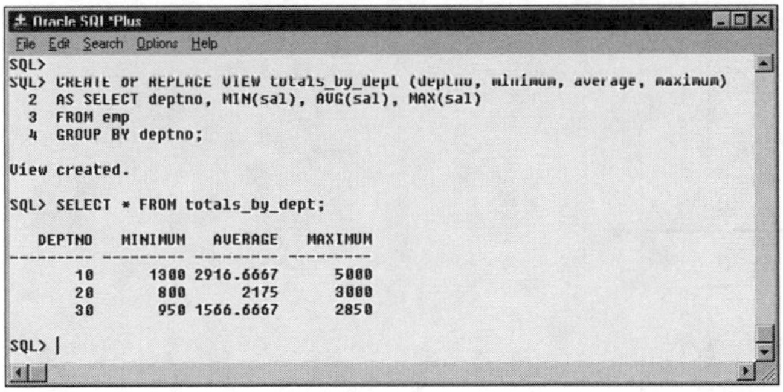

```
Oracle SQL*Plus
File  Edit  Search  Options  Help
SQL>
SQL> CREATE OR REPLACE VIEW totals_by_dept (deptno, minimum, average, maximum)
  2  AS SELECT deptno, MIN(sal), AVG(sal), MAX(sal)
  3  FROM emp
  4  GROUP BY deptno;

View created.

SQL> SELECT * FROM totals_by_dept;

   DEPTNO   MINIMUM   AVERAGE   MAXIMUM
--------- --------- --------- ---------
       10      1300 2916.6667      5000
       20       800      2175      3000
       30       950 1566.6667      2850

SQL> |
```

Figure 7.33: Complex view example.

Views can also be created with the READ ONLY option (as illustrated in Figure 7.34) to ensure that there will be no DML SQL statements processed against them.

```
Oracle SQL*Plus                                              _ □ ×
File  Edit  Search  Options  Help
SQL>
SQL>
SQL> CREATE OR REPLACE VIEW employee_job_sal (empno, ename, job, sal)
  2  AS SELECT empno, ename, job, sal
  3  FROM emp
  4  WITH READ ONLY;

View created.

SQL> INSERT INTO employee_job_sal VALUES (55555,'Dan Hotka','Author',1000);
INSERT INTO employee_job_sal VALUES (55555,'Dan Hotka','Author',1000)
*
ERROR at line 1:
ORA-01733: virtual column not allowed here

SQL>
SQL
```

Figure 7.34: *Read-only view example.*

Read Consistency

The Oracle RDBMS has always supported read consistency. Read consistency ensures that the data will remain consistent for the duration of a SQL query from the start of the query. What this really means is if User A starts a query at 10:00 A.M. and User B makes an insert to data at 10:05 A.M., when User A's process gets to the change of User B, the SQL statement will see the data as it existed prior to the change made by User B. Figure 7.35 illustrates read consistency as depicted in this example.

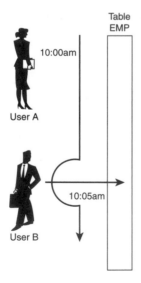

Figure 7.35: *Read consistency example.*

In any environment with more than one user trying to use resources, a mechanism for sharing must be established. Oracle9i uses various locking mechanisms to ensure that only one resource is updating a particular row at a time. Oracle supports two kinds of locking: exclusive and share. An exclusive lock would prevent any other user from making any changes to the object. A share lock allows multiple users to manipulate data in different parts of the object. Most locking is implicit, in that Oracle9I automatically locks rows, blocks, and tables for certain types of operations. Figure 7.36 shows an explicit share lock on the rows being affected by this particular SQL statement. All locks are released with a COMMIT or ROLLBACK statement. Figure 7.37 shows the lock created by Figure 7.36 (user 11). You will learn more about locks and interpreting the information in Chapter 14, "Oracle9i Application SQL Tuning."

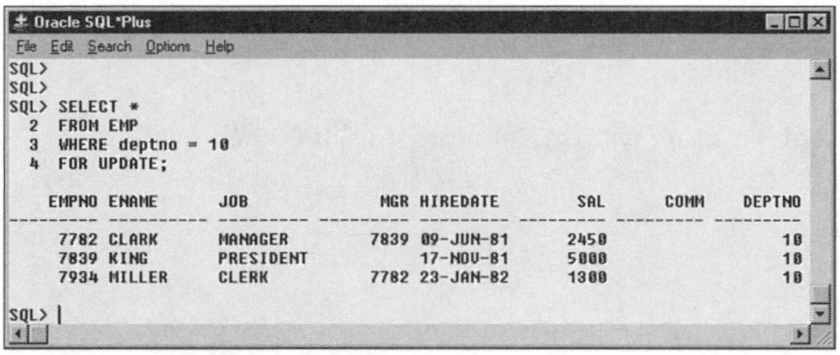

Figure 7.36: Row-level locking example.

Figure 7.37: V$Lock example.

Oracle9i supports a new feature called flash back queries. This allows for a query user to invoke a read-consistent view of the database as of a certain date and time. This feature can be helpful to identify (or even build a recovery script!) accidentally deleted rows or to create a report before an update occurred. Listing 7.1 illustrates a query of the EMP table, an update, the same query showing the update and flash back enabled. Notice first the date and time. Then the query is first run, showing dept 10 having a combined salary of 8,750. The department 10 salaries are then doubled with the update SQL statement. The same query is run again showing the department salaries now of 17,500.

Figure 7.38 illustrates a SQL query before and after an update, showing the same results. Notice the execute `dbms_flashback.enable_at_time` syntax. The same query is again ran that shows the data as it appeared at 5:08.

Listing 7.1: Flash Back Query

```
SQL> select sysdate from dual;

SYSDATE
-- -- -- -- -
11-AUG-01

SQL> select to_char(sysdate,'hh:mm:ss') TIME from dual;

TIME
-- -- -- --
05:08:35

SQL> get test_flash
  1  select dept.deptno, dname, sum(sal)
  2  from emp, dept
  3  where emp.deptno = dept.deptno
  4* group by dept.deptno, dname
SQL> /

    DEPTNO DNAME           SUM(SAL)
-- -- -- -- --  -- -- -- -- -- -- --  -- -- -- -- --
        10 ACCOUNTING          8750
        20 RESEARCH           10875
        30 SALES               9400

SQL> update emp
  2  set sal = sal * 2
  3  where deptno = 10;

3 rows updated.

SQL> get test_flash
  1  select dept.deptno, dname, sum(sal)
  2  from emp, dept
  3  where emp.deptno = dept.deptno
  4* group by dept.deptno, dname
SQL> /
```

Listing 7.1:   continued

```
    DEPTNO DNAME            SUM(SAL)
-- -- -- -- -- -- -- -- -- -- -- -- -- -- -- -- -- --
        10 ACCOUNTING         17500
        20 RESEARCH           10875
        30 SALES               9400



SQL> execute dbms_flashback.enable_at_time ('11-AUG-01 05:08');

PL/SQL procedure successfully completed.


SQL> get test_flash
  1  select dept.deptno, dname, sum(sal)
  2  from emp, dept
  3  where emp.deptno = dept.deptno
  4* group by dept.deptno, dname

SQL> /


    DEPTNO DNAME            SUM(SAL)
-- -- -- -- -- -- -- -- -- -- -- -- -- -- -- -- -- --
        10 ACCOUNTING          8750
        20 RESEARCH           10875
        30 SALES               9400

SQL> spool off
```

Advanced SQL*Plus Reporting Features Techniques

This is the final section of Chapter 7. "Using Advanced SQL Techniques and SQL*Plus Reporting Features," discusses more advanced reporting features of SQL*Plus: creating a cross-tabular report, using substitution variables from the operating-system command line along with a pre-formatted output result, and creating a master/detail report.

Cross-tabular reports are easy to do with a mix of SQL and SQL*Plus formatting commands. Listing 7.2 shows the CH3_XREF.SQL SQL*Plus script file and Listing 7.3 shows the output cross-tabular report from this script file. Notice again that there is a command line field that is passed in and appears in the heading. In this case, it is a report date. Notice the new format of the TTITLE at lines 28 and 29 (the - at the end of line 28 is a line-continuation character). The column format commands (lines 15 through 20) control the appearance of the columns. The DECODE lines 32 through 36 control which salary gets added to which bucket. Notice that the substr is only looking at the first column of job. This is simply because all the jobs are unique by the first position of the field. The combination of compute commands (lines 22 through 27), the SUM statements in the query (lines 32 through 37), and the Group By clause in the query (line 39) give the report output the appearance of a cross-tabular report.

Listing 7.2: CH3_XREF.SQL Script

```
1:  rem
2:  rem CH7_XREF.SQL - Creates a Cross Reference Matrix Report
3:  rem
4:  rem      Oracle9i by Example
5:  rem            by Dan Hotka
6:  rem          Que Publications June 2001
7:  rem          All Rights Reserved
8:  rem
9:  define RPT_DATE = &1
10: SET FEEDBACK OFF
11: SET VERIFY OFF
12: SET TERMOUT OFF
13: SET ECHO OFF
14: SET LINESIZE 60
15: COLUMN CLERK                       format 999999    heading 'Clerk'
16: COLUMN MANAGER          format 999999  heading 'Manager'
17: COLUMN SALESMAN         format 999999  heading 'Salesman'
18: COLUMN ANALYST          format 999999  heading 'Analyst'
19: COLUMN PRESIDENT        format 999999  heading 'President'
20: COLUMN TOTALS           format 999999  heading 'Totals'
21: BREAK ON REPORT SKIP 2
22: COMPUTE SUM OF CLERK on report
23: COMPUTE SUM OF ANALYST on report
24: COMPUTE SUM OF MANAGER on report
25: COMPUTE SUM OF SALESMAN on report
26: COMPUTE SUM OF PRESIDENT on report
27: COMPUTE SUM OF TOTALS on report
28: TTITLE left '&RPT_DATE' center 'Salary Cross-Tabular'  RIGHT 'Page: ' format
999 -
29: SQL.PNO skip CENTER ' by Job/Department '
30: SPOOL CH3_XREF.OUT
31: SELECT deptno,
32:     SUM(DECODE(SUBSTR(job,1,1),'C',sal,0)) CLERK,
33:     SUM(DECODE(SUBSTR(job,1,1),'A',sal,0)) ANALYST,
34:     SUM(DECODE(SUBSTR(job,1,1),'M',sal,0)) MANAGER,
35:     SUM(DECODE(SUBSTR(job,1,1),'S',sal,0)) SALESMAN,
36:     SUM(DECODE(SUBSTR(job,1,1),'P',sal,0)) PRESIDENT,
37:     SUM(sal) TOTALS
38: FROM emp
39: GROUP BY deptno
```

Listing 7.2:   continued

```
40: /
41: SPOOL OFF
42: EXIT
```

Listing 7.3:   Output Cross-Matrix Report from Listing 7.2

```
06/14/2001             Salary Cross-Tabular        Page:    1
                         by Job/Department

   DEPTNO   Clerk Analyst Manager Salesman President  Totals
   ........  ............. ....... ................  .......
       10    1300       0    2450        0     5000    8750
       20    1900    6000    2975        0        0   10875
       30     950       0    2850     5600        0    9400

         .. .. .. . .. .. .. .. .. .. .. .. .. .. . .. .. .. .. .

   sum     4150    6000    8275     5600     5000   29025
```

Listing 7.4 illustrates how to load SQL*Plus define variables with data from a table. This technique is useful any time there is a need to create an output file (be it in a report format, SQL*Plus, or operating-system command-language scripts, and so on) that is based on data from inside a table. The importance of this concept is that these variables can be loaded from the Oracle database and their values referenced again in other SQL queries. The example is simple but the technique is powerful.

The important technique to observe in Listing 7.4 is the COLUMN commands (lines 20 and 21) and the select statement that loads the DNAME column (lines 23 through 25). Notice that the COLUMN name is referenced in the SQL statement but the NEW_VALUE name is referenced in the SQL statement (lines 28 and 29) that uses the contents of the variable. Also notice that there is one line of output for each combination of SELECT... FROM dual lines 28 and 29, 31 and 32, and 34 and 35. Also notice line 15, which is setting PAGESIZE to 0. This will cause no heading breaks, or even the blank line that appears even if SET HEADING OFF is used (line 16). This technique can be used to create SQL*Loader control files from information stored in the USER_TAB_COLUMNS or CREATE TABLE statements from the same USER_TAB_COLUMNS, fixed formatted reports, and so on. See Listing 7.5 for the output from Listing 7.4.

Listing 7.4:   CH7_LVAR.SQL Script

```
1:  rem
2:  CH7_LVAR.SQL - Demonstrates how to load variables from the contents
3:  rem                  of a table.w to load variables from the contents
4:  rem      Oracle9i by Example
5:  rem           by Dan Hotka
6:  rem         Que Publications June 2001
7:  rem         All Rights Reserved
```

Listing 7.4: continued

```
8:  rem
9:
10: SET FEEDBACK OFF
11: SET VERIFY OFF
12: SET TERMOUT OFF
13: SET ECHO OFF
14: SET LINESIZE 60
15: SET PAGESIZE 0
16: SET HEADING OFF
17:
18: define DEPTNO = &1
19:
20: column DNAME new_value VAR_DNAME noprint
21: column LOC new_value VAR_LOC noprint
22:
23: SELECT dname, loc
24: FROM dept
25: WHERE deptno = &DEPTNO
26: /
27: spool  CH3_LVAR.TXT
28: select 'This Department ' || ' &VAR_DNAME' || ' was loaded into a variable'
29: FROM dual
30: /
31: select 'from a database table that returned 1 row.  This technique '
32: FROM dual
33: /
34: select 'can be used to build any fixed formatted report, code syntax, etc.'
35: FROM dual
36: /
37: SPOOL OFF
38: EXIT
```

Listing 7.5: Output from CH7_LVAR.SQL in Listing 7.4

```
This Department  ACCOUNTING was loaded into a variable
from a database table that returned 1 row.  This technique
can be used to build any fixed formatted report, code syntax, and so on.
```

TIP

Use the column command with the NEW_VALUE option to load variables from Oracle9i tables to use in other SQL queries in the SQL*Plus script.

The final example in this chapter will make use of the UNION operator to create a master/detail type report.

Listing 7.6 creates a Master/Detail SQL*Plus Report by utilizing the SQL UNION command. In this example, there are six distinct separate types of lines to be printed: the Department line (line 27), a line of dashes under the department name (line 30), the employee detail line (line 33), a line of dashes under the detail total (line 36), a total line (lines 39 through 42), and a blank line between the groups (line 44). There are six separate queries that have their output merged and sorted together by the SQL JOIN statement (see lines 29, 32, 35, 38, and 43). When using JOIN to merge the output of two or more queries, the output result set MUST have the same number of columns and column types.

The headings are turned off (line 19) because regular SQL*Plus column headings are not desired for this type of report. The first column of each query has an alias column name of DUMMY. This DUMMY column is used to sort the order of the six types of lines (denoted by each of the six queries). The DUMMY column's only role is to maintain the order of the lines within the major sort field (DEPTNO in this example), so the NOPRINT option is specified in line 23. The final ORDER BY (line 46) actually merges the result set lines together to form the report in Listing 7.7. Notice line 33 uses a TO_CHAR function to ensure the output from this query is indeed character mode for the UNION operator. Also notice that each of the queries returns three columns: DUMMY, DEPTNO, and a character string. The INLINE view or a sub-query in the FROM clause at lines 40 through 44, which allows for the SUM function to occur for the totals at the deptno breaks. The BREAK ON command (line 24) is to eliminate the duplicate DEPTNOs from the output report.

Listing 7.6: CH7_MDET.SQL Script

```
 1:  rem
 2:  rem CH7_MDET.SQL - Demonstrates how to create a Master/Detail report
 3:  rem                        using the UNION operator.  This technique is useful
 4:  rem                        when ever records/text from different tables nees
 5:  rem                        to appear in the same report.
 6:  rem
 7:  rem      Oracle9i by Example
 8:  rem            by Dan Hotka
 9:  rem          Que Publications June 2001
10:  rem          All Rights Reserved
11:  rem
12:
13:  SET FEEDBACK OFF
14:  SET VERIFY OFF
15:  SET TERMOUT OFF
16:  SET ECHO OFF
17:  SET LINESIZE 60
18:  SET PAGESIZE 55
19:  SET HEADING OFF
20:
```

Listing 7.6: continued

```
21: TTITLE 'Employee Detail | by Department'
22:
23: COLUMN DUMMY NOPRINT
24: BREAK ON deptno
25:
26: SPOOL CH3_MDET.OUT
27: SELECT 1 DUMMY, deptno,'Department: ' || dname
28: FROM dept
29: UNION
30: SELECT 2 DUMMY,deptno,'-- -- -- -- -- -- -- -- -- -- -'
31: FROM dept
32: UNION
33: SELECT 3 DUMMY,deptno, ename || '    ' || TO_CHAR(sal,'$999,999')
34: FROM emp
35: UNION
36: SELECT 4 DUMMY,deptno,'        -- -- -- -- -- '
37: FROM dept
38: UNION
39: SELECT 5 DUMMY,deptno,'Total:  ' || TO_CHAR(sal,'$999,999')
40: FROM (SELECT deptno, SUM(sal) sal
41:       FROM emp
42:       GROUP BY deptno)
43: UNION
44: SELECT 6 DUMMY,deptno,'            '
45: FROM dept
46: ORDER BY 2,1,3
47: /
48: SPOOL OFF
49: EXIT
```

Listing 7.7: Output from CH7_MDET.SQL in Listing 3.9

```
Thr Jun 14                                          page    1
                         Employee Detail
                          by Department


        10 Department: ACCOUNTING
           -- -- -- -- -- -- -- -- -- -- -
           CLARK      $2,450
           KING       $5,000
           MILLER     $1,300
                      -- -- -- -- --
           Total:     $8,750


        20 Department: RESEARCH
           -- -- -- -- -- -- -- -- -- -- -
           ADAMS      $1,100
```

Listing 7.6: continued

```
            FORD        $3,000
            JONES       $2,975
            SCOTT       $3,000
            SMITH         $800
            -- -- -- -- --
            Total:     $10,875

    30 Department: SALES
    -- -- -- -- -- -- -- -- -- -- -- ·
            ALLEN       $1,600
            BLAKE       $2,850
            JAMES         $950
            MARTIN      $1,250
            TURNER      $1,500
            WARD        $1,250
            -- -- -- -- --
            Total:      $9,400
```

Summary

This chapter built on the syntax learned in Chapters 2 and 6, illustrating more advanced features of both the SQL language and how these features can be used to enhance reports and used in business applications.

REVIEW

Reviewing It

1. What is the purpose of SQL functions?

2. What is the DUAL table useful for?

3. Explain SQL concatenation.

4. The DECODE statement is what?

5. When might you use the HAVING clause?

6. Briefly describe what a JOIN is.

7. What is 'qualification' and why is it important to a self-join?

8. Name the four types of sub-queries.

9. What is an IN-LINE view?

Checking It

1. SQL functions falls into

   a) 1 Category

   b) 2 Categories

   c) 3 Categories

   d) Does not have categories

2. A single-row function can only return one row.

   True/False

3. In a DATE mask, the RR means

   a) Current century if the year tested is between 00 and 49 and the current year is between 50 and 99

   b) Current century if the year tested is between 00 and 49 and the current year is between 00 and 49

   c) Next century if the year tested is 00 through 49 and the current year is 50 through 99

   d) Current century if the year tested is 50 and 99 and the current year is between 00 and 49

4. When might a group function return more than one row?

   a) When used with a WHERE clause

   b) When used with an ORDER BY clause

   c) When used with a GROUP BY clause

   d) Cannot have more than one row returned

5. Cartesian Joins have a valid use.

   True/False

6. Oracle9i supports a subquery in the FROM clause.

   True/False

7. SQL*Plus can

   a) Take input from the command line

   b) Format column output

   c) Sum the contents of a column

   d) All of the above

8. SQL*Plus can be used to create GUI reports.

   True/False

APPLY

Applying It

Independent Exercise 1:

- SELECT the departments with a count of the rows for each department.

Independent Exercise 2:

- Build a Master/Detail report using DEPT and EMP.

- Show just the Department Name on the master record.

- Show the employees name and salary in the Detail.

- Create a Cross-matrix report using EMP, showing the salaries summed by JOB and by DEPTNO.

Independent Exercise 3:

- UPDATE the EMP table, give everyone a 10% increase in salary.

- Show the values of ENAME and SAL prior to the UPDATE.

What's Next?

In this chapter, you learned some advanced SQL features as well as some advanced SQL*Plus reporting techniques. Chapter 8, "Building Web Sites with Oracle 9i," takes what you have learned so far about SQL and PL/SQL and uses these skills to build an interactive series of Web pages.

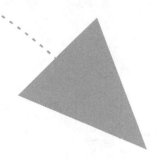

Building Web Sites with Oracle9i

Several ways are available to process HTML (*Hypertext Markup Language*), the language that Web browsers understand. Figure 8.1 illustrates the typical static Web environment in which all the files are generated ahead of time in an HTML format that contains tags telling the Web browser how to display various items. Each computer hosting a Web server has an HTTP (*Hypertext Transfer Protocol*) listener or a Web listener—these are the same. An HTTP or Web listener is assigned to a specific TCP/IP port on the computer and listens for *URLs* addressed to that particular computer and port.

This chapter teaches you the following:

- How does a Web browser access Oracle9i?

- Planning a Web site—buy a car

- What is Oracle9 iAS?

- Web-based strategies

NOTE

URL—Stands for Uniform Resource Locator, which is the addressing mechanism of the World Wide Web. It contains the computer's TCP/IP address (or a name that translates to the computer's TCP/IP address), the port number on that computer, and the resource to be first accessed. When WWW is part of a URL, this name is registered with a name-server that interprets this WWW URL address (such as www.oracle.com) into the computer's name (known as a hostname) and the port for the listener.

TCP/IP—A common computer network, which also supports the World Wide Web.

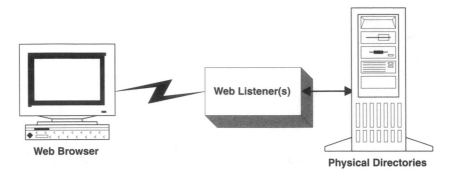

Web Browser

Physical Directories

Figure 8.1: Web browser accessing an HTML file.

NOTE

HTTP (Hypertext Transfer Protocol)—The communication layer between the Web browser and the HTTP or Web listener. HTTP is a transmission protocol that works over TCP/IP and the Internet.

NOTE

HTML (Hypertext Markup Language)—Used to build Web pages by specifying various display attributes, accessing computer files for display, and using tags. These tags tell the Web browser whether to bold, highlight, link, access computer files, and so on.

Another method for creating and processing Web requests is through a *CGI* (Common Gateway Interface) program, illustrated in Figure 8.2. In Figure 8.2, where a computer system file containing HTML is being accessed, the CGI method executes a program that can be written in almost any language and produces files (in HTML format, or referenced by an HTML-formatted file) that are returned to the Web browser. This method consumes quite a bit more resources than the one shown in Figure 8.1 because a program has to start, execute, possibly log in to a database, and perform some work there (such as data extraction) before it can return anything to the Web browser. In addition, each Web listener request starts a new program. You can see that if this method is employed on a popular Web site, it could create quite a load on the computer system.

NOTE

CGI (Common Gateway Interface)—Usually a program being accessed instead of a computer file, as in Figure 8.2.

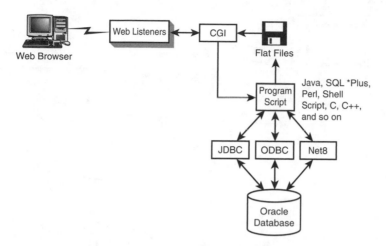

Figure 8.2: Web browser accessing a CGI interface.

Applets are Java programs that are parts of Web pages. They are down-loaded through the listener to a compliant Web browser (Netscape and Microsoft Explorer both support applets) and are executed on the client machine. Servlets are host-based Java programs that build dynamic Web pages that are then passed back to the Web browser.

A series of servlets remains running to handle requests from the Java Web server. Two versions of Java Database Connectivity (JDBC) exist—thin JDBC and thick JDBC.

- Thin JDBC is used by applets and provides database connectivity for a particular client session.

- Thick JDBC is used to maintain connectivity for the duration of the servlet process.

Both kinds of JDBC connect to Oracle9i via Net8. Figure 8.3 illustrates how the servlets work and how the applets work. The applet is downloaded to the client's Web browser via a Web page; it then connects and processes Java requests from the client's computer. Servlets maintain connectivity and are designed to be shared across requests coming through the Java Web server.

The HTTP or Web listener can be one of many products, such as Microsoft IIS, Netscape FastTrack, or Oracle iAS (internet Application Server). Each complete URL contains many parts. The first part up to the first / is the machine address. Somewhere along the way, this WWW name gets relayed back to a host and domain name and a TCP/IP address and port number for a particular computer. On that computer is a listener process waiting for requests for that computer. What follows the first / is the virtual address.

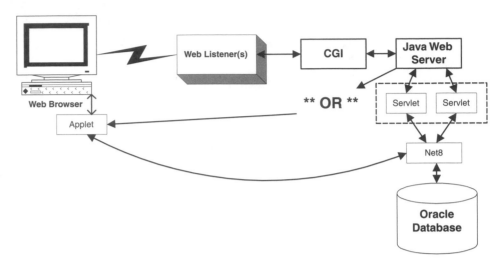

Figure 8.3: *CGI interface with applets versus servlets.*

Figure 8.4 shows how that virtual address relates to a physical location on the particular computer. Whatever follows the final / is what is accessed, started, or executed on that computer. If nothing follows the final /, a default, such as Index.html, is used.

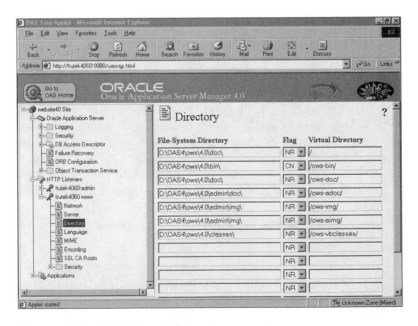

Figure 8.4: *Web Virtual Directory mappings.*

Several different kinds of URLs exist. An HTTP URL is used to connect with a Web server that handles HTML documents (Web pages)—for example, http://www.quest.com/, which accesses the Quest Web server and returns the HTML document Index.HTML. Other URLs are used for file transfer, such as ftp://www.some_ftp_server.com/, which uploads or downloads files using the FTP program and protocol. In addition, many kinds of servers are available, each with its own protocol, such as Usenet (uses the News URL), and so on.

URLs can also contain parameters. Parameters begin following a ?, where the parameters are then named and values passed. A URL with parameters might look like this:

```
http://yourdomain.com/virtual_path_for_plsqlcart/stored_proc?param=1
```

Planning a Web Site—Buy a Car

As cars are prepared for sale, they are added to the ST_CARS_FOR_SALE table (see Figure 8.5). This object tracks the inventory ID, the description of the car, and the location of the picture image on disk. HTML output can pick up images from only the disk, so all you need to do is store the location of the image in the database, not necessarily the whole picture. If the picture is stored in the database, the get_lob PL/SQL built-in procedure can be used to extract it to a specific location with a specific name, which can then be referenced by the HTML output. An additional Oracle form could be added to maintain the ST_CARS_FOR_SALES, and of course, a report or form would be needed to display or process the BUYER information when offers are made.

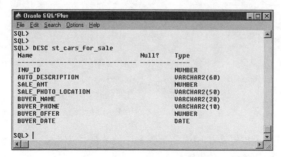

Figure 8.5: *Sales Tracking Cars For Sale object.*

The Sales Tracking Web site dynamically displays auto information on those vehicles that have been added to the ST_CARS_FOR_SALE table object. Figure 8.6 shows the 1992 Camry Deluxe auto information that is in the

ST_CARS_FOR_SALE object. This is the information that will be pulled from the database to be displayed on the actual Web site.

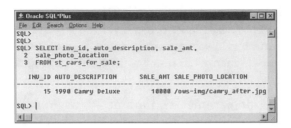

Figure 8.6: ST_CARS_FOR_SALE data.

The Web site will then be capable of displaying information stored in this table object. Figure 8.7 shows the Web site that will be built in Chapters 9, "Using PL/SQL to Build Web Sites," and 10, "Using Java to Build Web Sites."

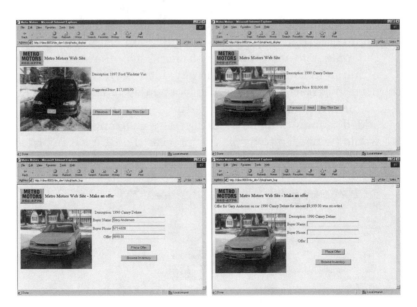

Figure 8.7: These four windows (starting at the upper left) show the navigation of the actual Sales Tracking Web site.

Three buttons control the navigation of this Web page: Previous, Next, and Buy This Car (shown in the main screen in the upper-left window). The

Previous and Next buttons display information from the previous or next row in the ST_CARS_FOR_SALE object. For example, clicking the Next button displays the Camry information as illustrated in the upper-right window. If you click the Place Offer button here, you then see the entry boxes displayed on the Web page in the bottom-left window. After you enter the offer information and click Place Offer, you will see the summary information displayed as in the bottom-right window. The Browse Inventory button in this panel then returns the Web user back to the original screen, as seen in the upper left.

Figure 8.8 shows the data stored in ST_CARS_FOR_SALE after the Place Offer button has been clicked. This shows the information from the Web page has been written into the database.

NOTE

This is a sample application. A real application that takes offers over the Web would collect as many offers as possible, storing them in yet another table object. The author is interested in showing functionality in these examples.

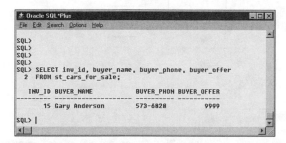

Figure 8.8: ST_CARS_FOR_SALE *offer data recorded.*

What Is Oracle9iAS?

Oracle9iAS is Oracle Corporation's integrated Web server. Figure 8.9 illustrates Oracle's Web server technology. This offering from Oracle Corp is a web server and application server combined. Along with processing HTTP/HTML/XML type requests, it can host Oracle Forms, Java, Perl, PL/SQL, and many more engines as well as cache both HTTP and database requests. When a listener receives an HTTP transaction from a Web browser (end user), the transaction is passed to the Oracle/Apache HTTP Server. The HTTP Server then decides what kind of request this is and routes it properly through the Web server to the appropriate facilities. For example, if you are running a Web-based Oracle Form, the request will be routed to the business logic service that is running the Oracle Form itself (as discussed in Chapter 5, "Building Oracle Forms").

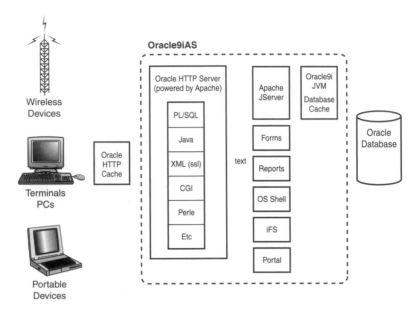

Figure 8.9: Oracle9iAS.

NOTE

Virtual Mappings—The part of the URL that can specify a location after the computer's address. This location is virtual in that it is converted by the Web listener process into a real computer directory location on the computer hosting the Web server. This virtual address can be named anything because it is simply a name to be looked up and converted by the Web listener.

Oracle refers to this technology as 3-tier because the client is the first tier, the iAS is the middle tier, and the database server is the third tier. For scalability and performance reasons, there is no reason that the various components of Oracle9iAS cannot reside on different physical machines in the computing network. Oracle9iAS has many features such as multiple caching mechanisms, high availability features, and redundant features to ensure connectivity. An in-depth look at Oracle9iAS is beyond the scope of this book.

Web-Based Strategies

This book considers three different strategies for creating Web sites that will access the Sales Tracking database. Chapter 9 introduces you to creating Web pages with PL/SQL; Chapter 10 introduces you to creating Web pages with Java; Chapter 11, "Using XML to Build Web Sites," shows you how to use XML to reformat the Web site for use with wireless devices, and Chapter 12, "Using Portal v3.0 (WebDB) Web Development Software," introduces you to creating Web pages with Oracle Portal. Each strategy has its purpose and has different levels of efficiency.

PL/SQL

PL/SQL is Oracle's proprietary procedural language. The Web Toolkit has given PL/SQL Web extensions by supplying an additional set of built-in procedures that handle the various aspects of HTML.

ADVANTAGES

The only advantage of using PL/SQL to build Web pages is a lower learning curve. PL/SQL is a fairly straightforward programming language with which many Oracle programmers are already familiar.

DISADVANTAGES

Disadvantages of using PL/SQL to build Web pages include the following:

- Less flexibility
- Performs more slowly than Java
- Proprietary to Oracle databases

PL/SQL is less flexible than full-featured languages such as Java. The execution of the PL/SQL code is still runtime interpreted; that is, it is not compiled into machine language as many programming languages are. PL/SQL is also proprietary to the Oracle database environment. If a possibility ever exists that the application being coded will be required to run in a different database environment, PL/SQL should not be used; one of the other languages available should be used instead to code the application.

Java

Java is an open language, meaning it is not constrained to a particular database or computing environment. Java is also an object-oriented language that can be difficult for some folks to understand. However, it is capable of easily handling Web page HTML needs as well as a variety of other computer tasks.

ADVANTAGES

The advantages of using Java to build Web pages include the following:

- Code execution time is faster as compared to PL/SQL.
- It's a full-featured programming language.
- Code is portable between database and computing environments.
- Java resources are possibly easier to find.
- It's useful if Oracle might not be the only database environment for the application.

Java compiles into intermediate code that executes much more quickly in most computing environments when compared to PL/SQL. Java is a full-featured programming language with a lot more capability than PL/SQL. Additionally, when coded correctly, Java is portable between computing environments and even between different kinds of databases. This is the purpose of philosophies such as Enterprise Java Beans, JDBC, and so on. Because Java covers many database and computing environments, Java programmers might be easier to find than PL/SQL programmers. And, Java would be useful if the database environment might not always be Oracle.

DISADVANTAGES

Disadvantages of using Java to build Web pages include the following:

- Possible steep learning curve
- Still have to use PL/SQL

Java is an object-oriented language that is much more powerful than PL/SQL. Being a full-featured programming language, Java might be too much for some to learn for one or two Web-based projects. When using Java for Oracle triggers and so on, the Java code needs to be called by a PL/SQL procedure. This is known as *wrapping the Java in PL/SQL*.

Portal V3.0

Portal V3.0 is Oracle's wizard-based Web application and Web site building environment. Portal V3.0 has significant improvements over its predecessor, WebDB, and allows users to quickly build Web-based applications and Web sites with very little knowledge of the Web environment.

ADVANTAGES

Advantages of using Portal V3.0 to build Web pages include the following:

- Virtually no learning curve
- Ease of use

The Portal Wizard walks the Web page builder through all the steps necessary to build complete, functional applications and Web sites. The wizard-based development takes all the guesswork out of building Web-based applications.

DISADVANTAGES

Disadvantages of using Portal to build Web pages include the following:

- Limited flexibility in appearance
- Slow performance as compared to Java

Summary

In this chapter, you learned what the Oracle Application Server is. The first part of this chapter provided an in-depth overview of how a Web browser can interact with a host computer. The topics of applets and servlets were introduced, as well as how the Oracle Application Server works to provide services (HTML output) to requesting Web browsers. This chapter also summarized the three Web-based programming environments that will be covered in the remainder of this book: PL/SQL, Java, and WebDB. The final section of this chapter summarized the uses and differences of these three programming environments as they apply to Web page development.

REVIEW

Reviewing It

1. What kind of networks do Web browsers support?
2. Explain what a CGI is.
3. What is the difference between an Applet and a Servlet?
4. What is the difference between thin and thick JDBC Drivers?
5. What is a virtual address?
6. Briefly describe why one might use PL/SQL or Java or Portal (and vice versa).

Checking It

1. HTTP is

   a) The Internet

   b) The protocol between the Web browser and the Web server

   c) The language used to build Web pages

   d) The CGI program

2. HTML is

   a) The Internet

   b) The protocol between the Web browser and the Web server

   c) The language used to build Web pages

   d) The CGI program

3. A URL is a Universal Resource Locator.

   True/False

4. Oracle9iAS is

   a) Oracle's latest database engine

   b) Oracle's latest Web server

   c) Oracle's latest forms server

   d) Oracle's latest clustered database technology

5. Oracle Corp refers to Oracle9iAS as a

   a) 1-Tier environment

   b) 2-Tier environment

   c) 3-Tier environment

   d) 4+-Tier environment

6. PL/SQL is

    a) Runtime interpreted

    b) Full-featured open language

    c) Wizard-based Web development

7. Java is

    a) Runtime interpreted

    b) Full-featured open language

    c) Wizard-based Web development

8. Portal V3.0 is

    a) Runtime interpreted

    b) Full-featured open language

    c) Wizard-based Web development

Applying It

APPLY

Independent Exercise 1:

- Web browse www.quepublishing.com.

- On your browser tool bar (Netscape), select View, Page Source, (Internet Explorer) select View,Source.

- Review the various HTML tags and commands that make up this Web page.

- Notice the tags around any pictures or objects that downloaded.

What's Next?

The next chapter will introduce you to PL/SQL with HTML extensions. You first will learn the PL/SQL Web page basics by building several modules that will then be used throughout the remainder of the chapter. You will also learn how to build the Sales Tracking Web site that was outlined in this chapter.

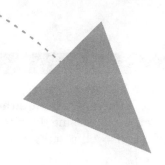

Using PL/SQL to Build Web Sites

The "Using PL/SQL" section of this chapter builds a basic HelloWorld display-type Web page using simple PL/SQL HTML-type commands. The HelloWorld example begins with passing text strings from PL/SQL to the HTML output (and subsequently being passed back to a Web browser). We will then build on the example by building a heading and displaying a picture. We will learn by updating the HelloWorld example to include either a parameter being passed or the Web page prompting the user for the parameter. Then, the "Building the Web Site" section of this chapter uses these skills from the HelloWorld example to build the Sales Tracking Web site.

This chapter teaches you the following:

- Using PL/SQL to build HTML Web pages
- Building the Web site with PL/SQL

Using PL/SQL

The Oracle9iAS processes requests from users (Web browsers) and replies to these users with an HTML document. This document can be built either using a variety of methods, such as Java (see Chapter 10, "Using Java to Build Web Sites"), a CGI program, or using PL/SQL, as well as may other options.

The incoming URL has a virtual mapping to the PL/SQL cartridge in the Web server. Figure 8.9 in Chapter 8, "Building Web Sites with Oracle9i," illustrates how the Web server knows to use the PL/SQL interface to process incoming requests from Web browsers. Listing 9.1 shows the simplest of PL/SQL Web sites, the classic "Hello World" message. Notice that this PL/SQL procedure is created in the normal manner with the CREATE OR REPLACE syntax. Two types of PL/SQL built-in packages handle the HTML code. The *HTP* package contains PL/SQL procedures that generate HTML output, whereas the *HTF* package contains PL/SQL functions that return HTML code as the return value. The HTP. syntax tells PL/SQL that this is an HTML command and is passed through to the HTML output. The htp.htmlOpen syntax tells PL/SQL that this is the beginning of the HTML document, and htp.htmlClose tells PL/SQL that this is the end of the HTML document. The same is true of htp.bodyOpen and htp.bodyClose. The htp.p command, on the other hand, is used to print or place items in the HTML document. In this example, htp.p is used to display the HelloWorld message. Figure 9.1 shows how to access this procedure through a Web browser, as well as display the output of the PL/SQL procedure. Notice the URL used to access the HelloWorld PL/SQL procedure.

EXAMPLE

Listing 9.1:   HelloWorld PL/SQL Procedure Syntax

```
CREATE OR REPLACE PROCEDURE helloworld
AS
BEGIN
    htp.htmlOpen;
    htp.bodyOpen;
    htp.p('HelloWorld');
    htp.bodyClose;
    htp.htmlClose;
END;
/
```

Notice that Listing 9.2 shows the actual HTML code generated by the HelloWorld PL/SQL procedure. Also notice how the htp.htmlOpen syntax in Listing 9.1 generated the <HTML> document tag in Listing 9.2.

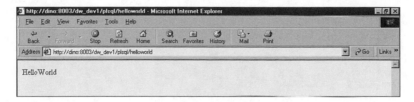

Figure 9.1: HelloWorld *PL/SQL procedure.*

EXAMPLE

Listing 9.2: HTML Output Created by the HelloWorld PL/SQL Procedure

```
<HTML>
<BODY>
HelloWorld
</BODY>
</HTML>
```

Listing 9.3 shows how the htp.p command can be used to pass HTML tags to the HTML output. In Listing 9.1, htp.htmlOpen was used to generate the <HTML> tag, whereas Listing 9.3 illustrates how htp.p can be used to pass the text <HTML> to the HTML output.

EXAMPLE

Listing 9.3: HelloWorld PL/SQL Procedure Using Just htp.p

```
CREATE OR REPLACE PROCEDURE helloworld
AS
BEGIN
    htp.p('<HTML>');
    htp.p('<BODY>');
    htp.p('HelloWorld');
    htp.p('</HTML>');
    htp.p('</BODY>');
END;
/
```

The owa_util.showpage package can be used to display the HTML output in SQL*Plus. Figure 9.2 illustrates how to execute the HelloWorld procedure in SQL*Plus and then immediately use the owa_util.showpage package to display the HTML output generated by the HelloWorld procedure.

Displaying Pictures with PL/SQL and HTML

Creating simple PL/SQL procedures that display common things, such as banner information and default items, on a Web page is easy. This gives the Web page a consistent look and enables PL/SQL to be coded once and reused many times.

```
SQL> set serveroutput on size 999999
SQL> exec helloworld;

PL/SQL procedure successfully completed.

SQL> exec owa_util.showpage;
<HTML>
<BODY>
HelloWorld
</BODY>
</HTML>

PL/SQL procedure successfully completed.

SQL>
```

Figure 9.2: *Showing the* HelloWorld *PL/SQL procedure's HTML output in SQL*Plus.*

Listing 9.4 builds on Listing 9.3 by adding the code to create the banner Web page information, as illustrated by Figure 9.3. Notice the htp.tableOpen and the htp.tableRowOpen syntax in lines 9 and 10. Within the table row, also notice that two references to htp.tableData exist (lines 14 and 22). Each of these tableData references is creating a column in the HTML table. This gives the HTML output the capability to display text and images in a very specific and consistent position. The first column gets the metro_motors.jpg image file (lines 14 through 21). The htf.img function is used to return the location of the picture (in this case the Metro Motors jpeg file) stored in the virtual location ows-img. Refer to Figure 8.4 in Chapter 8 and notice that ows-img maps to the computer directory D:\OAS4\ows\4.0\admin\img\. The metro_motors.jpg must be in this physical location for the htf.img function to find it, and the htf.img function generates an <IMG> tag that tells HTML where an image is stored in the virtual path. The second column receives the text Metro Motors Web Site (lines 22–25).

EXAMPLE

Listing 9.4: HelloWorld PL/SQL Procedure Displaying a Banner (helloworld2.sql)

```
1: CREATE OR REPLACE PROCEDURE helloworld
2: AS
3: BEGIN
4:     htp.htmlopen;
5:     htp.bodyOpen;
6:     -- ------------------------------------------------
7:     -- start of our heading / banner
8:     -- ------------------------------------------------
9:     htp.tableOpen;
10:    htp.tableRowOpen
11:    (
12:        cvalign => 'CENTER'
13:    );
14:    htp.tableData
15:    (
```

Listing 9.4: continued

```
16:         cvalue       => htf.img
17:                      (
18:                       curl        => '/ows-img/metro_motors.jpg'
19:                     , cattributes => 'WIDTH=100'
20:                      )
21:    );
22:    htp.tableData
23:    (
24:       cvalue  => htf.big('Metro Motors Web Site')
25:    );
26:    htp.tableRowClose;
27:    htp.tableClose;
28:    -- ------------------------------------------------
29:    -- End of our heading / banner
30:    -- ------------------------------------------------
31:    htp.p('HelloWorld');
32:    htp.bodyClose;
33:    htp.htmlClose;
34: END;
35: /
```

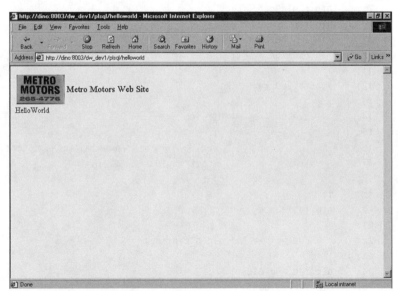

Figure 9.3: Metro Motors Web site banner page.

NOTE

If your browser does not show the graphic, check your Web server virtual mappings to ensure that the jpg image file is in the directory for which the virtual directory is configured (illustrated in Figure 8.4 in Chapter 8).

Now, creating a procedure called `display_banner` and calling it whenever we create a new Web page is easy and enables the banner information to be coded once and then reused throughout the Web application. If a change to the banner information needs to be made, one procedure is changed and the change is then automatically reflected throughout the application upon its next Web browser access.

To do this, review the `display_banner` procedure in Listing 9.5, and you will see that it is very similar to the code in Listing 9.4. Notice that lines 7–25 in Listing 9.5 are very similar to lines 9–27 in Listing 9.4. The only real difference is at lines 3 and 22—the `p_caption` variable replaces the hard-coded Metro Motors banner text so this procedure can be used for any banner by simply inserting `?p_caption=<some text>` on the URL line.

EXAMPLE

Listing 9.5: DISPLAY_BANNER PL/SQL Procedure (`display_banner.sql`)

```
1: CREATE OR REPLACE PROCEDURE display_banner
2: (
3:     p_caption    IN VARCHAR2 DEFAULT 'Metro Motors Web Site'
4: )
5: AS
6: BEGIN
7:     htp.tableOpen;
8:     htp.tableRowOpen
9:     (
10:        cvalign => 'CENTER'
11:     );
12:     htp.tableData
13:     (
14:        cvalue       => htf.img
15:                       (
16:                        curl        => '/ows-img/metro_motors.jpg'
17:                       ,  cattributes => 'WIDTH=100'
18:                       )
19:     );
20:     htp.tableData
21:     (
22:        cvalue  => htf.big(p_caption)
23:     );
24:     htp.tableRowClose;
25:     htp.tableClose;
26: END;
27: /
```

Note that we added an input parameter `p_caption` to the procedure. This enables us to specify a caption other than just `Metro Motors Web Site`.

Now we can change our `HelloWorld` procedure to call the `display_banner` procedure, as shown in Listing 9.6.

Listing 9.6: HelloWorld PL/SQL Procedure Using display_banner Procedure (helloworld3.sql)

```
CREATE OR REPLACE PROCEDURE helloworld
AS
BEGIN
    htp.htmlOpen;
    htp.bodyOpen;
    -- -------------------------------------------------
    -- start of our heading / banner
    -- -------------------------------------------------
    display_banner
    (
        p_caption => 'Metro Motors Web Site'
    );
    -- -------------------------------------------------
    -- End of our heading / banner
    -- -------------------------------------------------
    htp.p('HelloWorld');
    htp.bodyClose;
    htp.htmlClose;
END;
/
```

Both versions of this procedure, outlined in Listings 9.4 and 9.6, produce the same identical output as illustrated in Figure 9.3. If you were to look at the HTML output as illustrated in Figure 9.2, you would notice that the HTML output is also identical. The display_banner procedure creates the same HTML output, and it is now easy to use in other Web pages related to this application to give the identical visual attributes without having to add the code to each additional Web page.

Passing Parameters from PL/SQL to HTML

The final example in this section can accept a parameter from the URL and also accepts data from a field. Listing 9.7 illustrates the HelloWorld PL/SQL procedure with the additional code necessary to create a frame for data entry, as well as to process a parameter passed to the procedure. Lines 19–24 process any information in variable p_name. This value is populated if a parameter is passed from the URL (see Figure 9.4); otherwise, the generic message HelloWorld is displayed (see Figure 9.5).

Lines 26–30 in Listing 9.7 create an HTML form tag. This form is further defined by lines 31–43, where a submit button is defined (lines 33–36) and an entry box is defined (lines 38–43).

The HTML form tag has two parameters. curl defines the procedure to call when the form is submitted, whereas ctarget is the Web page where the results of the procedure should be displayed. This field is intentionally set to blank so the results are displayed on the same Web page.

The submit button contains only one value, cvalue, which will contain any text to place inside the button.

The entry field has three parameters. cname is the variable name where the contents of the entry field will be placed after the submit button is clicked. csize is the maximum length of the entered value to be placed in cname, and cmaxlength is the total width of the entry box being displayed.

EXAMPLE

Listing 9.7: HelloWorld PL/SQL Procedure Accepting a Parameter/Prompting for a Parameter
(`helloworld4_num.sql`)

```
1:   CREATE OR REPLACE PROCEDURE helloworld
2:    (
3:         p_name IN VARCHAR2 DEFAULT NULL
4:    )
5:   AS
6:   BEGIN
7:         htp.htmlopen;
8:         htp.bodyOpen;
9:         -- --------------------------------------------------
10:        -- start of our heading / banner
11:        -- --------------------------------------------------
12:        display_banner
13:          (
14:              p_caption => 'Metro Motors Web Site'
15:          );
16:        -- --------------------------------------------------
17:        -- End of our heading / banner
18:        -- --------------------------------------------------
19:        IF p_name IS NULL THEN
20:            htp.p('HelloWorld');
21:        ELSE
22:            htp.p('Hello '||p_name||'. The time here is '
23:                ||TO_CHAR(SYSDATE,'HH24:MI:SS'));
24:        END IF; -- p_name IS NULL
25:
26:        htp.formOpen
27:          (
28:            curl        => 'helloworld'
29:          , ctarget     => ''
30:          );
31:        htp.hr;
32:
33:        htp.formSubmit
34:          (
35:            cvalue      => 'Say Hello to '
36:          );
37:
```

Listing 9.7: continued

```
38:        htp.formText
39:        (
40:            cname        => 'p_name'
41:          ,  csize       => 30
42:          ,  cmaxlength  => 20
43:        );
44:
45:        htp.formclose;
46:        htp.bodyClose;
47:        htp.htmlClose;
48:     END;
49:     /
```

Line 3 of Listing 9.7 identifies the p_name parameter, defines it as a variable length character field, and gives it the default value NULL. The reason for the default value is that this procedure might not have a parameter passed to it. If the parameter did not have a default value, we would be forced to always provide one on the URL line:

```
http://yourdomain.com/virtual_path_for_plsqlcart/helloworld?p_name=Dave
```

If this parameter was not passed, the missing parameter error would be returned to the Web browser, as illustrated by Figure 9.4.

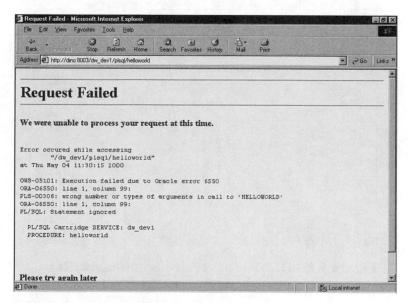

Figure 9.4: *Parameter missing Web error.*

Figure 9.5 shows the HelloWorld procedure with the just-added enterable field. Enter the value Dave in the text entry field and click the Say Hello to button. The Web page illustrated in Figure 9.6 will appear.

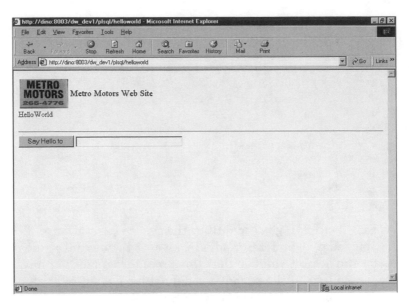

Figure 9.5: HelloWorld *procedure prompting for input.*

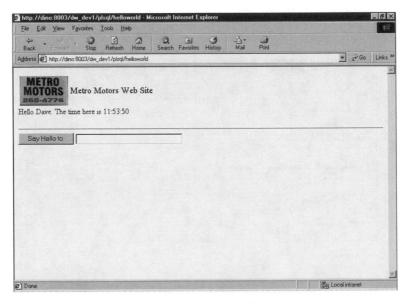

Figure 9.6: HelloWorld *procedure displaying results.*

Building the Web Site

NOTE

The remainder of this chapter builds the Web site (illustrated in Figure 9.7) of Chapter 8, reprinted here.

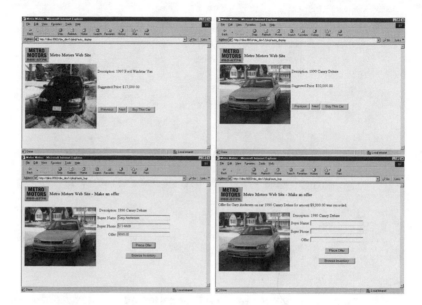

Figure 9.7

The Sales Tracking Web site will be based on two PL/SQL procedures: auto_display (see Listing 9.9) and auto_buy (see Listing 9.10). The Web site will also reuse the display_banner PL/SQL procedure built in Listing 9.5 and make reference to the PL/SQL procedure display_error used in Listing 9.8.

The display_error PL/SQL procedure (see Listing 9.8) is a simple Web page that accepts a parameter, p_text, (see line 3) and displays this text on the Web page at line 15. The show errors syntax in line 23 is a SQL*Plus command that's useful in displaying any errors that might have occurred when creating the procedure.

NOTE

The procedures detailed in this chapter can also be created using the Quest SQL Navigator tool.

EXAMPLE

Listing 9.8: DISPLAY_ERROR PL/SQL Procedure Syntax

```
1: CREATE OR REPLACE PROCEDURE display_error
2: (
3:     p_text  IN VARCHAR2 DEFAULT NULL
4: ) IS
5: BEGIN
6:     htp.htmlopen;
7:     htp.headOpen;
8:     htp.title('Error Page');
9:     htp.headClose;
10:    htp.bodyOpen;
11:
12:    htp.big('An Error has occurred');
13:
14:    htp.hr;
15:    htp.p('The following error occurred: '||p_text);
16:    htp.br;
17:    htp.p('Please contact Metro Motors directly at: 265-4776');
18:
19:    htp.bodyClose;
20:    htp.htmlClose;
21: END;
22: /
23: show errors
```

The main page of our Web site relies on the auto_display PL/SQL procedure. Because each car has a unique inventory number (INV_ID), easy access to the rows in the ST_CARS_FOR_SALE table object is enabled. This INV_ID column also makes a convenient parameter to look up a specific row if a parameter is passed to this Web page. The page should allow us to browse forward and backward through our entire inventory and should display a link to the auto_buy screen—so that customers can make an offer on the car. This is accomplished with lines 26–69 in Listing 9.9.

Lines 1–5 highlight the procedure and the parameters that can be passed to it. The procedure accepts a source (p_source), which tells the Web page to go to the next or previous record in the ST_CARS_FOR_SALE table object. The p_source parameter defaults to DISPLAY_NEXT if no parameter is passed. As discussed earlier in this chapter, this Web page can be called with parameters or with no parameters without causing any kind of parameter passing violation. The other parameter that can be passed is an inventory number (p_inv_id) that provides the row in the ST_CARS_FOR_SALE table object from which to perform the previous or next row function. The URL for this Web page is http://<computer name or IP address> / virtual_path/auto_display, which, with no parameters, will display the first auto in the ST_CARS_FOR_SALE table object.

Listing 9.9 shows the entire code for the display_auto PL/SQL procedure. Lines 6–14 are a cursor that selects the information about the next car in our inventory. If the inventory ID passed is NULL, the Web page starts at the beginning of the ST_CARS_FOR_SALE table object. Lines 15–23 are a cursor that selects the information about the previous row in ST_CARS_FOR_SALE. If the inventory ID passed is NULL, this procedure starts with the last row in the ST_CARS_FOR_SALE table object. Line 24 declares a PL/SQL record for the cursor defined in lines 6–23. When this cursor is opened, Oracle returns the row identified by the SQL select statement. Lines 26–30 verify that any passed parameters are valid. If any passed parameters are not found to be valid, the PL/SQL procedure display_error is then called at line 31. Lines 39–69 determine the row (previous or next) and use the appropriate cursor to select the correct row from ST_CARS_FOR_SALE.

Line 75 begins to build the actual Web page. Lines 81–84 call the display_banner PL/SQL procedure that we created in the previous section of this chapter (refer to Listing 9.5). This displays the standard Metro Motors banner at the top of the Web page. Review Figure 8.7 and you will notice that the picture is on the left with the description, pricing, and navigational buttons on the right. To accomplish this, an HTML table with 4 columns and 3 rows is used. The picture takes up column 1 and rows 1–3. The description takes up row 1 and columns 2–4. The price takes up row 2 and columns 2–4. The navigation buttons take up row 3 and each button takes up one column. Lines 89–113 display the information from the database stored in sale_row (see line 24). Lines 117–139 create the Previous button, and lines 141–166 create the Next button. Finally, lines 171–193 create the Buy This Car button. This button is created in a similar fashion to the Previous and Next buttons except that it calls the auto_buy PL/SQL procedure.

EXAMPLE

Listing 9.9: AUTO_DISPLAY PL/SQL Procedure Syntax

```
1:    CREATE OR REPLACE PROCEDURE auto_display
2:    (
3:        p_source        IN VARCHAR2 DEFAULT 'DISPLAY_NEXT'
4:      , p_inv_id        IN NUMBER DEFAULT NULL
5:    ) AS
6:    CURSOR next_CUR
7:    (
8:        p_inv_id IN NUMBER
9:    ) IS
10:      SELECT inv_id, auto_description
11:        ,  sale_amt, sale_photo_location
12:        FROM st_cars_for_sale
13:        WHERE inv_id > NVL(p_inv_id,0)
14:        ORDER BY inv_id ASC;
```

Listing 9.9: continued

```
15:    CURSOR prev_CUR
16:    (
17:       p_inv_id IN NUMBER
18:    ) IS
19:       SELECT inv_id, auto_description
20:       ,   sale_amt, sale_photo_location
21:       FROM st_cars_for_sale
22:       WHERE inv_id < NVL(p_inv_id,10000000)
23:       ORDER BY inv_id DESC;
24:    sale_row prev_CUR%ROWTYPE;
25:    BEGIN
26:       IF p_source NOT IN
27:       (
28:          'DISPLAY_NEXT'
29:       ,  'DISPLAY_PREV'
30:       ) THEN
31:          display_error
32:          (
33:             p_text  => p_source
34:          );
35:       ELSE
36:          -- -------------------------------------------------
37:          -- Retrieve the car that we want to display
38:          -- -------------------------------------------------
39:          IF p_source = 'DISPLAY_NEXT' THEN
40:             OPEN next_CUR
41:             (
42:                p_inv_id
43:             );
44:             FETCH next_CUR INTO sale_row;
45:             IF next_CUR%NOTFOUND THEN
46:                OPEN prev_CUR
47:                (
48:                   p_inv_id
49:                );
50:                FETCH prev_CUR INTO sale_row;
51:                CLOSE prev_CUR;
52:             END IF; -- next_CUR%NOTFOUND
53:             CLOSE next_CUR;
54:          ELSIF p_source = 'DISPLAY_PREV' THEN
55:             OPEN prev_CUR
56:             (
57:                p_inv_id
58:             );
59:             FETCH prev_CUR INTO sale_row;
```

Listing 9.9: continued

```
60:                 IF prev_CUR%NOTFOUND THEN
61:                   OPEN next_CUR
62:                   (
63:                       p_inv_id
64:                   );
65:                   FETCH next_CUR INTO sale_row;
66:                   CLOSE next_CUR;
67:                 END IF; -- prev_CUR%NOTFOUND
68:                 CLOSE prev_CUR;
69:               END IF; -- p_source = 'DISPLAY_NEXT'
70:
71:               -- ------------------------------------------------
72:               -- Now that we have the auto to display lets
73:               -- build our display screen
74:               -- ------------------------------------------------
75:               htp.htmlopen;
76:               htp.headOpen;
77:               htp.title('Metro Motors');
78:               htp.headClose;
79:               htp.bodyOpen;
80:
81:               display_banner
82:               (
83:                   p_caption   => 'Metro Motors Web Site'
84:               );
85:
86:               -- ------------------------------------------------
87:               -- Display the dynamic content - the selected car
88:               -- ------------------------------------------------
89:               htp.tableOpen;
90:               htp.tableRowOpen;
91:               htp.tableData
92:               (
93:                   cvalue      => htf.img
94:                   (
95:                   curl    => sale_ROW.sale_photo_location
96:                       ,   cattributes => 'WIDTH=300'
97:                   )
98:               ,   crowspan    => 3
99:               );
100:              htp.tableData
101:              (
102:                cvalue => 'Description: '||sale_ROW.auto_description
103:                ,  ccolspan    => 3
104:                );
105:              htp.tableRowClose;
```

Listing 9.9: continued

```
106:             htp.tableRowOpen;
107:             htp.tableData
108:              (
109:              cvalue => 'Suggested Price:'||TO_CHAR(sale_ROW.sale_amt,
➥ '$999,990.00')
110:              ,   ccolspan    => 3
111:              );
112:             htp.tableRowClose;
113:             htp.tableRowOpen;
114:             -- -------------------------------------------------
115:             -- previous button
116:             -- -------------------------------------------------
117:             htp.p('<TD>');
118:             htp.formOpen
119:              (
120:                curl        => 'auto_display'
121:              ,   cmethod     => 'post'
122:              ,   ctarget     => ''
123:              );
124:             htp.formHidden
125:              (
126:                cname       => 'p_source'
127:              ,   cvalue      => 'DISPLAY_PREV'
128:              );
129:             htp.formHidden
130:              (
131:                cname       => 'p_inv_id'
132:              ,   cvalue      => TO_CHAR(sale_ROW.inv_id)
133:              );
134:             htp.formSubmit
135:              (
136:                cvalue      => 'Previous'
137:              );
138:             htp.formClose;
139:             htp.p('</TD>');
140:
141:             -- -------------------------------------------------
142:             -- next button
143:             -- -------------------------------------------------
144:             htp.p('<TD>');
145:             htp.formOpen
146:              (
147:                curl        => 'auto_display'
148:              ,   cmethod     => 'post'
149:              ,   ctarget     => ''
```

Listing 9.9:   continued

```
150:          );
151:          htp.formHidden
152:          (
153:              cname       => 'p_source'
154:            , cvalue      => 'DISPLAY_NEXT'
155:          );
156:          htp.formHidden
157:          (
158:              cname       => 'p_inv_id'
159:            , cvalue      => TO_CHAR(sale_ROW.inv_id)
160:          );
161:          htp.formSubmit
162:          (
163:              cvalue      => 'Next'
164:          );
165:          htp.formClose;
166:          htp.p('</TD>');
167:
168:          -- ------------------------------------------------
169:          -- Buy this car
170:          -- ------------------------------------------------
171:          htp.p('<TD>');
172:          htp.formOpen
173:          (
174:              curl        => 'auto_buy'
175:            , cmethod     => 'post'
176:            , ctarget     => ''
177:          );
178:          htp.formHidden
179:          (
180:              cname       => 'p_source'
181:            , cvalue      => 'MAKE_OFFER'
182:          );
183:          htp.formHidden
184:          (
185:              cname       => 'p_inv_id'
186:            , cvalue      => TO_CHAR(sale_ROW.inv_id)
187:          );
188:          htp.formSubmit
189:          (
190:              cvalue      => 'Buy This Car'
191:          );
192:          htp.formClose;
193:          htp.p('</TD>');
194:
195:          htp.tableRowClose;
```

Listing 9.9: continued

```
196:             htp.tableClose;
197:
198:
199:             htp.bodyClose;
200:             htp.htmlClose;
201:        END IF; -- p_source NOT IN
202:     END auto_display;
203:     /
```

The auto_display PL/SQL procedure is accessed by pointing a Web browser to http://<computer name or IP address>/virtual_path/auto_display. Notice that the Web page functions perfectly when no parameters are passed. This same Web page (refer to the bottom-left panel of Figure 8.7) also processes parameters correctly, as in this example:

http://<computer name or IP address>/virtual_path/auto_display?p_
➡source=DISPLAY_PREV&p_inv_id=15

The auto_buy PL/SQL procedure is called from the Web page auto_display and updates the BUYER information in the ST_CARS_FOR_SALE table object (refer to the bottom-left panel of Figure 9.7).

Lines 1–8 name the procedure (auto_buy) and define the parameters it will accept. Note that all the parameters have a default value that will allow this procedure to be called without having to supply any parameters at all. Lines 20–24 check to see whether any supplied parameters are correct and display an error (using the display_error routine built earlier in this chapter) if they are not (lines 25–28).

Lines 33–45 select the car from inventory (based on the passed p_inv_id). If the car is not found, the user is directed again to the error page.

Line 46 checks to see whether the p_source variable is set to RECORD_OFFER. If it is, the UPDATE statement in lines 47–72 is executed.

Lines 46–72 check to see whether our source should record our offer or not. If the variable p_source does not contain RECORD_OFFER, the MAKE_OFFER Web page is displayed (roughly the remainder of this PL/SQL procedure). Notice that line 101 sets the p_source variable to RECORD_OFFER so that, when the Web page is returned, this UPDATE code is then executed.

If any Oracle error codes are returned, the failure message at lines 50–53 is shown.

Lines 54–56 check the parameters to make sure that a person making the offer has filled out the name, phone, and amount fields.

Lines 58–63 are the actual UPDATE to the ST_CARS_FOR_SALE table object.

NOTE

If this were a realistic situation, we would insert a record in a separate table so that multiple buyers and offers could be tendered. This example is just to show functionality between the Web page and the Oracle database.

Lines 64–67 set the status message indicating that the offer was successfully recorded.

Lines 68–69 catch any Oracle errors that might have occurred from the UPDATE statement. If an error does occur, the new status message is not set and we are left with the failure message.

Lines 76–203 create the HTML output. Lines 82–85 display the Metro Motors standard banner, whereas lines 87–90 display the status message (if one was created) from lines 50–69. Lines 92–107 open up an HTML form and set some hidden values (parameters) that are not to be displayed but are important to the Web page when it is returned. Lines 113–195 generate the main structure of the HTML table, laying out elements similar to the way auto_display was laid out.

Notice in lines 143 and 166 that the htp.p procedure is used to hard code the HTML <TD> tags. Lines 144–149 call the htp.formtext procedure, which generates a text input box.

Lines 196–216 create a second HTML form and button that take the Web user back to the display_auto page.

EXAMPLE

Listing 9.10:   AUTO_BUY PL/SQL Procedure Syntax

```
1:    CREATE OR REPLACE PROCEDURE auto_buy
2:    (
3:        p_source        IN VARCHAR2 DEFAULT 'MAKE_OFFER'
4:    ,   p_inv_id        IN NUMBER DEFAULT NULL
5:    ,   p_buyer_name    IN VARCHAR2 DEFAULT NULL
6:    ,   p_buyer_phone   IN VARCHAR2 DEFAULT NULL
7:    ,   p_buyer_offer   IN VARCHAR2 DEFAULT NULL
8:    ) AS
9:    CURSOR inv_CUR
10:   (
11:       p_inv_id IN NUMBER
12:   ) IS
13:       SELECT inv_id, auto_description
14:       ,  sale_amt, sale_photo_location
15:       FROM st_cars_for_sale
16:       WHERE inv_id = p_inv_id;
17:   inv_ROW inv_CUR%ROWTYPE;
18:   v_status_msg VARCHAR2(200);
```

Listing 9.10:   continued

```
19:    BEGIN
20:       IF p_source NOT IN
21:         (
22:             'MAKE_OFFER'
23:         ,   'RECORD_OFFER'
24:         ) THEN
25:           display_error
26:             (
27:                 p_text  => p_source
28:             );
29:         ELSE
30:             -- -----------------------------------------------
31:             -- get the car they are interested in
32:             -- -----------------------------------------------
33:             OPEN inv_CUR
34:             (
35:                 p_inv_id
36:             );
37:             FETCH inv_CUR INTO inv_ROW;
38:             IF inv_CUR%NOTFOUND THEN
39:                 CLOSE inv_CUR;
40:                 display_error
41:                 (
42:                 p_text  => 'The auto selected could not be found'
43:                 );
44:             ELSE
45:                 CLOSE inv_CUR;
46:                 IF p_source = 'RECORD_OFFER' THEN
47:         -- -----------------------------------------------
48:         -- update the table with the offer
49:         -- -----------------------------------------------
50:     v_status_msg := 'Offer could not be recorded at this time for '
51:     ||p_buyer_name||'.<BR> Please make sure the name and phone '
52:     ||' are filled in and that the offer ('||p_buyer_offer
53:     ||') is a number.<BR> Please correct your data and try again.';
54:             IF p_buyer_name IS NOT NULL
55:                 AND p_buyer_phone IS NOT NULL
56:                 AND p_buyer_offer IS NOT NULL THEN
57:                 BEGIN
58:                     UPDATE st_cars_for_sale
59:                     SET buyer_name = p_buyer_name
60:                     , buyer_phone = p_buyer_phone
61:                     , buyer_offer = TO_NUMBER(p_buyer_offer)
62:                     , buyer_date = SYSDATE
63:                     WHERE inv_id = p_inv_id;
64:             v_status_msg := 'Offer for '||p_buyer_name||' on car '
```

Listing 9.10:   continued

```
65:                 ||inv_ROW.auto_description||' for amount '
66:                 ||TO_CHAR(TO_NUMBER(p_buyer_offer),'$999,990.00')
67:                 ||' was recorded.';
68:                 EXCEPTION WHEN OTHERS THEN
69:                 NULL; -- leave the original status message as is...
70:                 END;
71:             END IF; -- p_buyer_name IS NOT NULL AND ...
72:         END IF; -- p_source = 'RECORD_OFFER'
73:         -- -------------------------------------------------
74:         -- display the offer form...
75:         -- -------------------------------------------------
76:                 htp.htmlopen;
77:                 htp.headOpen;
78:                 htp.title('Metro Motors');
79:                 htp.headClose;
80:                 htp.bodyOpen;
81:
82:                 display_banner
83:                     (
84:             p_caption   => 'Metro Motors Web Site - Make an offer'
85:                     );
86:
87:             IF v_status_msg IS NOT NULL THEN
88:                 htp.p(v_status_msg);
89:                 htp.br;
90:             END IF; -- v_status_msg IS NOT NULL
91:
92:             htp.formOpen
93:                 (
94:                 curl        => 'auto_buy'
95:                 , cmethod    => 'post'
96:                 , ctarget    => ''
97:                 );
98:             htp.formHidden
99:                 (
100:                 cname       => 'p_source'
101:                 , cvalue      => 'RECORD_OFFER'
102:                 );
103:             htp.formHidden
104:                 (
105:                 cname       => 'p_inv_id'
106:                 , cvalue      => TO_CHAR(p_inv_id)
107:                 );
108:
109:
110:
111:             htp.tableOpen;
```

Listing 9.10: continued

```
112:
113:                    htp.tableRowOpen;
114:                    htp.tableData
115:                (
116:                        cvalue        => htf.img
117:                        (
118:                            curl      => inv_ROW.sale_photo_location
119:                        ,   cattributes => 'WIDTH=300'
120:                        )
121:                    ,   crowspan     => 5
122:                    );
123:
124:                    htp.tableData
125:                (
126:                        cvalue        => 'Description: '
127:                    ,   calign        => 'RIGHT'
128:                    );
129:                    htp.tableData
130:                (
131:                        cvalue        => inv_ROW.auto_description
132:                    ,   calign        => 'LEFT'
133:                    );
134:
135:                    htp.tableRowClose;
136:
137:                    htp.tableRowOpen;
138:                    htp.tableData
139:                (
140:                        cvalue        => 'Buyer Name:'
141:                    ,   calign        => 'RIGHT'
142:                    );
143:                    htp.p('<TD ALIGN=LEFT>');
144:                    htp.formText
145:                (
146:                        cname         => 'p_buyer_name'
147:                    ,   csize         => 30
148:                    ,   cmaxlength    => 20
149:                    );
150:                    htp.p('</TD>');
151:                    htp.tableRowClose;
152:
153:                    htp.tableRowOpen;
154:                    htp.tableData
155:                (
156:                        cvalue        => 'Buyer Phone:'
```

Listing 9.10: continued

```
157:                  ,   calign      => 'RIGHT'
158:                  );
159:                  htp.p('<TD ALIGN=LEFT>');
160:                  htp.formText
161:                  (
162:                      cname       => 'p_buyer_phone'
163:                  ,   csize       => 30
164:                  ,   cmaxlength  => 10
165:                  );
166:                  htp.p('</TD>');
167:                  htp.tableRowClose;
168:
169:                  htp.tableRowOpen;
170:                  htp.tableData
171:                  (
172:                      cvalue      => 'Offer:'
173:                  ,   calign      => 'RIGHT'
174:                  );
175:                  htp.p('<TD ALIGN=LEFT>');
176:                  htp.formText
177:                  (
178:                      cname       => 'p_buyer_offer'
179:                  ,   csize       => 30
180:                  ,   cmaxlength  => 10
181:                  );
182:                  htp.p('</TD>');
183:                  htp.tableRowClose;
184:
185:                  htp.tableRowOpen;
186:                  htp.tableData
187:                  (
188:                      cvalue      => ''
189:                  );
190:                  htp.p('<TD ALIGN=CENTER>');
191:                  htp.formSubmit
192:                  (
193:                      cvalue      => 'Place Offer'
194:                  );
195:                  htp.formClose;
196:                  htp.formOpen
197:                  (
198:                      curl        => 'auto_display'
199:                  ,   cmethod     => 'post'
200:                  ,   ctarget     => ''
201:                  );
202:                  htp.formHidden
```

Listing 9.10: continued

```
203:                (
204:                    cname        => 'p_source'
205:                  , cvalue       => 'DISPLAY_NEXT'
206:                );
207:                htp.formHidden
208:                (
209:                    cname        => 'p_inv_id'
210:                  , cvalue       => '0'
211:                );
212:                htp.formSubmit
213:                (
214:                    cvalue       => 'Browse Inventory'
215:                );
216:                htp.formClose;
217:                htp.p('</TD>');
218:                htp.tableRowClose;
219:
220:
221:                htp.tableClose;
222:
223:                htp.bodyClose;
224:                htp.htmlClose;
225:            END IF; -- inv_CUR%NOTFOUND
226:        END IF; -- p_source NOT IN
227:    END auto_buy;
228:    /
```

Summary

This chapter introduced you to the creation of PL/SQL procedures, which create HTML output that will be returned to a Web browser. You were able to use simple but effective techniques to understand basic Web page building techniques. You then learned how to use these techniques to build the Sales Tracking Web site using PL/SQL and HTML.

REVIEW

Reviewing It

1. Explain the difference between the HTP package and the HTF package.

2. What is htp.p used for?

3. Why would you want to call another PL/SQL procedure in a Web environment?

4. In Listing 9.9, line 4, why is the `p_inv_id` variable set to null?

5. In Listing 9.10, what error message will be displayed if the car requested cannot be found?

Checking It

1. If you have an `htp.bodyopen` command you need an

    a) `Htp.htlmopen`

    b) `Htp.htlmclose`

    c) `Htp.bodyclose`

    d) `Htp.textopen`

CHECK

2. What happens if an input parameter does not have a default value and none is passed?

    a) Nothing happens, the Web page displays as programmed

    b) An error is returned to the user complaining about a missing mandatory parameter

    c) The results may be unpredictable as the Web page will try to display the variable

    d) The Web server will crash

3. When using PL/SQL, you do not need a virtual path at all.

    True/False

APPLY

Applying It

Independent Exercise 1:

- Start your favorite editor and put the few HTML commands in to simply display your name.

- Name this file Ch9_ex1.htm.

- Access this file with your favorite Web browser.

Independent Exercise 2:

- Start your favorite editor and build and compile a simple PL/SQL procedure that performs the same task as Exercise 1 except use the PL/SQL htp package to create the HTML.

Independent Exercise 3:

- Create a small table object with one character field.
- Build a simple PL/SQL Web-based procedure that
    - Prompts the user for a variable.
    - Checks to make sure something was entered.
    - Inserts into your table object the contents of this variable.
    - Displays what has been inserted.
    - Clears the entry field so that additional information can be entered.

What's Next?

The next chapter introduces you to Java, another language useful in creating Web pages. You will learn how to use JDeveloper v3.0 to learn the basics of JDeveloper and Java, as well as how to build a simple Web page using Java. Similar to this chapter, you will then use these simple Java skills to build the same Web site, which is illustrated in this chapter.

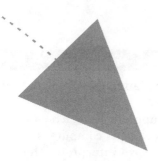

Using Java to Build Web Sites

Oracle9i supports procedures, functions, packages, and triggers to be coded in Java instead of PL/SQL. Because Java is a much more open language (supported by many platforms and databases) than the Oracle proprietary language, PL/SQL, it should provide Oracle environment performance improvements.

In this chapter, you will learn the following:

- What is Java VM
- What are Java development tools
- How to Use Java
- How to build a Web site with Java

Java can perform any task that PL/SQL can perform. The AS LANGUAGE JAVA syntax is added to the Oracle procedure, function, package body, or trigger. In addition, these procedures, functions, and packages are executed in the same manner as their PL/SQL equivalents.

Java stored procedures execute much more quickly than their PL/SQL counterparts. Java stored procedures with SELECT or DML type SQL statements typically execute 20 to 40% faster, and Java stored procedures without any SQL statements run about 10 times faster than their PL/SQL counterparts.

What Is Java VM?

Java is a cross–operating-system, cross-database language. This versatility is accomplished by the Java Virtual Machine (JVM), which is *ported* to each specific hardware platform and database that supports Java. The JVM enables Java code to be entirely portable across various computers and database environments. In addition, JVM is the Java interpreter that eliminates the need for a Java compiler for specific computing environments. Plus, it is part of the Oracle9i database, which makes it possible to have either Java-based procedures or PL/SQL-based procedures (or both). One JVM exists for each Oracle Application Server (Oracle9iAS), and it is started when the Apps Server is started.

> **NOTE**
>
> **Port**—To have a *port* of software means to have a version that runs in a particular computing environment. Previously in this book, I referred to *runtime* interpreters. A port exists for each computing environment that will support a particular software.

Java Development Tools

Chapter 8, "Building Web Sites with Oracle9i," discusses various methods of deploying Java-based programs across a computing network. The *applets*, *servlets*, and Java-based programs all must be developed with some kind of Java development language. Many of these are available on the market today, such as Visual Café, Visual Age, and JBuilder.

> **NOTE**
>
> **Applet**—When accessed, it is loaded to the user's Web browser and run on the local PC or workstation.
>
> **Servlet**—When accessed, it is run on the server, returning the output to the user's Web browser.

This chapter uses Oracle's JDeveloper v3.0.

Using Java

This part of the chapter explains and illustrates building a servlet, a server-side Java program that will be accessed by using the Oracle9iAS. To review how these pieces fit together, please refer to Figure 8.3 and its accompanying description in Chapter 8.

Building a Java Servlet with JDeveloper v3.0

Figure 10.1 shows the JDeveloper interface. Access the Project Wizard from the File, New Project menu item. This wizard guides you through all the necessary pieces to build a server-side Java program that will access the EMP demonstration table.

Figure 10.1: *JDeveloper v3.0 Project Wizard.*

After you click the Next button, the Project Wizard begins a three-step project setup. You must name the project and tell JDeveloper where to store it on your computer's hard disk. Notice in Figure 10.2 that the name of the new servlet is Empservlet.jar. Also notice that DbServlet is selected from the A Project containing a new option. Step 2 of 3 defines the project name, where to store the actual servlet code, and the Java classes code. Step 3 of 3 tracks where the project is documented. None of these fields is actually required, but the information might be convenient for others who might be making future changes to this program.

NOTE

.jar file—It's being created by JDeveloper and contains all the code necessary for the Web browser to access and run this particular Java program. Jar stands for Java archive file.

Figure 10.3 shows all the recently entered project information. If this information is correct, click Finished. If this information is not correct, use the Back button to return to where the incorrect information was entered and correct it.

NOTE

If you have clicked Finish and you later find that some of the information is incorrect, you probably should start again. JDeveloper uses some of this information inside various components being generated. Some of the options, such as source path and output directory, can be changed via the preferences selection in the menu bar.

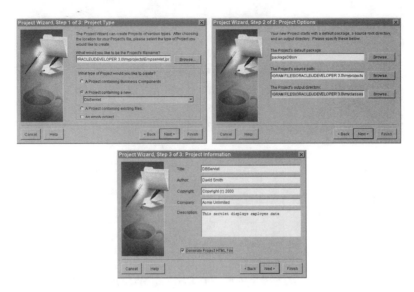

Figure 10.2: *JDeveloper v3.0 project setup steps 1–3.*

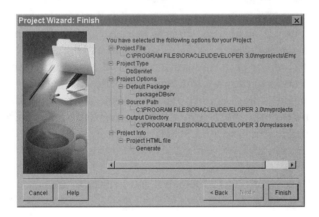

Figure 10.3: *JDeveloper v3.0 project setup finish.*

The DbServlet Wizard automatically starts based on selections made in the Project Wizard. This wizard can also be started from the menu bar by selecting File, New, DbServlet. This wizard actually builds the Java code needed to access a database table. It automatically stores its resulting code in the project that is highlighted—if the wizard started automatically, it will be stored in the project you just created. If you have to manually start the wizard, be sure to highlight the project for which you want to create the DbServlet. The wizard walks you through the process of creating the DbServlet with the following five steps:

1. In the first wizard window, be sure to select whether this is an individual table or a master-detail relationship type database access. Click Next.

2. Next, name the actual servlet and establish the type of connection to the database (see Figure 10.4). Notice that the DBServlet connection type is selected. This fills in the default URL needed to access this Java servlet from a Web browser. Also notice the check box designed to prompt the user for a valid password. Click Next.

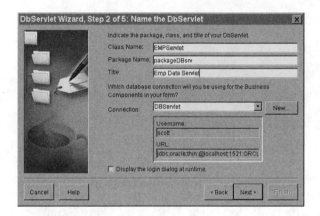

Figure 10.4: *DbServlet Wizard step 2—name and connection information.*

3. In this step you define the database object the servlet will reference. Notice in Figure 10.5 that the user SCOTT is used. When you click the Tables check box, the table objects appear in the window. Highlight the EMP table by clicking.

Figure 10.5: *DbServlet Wizard step 3—database object selection.*

4. Next, the available database columns are displayed. Use the >> button to select all the columns, as shown in Figure 10.6. When all the desired columns are moved to the Selected Attributes column, click Next.

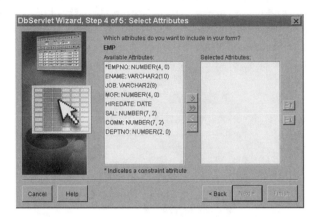

Figure 10.6: *DbServlet Wizard step 4—database column selection.*

5. Figure 10.7 shows the final step, which is to select a color pattern for the servlet. When you have chosen your desired color theme, click Next. The final step is the DBWizard Completion screen. This lists all the pertinent information about the name, the table being accessed, and the name and full path of the project where all these items will be stored. To exit the wizard, click Finish.

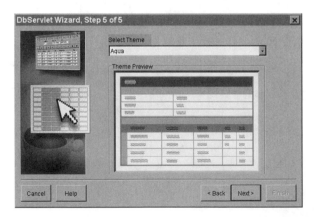

Figure 10.7: *DbServlet Wizard step 5—form template layout selection.*

Select File, Save As to save the JDeveloper workspace (see Figure 10.8). Notice the items in the recently created project in Figure 10.9. The HTML file will be accessed by the Web browser. This file contains the necessary HTML code to access the Empservlet.java program.

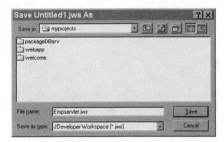

Figure 10.8: Items developed with JDeveloper.

Figure 10.9: Saving the JDeveloper workspace.

Deploying the Java Servlet Application

Because this is a server-side piece of code, it needs to be copied to the computer that has the Web server with the Java interface. This is accomplished by using the deployment feature of JDeveloper.

Figure 10.10 shows the EmpServlet project with the DBServlet package inside. From the menu, select Project, Deploy to start the Deployment Wizard. Walk through the wizard and complete the information as it pertains to your computing environment. Figure 10.11 shows the actual deployment. Make sure to check this screen for any errors that might have occurred.

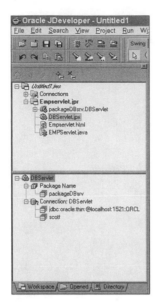

Figure 10.10: *Deploying the Java DBServlet.*

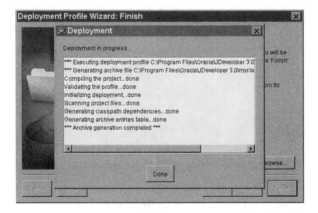

Figure 10.11: *Deployment Wizard finished screen.*

Running the Java Servlet Application

Chapter 8 covered some basic administrative issues, such as virtual paths. Figure 10.12 uses one of these virtual paths to point to where the DBServlet was deployed. Notice the URL in Figure 10.12. You see the `http://<IP Address>:<Port Number>` of the computer with the Oracle Application Server. Servlets is the virtual path that will be translated by Oracle9iAS into a directory path on this computer, and DBServlet is the name of the previously created and deployed servlet that will be found in this virtual path. Because this servlet is using the JDBC thin drivers, it will prompt the Web browser user for a user ID and password.

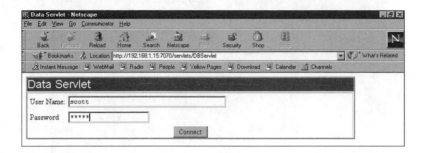

Figure 10.12: Netscape browser accessing the DBServlet.

DBServlet then prompts the Web browser user for the information to be displayed from the EMP table. Notice the pick list buttons that display the various options in Figure 10.13.

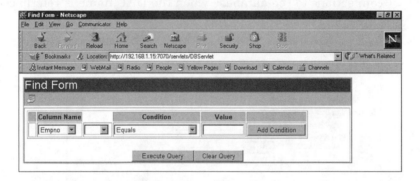

Figure 10.13: DBServlet query screen.

Figure 10.14 illustrates the DBServlet displaying information from the SCOTT.EMP table. Notice the buttons across the top of the displayed form. The + enables a record to be added, and the X enables a record to be deleted. The next set of blue buttons controls the capability to access the next or previous records in the table, and the key buttons enable the Web browser user to lock a record or unlock a record for update purposes.

iAS and Java Setup

The iAS environment needs to know about the servlets it is to manage, how to access the database (the DAD configuration), and even the installation and setup of the Java cartridge.

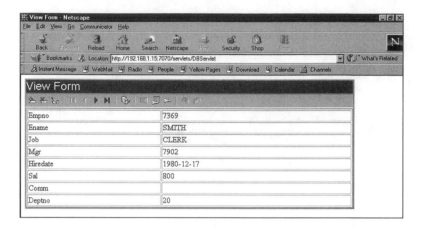

Figure 10.14: *DBServlet displaying SCOTT.EMP table information.*

Figure 10.15 shows the configuration of the DAD in the iAS Server Manager. This database descriptor is used by servlets to make automatic connections to the database when the DAD name is referenced in the URL.

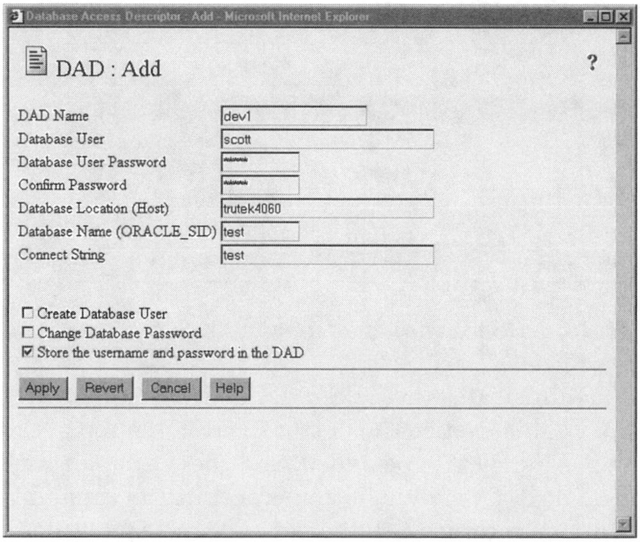

Figure 10.15: *DAD configuration for Web site examples.*

Figure 10.16 shows the virtual path-mapping configuration of the samplej virtual path. Notice the URL in Figure 10.17. The hostname trutek4060 matches the description of the DAD, and the virtual path samplej is also illustrated when accessing a HelloWorld servlet (which will be built in the next section of this chapter).

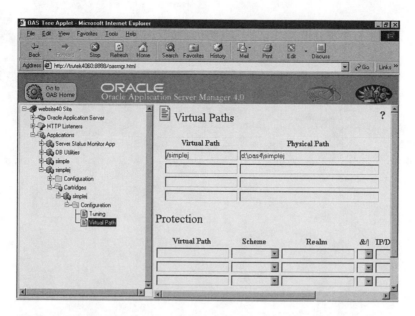

Figure 10.16: *Virtual path configuration for Web site examples.*

Figure 10.17: *URL example for Web site examples.*

Figure 10.18 illustrates the `simplej` Java cartridge configuration area. The `simplej` in this case is both a virtual path and an indication to the iAS that this is Java code that will need to be passed to the Java cartridge.

Figures 10.19 and 10.20 illustrate how to manually configure a Java cartridge. Notice in Figure 10.19 that the manual radio button is selected and that in Figure 10.20 the cartridge is named (`test`, in this example) and is assigned a virtual path.

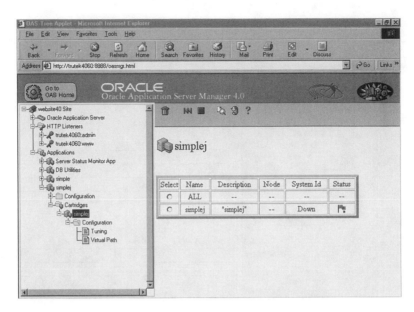

Figure 10.18: `simplej` *Java cartridge configuration.*

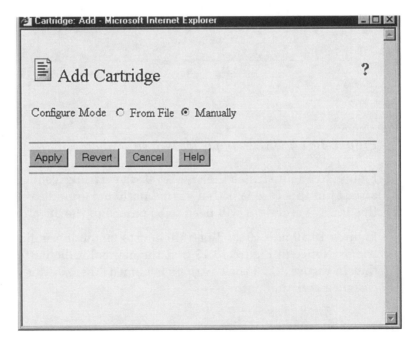

Figure 10.19: *Manually defining a Java cartridge.*

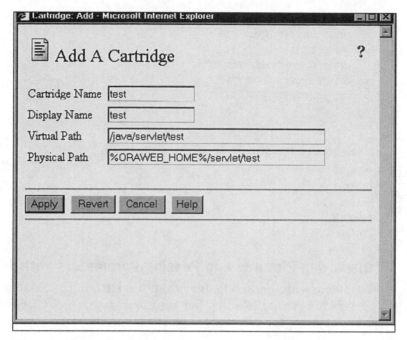

Figure 10.20: *Configuring the manually defined Java cartridge.*

To test the Java cartridge, build the `HelloWorld` servlet illustrated in
Listing 10.1, locate the output in the physical path as defined by the virtual
path configuration (refer to Figure 10.16), and use the URL (as defined in
Figure 10.17) to display the output as shown in Figure 10.17. Listing 10.2
shows the generated HTML output by the `out.println` code in Listing 10.1.
This can be seen from your browser by displaying Source Code.

EXAMPLE

Listing 10.1:   HelloWorld Java Servlet Syntax

```
import java.io.*;
import java.sql.*;
import javax.servlet.*;
import javax.servlet.http.*;
import java.util.*;

public class HelloWorld extends HttpServlet {


  public void doGet(HttpServletRequest req, HttpServletResponse res)
        throws ServletException, IOException{

    res.setContentType("text/html");
    PrintWriter out = res.getWriter();
```

Listing 10.1: continued

```
    out.println("<HTML>");
    out.println("<BODY>");
    out.println("Hello World!");
    out.println("</BODY>");
    out.println("</HTML>");
  }
}
```

Listing 10.2: HTML Output from `HelloWorld` Java Servlet

```
<HTML>
<BODY>
HelloWorld
</BODY>
</HTML>
```

EXAMPLE

Displaying Pictures and Passing Parameters with Java

Parameters are passed to Java from the URL in the same manner as parameters are passed to any other Web process: `http://yourdomain.com/virtual_path_for_servlet/servlet?param=1` .

Listing 10.3 expands on the `HelloWorld` example by building the Metro Motors banner page (see Figure 10.21) and prompts the Web browser user for input if a parameter is not supplied. Notice that `req.getParameter` in line 12 retrieves a parameter, `p_name`, and puts this parameter's contents into the variable `myname`. If the parameter does not exist on the URL line, `myname` is set to null. `myname` is then used later in the program in line 29. Notice that this will be displayed only if something exists in `myname`. This enables the program to have a parameter or to continue without error even if no parameter is supplied.

Lines 16–26 process the Metro Motors banner. Notice line 21 makes reference to the virtual address `ows-img` where the `metro_motors.jpg` file should be located.

Line 36 defines the input text box, and line 37 defines the submit button.

Listing 10.3: `HelloWorld` Displaying Metro Motors Banner and Accepting a Parameter

```
1:  import java.io.*;
2:  import java.sql.*;
3:  import javax.servlet.*;
4:  import javax.servlet.http.*;
5:  import java.util.*;
6:
7:  public class HelloWorld extends HttpServlet {
8:
```

EXAMPLE

Listing 10.3: continued

```
9:  public void doGet(HttpServletRequest req, HttpServletResponse res)
10:         throws ServletException, IOException{
11:
12:     String myname = req.getParameter("p_name");
13:
14:     res.setContentType("text/html");
15:     PrintWriter out = res.getWriter();
16:     out.println("<HTML>");
17:     out.println("<HEAD><TITLE>Metro Motors Web Site</TITLE></HEAD>");
18:     out.println("<BODY>");
19:     out.println("<TABLE><TR VALIGN=CENTER>");
20:     out.println("<TD>");
21:     out.println("<IMG WIDTH=100 SRC=/ows-img/metro_motors.jpg>");
22:     out.println("</TD>");
23:     out.println("<TD>");
24:     out.println("<B>Metro Motors Web Site</B>");
25:     out.println("</TD>");
26:     out.println("</TR></TABLE>");
27:
28:     if ( myname != null ) {
29:       out.println("Hello " + myname);
30:     }
31:     else {
32:       out.println("HelloWorld");
33:     }
34:
35:     out.println("<FORM URL=HelloWorld METHOD=get>");
36:     out.println("<INPUT TYPE=TEXT NAME=p_name maxlength=20>");
37:     out.println("<INPUT TYPE=SUBMIT VALUE='Say Hello to'>");
38:     out.println("</FORM>");
39:     out.println("</BODY></HTML>");
40:  }
41: }
```

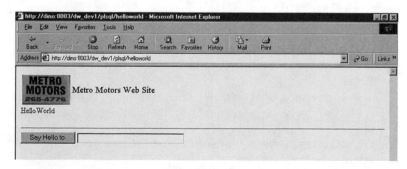

Figure 10.21: HelloWorld Java servlet.

Java Code Reuse

Java enables the easy reuse of code in the form of modules or public classes. Notice that lines 7–14 in Listing 10.4 is the same code as lines 19–26 in Listing 10.3.

Listing 10.4: Java stcarsutil Public Class

```
1:  import java.io.*;
2:
3:  public class stcarsutil {
4:
5:  public static void banner(PrintWriter out, String caption) {
6:
7:     out.println("<TABLE><TR VALIGN=CENTER>");
8:     out.println("<TD>");
9:     out.println("<IMG WIDTH=100 SRC=/ows-img/metro_motors.jpg>");
10:    out.println("</TD>");
11:    out.println("<TD>");
12:    out.println("<B>" + caption + "</B>");
13:    out.println("</TD>");
14:    out.println("</TR></TABLE>");
15:    }
16: }
```

To use the new public class, notice line 20 in Listing 10.5 makes reference to the class stcarsutil and the routine banner and passes the text string Metro Motors Web Site. As in the PL/SQL example of Chapter 9, "Using PL/SQL to Build Web Sites," this routine or Java class can now be used to give constant visual attributes to our Web site, without having to add the same code to each Web page.

Listing 10.5: Java HelloWorld Calling Public Class stcarsutil.banner

```
1: import java.io.*;
2: import java.sql.*;
3: import javax.servlet.*;
4: import javax.servlet.http.*;
5: import java.util.*;
6:
7: public class HelloWorld extends HttpServlet {
8:
9:
10:  public void doGet(HttpServletRequest req, HttpServletResponse res)
11:       throws ServletException, IOException{
12:
13:   String myname = req.getParameter("p_name");
14:
15:   res.setContentType("text/html");
```

Listing 10.5:   continued

```
16:    PrintWriter out = res.getWriter();
17:    out.println("<HTML>");
18:    out.println("<HEAD><TITLE>Metro Motors Web Site</TITLE></HEAD>");
19:    out.println("<BODY>");
20:    stcarsutil.banner(out,"Metro Motors Web Site");
21:    if ( myname != null ) {
22:      out.println("Hello " + myname);
23:    }
24:    else {
25:      out.println("HelloWorld");
26:    }
27:
28:    out.println("<FORM URL=HelloWorld METHOD=get>");
29:    out.println("<INPUT TYPE=TEXT NAME=p_name maxlength=20>");
30:    out.println("<INPUT TYPE=SUBMIT VALUE='Say Hello to'>");
31:    out.println("</FORM>");
32:    out.println("</BODY></HTML>");
33:  }
34: }
```

Building the Web Site with Java

The remainder of this chapter builds the Sales Tracking Web site as defined in Chapter 8 in Figure 8.7 (reprinted here). Figure 10.22 illustrates that Java can build the same Web site as was built in Chapter 9. Notice the URL, in Figure 10.22, makes reference to the simplej virtual path and Java cartridge (as defined in Figures 10.16 and 10.18).

The final example for this chapter illustrates two servlets—stcarsforsale and stcarsforsalebuy—to match the two Web pages of the Web site. Each will use the stcarsutil.banner to provide a consistent banner. These Java servlets also will select and update the ST_CARS_FOR_SALE table object, illustrated in Chapter 8 (refer to Figures 8.5 and 8.6).

The Java code will be listed and can be accessed and compiled using the Oracle JDeveloper v3.0 environment, discussed earlier in this chapter. This chapter also discusses the Java examples and the specific code necessary to build the Web site. Java is a complex code, and it is beyond the scope of this one chapter to discuss the intricacies of the Java language.

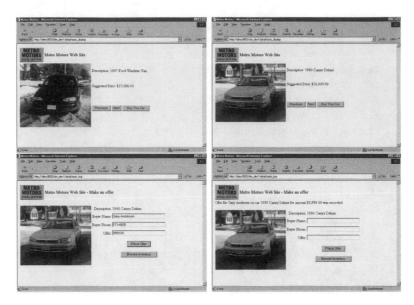

Figure 8.7: *These four windows (starting at the upper left) show the naviga-tion of the actual Sales Tracking Web site.*

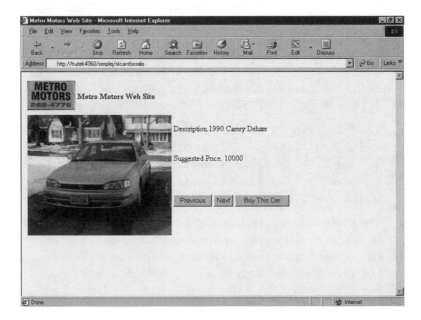

Figure 10.22: *Sales Tracking Web site.*

TIP

Many good books about the Java language are available, including *Java from Scratch* by Que.

The stcarsforsale Java servlet builds the Web page as illustrated in Figure 10.22. Lines 15 and 16 retrieve specific parameters coming in from the URL. If no parameters are passed, the inv_id and direction variables are set to null.

Lines 20–22 begin the HTML output. Notice in line 23 the call to stcarsutil.banner (from Listing 10.4) to display the Metro Motors banner page.

Line 31 connects to the database using the JDBC thin driver and connects to an Oracle database with a Net8 name of test, using the sales_tracking user ID and password. Remember from Chapter 8 that the thin connection will be maintained only for a single session initiated by a single Web browser access.

Some tasks, such as cursor management (retrieving a group of rows from the database and moving forward and backward through the rows), are best handled by PL/SQL. This Java servlet shows interaction between Java and PL/SQL (see line 33). The get_car PL/SQL procedure is similar to the auto_display PL/SQL developed in Chapter 9 (refer to Listing 9.9) in how it selects rows to be displayed. In Java, the CallableStatement routine is used to build the call statement and process any parameters. The six question marks (?) in line 33 are parameter placeholders: There are two input variables to this procedure and four variables returned. Lines 34–37 define the parameters that will be returned from the PL/SQL procedure, and lines 39–45 do some checking for the existence of URL input parameters. If they exist, they will be passed to the PL/SQL routine. Line 46 calls the PL/SQL routine.

Lines 48–84 prepare the bulk of the Web page illustrated in Figure 10.22. Notice how line 50 displays the automobile photo (its path was returned in variable 6 from the PL/SQL routine: line 66 of Listing 10.7) by defining an image IMG and making the source SRC reference the return variable from the PL/SQL get_car procedure.

The Previous and Next buttons are defined in lines 59–62 and lines 66–69, respectively. The URL is set to this Java servlet, whereas the Buy This Car button's URL (lines 73–75) is set to the other Java servlet, stcarsforsalebuy. This is how access to either Web page is defined.

The remainder of the code in this servlet, lines 87–99, is used to catch and handle any error conditions, and line 101 completes the HTML output.

EXAMPLE

Listing 10.6: stcarsforsale Java Servlet

```
1:  import java.io.*;
2:  import java.sql.*;
3:  import javax.servlet.*;
4:  import javax.servlet.http.*;
5:  import java.util.*;
6:
7:  public class stcarsforsale extends HttpServlet {
8:
9:    public void doGet(HttpServletRequest req, HttpServletResponse res)
10:       throws ServletException, IOException{
11:       Connection con = null;
12:       Statement stmt = null;
13:       ResultSet rs = null;
14:
15:       String inv_id = req.getParameter("p_inv_id");
16:       String direction = req.getParameter("p_direction");
17:
18:       res.setContentType("text/html");
19:       PrintWriter out = res.getWriter();
20:       out.println("<HTML>");
21: out.println("<HEAD><TITLE>Metro Motors Web Site</TITLE></HEAD>");
22:       out.println("<BODY>");
23:       stcarsutil.banner(out,"Metro Motors Web Site");
24:
25:       try {
26:       //Register Oracle Driver
27:       Class.forName("oracle.jdbc.driver.OracleDriver");
28:
29:       //Get a Connection to the database
30:       con = DriverManager.getConnection(
31:"jdbc:oracle:thin:@localhost:1521:test", "sales_tracking","sales_tracking");
32:
33:    CallableStatement cstmt = con.prepareCall("{call get_car(?,?,?,?,?,?)}");
34:       cstmt.registerOutParameter(3,java.sql.Types.FLOAT);
35:       cstmt.registerOutParameter(4,java.sql.Types.VARCHAR);
36:       cstmt.registerOutParameter(5,java.sql.Types.FLOAT);
37:       cstmt.registerOutParameter(6,java.sql.Types.VARCHAR);
38:       cstmt.setString(1,direction);
39:       if (inv_id != null) {
```

Listing 10.6: continued

```
40:        cstmt.setInt(2,Integer.parseInt(inv_id));
41:       }
42:     else
43:      {
44:         cstmt.setInt(2,0);
45:      }
46:      cstmt.execute();
47:
48:      out.println("<TABLE><TR>");
49:      out.println("<TD ROWSPAN=3>");
50:      out.println("<IMG WIDTH=300 SRC=" + cstmt.getString(6) + ">");
51:      out.println("</TD>");
52:      out.println("<TD COLSPAN=3>");
53:      out.println("Description:"+cstmt.getString(4));
54:      out.println("</TD></TR><TD COLSPAN=3>");
55:      out.println("Suggested Price: "+ cstmt.getInt(5));
56:      out.println("</TD></TR>");
57:      out.println("<TR>");
58:      out.println("<TD>");
59:      out.println("<FORM URL=stcarsforsale METHOD=get>");
60: out.println("<INPUT TYPE=hidden NAME=p_direction VALUE=DISPLAY_PREV>");
61: out.println("<INPUT TYPE=hidden NAME=p_inv_id VALUE="+cstmt.getInt(3)+">");
62:      out.println("<INPUT TYPE=SUBMIT VALUE=Previous>");
63:      out.println("</FORM>");
64:      out.println("</TD>");
65:      out.println("<TD>");
66:      out.println("<FORM URL=stcarsforsale METHOD=get>");
67: out.println("<INPUT TYPE=hidden NAME=p_direction VALUE=DISPLAY_NEXT>");
68: out.println("<INPUT TYPE=hidden NAME=p_inv_id VALUE="+cstmt.getInt(3)+">");
69:      out.println("<INPUT TYPE=SUBMIT VALUE=Next>");
70:      out.println("</FORM>");
71:      out.println("</TD>");
72:      out.println("<TD>");
73: out.println("<FORM URL=stcarsforsalebuy METHOD=get>");
74: out.println("<INPUT TYPE=hidden NAME=p_inv_id VALUE="+cstmt.getInt(3)+">");
75:      out.println("<INPUT TYPE=SUBMIT VALUE='Buy This Car'>");
76:      out.println("</FORM>");
77:      out.println("</TD>");
78:
79:      out.println("");
80:      out.println("");
81:      out.println("");
82:      out.println("");
```

Listing 10.6: continued

```
83:        out.println("</TR>");
84:        out.println("</TABLE>");
85:
86:
87:      }
88:      catch(ClassNotFoundException e) {
89:        out.println("Could not load db driver" + e.getMessage());
90:    }
91:      catch(SQLException e) {
92:        out.println("SQL Error: " + e.getMessage());
93:      }
94:      finally {
95:      try {
96:          if (con != null) con.close();
97:        }
98:        catch (SQLException e) {}
99:      }
100:
101:      out.println("</BODY></HTML>");
102:    }
103: }
```

The PL/SQL procedure get_car, Listing 10.7, is similar to Listing 9.9 in how it selects cars from the ST_CARS_FOR_SALE table object. It is passed two input variables. In line 3, the p_direction variable has a default value, in case no input values were passed from the Java servlet (Listing 10.6, line 33).

There is no connect string to the database. The Java servlet is already connected to the database and can call this procedure. The output of this procedure is in lines 63–66 and returns information from the current row in the open cursor.

EXAMPLE

Listing 10.7: get_car PL/SQL Procedure stcarsforsale Java Servlet

```
1:  CREATE OR REPLACE PROCEDURE get_car
2:  (
3:      p_direction          IN VARCHAR2 DEFAULT 'DISPLAY_NEXT'
4:  ,   p_inv_id             IN NUMBER DEFAULT NULL
5:  ,   x_inv_id             OUT NUMBER
6:  ,   x_auto_description   OUT VARCHAR2
7:  ,   x_sale_amt           OUT NUMBER
8:  ,   x_photo_location     OUT VARCHAR2
9:  ) IS
10: CURSOR next_CUR
11: (
```

Listing 10.7:   continued

```
12:      p_inv_id IN NUMBER
13: ) IS
14:      SELECT inv_id, auto_description
15:      ,   sale_amt, sale_photo_location
16:      FROM st_cars_for_sale
17:      WHERE inv_id > NVL(p_inv_id,0)
18:      ORDER BY inv_id ASC;
19: CURSOR prev_CUR
20: (
21:      p_inv_id IN NUMBER
22: ) IS
23:      SELECT inv_id, auto_description
24:      ,   sale_amt, sale_photo_location
25:      FROM st_cars_for_sale
26:      WHERE inv_id < NVL(p_inv_id,10000000)
27:      ORDER BY inv_id DESC;
28: sale_row prev_CUR%ROWTYPE;
29: BEGIN
30:      IF p_direction = 'DISPLAY_NEXT' THEN
31:          OPEN next_CUR
32:          (
33:              p_inv_id
34:          );
35:          FETCH next_CUR INTO sale_row;
36:          IF next_CUR%NOTFOUND THEN
37:              OPEN prev_CUR
38:              (
39:                  p_inv_id
40:              );
41:              FETCH prev_CUR INTO sale_row;
42:              CLOSE prev_CUR;
43:          END IF; — next_CUR%NOTFOUND
44:          CLOSE next_CUR;
45:      ELSE
46:          OPEN prev_CUR
47:          (
48:              p_inv_id
49:          );
50:          FETCH prev_CUR INTO sale_row;
51:          IF prev_CUR%NOTFOUND THEN
52:              OPEN next_CUR
53:              (
54:                  p_inv_id
55:              );
56:              FETCH next_CUR INTO sale_row;
```

Listing 10.7: continued

```
57:          CLOSE next_CUR;
58:       END IF;  — prev_CUR%NOTFOUND
59:       CLOSE prev_CUR;
60:    END IF;  — p_direction = 'DISPLAY_NEXT'
61:
62:    — Set return values
63:    x_inv_id         := sale_row.inv_id;
64:    x_auto_description  := sale_row.auto_description;
65:    x_sale_amt       := sale_row.sale_amt;
66:    x_photo_location   := sale_row.sale_photo_location;
67: END;
68: /
```

The stcarsforsalebuy Java servlet (see Listing 10.8) displays the Web page
as illustrated in Figure 8.9 of Chapter 8. This Web page enables the Web
browser user to make an offer on a car and record the information in the
ST_CARS_FOR_SALE table object. The UPDATE statement that performs this
task can be found in lines 43–47. If the UPDATE was successful (see line 48),
the offer information is displayed on the Web page.

The SELECT statement (lines 54–56) reread the information being displayed
on the original Web page (the stcarsforsale Java servlet). The remainder
of the code (beginning at line 58) builds the Web page and directs the Web
browser to the appropriate servlet for the selections made by the Web
browser user, similar to Listing 10.6 (lines 48–84).

EXAMPLE

Listing 10.8: stcarsforsalebuy Java Servlet

```
1: import java.io.*;
2: import java.sql.*;
3: import javax.servlet.*;
4: import javax.servlet.http.*;
5: import java.util.*;
6:
7:
8:
9:
10: public class stcarsforsalebuy extends HttpServlet {
11:
12:  public void doGet(HttpServletRequest req, HttpServletResponse res)
13:       throws ServletException, IOException{
14:   Connection con = null;
15:   Statement stmt = null;
16:   ResultSet rs = null;
17:   int counter = 0;
18:
```

Listing 10.8:   continued

```
19:    String inv_id = req.getParameter("p_inv_id");
20:    String buyer_name = req.getParameter("p_buyer_name");
21:    String buyer_phone = req.getParameter("p_buyer_phone");
22:    String buyer_offer = req.getParameter("p_buyer_offer");
23:
24:    res.setContentType("text/html");
25:    PrintWriter out = res.getWriter();
26:    out.println("<HTML>");
27:out.println("<HEAD><TITLE>Metro Motors Web Site Make Offer</TITLE></HEAD>");
28:    out.println("<BODY>");
29:    stcarsutil.banner(out,"Metro Motors Web Site - Make An Offer");
30:
31:    try {
32:    //Register Oracle Driver
33:    Class.forName("oracle.jdbc.driver.OracleDriver");
34:
35:    //Get a Connection to the database
36:    con = DriverManager.getConnection(
37:"jdbc:oracle:thin:@localhost:1521:test", "sales_tracking","sales_tracking");
38:
39:    stmt = con.createStatement();
40:
41:    if (buyer_name != null) {
42:    // update the record with the offer
43:    counter = stmt.executeUpdate(
44:    "UPDATE st_cars_for_sale SET buyer_name='" + buyer_name
45:      + "', buyer_phone='" + buyer_phone + "', buyer_offer="
46:      + buyer_offer + ", buyer_date=SYSDATE WHERE inv_id = " + inv_id
47:    );
48:    if (counter > 0) {
49:      out.println("Offer for $" + buyer_offer + " recorded<BR>");
50:      }
51:    counter = 0;
52:    }
53:
54:    rs = stmt.executeQuery("SELECT auto_description, sale_amt,
➥sale_photo_location, inv_id "
55:      + "FROM st_cars_for_sale WHERE inv_id="+inv_id);
56:
57:      while (rs.next()) {
58:        counter++;
59:        out.println("<TABLE><TR>");
60:        out.println("<TD ROWSPAN=6>");
61:        out.println("<IMG WIDTH=300 SRC=" + rs.getString
➥("sale_photo_location") + ">");
```

Listing 10.8: continued

```
62:        out.println("</TD>");
63:        out.println("<TD COLSPAN=2>");
64:        out.println("Description:"+rs.getString
➥("auto_description"));
65:        out.println("</TD></TR>");
66:        out.println("<TR>");
67:        out.println("<TD>");
68:        out.println("<FORM URL=stcarsforsale METHOD=get>");
69:   out.println("<INPUT TYPE=hidden NAME=p_direction VALUE=DISPLAY_PREV>");
70:        out.println("<INPUT TYPE=hidden NAME=p_inv_id
➥VALUE="+rs.getInt("inv_id")+">");
71:        out.println("Buyer Name:");
72:        out.println("</TD><TD>");
73:        out.println("<INPUT TYPE=TEXT NAME=p_buyer_name maxlength=20>");
74:        out.println("</TD><TD></TR>");
75:        out.println("<TR><TD>");
76:        out.println("Buyer Phone:");
77:        out.println("</TD><TD>");
78:        out.println("<INPUT TYPE=TEXT NAME=p_buyer_phone maxlength=10>");
79:        out.println("</TD></TR>");
80:        out.println("<TR><TD>");
81:        out.println("Offer:");
82:        out.println("</TD><TD>");
83:        out.println("<INPUT TYPE=TEXT NAME=p_buyer_offer maxlength=10>");
84:        out.println("</TD></TR>");
85:
86:        out.println("<TR>");
87:        out.println("<TD COLSPAN=2 ALIGN=CENTER>");
88:        out.println("<INPUT TYPE=SUBMIT VALUE='Make Offer'>");
89:        out.println("</FORM>");
90:        out.println("</TD></TR>");
91:        out.println("<TR><TD COLSPAN=2 ALIGN=CENTER>");
92:        out.println("<FORM URL=stcarsforsale METHOD=get>");
93:        out.println("<INPUT TYPE=hidden NAME=p_inv_id
➥VALUE="+rs.getInt("inv_id")+">");
94:        out.println("<INPUT TYPE=SUBMIT VALUE='Browse Inventory'>");
95:        out.println("</FORM>");
96:        out.println("</TD></TR>");
97:        out.println("</TABLE>");
98:        }
99:      if (counter==0) {
100:       out.println("Car Not found");
101:       }
102:
103:    }
```

Listing 10.8:   continued

```
104:    catch(ClassNotFoundException e) {
105:      out.println("Could not load db driver" + e.getMessage());
106:      }
107:    catch(SQLException e) {
108:    out.println("SQL Error: " + e.getMessage());
109:      }
110:      finally {
111:          try {
112:            if (con != null) con.close();
113:          }
114:          catch (SQLException e) {}
115:      }
116:
117:      out.println("</BODY></HTML>");
118:    }
119:
120:
121: }
```

Summary

In this chapter, you learned the basics of Java and the portability of Java across many computing platforms. You learned the basics of JDeveloper v3.0, Oracle's Java procedure building toolkit, while building a basic servlet that created a simple Web page based on the SCOTT.EMP table. You then applied this knowledge to build the Sales Tracking Web site, as illustrated in Chapter 8.

REVIEW

Reviewing It

1. Explain the purpose of a JAR file.

2. Why does the JDeveloper software create a HTML file when saving the Java program?

3. Why does the JDBC thin client software prompt for userid and password?

4. What is a DAD and why is it important?

5. What does the java function out.println() do.

Checking It

CHECK

1. What does JAR stand for?

    a) Java Archive Resource

    b) Java Archive File

    c) Java Active Repository

    d) Java Archive Repository

2. The DB Servlet runs on

    a) The client

    b) The database server

    c) The Web server

    d) Any of the above

3. You have to FTP the servlet code created to its intended target.

    True/False

Applying It

APPLY

Independent Exercise 1:

- Build the 'Hello World' example in Listing 10.1.

- Deploy it and run it.

Independent Exercise 2:

- Build a master/detail servlet that displays department information then displays the employees and their managers underneath.

- Deploy and run the servlet.

Independent Exercise 3:

- Build an applet and a servlet that prompts the user for a valid EMPNO in the EMP table, then displays the correct row from the EMP table.

- Deploy and run the code.

In the next chapter, you will learn about XML, how to extract information from the past two chapters' Web sites, and how to present that information on wireless devices such as cell phones and hand-held devices.

What's Next?

In the next chapter, you will learn about XML, how to extract information from the past two chapters' Web sites, and how to present that information on wireless devices such as cell phones and hand-held devices.

Using PL/SQL Pages, Java Pages, and XML with Apache/Oracle9iAS

This chapter focuses on adapting existing HTML to PL/SQL pages, Java Server Pages, and building Web and wireless applications with XML, using examples from both Chapters 9 and 10.

This chapter teaches you the following

- Oracle9iAS/Apache Web Server Setup Options
- Using PL/SQL Pages
- Using Java
- Using XML

Oracle9i provides many ways to present data on the Web. Oracle has embraced Java as an alternative to PL/SQL. Within Oracle 8i/9i Java is spoken natively inside the database. This means that developers have the freedom to program using either or both Java and PL/SQL, using whatever solution fits best for the given situation. Java is well suited to Internet applications through the use of Java Servlets (introduced in Chapter 10, "Using Java to Build Web Sites").

PL/SQL Pages are a way of imbedding PL/SQL into existing HTML Web applications (generated with tools such as Frontpage, Dreamweaver, and so on) and Java Server Pages are a way of imbedding Java into existing HTML Web applications.

Java server pages are loosely analogous to PSP pages and Java Servlets are analogous to PL/SQL packages. PL/SQL pages can do many things well, but it does tie your application to an Oracle-only database solution.

XML is the next generation of Web languages. Not only can you develop Web pages using XML but you can easily adapt Web-enabled applications to wireless devices such as cellular telephones, and so on. Oracle has made using XML data easy. A full XML implementation is included with later versions of Oracle8i and with Oracle9i. It can also be downloaded separately as the XML developer's kit.

The Oracle corporation has made a large investment in XML and has provided excellent tools and utilities for developers to use. They have made using XML in PL/SQL, Java, and C/C++ quite easy. They have also used their own technology to create another Web page generating facility called XSQL pages. These XSQL pages are simple to use and allow developers to get started with XML without worrying too much about XML details.

With Oracle9i (and later versions of Oracle8i) you have all these abilities built right into the database. Oracle has bundled the Apache Web server with the Oracle9iAS environment to make PL/SQL, Java, XML, PSP, JSP, and XSP as seamless as possible.

Oracle9iAS/Apache Web Server Setup Options

It is important that the Web environment options are set correctly. This allows for Web pages and code to make generic references to images and other objects and enables those generic references to get interpreted correctly into physical computer locations. It is also important that login information be hidden from Web users. This is accomplished with *Database Access Descriptors,* or DAD.

Apache Virtual Directory Setup

You can set up virtual directories in Oracle9iAS, in the httpd.conf file, as you would for any standard Apache installation. Setting up some aliases will allow for more Web-environment-neutral access to files (such as pictures, code, and so on).

Find the httpd.conf file. This file is the configuration file for Apache. It contains all the directives that customize Apache for your Web-server installation. This file is usually located in $ORACLE_HOME/Apache/Apache/conf/ httpd.conf.

NOTE

I HIGHLY recommend making a copy of any configuration file prior to making any changes to it!

Open the file in an edit session and find the section of the file that talks about directory aliases. This maps your logical directory structure to a physical location on your hard drive. The section in httpd.conf looks like Listing 11.1.

Listing 11.1: Apache `httpd.conf` File

```
#
# Aliases: Add here as many aliases as you need (with no limit). The format is
# Alias fakename realname
#
# Note that if you include a trailing / on fakename then the server will
# require it to be present in the URL.  So "/icons" isn't aliased in this
# example, only "/icons/"..
#
Alias /icons/ "C:\oracle\ora81\Apache\Apache\icons/"
Alias /jservdocs/ "C:\oracle\ora81\Apache\Jserv\docs/"
Alias /mm/ "C:\metromotors/"
Alias /mmimage/ "C:\metromotors/img/"
```

The last two lines, alias `mm` and `mmimage`, are the aliases that will be used throughout the coding examples in this chapter. The Apache listener will need to be stopped and started to implement any changes made to this file.

Apache Listener Setup and Database Access Descriptor (DAD) Setup

The listener for Oracle Web traffic is set by default to run on port 80. You may need to adjust this value if the computer running the Apache or Oracle9iAS Web server is running more than one Web server.

All these configuration values can be found in the `$ORACLE_HOME/Apache/Apache/conf/httpd.conf` file. If necessary, modify which the port that the Web server is configured to use by looking for a line similar to Listing 11.2. This is the port that the Apache or Oracle9iAS Web server will listen for requests on.

Listing 11.2: Apache `httpd.conf` Port Configuration

```
#
# Port: The port to which the standalone server listens. For
# ports < 1023, you will need httpd to be run as root initially.
#

Port 80
```

Once the port is determined the Web server needs to be started. Run the executable `ORACLE_HOME/Apache/Apache/bin/startapache.exe` starts the Apache Web server as background process and if no error messages are displayed the Web server should be running. Test this by attempting to navigate a Web browser to the machine serving the database. If your computer has a local database, navigate to `http://localhost`, if your port is 80. If your port is configured for anything else then navigate to `http://localhost:port`. You should now see something like Figure 11.1.

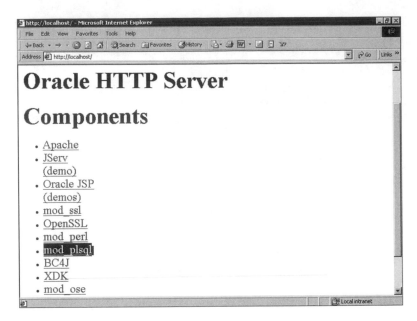

Figure 11.1: Oracle HTTP server splash screen.

Apache Database Access Descriptor (DAD) Setup

Any Web procedure needing access to the database will need a database access descriptor set up for it. This essentially hides the login process from the Web user and allows the oracle database administrator to control the type of access that the Web environment can have to this particular database.

Select the mod_plsql link (this is the Apache PL/SQL processor) on this page and you should get the Oracle Portal Homepage. From here select the Administer' tab. On this page you will see a Services section from which you will select Listener Gateway Settings. On the Gateway Configuration Menu, select Gateway Database Access Descriptor Settings to add additional DADs to this Web server. Scroll down until you see the configured DADs. Click on the edit icon of the SAMPLE DAD. You should now have a screen that will allow you to change or add DAD parameters (see Figure 11.2).

Configuring DADs will allow the pages being developed in the remainder of this chapter to be browsed. Leave all the defaults as they are, with the exception of the Oracle User Name, Oracle Password, and Oracle Connect String. Fill these in with the appropriate values (the same account that owns the PSP) and then click the OK button at the top of the screen.

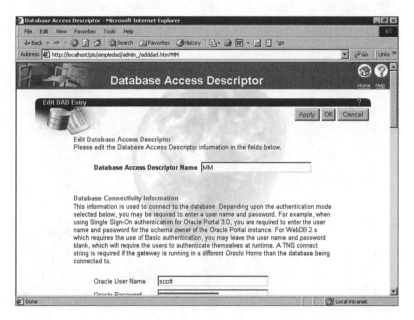

Figure 11.2: *Database Access Descriptor configuration screen.*

Using PL/SQL Pages

For developers familiar with PL/SQL, adding PL/SQL to existing HTML pages is possibly the quickest way to create great looking Web pages that are integrated with the database. You can use your in-house graphics department to create the look and feel of the Web pages required and then use PL/SQL to integrate the HTML Web pages with the Oracle9i database (creating PL/SQL Pages or PSP).

For example, standard HTML generators can create Web pages that look like page1.html (see Figure 11.3) and page2.html (see Figure 11.4). These are just base Web pages without any database interaction.

The previous pages can be easily created with a dozen different HTML generator products and these Web pages are static. They will appear the same with each access.

PL/SQL pages are simply static html pages with some special PL/SQL tags (PSP), becoming dynamic Web pages. This marked up psp file is then loaded into the Oracle 9i database and the dynamic content is made available to the world.

Listing 11.3 shows the page1.html, the static Web page illustrated in Figure 11.3.

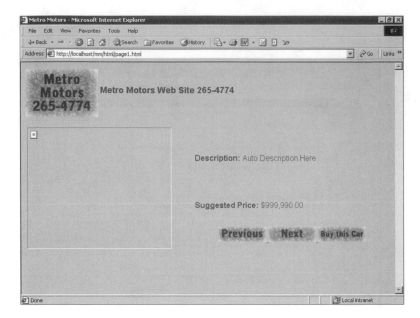

Figure 11.3: Basic Web page to be used to display autos.

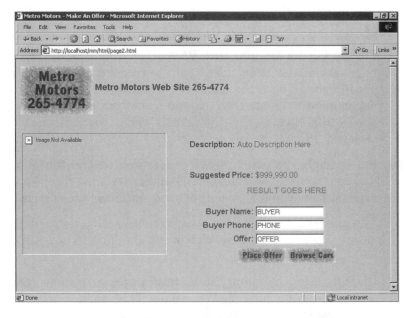

Figure 11.4: Basic Web page to be used to buy autos.

EXAMPLE

Listing 11.3: Page1.HTML Code

```
1:  <html>
2:  <head>
3:  <title>Metro Motors</title>
4:  <meta http-equiv="Content-Type" content="text/html; charset=iso-8859-1"/>
5:  </head>
6:  <body bgcolor="#CCCCCC" text="#990000">
7:  <p><img src="/mmimage/logo.gif" width="150" height="100" align="middle"/>
8:  <b><font face="Geneva, Arial, Helvetica, san-serif">
9:  <font size="4">Metro Motors Web Site 265-4774</font></font></b></p>
10: <table width="100%" border="0">
11: <tr>
12: <td rowspan="3" width="46%">
13: <img src="/mmimage/photo1.gif" width="300" height="250"/></td>
14: <td width="54%" height="83">
15: <font face="Geneva, Arial, Helvetica, san-serif"><b>Description:</b>
16: Auto Description Here</font></td>
17: </tr>
18: <tr>
19: <td width="54%" height="39">
20: <font face="Geneva, Arial, Helvetica, san-serif"><b>Suggested Price:</b>
21: $999,990.00</font></td>
22: </tr>
23: <tr>
24: <td align="center" width="54%">
25: <a href="page1?id=0">
26: <img src="/mmimage/prev.gif" width="100" height="30" border="0"
➥alt="Previous"/>
27: </a>
28: <a href="page1?id=2">
29: <img src="/mmimage/next.gif" width="100" height="30" border="0" alt="Next"/>
30: </a>
31: <a href="page2?id=1">
32: <img src="/mmimage/buy.gif" width="100" height="30"
33: border="0" alt="Buy This Car"/>
34: </a>
35: </td>
36: </tr>
37: </table>
38: </body>
39: </html>
```

Begin the transformation by renaming the Here is the original page1.html page to page1.psp. Listing 11.4 shows the PL/SQL Page.

Listing 11.4: Page1.psp Code

```
1:   <%@ page language="PL/SQL"%>
2:   <%@ plsql procedure="page1" %>
3:   <%@ plsql parameter="id" type="NUMBER" default="1" %>
4:   <%! l_id st_cars_for_sale.inv_id%TYPE :=id;%>
5:   <%! l_sale_photo_location st_cars_for_sale.sale_photo_location%TYPE;%>
6:   <%! l_auto_description st_cars_for_sale.auto_description%TYPE;%>
7:   <%! l_amount VARCHAR2(15);%>
8:   <%
9:   get_car
10:  (
11:  px_id          => l_id
12:  ,  x_description => l_auto_description
13:  ,  x_image       => l_sale_photo_location
14:  ,  x_amount      => l_amount
15:  );
16:  %>
17:  <html>
18:  <head>
19:  <title>Metro Motors</title>
20:  <meta http-equiv="Content-Type" content="text/html; charset=iso-8859-1"/>
21:  </head>
22:
23:  <body bgcolor="#CCCCCC" text="#990000">
24:  <p><img src="/mmimage/logo.gif" width="150" height="100" align="middle"/>
25:  <b><font face="Geneva, Arial, Helvetica, san-serif">
26:  <font size="4">Metro Motors Web Site 265-4774</font></font></b></p>
27:  <table width="100%" border="0">
28:  <tr>
29:  <td rowspan="3" width="46%">
30:  <img src="/mmimage<%=l_sale_photo_location%>" width="300"
➥height="250"/></td>
31:  <td width="54%" height="83">
32:  <font face="Geneva, Arial, Helvetica, san-serif"><b>Description:</b>
33:  <%=l_auto_description%></font></td>
34:  </tr>
35:  <tr>
36:  <td width="54%" height="39">
37:  <font face="Geneva, Arial, Helvetica, san-serif"><b>Suggested Price:</b>
38:  <%=l_amount%></font></td>
39:  </tr>
40:  <tr>
41:  <td align=center width="54%">
42:  <a href="page1?id=<%=l_id-1%>">
43:  <img src="/mmimage/prev.gif" width="100" height="30" border="0"
➥alt="Previous"/>
44:  </a>
```

Listing 11.4:   continued

```
45:    <a href="page1?id=<%=l_id+1%>">
46:    <img src="/mmimage/next.gif" width="100" height="30" border="0" alt="Next"/>
47:    </a>
48:    <a href="page2?id=<%=l_id%>">
49:    <img src="/mmimage/buy.gif" width="100" height="30"
50:    border="0" alt="Buy This Car"/>
51:    </a>
52:    </td>
53:    </tr>
54:    </table>
55:    <p> </p>
56:    </body>
57:    </html>
```

The first 16 lines of Listing 11.4 are where all the dynamic action occurs. Line 1 identifies this page as a PL/SQL language file. Line 2 specifies what PL/SQL procedure to create for this page. Ultimately PSP pages get stored in the database as PL/SQL procedures, so this is the name that it will be stored as. If this line is omitted then the name of the file is used by default.

Line 3 indicates that this page will have an optional parameter passed to it. This page will work exactly like the example in Chapters 9 and 10 where the first time the Web page is called, there is not an inventory id passed to it, so the default value of 1 is used. The syntax default="1" clause makes the parameter optional. Lines 4 through 7 are procedure-level variable declarations. Variables are declared here just as they are in PL/SQL and are enclosed in <%! %> tags.

Lines 8 through 16 are enclosed in a PL/SQL code block tag <% %>. This code is direct PL/SQL. Here we are calling a stored procedure called get_car (the concept was created in Chapters 9 and 10 but adapted to be a non-Web procedure, see Appendix C, "Web Sites and Product Codes," for the code listing) that takes the inventory id parameter in and returns the information about this car back out into the local variables (l_%). This get_car (see Appendix B, "Complete Sales Tracking Installation Scripts," for the procedure listing) simply opens up a cursor against the table object st_cars_for_sale table and finds an exact match if it can. If no car matches the inventory id passed, then it returns the next closest inventory id and related information. The id of the car selected and all the pertinent information is then returned.

This get_car logic could have been coded right in this page but the idea is to minimize mixing code with content, allowing simplicity in converting the Web pages and providing code sharing across the entire application.

The next line that changed is line 30. Here the hard-coded image of the car for sale is replaced with the results from the get_car procedure. The tag <%= %> is an output tag. Think of it as the left-hand side of a variable assignment statement. When you now see the syntax <%=l_sale_photo_ location%>, it will interpret this to the value of this location.

Lines 33 and 38 do the exact same thing for the description of the car and the suggested selling price (items from the get_car procedure again).

Lines 42, 45, and 48 show that more can be done than just displaying the contents of a variable. Math, string concatenation, and more (anything that can be the right-hand side of a PL/SQL assignment) can be inside a <%= %> tag combination. For example, the previous inventory id can be accessed with <%=l_id-1%> and the next inventory id with <%l_id+1%>. Line 48 is the link to making an offer. It calls page2 to handle accepting an offer, passing the inventory id as a parameter to it.

This PL/SQL page is now complete and it can now be loaded into the database. The command line tool loadpsp provides this function, see Figure 11.5.

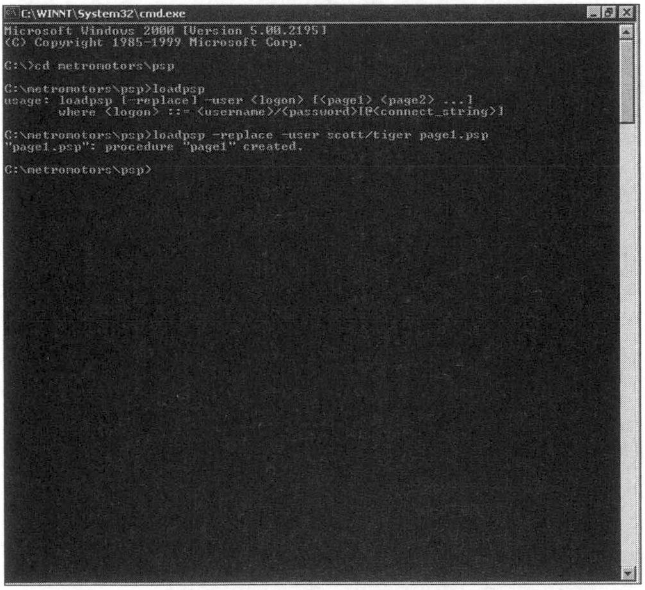

Figure 11.5: *Loading PL/SQL pages into Oracle.*

The -replace option allows you to overwrite the existing procedure with the new one you are passing in. The tool allows you to pass more than one page at a time as well. This allows compile time to link together pages to make one page. This technique of code sharing would be useful in a full-blown development framework where a standard header or footer is always wanted to include with every page, at compile time. This header or footer file is placed inside the PSP page wherever the `<%@ include file="includefile.inc" %>` tag is used.

NOTE

If you later changed your `includefile.inc` you would have to re-load every page that uses it with the `loadpsp` program. To achieve runtime dynamic linking you would just use the `<% %>` PL/SQL code tags and execute a stored procedure that uses some of the available owa/htp procedures to include whatever content you like.

Listing 11.5 shows the Web page for page2.html, the make-an-offer page. Listing 11.6 is the modified page2.psp code.

EXAMPLE

Listing 11.5:   Page2 HTML Code

```
1: <html>
2: <head>
3: <title>Metro Motors - Make An Offer</title>
4: <meta http-equiv="Content-Type" content="text/html; charset=iso-8859-1"/>
5: </head>
6:
7: <body bgcolor="#CCCCCC" text="#990000">
8: <p><img src="/mmimage/logo.gif" width="150" height="100" align="middle"/>
9:    <b><font face="Geneva, Arial, Helvetica, san-serif">
10:    <font size="4">Metro Motors Web Site 265-4774</font></font></b></p>
11: <form name="form2" method="post" action="page2">
12:    <input type="hidden" name="id" value="1"/>
13:    <table width="100%" border="0">
14:    <tr>
15:      <td rowspan="4" width="46%"><a href="page2.html">
16:        <img src="/mmimage/photo1.gif" width="300" height="250"
17:        border="0" alt="Image Not Available"/>
18:        </a>
19:      </td>
20:      <td width="54%" height="83"><font face="Geneva, Arial,
21:        Helvetica, san-serif">
22:        <b>Description:</b>
23:        Auto Description Here</font></td>
24:    </tr>
25:    <tr>
26:      <td width="54%" height="39"><font
27:        face="Geneva, Arial, Helvetica, san-serif"><b>Suggested Price:</b>
28:        $999,990.00</font></td>
29:    </tr>
```

Listing 11.6:   continued

```
30:   <tr>
31:        <td>
32:     <p align="CENTER"><b><font
33:       face="Geneva, Arial, Helvetica, san-serif" COLOR="Fuchsia">
34:       <font size="3">
35:       RESULT GOES HERE</font></font></b>
36:     </p>
37:       <table width="100%" border="0">
38:         <tr>
39:           <td width="33%">
40:             <div align="right">
41:             <font face="Geneva, Arial, Helvetica, san-serif"><b>Buyer
42:               Name:</b></font></div>
43:           </td>
44:             <td width="67%">
45:               <input type="text" name="buyer"
46:               maxlength="50" value="BUYER"/>
47:             </td>
48:         </tr>
49:         <tr>
50:           <td width="33%">
51:             <div align="right">
52:             <font face="Geneva, Arial, Helvetica, san-serif"><b>Buyer
53:               Phone:</b></font></div>
54:           </td>
55:           <td width="67%">
56:               <input type="text" name="phone"
57:               maxlength="15" value="PHONE"/>
58:             </td>
59:         </tr>
60:         <tr>
61:           <td width="33%">
62:             <div align="right">
63:             <font face="Geneva, Arial, Helvetica, san-serif">
64:             <b>Offer:</b></font></div>
65:           </td>
66:           <td width="67%">
67:               <input type="text" name="offer"
68:               maxlength="15" value="OFFER"/>
69:             </td>
70:         </tr>
71:       </table>
72:     </td>
73:   </tr>
74:   <tr>
```

Listing 11.5: continued

```
75:        <td align="center" width="54%">
76:          <input type="image" border="0"
77:          src="/mmimage/offer.gif" width="100" height="30" alt="Place Offer" />
78:          <a href="page1?id=1">
79:          <img src="/mmimage/browse.gif" width="100"
80:          height="30" border="0" alt="Browse Cars"/></a>
81:          </td>
82:          </tr>
83: </table>
84: </form>
85: <p> </p>
86: </body>
87: </html>
```

Listing 11.6 shows the page2 as a PL/SQL PSP.

EXAMPLE

Listing 11.6: Page2.PSP Code

```
1:   <%@ page language="PL/SQL"%>
2:   <%@ plsql procedure="page2" %>
3:   <%@ plsql parameter="id" %>
4:   <%@ plsql parameter="buyer" default="NULL"%>
5:   <%@ plsql parameter="phone" default="NULL"%>
6:   <%@ plsql parameter="offer" default="NULL"%>
7:   <%@ plsql parameter="x" default="NULL"%>
8:   <%@ plsql parameter="y" default="NULL"%>
9:   <%! l_id st_cars_for_sale.inv_id%TYPE:=id;%>
10:  <%! l_sale_photo_location st_cars_for_sale.sale_photo_location%TYPE;%>
11:  <%! l_auto_description st_cars_for_sale.auto_description%TYPE;%>
12:  <%! l_amount VARCHAR2(15);%>
13:  <%! l_buyer st_cars_for_sale.buyer_name%TYPE := buyer;%>
14:  <%! l_phone st_cars_for_sale.buyer_phone%TYPE :- phone;%>
15:  <%! l_offer VARCHAR2(50) := offer;%>
16:  <%! l_success BOOLEAN;%>
17:  <%! l_result VARCHAR2(1000);%>
18:  <%
19:  get_car
20:  (
21:      px_id         => l_id
22:  ,   x_description => l_auto_description
23:  ,   x_image       => l_sale_photo_location
24:  ,   x_amount      => l_amount
25:  );
26:  IF l_offer IS NOT NULL THEN
27:    make_offer
28:    (
29:        p_id      => l_id
```

Listing 11.6: continued

```
30:    ,   p_buyer   => l_buyer
31:    ,   p_phone   => l_phone
32:    ,   p_offer   => l_offer
33:    ,   x_success => l_success
34:    ,   x_result  => l_result
35:    );
36:    IF l_success THEN
37:       l_buyer := NULL;
38:       l_phone := NULL;
39:       l_offer := NULL;
40:     END IF;
41:   END IF;
42:   %>
43:   <html>
44:   <head>
45:   <title>Metro Motors - Make An Offer</title>
46:   <meta http-equiv="Content-Type" content="text/html; charset=iso-8859-1"/>
47:   </head>
48:
49:   <body bgcolor="#CCCCCC" text="#990000">
50:   <p><img src="/mmimage/logo.gif" width="150" height="100" align="middle"/>
51:     <b><font face="Geneva, Arial, Helvetica, san-serif">
52:     <font size="4">Metro Motors Web Site 265-4774</font></font></b></p>
53:   <form name="form2" method="post" action="page2">
54:     <input type="hidden" name="id" value="<%=l_id%>">
55:     <table width="100%" border="0">
56:     <tr>
57:       <td rowspan="4" width="46%"><a href="page2.html">
58:         <img src="/mmimage<%=l_sale_photo_location%>" width="300"
➥height="250"
59:         border="0" alt="Image Not Available"/>
60:         </a>
61:       </td>
62:       <td width="54%" height="83"><font face="Geneva, Arial,
63:         Helvetica, san-serif">
64:         <b>Description:</b>
65:         <%=l_auto_description%></font></td>
66:     </tr>
67:     <tr>
68:       <td width="54%" height="39"><font
69:         face="Geneva, Arial, Helvetica, san-serif"><b>Suggested Price:</b>
70:         <%=l_amount%></font></td>
71:     </tr>
72:     <tr>
73:           <td>
74        <p align="CENTER"><b><font
```

Listing 11.6:   continued

```
75:           face="Geneva, Arial, Helvetica, san-serif" COLOR="Fuchsia">
76:           <font size="3">
77:           <%=l_result%></font></font></b>
78:        </p>
79:        <table width="100%" border="0">
80:          <tr>
81:            <td width="33%">
82:              <div align="right">
83:              <font face="Geneva, Arial, Helvetica, san-serif"><b>Buyer
84:                Name:</b></font></div>
85:            </td>
86:              <td width="67%">
87:                <input type="text" name="buyer"
88:                maxlength="50" value="<%=l_buyer%>"/>
89:              </td>
90:          </tr>
91:          <tr>
92:            <td width="33%">
93:              <div align="right">
94:              <font face="Geneva, Arial, Helvetica, san-serif"><b>Buyer
95:                Phone:</b></font></div>
96:            </td>
97:            <td width="67%">
98:                <input type="text" name="phone"
99:                maxlength="15" value="<%=l_phone%>"/>
100:              </td>
101:          </tr>
102:          <tr>
103:            <td width="33%">
104:              <div align="right">
105:              <font face="Geneva, Arial, Helvetica, san-serif">
106:                <b>Offer:</b></font></div>
107:            </td>
108:              <td width="67%">
109:                <input type="text" name="offer"
110:                maxlength="15" value="<%=l_offer%>"/>
111:              </td>
112:          </tr>
113:          </table>
114:        </td>
115:      </tr>
116:      <tr>
117:        <td align=center width="54%">
118:          <input type="image" border="0"
119:          src="/mmimage/offer.gif" width="100" height="30" alt="Place Offer"
➥/>
```

Listing 11.6: continued

```
120:            <a href="page1?id=<%=l_id%>">
121:            <img src="/mmimage/browse.gif" width="100"
122:            height="30" border="0" alt="Browse Cars"/></a>
123:        </td>
124:    </tr>
125:  </table>
126:  </form>
127:  <p> </p>
128:  </body>
129:  </html>
```

Lines 1–2 indicate that the page is a PL/SQL page and that the procedure is to be named page2. Because this file is named page2.psp, declaring that the page is to be called page2 is redundant but a good practice anyway. Lines 3–8 are the parameters to the procedure. They are the HTML variables that will be passed from the HTML Web page. Notice that the id parameter (line 3) is NOT declared with a default value. This means that whenever this page is requested it must be requested with a parameter, in this case an inventory id. If the inventory id parameter is not passed then the default error page will be displayed.

TIP

The default error page can be overridden by declaring the name of a PSP to call in the event of an error as the following: `<%@ page language="PL/SQL" errorPage="customerror.psp"%>`.

The buyer, phone, and offer parameters are input fields on the form to fill in the name of the buyer, their contact phone, and the amount of the offer. At first glance, parameters 7 and 8 don't seem to make much sense. Lines 117–123 show that an image is being used as the submit button. When using an image as a submission button Oracle defines the image as an image map and so the coordinates of the mouse inside the image are passed to the form. Because this image is simply a label, the mouse coordinates are irrelevant, so they can be ignored, but they are necessary to define as variables so the form will process correctly when the button is pressed.

Lines 9–17 define the local variables that are used in the program. Some of the variables are defined as static types for example, VARCHAR2(15) and other types based off the column definitions. Basing your variables on database columns improves readability and avoids database runtime errors due to column sizes changing. Notice that some of the variables (id, buyer, phone, offer) are initialized with the value passed in from the parameter. Local variables are defined within the <%! %> tag.

Line 19 is the same call, get_car, that was used in page1 line 9. Line 26 checks to see if there is an offer amount or not. If there is an offer then the make_offer procedure will be called (see Appendix C for the make_offer procedure listing). The make_offer procedure returns a boolean variable into 1_success and a resulting message in 1_result (positive or negative). Line 36 uses the 1_success boolean variable. If it was successful then the local 1_buyer, 1_phone, and 1_offer variables are cleared so that they do not show up on the screen (lines 36 through 40).

Line 53 sets up an HTML form and declares that the parameters are passed to the page as post parameters instead of get parameters. So far, only get parameters have been used. When the user clicks on our submit button (the place offer button) all input values are posted to page2 for processing.

Lines 58, 65, and 70 show the same features of page1. The hard-coded values were replaced with dynamic results from the <%= %> tags. These are the same values that give the information about the car for sale.

Line 77 echoes out the 1_result variable. If an offer was attempted then some status message will be displayed. If there was no offer attempted (in other words, no value passed into the 1_offer parameter) then no message is displayed. Lines 86 through 89 create an input box for the name of the buyer. Line 88 sets the default value of the text field. Lines 97 through 100 set up an input box for the buyer's phone number. The default value for the phone number is set with the <%=1_phone%> tag. Lines 108 through 111 create the text box to accept the buyers offer amount. The default value is set in the <%= %> tag.

Lines 118 and 119 create a submit button. For the submit button, an image is used. This image is actually turned into an image map and when the image is clicked, the click is translated into an x, y coordinate that is then passed to the form as the x and y parameters. Line 120 sets up a link back to the car browsing page (page1).

Use the same `loadpsp` command (used with page1) to load the page into the database. Tools like TOAD (see Figure 11.6—using TOAD is covered in Chapter 16, "Using TOAD in the Development Arena") can then be used to view and make additional changes to the page.

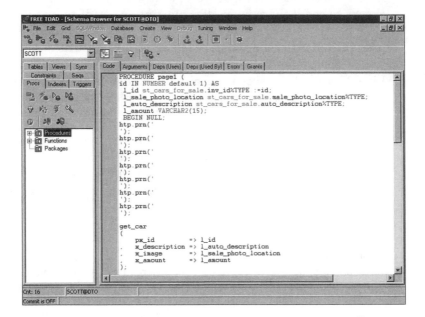

Figure 11.6: *Using TOAD with PL/SQL pages.*

Our DAD setup is now complete. We are ready to browse our page.

You can now access the new procedure with a URL something like this: http:// localhost/pls/simpledad/page1. You should see the Web page, with database access as in Figure 11.7. If you received an error or you are encountering a configuration error, check with the section earlier in this chapter about setting up the Apache Listener and Database Access Descriptors.

Because this procedure is now inside of the Oracle database, the `.psp` extension is not needed—it is not part of the procedure name inside the database. On the URL line, the `/pls/` tells the Apache Web server to use the modplsql module to process this request. The `/simpledad/` indicates which DAD to use, and the last part is the procedure being requested.

The next and previous buttons walk the user through the car inventory loaded in the ST_CARS_FOR_SALE table. The "Buy This Car" button accesses the page2 procedure, see Figure 11.8. Notice in the URL that the procedure page2 is being accessed and being passed the id of 2. As in Chapters 9 and 10, when an offer is made, it updates the ST_CARS_FOR_SALE table, see Figure 11.9.

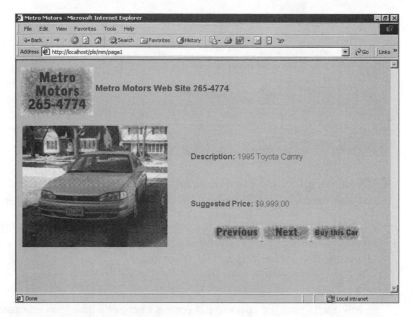

Figure 11.7: *Buy This Car—procedure page1.*

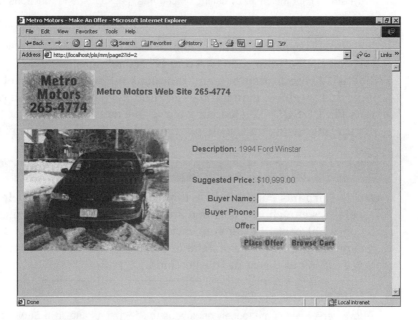

Figure 11.8: *Buy This Car—procedure page2.*

```
SQL> select * from st_cars_for_sale where inv_id = 2;

    INV_ID AUTO_DESCRIPTION
---------- ------------------------------------------------
  SALE_AMT SALE_PHOTO_LOCATION
---------- ------------------------------------------------
BUYER_NAME               BUYER_PHON BUYER_OFFER BUYER_DAT
------------------------ ---------- ----------- ---------
         2 1994 Ford Winstar
     10999 /ford_van_after.jpg
JJ                       944-8354          8999 02-AUG-01


SQL>
```

Figure 11.9: *Verify update with SQL*Plus.*

If you were to view the source (in Web browser View, Source), you would not see any of the PSP tags—the HTML looks like any other static page.

PL/SQL pages are simple but powerful. This chapter covered a simple but effective example. PSP made it easy for an Oracle developer to quickly get Oracle information out to the Internet.

TIP

PSP pages have the ability to pull code in at compile time from external files. This can be accomplished with the `<% include file="..."%>` tag. Developers can also have dynamic script inclusion by calling procedures, packages, and functions from within the PSP.

The Oracle corporation has also provided a comprehensive set of utilities that can be found in the OWA and UTL packages (see the PL/SQL Web Toolkit). These procedures and functions allow PL/SQL developers to send mail, dump tables, manage cookies, and perform other powerful Web functions via PL/SQL. The learning curve is extremely short and because it is all running inside an Oracle database the solution can scale well.

Using Java Pages

Oracle Corp has supported Java in the database since Oracle v8.0. Developers can choose between Java and PL/SQL or even use both, depending on what best fits the application. Java is well suited for Internet applications through the use of Java Servlets (see Chapter 10) and Java Server Pages (JSP, discussed in this section).

NOTE

Java server pages are loosely analogous to PSP pages and Java Servlets are analogous to PL/SQL packages.

Java is not just an Oracle language. Many computing environments as well as other database environments have embraced Java as well. You can deploy Java in the database, on the middle tier application server, in the Web server, or even on the client. With so many deployment options the complexity increases as well.

This section takes the page1 and page2 HTML (Car Inventory examples) examples from the prior section and converts them to Java Server Pages or JSP. This example will also deploy the pages in the Apache Web server that is integrated with Oracle versions 8i and 9i. You have the option of deploying these pages in Oracle 9i Application server or directly inside the Oracle database.

When the jsp pages are accessed through the Web browser the first time, the jsp page is compiled into a servlet, a java class file. This servlet is then executed.

If you look at the `ojsp.conf` file located in `$ORACLE_HOME/apache/jsp/conf/ojsp.conf`, see Listing 11.7, you can see that Apache is setup to handle jsp files. The directive on line 5 says that any page with the `.jsp` ending (or `.sqljsp` line 6) should be processed by the servlet `/servlets/oracle.jsp.JspServlet`.

EXAMPLE

Listing 11.7: Apache JSP Configuration

```
1:  # Set aliases for Oracle JSP
2:  Alias /jspdocs/ "C:\oracle\ora81\jsp\doc/"
3:  #
4:  # Associate OJSP extension with OJSP class to be called
5:  ApJServAction .jsp /servlets/oracle.jsp.JspServlet
6:  ApJServAction .sqljsp /servlets/oracle.jsp.JspServlet
7:  #
```

JSP pages are similar to PSP pages in that the idea is to separate content from presentation. Listing 11.3 shows the Page1.HTML, or the presentation, as it was designed using a HTML generator. Listing 11.8 shows the converted Page1.jsp page.

EXAMPLE

Listing 11.8: Page1.jsp Page

```
1:   <html>
2:   <head>
3:   <title>Metro Motors</title>
4:   <meta http-equiv="Content-Type" content="text/html; charset=iso-8859-1"/>
5:   </head>
6:   <jsp:usebean id="getcar" class="beans.CarGetCar" scope="page" />
7:   <jsp:setProperty name="getcar" property="id" param="id" />
8:   <body bgcolor="#CCCCCC" text="#990000">
9:   <p><img src="/mmimage/logo.gif" width="150" height="100" align="middle"/>
10:    <b><font face="Geneva, Arial, Helvetica, san-serif">
11:    <font size="4">Metro Motors Web Site 265-4774</font></font></b></p>
```

Listing 11.8:   continued

```
12:    <table width="100%" border="0">
13:      <tr>
14:        <td rowspan="3" width="46%">
15:          <img src="/mmimage<jsp:getProperty name="getcar" property="image" />"
16:             width="300" height="250"/></td>
17:        <td width="54%" height="83">
18:          <font face="Geneva, Arial, Helvetica, san-serif"><b>Description:</b>
19:          <jsp:getProperty name="getcar" property="description" /></font></td>
20:      </tr>
21:      <tr>
22:        <td width="54%" height="39">
23:          <font face="Geneva, Arial, Helvetica, san-serif"><b>Suggested
➥Price:</b>
24:            <jsp:getProperty name="getcar" property="amount" /></font></td>
25:      </tr>
26:      <tr>
27:        <td align=center width="54%">
28:          <a href="page1.jsp?id=<%=getcar.getId()-1%>">
29:          <img src="/mmimage/prev.gif" width="100" height="30" border="0"
➥alt="Previous"/>
30:          </a>
31:          <a href="page1.jsp?id=<%=getcar.getId()+1%>">
32:          <img src="/mmimage/next.gif" width="100" height="30" border="0"
➥alt="Next"/>
33:          </a>
34:          <a href="page2.jsp?id=<%=getcar.getId()%>">
35:          <img src="/mmimage/buy.gif" width="100" height="30"
36:          border="0" alt="Buy This Car"/>
37:          </a>
38:        </td>
39:      </tr>
40:    </table>
41:    </body>
42:    </html>
```

Line 6 is the first custom jsp tag. It indicates that a java bean (a Java class used to do something specific) will be used in this program. Page1.jsp uses a java bean called beans.CarGetCar. This jsp refers to this bean as getcar. The java bean code (see Appendix B) is compiled using the javac compiler and placed in the apache java classpath. The scope directive indicates the scope that the java bean should have. The default value of scope is 'page' indicating that the bean has accessibility throughout the entire page but not between pages.

NOTE

It is beyond the scope of this chapter to cover all the intricacies of Java and Java beans. I intend to provide a simple functional example to show this language in use.

NOTE

There is no reason that the code in the java bean could not be added to this or any JSP but this practice does not promote code reuse. You will notice that the java bean does nothing more than call the PL/SQL procedure used in the PSP examples.

Line 7 illustrates how to pass parameters to the java bean. In this example, the inventory id passed to the java bean via the setProperty syntax. The java bean will return values (lines 15, 19, and 24), in this example the image location, the auto description, and the sale amount.

Lines 28, 31, and 34 uses the familiar <%= %> tag to execute some generic java code. Line 28 returns the next lower inventory id, line 31 returns the next higher inventory id, and line 34 sets up the call to page2, the make offer page.

This is all the code that is necessary to convert the page1.html to java server pages. Most of the work is done via the java beans (see Appendix B for these listings). Listing 11.9 shows page2.jsp after being converted from Page2.HTML (refer to Listing 11.5).

EXAMPLE

Listing 11.9: Page1.jsp Page

```
1:    <html>
2:    <head>
3:    <title>Metro Motors - Make An Offer</title>
4:    <meta http-equiv="Content-Type" content="text/html; charset=iso-8859-1"/>
5:    </head>
6:    <jsp:usebean id="getcar" class="beans.CarGetCar" scope="page" />
7:    <jsp:setProperty name="getcar" property="id" param="id" />
8:    <jsp:usebean id="makeoffer" class="beans.MakeOffer" scope="page" />
9:    <jsp:setProperty name="makeoffer" property="id" param="id" />
10:   <jsp:setProperty name="makeoffer" property="buyer" param="buyer" />
11:   <jsp:setProperty name="makeoffer" property="phone" param="phone" />
12:   <jsp:setProperty name="makeoffer" property="offer" param="offer" />
13:
14:   <body bgcolor="#CCCCCC" text="#990000">
15:   <p><img src="/mmimage/logo.gif" width="150" height="100" align="middle"/>
16:     <b><font face="Geneva, Arial, Helvetica, san-serif">
17:     <font size="4">Metro Motors Web Site 265-4774</font></font></b></p>
18:   <form name="form2" method="post" action="page2.jsp">
19:     <input type="hidden" name="id" value="<jsp:getProperty name="makeoffer"
➥property="Id" />" />
```

Listing 11.9:   continued

```
20:     <table width="100%" border="0">
21:       <tr>
22:         <td rowspan="4" width="46%"><a href="page2.html">
23:           <img src="/mmimage<jsp:getProperty name="getcar" property="image" />"
➥width="300" height="250"
24:           border="0" alt="Image Not Available"/>
25:           </a>
26:         </td>
27:         <td width="54%" height="83"><font face="Geneva, Arial,
28:           Helvetica, san-serif">
29:           <b>Description:</b>
30:           <jsp:getProperty name="getcar" property="description" /></font></td>
31:       </tr>
32:       <tr>
33:         <td width="54%" height="39"><font
34:           face="Geneva, Arial, Helvetica, san-serif"><b>Suggested Price:</b>
35:            <jsp:getProperty name="getcar" property="amount" /></font></td>
36:       </tr>
37:       <tr>
38:             <td>
39:         <p align="CENTER"><b><font
40:           face="Geneva, Arial, Helvetica, san-serif" COLOR="Fuchsia">
41:           <font size="3">
42:           <jsp:getProperty name="makeoffer" property="Result" />
43:           </font></font></b>
44:         </p>
45:           <table width="100%" border="0">
46:             <tr>
47:               <td width="33%">
48:                 <div align="right">
49:                 <font face="Geneva, Arial, Helvetica, san-serif"><b>Buyer
50:                   Name:</b></font></div>
51:               </td>
52:                 <td width="67%">
53:                   <input type="text" name="buyer"
54:                   maxlength="50" value="<jsp:getProperty name="makeoffer"
➥property="Buyer"/>"/>
55:                 </td>
56:             </tr>
57:             <tr>
58:               <td width="33%">
59:                 <div align="right">
60:                 <font face="Geneva, Arial, Helvetica, san-serif"><b>Buyer
61:                   Phone:</b></font></div>
62:               </td>
63:               <td width="67%">
```

Listing 11.9:   continued

```
64:                    <input type="text" name="phone"
65:                    maxlength="15" value="<jsp:getProperty name="makeoffer"
➥property="Phone"/>"/>
66:                </td>
67:            </tr>
68:            <tr>
69:              <td width="33%">
70:                <div align="right">
71:                <font face="Geneva, Arial, Helvetica, san-serif">
72:                <b>Offer:</b></font></div>
73:              </td>
74:              <td width="67%">
75:                    <input type="text" name="offer"
76:                    maxlength="15" value="<jsp:getProperty name="makeoffer"
➥property="Offer"/>"/>
77:                </td>
78:            </tr>
79:          </table>
80:        </td>
81:      </tr>
82:      <tr>
83:        <td align="center" width="54%">
84:          <input type="image" border="0"
85:          src="/mmimage/offer.gif" width="100" height="30" alt="Place Offer"
➥/>
86:            <a href="page1.jsp?id=<%=getcar.getId()%>">
87:            <img src="/mmimage/browse.gif" width="100"
88:            height="30" border="0" alt="Browse Cars"/></a>
89:        </td>
90:      </tr>
91:    </table>
92:    </form>
93:    <p> </p>
94:    </body>
95:    </html>
```

Lines 6 and 7 are the same as in page1.jsp (Listing 11.8) in the use of the java bean CarGetCar, passing it the inventory id. Lines 8 through 12 make use of a second java bean called beans.MakeOffer (see Appendix B for code examples). Lines 9 through 12 setup the needed properties for the makeoffer java bean.

NOTE

If the parameters were not passed to the page then the null string is passed onto the java bean.

Line 18 sets up the page2 HTML form to call page2.jsp and passes the parameters to the page with the post method. Page1.jsp (see line 15 for example) used the get method to retrieve parameters. The post method is just another way to pass parameters.

Line 19 sets a hidden input id field to the id property of the makeoffer java bean. Lines 23, 30, and 35 get the item properties from the java bean getcar and dynamically fill in the values. Notice the alt or alternate option on line 23. If no value is returned then this text will appear.

Line 42 gets the result property of the makeoffer bean. If there was no offer entered then no message is returned. If an offer was attempted then either a success or failure message will be returned.

Lines 54, 65, and 76 put default values into input text fields from the makeoffer java bean.

Lines 84 and 85 set up the Submit button. Clicking on this image submits the form, passing in all the input values. Line 86 is a link back to page1.jsp, the car browse page. The <%= %> tags are used to retrieve some value from java.

Figures 11.10 and 11.11 illustrate page1 and page2 jsp pages. Because the same HTML page was used, note the similarities in the appearance. Also note the URL line, Figures 11.10 and 11.11 call the jsp Apache module and both URLs have the .jsp suffix on the jsp page name.

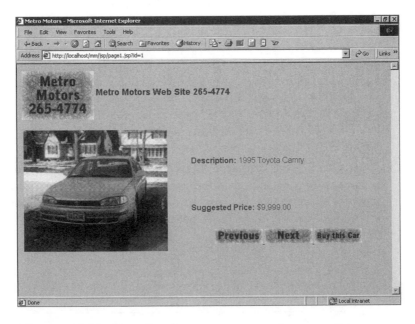

Figure 11.10: *View Car Inventory—procedure page1.jsp.*

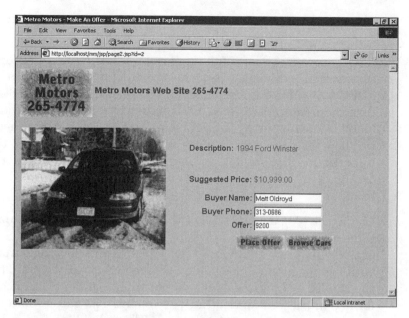

Figure 11.11: *Buy This Car—procedure page2.jsp.*

Java Server Pages offer an incredible depth and breadth of functionality for developers—including session management and custom tag libraries (beyond the scope of this section). Because these JSP pages are in fact java code, they can be moved and executed where it makes the most sense. If the JSP pages are database intensive then the page can be stored and executed directly from inside of the Oracle JVM. The pages can also reside on the same server as the database server, inside Oracle 9iAS, or in any JSP compatible environment.

The learning curve for Java is quite a bit higher than for PL/SQL. Entire books are devoted to this topic including "Special Edition Using Java 2 Standard Edition," ISBN: 0-7897-2468-5, published by Que.

Using XML

Oracle9i has adapted XML to the database much as Oracle8 did with Java. XML is a HTML like language that is very useful in formatting data for all kinds of environments such as the Web and wireless devices. Oracle's implementation of XML is easy to use and can easily be incorporated with other languages such as PL/SQL, Java, and C++. Oracle has also used their own technology to create another Web page-generating facility called XSQL pages. These XSQL pages are simple to use and allow developers to easily get started with XML.

This final section will build a Web site using XML and then will adapt the same example for use with a cellular phone.

XSQL pages make use of the xsql servlet that Oracle developed. This servlet enables the user to connect to an Oracle database (actually any JDBC accessible database will do) and take the results of SQL queries and turn them into well-formed XML documents. This XML document can then be translated using XML Stylsheets (XSLT). These style sheets in turn control how the output will appear and on what kind of device the output is intended for. The servlet can also be used from the computer command line or from a java program to emit structured (or unstructured) data in any form.

Listing 11.10 is a simple query that produces an XML document that contains all the cars in our inventory. Figure 11.12 shows the SQL*Plus output of the SQL query and Figure 11.13 illustrates what the output looks like with the command line syntax: `xsql.bat inventory.xsql`. The output from the servlet is the same as the output from SQL*Plus but it has been transformed into a well-formed XML document. The output data is enclosed in `<ROWSET><ROW></ROW></ROWSET>` tags. The individual data values are further delimited by tags named after their column name.

EXAMPLE

Listing 11.10:   Simple XML Program—`inventory.xsql`

```
 1:  <?XML version='1.0'?>
 2:  <xsql:query XMLns:xsql="urn:oracle-xsql" connection="scott">
 3:     SELECT inv_id
 4:     , auto_description
 5:     , sale_photo_location
 6:     , sale_amt
 7:     FROM st_cars_for_sale
 8:     ORDER BY inv_id
 9:
10:  </xsql:query>
```

NOTE

The Web server knows how to process the xsql pages through the directive found in the `$ORACLE_HOME/xdk/admin/XML.conf` file as follows:

```
#
# Associate .xsql extension to XSQL Servlet
ApJServAction .xsql /servlets/oracle.xml.xsql.XSQLServlet
#
```

This directive says that any file ending in .xsql should be processed with the XSQLServlet servlet.

```
SQL>    SELECT inv_id
  2     , auto_description
  3     , sale_photo_location
  4     , sale_amt
  5     FROM st_cars_for_sale
  6     ORDER BY inv_id
  7  /

    INV_ID AUTO_DESCRIPTION
---------- ---------------------------------
SALE_PHOTO_LOCATION                              SALE_AMT
------------------------------------------- ----------
         1 1995 Toyota Camry
/camry_after.jpg                                     9999

         2 1994 Ford Winstar
/ford_van_after.jpg                                 10999

         3 1965 Ford Galaxie V8 Automatic
/galaxie.jpg                                         3000


    INV_ID AUTO_DESCRIPTION
---------- ---------------------------------
SALE_PHOTO_LOCATION                              SALE_AMT
------------------------------------------- ----------
```

Figure 11.12: *SQL*Plus simple query illustration.*

Figure 11.13: *Inventory.xsql output example.*

Because XSQL pages are themselves XML documents they must be well formed and follow the rules for any XML document. In Listing 11.10, the XML tag <? ?> tells the parser to follow version 1 XML standards. The second line defines the namespace of the document to be urn:oracle-xsql. If this namespace is not named exactly then the servlet will not understand what to do with the tags and will most likely emit nothing. The attribute connection="scott" indicates a named database connection to use.

This named connection is defined in the `$ORACLE_HOME/xdk/lib/XSQLConfig.xml` file (see Listing 11.11). This file contains a number of parameters that the XSQL servlet uses to define its operating parameters. In the `<connectiondefs>` tag there are a number of "example" connections. Define one with the username, password, jdbc driver url, and the name of the database driver for your examples.

TIP

Oracle's XDK is geared to work with Oracle databases but could easily be used with other databases as well as long as they have a JDBC driver for it.

EXAMPLE

Listing 11.11: `XSQLConfig.xml` File

```
<connectiondefs>

  <connection name="demo">
    <username>scott</username>
    <password>tiger</password>
    <dburl>jdbc:oracle:thin:@localhost:1521:ORCL</dburl>
    <driver>oracle.jdbc.driver.OracleDriver</driver>
  </connection>
  ...
    <connection name="scott">
      <username>scott</username>
      <password>tiger</password>
      <dburl>jdbc:oracle:thin:@localhost:1521:dto</dburl>
      <driver>oracle.jdbc.driver.OracleDriver</driver>
    </connection>

</connectiondefs>
```

In Listing 11.10, lines 3 through 9 are simply the SQL query. The query can be as simple or complex as need be and you will learn later how to use parameters. Other things it can also do is execute stored procedures, insert/update/delete data, return only the first N rows, return rows x-y, and generally do most anything (with user defined actions—see Oracle XDK documentation complete details). Line 10 is the closing tag to the XML page.

Any query that is executed using this XML servlet will return the same ROWSET-ROW tag combination. Do not think of this as a limitation but do think of it as a standardization of output. Now SML stylesheets can be applied to the SQL page and turn the data into any format desired.

The first thing to notice is that XML looks a whole lot like HTML. HTML is not nearly as strict about closing tags and the browser manufacturers quickly adapted and made their browsers less strict in how they parsed the HTML.

TIP

There is a utility that cleans up html files, it is called tidy and can be found at http://www.w3.org/People/Raggett/tidy.

XML is very unforgiving in that all tags are case sensitive and all tags must have ending tags. Unfortunately the programs that generated the page1.html (Listing 11.3) and page2.html (Listing 11.5) are less-than-perfect and many of the closing tags are missing. These will need to be fixed before proceeding to XML.

Before starting on a XML document with a XSLT stylesheet, the page1.html and page2.html need to be valid XML documents. We need our template (page1.html, page2.html) to be a valid XML document.

Page1.html will be the template for the transformation. It has been renamed to page1.xsl and has some minor changes made to it, see Listing 11.12.

EXAMPLE

Listing 11.12:   Page1.xsl

```
1:   <html xsl:version="1.0" XMLns:xsl="http://www.w3.org/1999/XSL/Transform">
2:   <head>
3:   <title>Metro Motors</title>
4:   <meta http-equiv="Content-Type" content="text/html; charset=iso-8859-1"/>
5:   </head>
6:   <body bgcolor="#CCCCCC" text="#990000">
7:   <xsl:for-each select="RESULTS/CAR">
8:   <p><img src="/mmimage/logo.gif" width="150" height="100" align="middle"/>
9:     <b><font face="Geneva, Arial, Helvetica, san-serif">
10:     <font size="4">Metro Motors Web Site 265-4774</font></font></b></p>
11:   <table width="100%" border="0">
12:     <tr>
13:       <td rowspan="3" width="46%">
14:         <img src="/mmimage{IMAGE}" width="300" height="250"/></td>
15:       <td width="54%" height="83">
16:         <font face="Geneva, Arial, Helvetica, san-serif"><b>Description:</b>
17:         <xsl:value-of select="DESCRIPTION"/></font></td>
18:     </tr>
19:     <tr>
20:       <td width="54%" height="39">
21:         <font face="Geneva, Arial, Helvetica, san-serif"><b>Suggested
➥Price:</b>
22:          <xsl:value-of select="AMOUNT"/></font></td>
23:     </tr>
24:     <tr>
25:       <td align="center" width="54%">
26:         <a href="page1.xsql?id={ID+ (-1)}">
```

Listing 11.12: continued

```
27:            <img src="/mmimage/prev.gif" width="100" height="30" border="0"
⮩alt="Previous"/>
28:            </a>
29:            <a href="page1.xsql?id={ID+1}">
30:            <img src="/mmimage/next.gif" width="100" height="30" border="0"
⮩alt="Next"/>
31:            </a>
32:            <a href="page2.xsql?id={ID}">
33:            <img src="/mmimage/buy.gif" width="100" height="30"
34:            border="0" alt="Buy This Car"/>
35:            </a>
36:         </td>
37:      </tr>
38:   </table>
39:   </xsl:for-each>
40:   </body>
41:   </html>
```

Line 1 starts off with the HTML tag. It has a few attributes that are not found in most HTML pages, such as the version of XSL being used and the namespace for the HTML pages.

Line 4 contains some meta data being sent with the header of the HTML page. This tells the browser to treat the results of this page as mime type text/html and also tells the browser which character set to use.

Line 7 introduces a new XSLT tag—the for-each tag. The for-each tag is basically the looping construct that XSLT uses to search through the raw XML document. The for-each is not wide open so a search path needs to be supplied for it to search for elements. Otherwise it will just take the 1 instance of the root document. In this example all the tags under RESULTS/ CAR tags are desired.

Lines 14 and 17 show how to pull dynamic XML data from the XML query and put it into this template. The first method illustrated by line 14 is where you are inside quoted text, {tagname}. Line 17 shows how to pull information for a regular text node.

TIP

Use the {XPATH} notation to pull dynamic data from inside a static attribute tag. XPATH is the W3C standard XML declarative query language. It defines how to select interesting subsets of XML information from within an XML file.

Line 22 selects the suggested price (AMOUNT) from the XML query document. Lines 26, 29, and 32 again show use of XPATH expressions to pull data from inside an attribute. The XPATH language allows us to perform mathematical operations on the result before emitting the final result. Notice the href setting up the previous (line 26) and next (line 29) buttons and the page2.xsql reference on line 32. This is setting up the link to the previous and next car in the inventory and allowing the user to navigate to the offer page (page2.xsql).

These are all the changes that are required to make the page1.xsl stylesheet.

The data page that generates this XML document is illustrated in Listing 11.13, data.xsql.

EXAMPLE

Listing 11.13: Data.xsql

```
1:  <?XML version="1.0" encoding='ISO-8859-1'?>
2:
3:  <RESULTS XMLns:xsql="urn:oracle-xsql" connection="scott" id="1">
4:  <xsql:include-owa>
5:  get_car_XML({@id});
6:  </xsql:include-owa>
7:
8:  </RESULTS>
```

Line 3 sets up the XSQL namespace and tells Oracle to use the "scott" connection. The attribute id="1" sets up a default value for the id parameter. If a value for ID is passed in then it overrides the default but if nothing is passed in then ID will take the default value of 1 and passes it to the function get_car_XML on line 5.

Line 4 shows the use of the include-owa action element. The include-owa element allows the use of PL/SQL skills inside a procedure to produce any arbitrary XML document. The include-owa element can be used any time that the desired results cannot be created from a query or queries. The get_car_XML (see the listing in Appendix B) procedure makes use of the get_car PL/SQL procedure used with the PSP earlier in this chapter. XML is used to create an XML page that looks like Listing 11.14.

EXAMPLE

Listing 11.14: Output from Data.xsl (Listing 11.14)

```
<RESULTS>
<CAR>
<ID>1</ID>
<DESCRIPTION>1995 Toyota Camry</DESCRIPTION>
<IMAGE>/camry_after.jpg</IMAGE>
<AMOUNT>9999</AMOUNT>
</CAR>
</RESULTS>
```

Now all that is needed is to combine this data (Listing 11.14) with the stylesheet. Listing 11.15 brings all the pieces together as page1.xsql.

Notice that the page1.xsl is referenced in line 2 and that the data.xsql is referenced in line 3. Figure 11.14 illustrates the output results from Page1.xsql. Notice the URL line, calling the Page1.xsql directly.

Listing 11.15: Page1.xsql

```
1:  <?XML version="1.0" encoding='ISO-8859-1'?>
2:  <?XML-stylesheet type="text/xsl" href="page1.xsl"?>
3:  <xsql:include-xsql href="data.xsql" XMLns:xsql="urn:oracle-xsql"/>
```

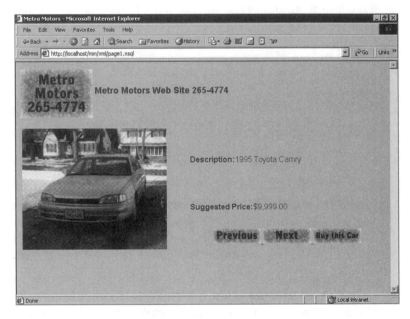

Figure 11.14: Page1.xsql output example.

Use the same method from page1.xsql for page2.xsql. First, create the data2.xsql as illustrated in Listing 11.16.

Listing 11.16: data2.xsql

```
1:   <?XML version="1.0" encoding='ISO-8859-1'?>
2:   <RESULTS XMLns:xsql="urn:oracle-xsql" connection="scott" id="1">
3:
4:   <xsql:include-owa>
5:   get_car_XML({@id});
6:   </xsql:include-owa>
7:
8:   <xsql:include-owa>
9:   make_offer_XML(
10:     {@id}
11:   , '{@buyer}'
12:   , '{@phone}'
```

Listing 11.16: continued

```
13:    , '{@offer}'
14:    );
15:    </xsql:include-owa>
16:
17:  </RESULTS>
```

Listing 11.16 looks very similar to data.xsql, Listing 11.13. The only difference is that data2.xsql is passing parameters to the make_offer_XML procedure (see Appendix B for the make_offer_XML listing).

Lines 5, 10, 11, 12, and 13 use the XPATH expressions: {@}. These expressions are how parameters are used. Notice that on line 2 the only default
parameter is id=1. All the other parameters must either be passed in to the
page or NULL will be passed. The output XML page from data2.xsql looks
like Listing 11.17.

Line 6 is another xsql action element that directs the page to include all
the requested parameters into the page. It creates the tag illustrated in
Listing 11.18.

EXAMPLE

Listing 11.17: Output from Data2.xsql

```
<PAGE>
<RESULTS id="1">
<CAR>
<ID>1</ID>
<DESCRIPTION>1995 Toyota Camry</DESCRIPTION>
<IMAGE>/camry_after.jpg</IMAGE>
<AMOUNT>$9,999.00</AMOUNT>
</CAR>
<OFFER />
</RESULTS>
<request>
<id>1</id>
<parameters />
<session />
<cookies />
</request>
</PAGE>
```

Now this data page needs to be transformed into HTML with the Page2.xsl
stylesheet that was modified from the original Page2.html (back in Listing
11.5). Listing 11.18 illustrates the Page2.xsl stylesheet.

Listing 11.18: Page2.xsl

```
1:    <html xsl:version="1.0" XMLns:xsl="http://www.w3.org/1999/XSL/Transform">
2:    <head>
3:    <title>Metro Motors - Make An Offer</title>
4:    <meta http-equiv="Content-Type" content="text/html; charset=iso-8859-1"/>
5:    </head>
6:    <xsl:variable name="updateresult" select="PAGE/RESULTS/OFFER"/>
7:    <xsl:variable name="buyer" select="PAGE/request/parameters/buyer"/>
8:    <xsl:variable name="phone" select="PAGE/request/parameters/phone"/>
9:    <xsl:variable name="offer" select="PAGE/request/parameters/offer"/>
10:   <body bgcolor="#CCCCCC" text="#990000">
11:   <xsl:for-each select="PAGE/RESULTS/CAR">
12:   <p><img src="/mmimage/logo.gif" width="150" height="100" align="middle"/>
13:     <b><font face="Geneva, Arial, Helvetica, san-serif">
14:     <font size="4">Metro Motors Web Site 265-4774</font></font></b></p>
15:   <form name="form2" method="post" action="page2.xsql">
16:     <input type="hidden" name="id" value="{ID}"/>
17:     <table width="100%" border="0">
18:     <tr>
19:       <td rowspan="4" width="46%"><a href="page2.html">
20:         <img src="/mmimage{IMAGE}" width="300" height="250"
21:         border="0" alt="Image Not Available"/>
22:         </a>
23:       </td>
24:       <td width="54%" height="83"><font face="Geneva, Arial,
25:         Helvetica, san-serif">
26:         <b>Description:</b>
27:         <xsl:value-of select="DESCRIPTION"/></font></td>
28:     </tr>
29:     <tr>
30:       <td width="54%" height="39"><font
31:         face="Geneva, Arial, Helvetica, san-serif"><b>Suggested Price:</b>
32:          <xsl:value-of select="AMOUNT"/></font></td>
33:     </tr>
34:     <tr>
35:           <td>
36:       <p align="CENTER"><b><font
37:         face="Geneva, Arial, Helvetica, san-serif" COLOR="Fuchsia">
38:         <font size="3">
39:         <xsl:value-of select="$updateresult"/></font></font></b>
40:       </p>
41:         <table width="100%" border="0">
42:           <tr>
43:             <td width="33%">
44:                <div align="right">
45:                <font face="Geneva, Arial, Helvetica, san-serif"><b>Buyer
```

Listing 11.18: continued

```
46:                    Name:</b></font></div>
47:                </td>
48:                <td width="67%">
49:                    <input type="text" name="buyer"
50:                    maxlength="50" value="{$buyer}"/>
51:                </td>
52:            </tr>
53:            <tr>
54:                <td width="33%">
55:                    <div align="right">
56:                    <font face="Geneva, Arial, Helvetica, san-serif"><b>Buyer
57:                    Phone:</b></font></div>
58:                </td>
59:                <td width="67%">
60:                    <input type="text" name="phone"
61:                    maxlength="15" value="{$phone}"/>
62:                </td>
63:            </tr>
64:            <tr>
65:                <td width="33%">
66:                    <div align="right">
67:                    <font face="Geneva, Arial, Helvetica, san-serif">
68:                    <b>Offer:</b></font></div>
69:                </td>
70:                <td width="67%">
71:                    <input type="text" name="offer"
72:                    maxlength="15" value="{$offer}"/>
73:                </td>
74:            </tr>
75:            </table>
76:        </td>
77:    </tr>
78:    <tr>
79:        <td align="center" width="54%">
80:            <input type="image" border="0"
81:            src="/mmimage/offer.gif" width="100" height="30" alt="Place Offer" >
82:            <a href="page1.xsql?id={ID}">
83:            <img src="/mmimage/browse.gif" width="100"
84:            height="30" border="0" alt="Browse Cars"/></a>
85:            </input>
86:        </td>
87:    </tr>
88:    </table>
89:    </form>
90  <p> </p>
```

Listing 11.18: continued

```
91:     </xsl:for-each>
92:   </body>
93: </html>
```

Lines 6 through 9 create and use stylesheet variables. They use XPATH queries against the data page to populate the variables.

Line 39 then uses one of these variables in the XPATH. Variables are referenced by using the $ prefix.

Lines 50, 61, and 72 use the input parameters as default values for the text boxes. Notice how the input length from the user is controlled.

The Page2.XSQL (see Listing 11.19) brings all the pieces together and produces the output in Figure 11.15.

EXAMPLE

Listing 11.19: Page2.xsql

```
1: <?XML version="1.0" encoding='ISO-8859-1'?>
2: <?XML-stylesheet type="text/xsl" href="page2.xsl"?>
4: <PAGE XMLns:xsql="urn:oracle-xsql">
5: <xsql:include-xsql href="data2.xsql"/>
6: <xsql:include-request-params/>
7: </PAGE>
```

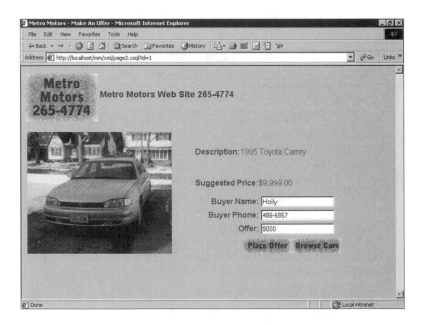

Figure 11.15: *Page2.xsql output example.*

XML for Wireless Devices

Part of the promise of XML is that it can easily transform data from one format to another. The remainder of this chapter shows how to display this information upon a cell phone or a PDA (personal data assistant) using WML and WML stylesheets.

The XSQL solution has proven to successfully separate the data from the presentation of the data. All that is needed now is a different stylesheet, one that creates WML presentation (for wireless devices) instead of HTML presentation.

For this example, the WML examples for page1 and page2 will be page1w.xsl and page2w.xsl respectively. All that is needed now are new WML stylesheets and a small modification to the page1.xsql and page2.xsql scripts.

All we need to do to support our WML phones is create our stylesheets and make a modification to our driving page1.xsql (see Listing 11.20) and page2.xsql (see Listing 11.21).

EXAMPLE

Listing 11.20:   Page1.xsql Modified for WML

```
1:   <?XML version="1.0" encoding='ISO-8859-1'?>
2:   <?XML-stylesheet type="text/xsl" href="page1.xsl" media="MSIE"?>
3:   <?XML-stylesheet type="text/xsl" href="page1w.xsl" media="UP"?>
4:   <xsql:include-xsql href="data.xsql" XMLns:xsql="urn:oracle-xsql"/>
```

Notice that the only differences are on line 2 and line 3 where the stylesheet is declared. Notice the media="MSIE" on line 2 and media="UP" on line 4. When a browser makes a request it sends a user-agent string as part of the header. XSQL pages compare the user-agent string with the media value. If the media value is found in the string then that stylesheet is used. Line 2 says that if the user-agent string contains MSIE then use the page1.xsl stylesheet.

NOTE

Both Netscape and Microsoft Explorer have MSIE in their user-agent string so they will use the standard html stylesheet presented here.

EXAMPLE

Listing 11.21:   Page2.xsql Modified for WML

```
<?XML version="1.0" encoding='ISO-8859-1'?>
<PAGE XMLns:xsql="urn:oracle-xsql">
<?XML-stylesheet type="text/xsl" href="page2.xsl" media="MSIE"?>
<?XML-stylesheet type="text/xsl" href="page2w.xsl" media="UP"?>
<xsql:include-xsql href="data2.xsql"/>
<xsql:include-request-params/>
</PAGE>
```

The phone that has been chosen to support this example is from www. phone.com (openwave system sdk) and it sends UP as part of its user-agent string so the cell phone will use the page1w.xsl stylesheet.

Now all that is left to support WML is to come up with appropriate stylesheets. Cell phones cannot handle the graphics and colors (yet anyway) as in html. These types of items are removed and the page1.xsl is formatted to WAP/WML standards. The resulting page1w.xsl stylesheet is illustrated in Listing 11.22, page2w.xsl stylesheet is illustrated in Listing 11.23.

EXAMPLE

Listing 11.22: Page1w.sxl WML Stylesheet

```
<xsl:stylesheet XMLns:xsl="http://www.w3.org/1999/XSL/Transform" version="1.0">
<xsl:output method="XML" doctype-public="-//WAPFORUM//DTD WML 1.1//EN"
    media-type="text/vnd.wap.wml" doctype-system="http://www.wapforum.org/DTD/
    wml_1.1.xml" />
<xsl:template match="/">
<wml>
<card id="page1" title="Metro Motors Cars">
<p><b>Metro Motors:</b></p>
<xsl:for-each select="RESULTS/CAR">
<p><xsl:value-of select="DESCRIPTION"/></p>
<p>Price:$<xsl:value-of select="AMOUNT"/></p>
<p align="center">
<anchor><go><xsl:attribute name="href">
page1.xsql?id=<xsl:value-of select="ID - 1"/></xsl:attribute> </go>
Prev   </anchor>
<anchor><go><xsl:attribute name="href">
page1.xsql?id=<xsl:value-of select="ID + 1"/></xsl:attribute> </go>
Next</anchor>
</p>
<p align="center">
<anchor><go><xsl:attribute name="href">
page2.xsql?id=<xsl:value-of select="ID + 0"/></xsl:attribute> </go>
Make Offer</anchor>
</p>

</xsl:for-each>
</card>
</wml>
</xsl:template>
</xsl:stylesheet>
```

EXAMPLE

Listing 11.23: Page2w.sxl WML Stylesheet

```
<xsl:stylesheet XMLns:xsl="http://www.w3.org/1999/XSL/Transform" version="1.0">
<xsl:output method="XML" doctype-public="-//WAPFORUM//DTD WML 1.1//EN" media-
type=
    "text/vnd.wap.wml" doctype-system="http://www.wapforum.org/DTD/wml_1.1.xml"
```

Listing 11.23:   continued

```
/>
<xsl:template match="/">
<wml>
<xsl:variable name="ID" select="PAGE/request/parameters/id"/>
<xsl:variable name="buyer" select="PAGE/request/parameters/buyer"/>
<xsl:variable name="phone" select="PAGE/request/parameters/phone"/>
<xsl:variable name="offer" select="PAGE/request/parameters/offer"/>
<card>
<p><b>Metro Motors Offer:</b></p>
<p><b><xsl:value-of select="PAGE/RESULTS/OFFER"/></b></p>
<xsl:for-each select="PAGE/RESULTS/CAR">
<p><xsl:value-of select="DESCRIPTION"/></p>
<p>Price:$<xsl:value-of select="AMOUNT"/></p>
<p>
Buyer: <input name="buyer" size="10"/><br/>
Phone: <input name="phone" size="10"/><br/>
Offer: <input name="offer" size="10" format="*N"/><br/>
</p>
<p align="center">
<anchor><go><xsl:attribute name="href">
page1.xsql?id=<xsl:value-of select="ID + 0"/></xsl:attribute> </go>
Browse   </anchor>
<anchor>
<go href="page2.xsql" method="post">
<postfield name="id" value="{$ID}" />
<postfield name="buyer" value="$(buyer)" />
<postfield name="phone" value="$(phone)" />
<postfield name="offer" value="$(offer)" />
</go>
Make Offer</anchor>
</p>

</xsl:for-each>
</card>
</wml>
</xsl:template>
</xsl:stylesheet>
```

WML documents must be valid XML documents and have special tags of their own that don't conform to the HTML standard. Discussing WML is beyond the scope of this book. Additional WML information is available at www.phone.com.

The results of running these pages through the www.phone.com cellular phone emulator can be seen in Figures 11.16 and 11.17.

Figure 11.16: Page1s.xsql *output example.*

Figure 11.17: Page2w.xsql *output example.*

Oracle XSQL pages are very powerful. XSQL allows you to truly separate data from presentation. XSLT and XPATH make translating data into any format easy. XML can be manipulated through the XSQL servlet, Java, PL/SQL, and any combination thereof. This section is intended to give you a functioning example, once again, entire books are devoted to XML including "XML by Example," ISBN: 0-7897-2504-5, also published by Que.

Summary

Hopefully you have a better understanding of PL/SQL pages, Java Server Pages, and to XML. This chapter also covered important Apache configuration issues such as Database Access Descriptors and virtual to physical directory mappings.

REVIEW

Reviewing It

1. What is a PL/SQL Page?

2. Why would you want to use PL/SQL procedures in a JSP?

3. What are Apache Virtual Directories useful for?

4. What does DAD stand for and what is it useful for?

5. What is the purpose of JSP and PSP?

6. What is a Java Bean?

7. What functions are used in JSPs to pass parameters?

8. What is the purpose of a stylesheet?

CHECK

Checking It

1. JSP stands for

    a) Java Servlet Pages

    b) Java Server Procedures

    c) Java Servlet Procedures

    d) Java Server Pages

2. XML can only create HTML pages.

    True/False

3. The following syntax, `Alias /icons/ "C:\oracle\ora81\Apache\Apache\icons/"` is from which Apache configuration file:

    a) `ojsp.conf`

    b) Httpd.conf

    c) Page1.xsl

    d) Xml.conf

4. The `<% %>` tags are found in what syntax:

    a) PSP

    b) JSP

    c) XSP

    d) WML

5. What does XSQL produce?

    a) HTML

    b) JSP

    c) XML

    d) WML

6. The `<? ?>` tags are found in what syntax:

    a) PSP

    b) JSP

    c) XSP

    d) XML

7. XML stylesheets read XML data pages.

    True/False

APPLY

Applying It

Independent Exercise 1:

- Download the Chapter 11 examples from www.quepublishing.com.

- Build the PL/SQL procedures getcar and makeoffer.

- Build a simple PSP that gets the first record from getcar.

Independent Exercise 2:

- Download the java bean programs from www.quepublishing.com.

- Compile the java bean programs.

- Build a simple JSP that gets the first record from getcar.

Independent Exercise 3:

- Download the cell phone emulator from www.phone.com.

- Build a simple XML application using the following query:

```
Select DNAME, SUM(SAL)
From EMP, DEPT
Where EMP.DEPTNO = DEPT.DEPTNO
```

What's Next?

Chapter 12, "Using Portal v3.0 (WebDB) Web Development Software," focuses on Web Development using the Oracle Portal v3.0 software. You learn how to build user-personalized dynamic Web pages, build portlets to be added to portal Web pages, and cover some of the administrative features of the portal environment.

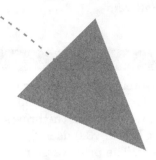

Using Portal v3.0 (WebDB) Web Development Software

Portal v3.0 is the next generation of Web-based development from Oracle Corp. WebDB is the prior version product name. Portal v3.0 is useful in Web-based database administration, database and Web-based application monitoring, Web-based forms access, and content-oriented Web sites.

This chapter teaches you the following:

- What is Portal v3.0?
- Using the Portal software for Database Administration
- Creating Web-based applications using Portal
- Creating Web sites using Portal

What Is Portal v3.0/WebDB?

Portal v3.0 has its own listener process with an integrated PL/SQL cartridge. Basically, Portal v3.0 generates HTML-related PL/SQL behind the scenes. Figure 12.1 illustrates how Portal v3.0 interacts with the browser community and the Oracle database. Notice that Portal v3.0 uses the Oracle9iAS environment to do all its management. The prior version, WebDB, had its own listener and you had to set up database access descriptors but because Portal v3.0 is integrated with Oracle9iAS, these features are all handled and contained within Oracle9iAS. Because Portal v3.0 is integrated with Oracle9iAS, it is also dependent upon Oracle9iAS and cannot run with prior versions of the Oracle Web Server products.

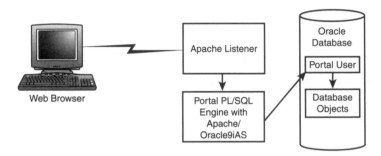

Figure 12.1: Portal v3.0 architecture.

NOTE

The URL to access Portal v3.0 is http://<hostname> or IP address/pls/portal30. The default administrator user id portal30, password is portal30.

Portal v3.0 Administration

Portal v3.0 has many administrative and monitoring capabilities. It can monitor tablespaces and Web-based application activity, and so on, and perform basic database-administration tasks such as create users, assign privileges, and so on. Figure 12.2 and Figure 12.3 show some of the database monitoring capabilities of Portal v3.0. Figure 12.4 illustrates some of the Web monitoring available with Portal v3.0. All the Portal monitoring capabilities are under the Monitor tab of the Portal Main Menu.

It is also easy to perform administrative tasks such as adding a user, changing a user password, and adding datafiles to the database.

To add a user, start with the Portal Main Menu Administer tab (see Figure 12.5). Click Create New User, which takes you to the next screen, where you can fill in the Portal Application Name, user name, password, and so on. If you wanted to change a password for a user, you would select Edit User, just under the Create New User item. All the administrative features of Portal v3.0 are under the Administer and Administer Database tabs.

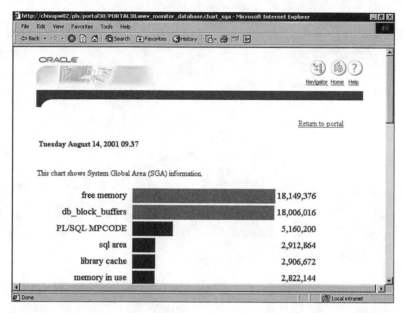

Figure 12.2: *SGA monitoring.*

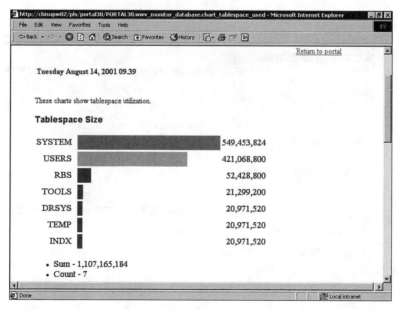

Figure 12.3: *Tablespace monitoring.*

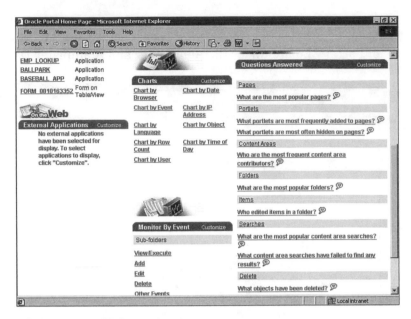

Figure 12.4: *Web monitoring.*

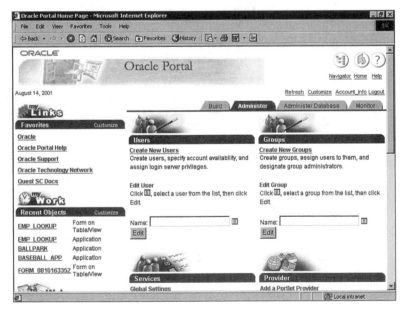

Figure 12.5: *Adding users.*

Using Portal v3.0 to Build Applications

Portal v3.0 is capable of producing Web-based forms to access various data objects in the Oracle database. Portal v3.0 is also capable of creating and maintaining content-oriented Web sites.

NOTE

A content-oriented Web site is one where everything displayed upon a browser is pre-determined, with no direct access to information in the database.

Creating a Portal v3.0 Application

Select Create a New Application from the Portal Main Menu Build tab. On the next screen, click Create New...Form from the Applications tab. Notice all the different kinds of things that can be built using Portal (see Figure 12.6). Select Form based on table or view and this will begin a seven-step wizard that will build a basic but functional forms-based application. Give this application a name and click Next>. Step 2 of 7 and the wizard asks you to choose a table or view. Continue through the wizard, selecting the table/view (SCOTT.EMP in this example), select a tabular form layout, accept the forms and validation options defaults, on Form Text select PUBLIC.SKY_TEMPLATE and a display name of Employee Lookup. There is no PL/SQL code to add at this time so click to continue and you should now see that the application has been build and its options in Figure 12.7. Notice that any primary keys appear in red.

By default, there are three buttons that allow you to insert new records, look up existing records, or reset the form to its default options. To lookup rows in the database, fill in any search criteria (see Figure 12.8) and click the Query button. This searches for the record and changes the button options, as illustrated in Figure 12.9.

NOTE

This application is actually a PL/SQL routine in the database. The URL to access this new application is //http:/<host name or IP address/pls/portal30/ <application name>.

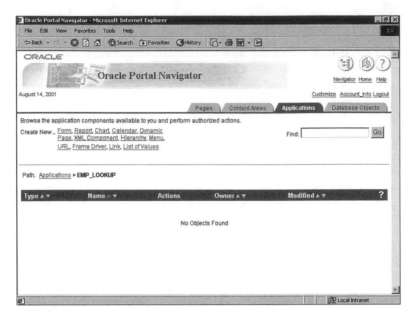

Figure 12.6: *Portal v3.0 form building.*

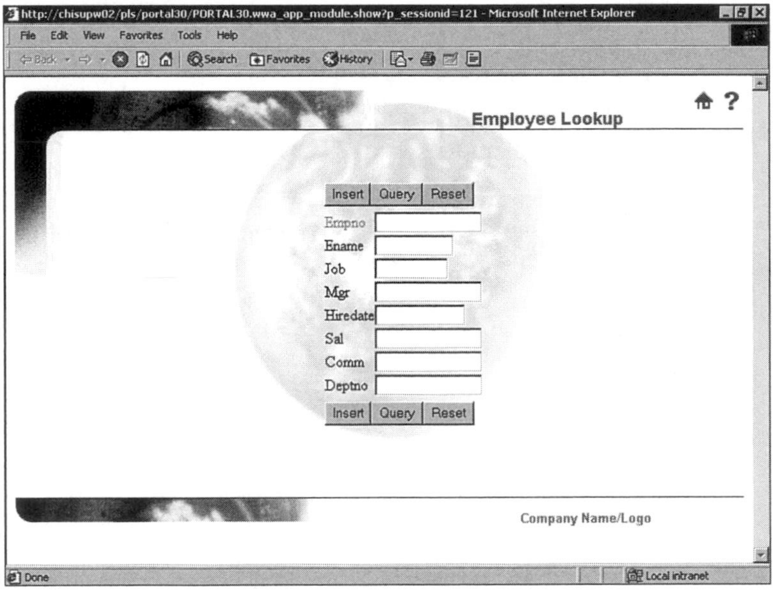

Figure 12.7: *Portal v3.0 tabular form on Table SCOTT.EMP.*

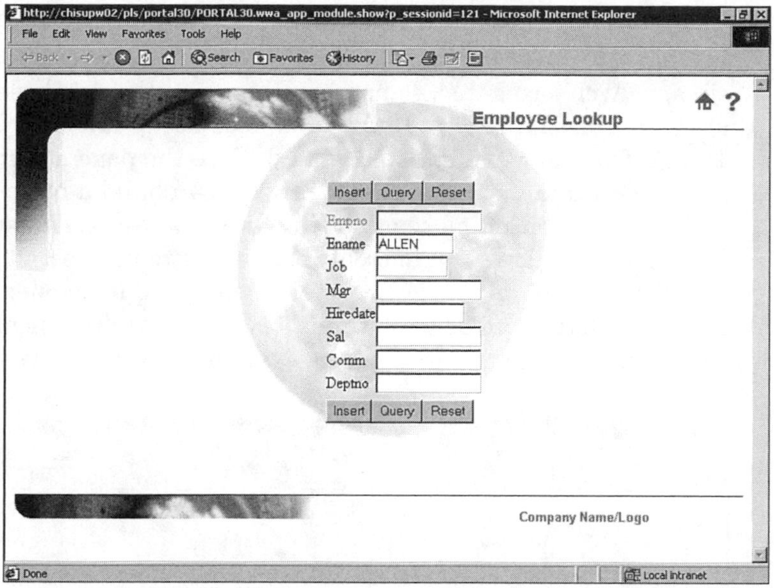

Figure 12.8: *Form Row Lookup.*

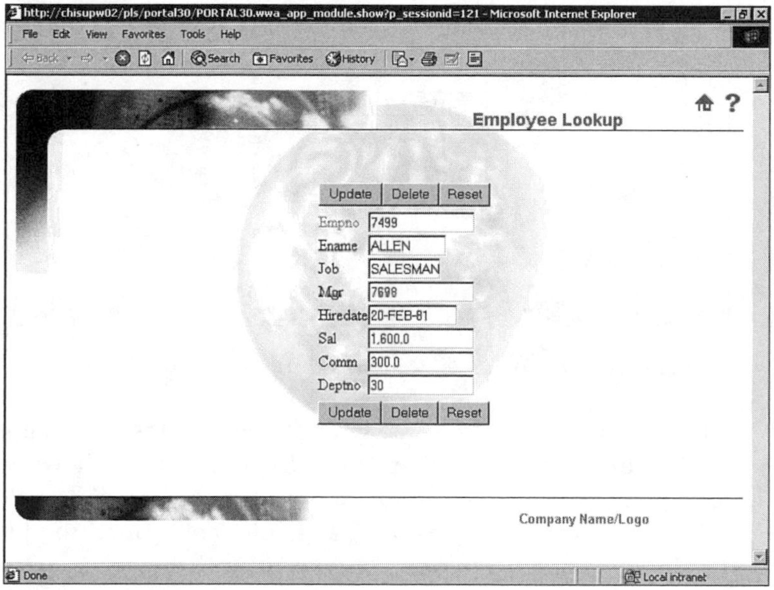

Figure 12.9: *Form Query Mode.*

Creating a Portal v3.0 Web Site

Portal v3.0 allows for the easy building and maintenance of content Web sites, or Web pages that do not directly access the database. To begin, start at the Portal Main Menu Build tab and select Create Page (see Figure 12.10). This begins a four-step wizard. Give the page a name and click Next' to continue. Notice that Portal v3.0 can build a basic Web page with just this little bit of information (the Finish button). The next screen, Figure 12.11, allows you to create the layout template and select a style. Portal builds column style pages, or regions and in the next step, you will select Portlets or items to place in these columns. This is about the only selectivity you have in where things will appear on the Web page.

Figure 12.10: *Portal v3.0 Create Page Wizard.*

Click Next> when you're ready to continue. This brings up the Add Portlets page. Click the button to display a list of portlets (shown in Figure 12.12). A region is one of the columns previously created. Select Set Language and People portlets. Your portal page should look something like Figure 12.13. Click Next> when you're ready to continue.

Select Expose Page To Everyone on the final screen and select Finish. Notice one of the options is to create this page as a portlet. This is one way of creating portlets. Portlets can then be included in other Portal Web Pages. Figure 12.14 shows the finished portal page.

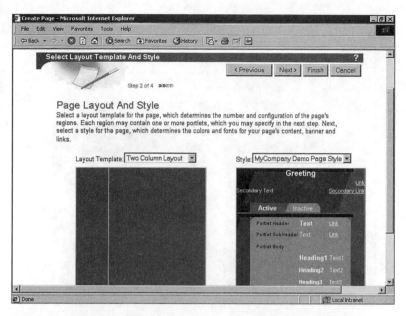

Figure 12.11: *Page Layout and Style.*

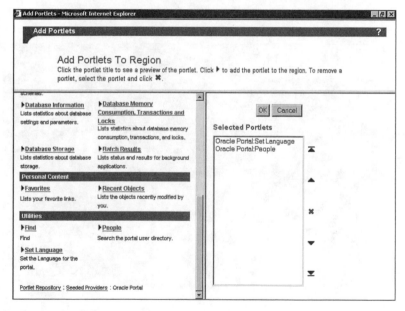

Figure 12.12: *Portlet selection page.*

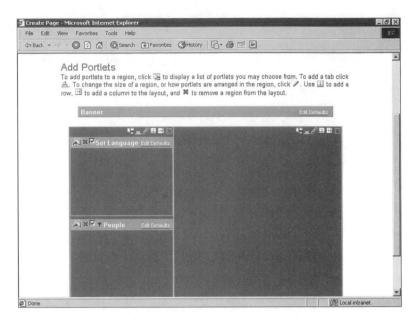

Figure 12.13: *Portal page with selected portlets.*

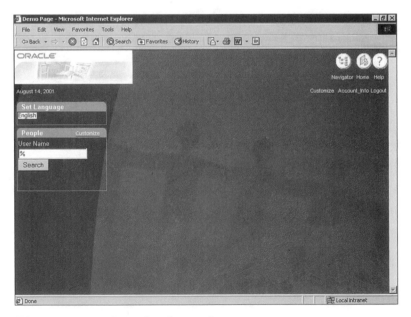

Figure 12.14: *Completed portal page.*

Summary

Portal v3.0 is a powerful Web-building tool. This chapter introduced you to the monitoring and administrative features of Portal but focused on Web site development using the Portal software. Figures 12.15 through 12.17 illustrate the flexibility available with Portal v3.0. You can see that Portal can create more than just your basic Web page. Portal pages can be user personalized as well, as illustrated by Figure 12.17.

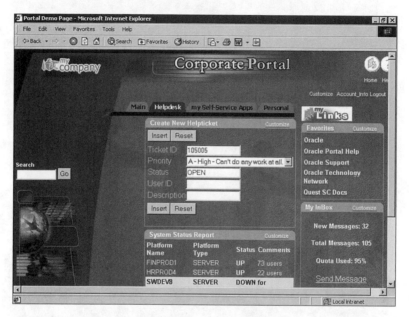

Figure 12.15: Portal Help-desk application.

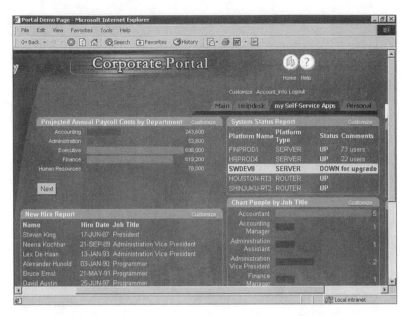

Figure 12.16: *Portal monitoring application.*

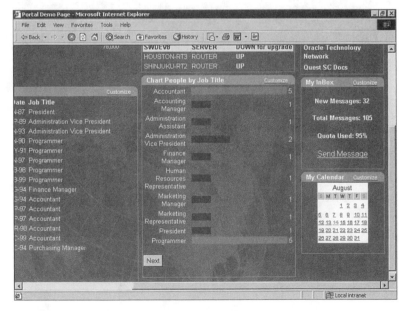

Figure 12.17: *Portal personal application.*

Reviewing It

1. What is Portal v3.0?

2. What are key differences between Portal v3.0 and its predecessor WebDB?

3. What is a portlet?

Checking It

1. What URL starts the Portal environment:

    a) `http://<host-name>/portal30`

    b) `http://10.4.50.100/pls/portal30`

    c) `http://<host-name>/portal30/portal30`

    d) All of the above

2. Portal is only a Web-development tool.

    True/False

3. Portal can build which of these:

    a) Form

    b) Report

    c) XML

    d) Menu

    e) List of Values

    f) All of the above

4. On the base tabular form, there are four buttons by default.

    True/False

Applying It

Independent Exercise 1:

- Build a simple Portal Application Form based on the EMP table.

- Query KING.

- Query all those making more than $2,000.

Independent Exercise 2:

- Build a Portal Application Report based on

  SELECT DNAME, SUM(SAL)

  FROM DEPT, EMP

  WHERE DEPT.DEPTNO = EMP.DEPTNO

Independent Exercise 3:

- Build a portal page with three columns.

- Populate these columns with various portlets.

- Run this newly created page.

What's Next?

The next section of this book focuses on tuning issues. Chapter 13, "Oracle9i Indexing Options," illustrates all of the Oracle9i indexing features, how they work, and techniques to consider when using each.

Part III

Oracle9i Tuning Issues

Oracle9i Indexing Options

Oracle9i Application SQL Tuning

Oracle9i Partitioning Features

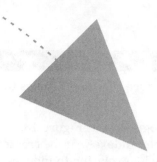

## 13

Oracle9i Indexing Options

This chapter begins the next section of the book that covers various tuning issues. Chapter 13 starts with coverage of the Oracle9i Indexing features and options. Since indexing plays a major role in the fast retrieval of information within the Oracle database, it is essential that the reader understands indexing, how it works, and the various options and features available in Oracle 9i.

This chapter teaches you the following:

- B-tree indexes
- How IOTs are useful
- Various Oracle9i indexing options and features
- How to use these options and features in a real application

Understanding Indexes

An *index* is a data structure that can greatly reduce the time it takes to find particular rows in the associated table.

A table object can have one or more indexes assigned to it. Figure 13.1 shows the syntax for creating an index on a table. Indexes can be created on one or more table columns. These columns, when relating to indexes, are known as *key fields*, or *keys*. A *composite* key uses more than one table column in a single index. Indexes are automatically created for the primary key constraint and can be unique—that is, have only one key value stored—or can have many keys with the same value. The more unique the key, the faster the access to the rows in the table.

Figure 13.1: SQL*Plus Help text about Create Index syntax.

Each row in a table has a unique identifier called *ROWID*. This ROWID is a *pseudocolumn* (false column) that contains the exact location of a row within the database. It also contains the following information: object ID, data file ID, block ID, and ROWID. In addition, ROWID is the fastest way to access a row in any version of Oracle. Any time the row is moved, exported, imported, and so on, this ROWID changes because the physical location of the row has changed. Indexes store ROWID along with the index key fields, and Oracle automatically updates all references to ROWID if and when a row is inserted or moved.

NOTE

Pseudocolumn—A column that can be selected with standard SQL syntax but does not occupy any space in the database. ROWID is a pseudocolumn that is really an exact physical location of that particular row.

NOTE

Using indexes greatly enhances the response time of most SQL statements. The rule of thumb here is if more than 20% of the rows of a table are going to be returned, you should consider not using indexes. The next sections cover the various indexing features of Oracle8i. Understanding the various available indexing options is important to choose the optimal indexing method for a given SQL statement.

B-Tree Indexes

A *b-tree (balanced-tree structured object)* index is the default indexing method of Oracle8i. Oracle adapted this indexing method from the start. The index structure resembles a tree in that the top block is read first, then a block in the next layer—which is known as a *branch* block—is read, and so on, until the index block (known as a *leaf* block) that contains the actual ROWID is retrieved.

This balancing-structure approach helps minimize I/O. Oracle9i keeps this type of index in order by the assigned key value or values, splitting the blocks if necessary, to keep the structure in sequence. The b-tree structure is stable in that it will take the same number of read operations to retrieve any table row, whatever the size of the table structure. Figure 13.2 illustrates how these branch blocks and leaf blocks might look using the EMP table. Notice that the branch blocks simply point to other blocks associated with this same index, in which the leaf blocks (along the bottom) contain an actual ROWID. Larger indexes have many rows or levels of branch blocks. The example in Figure 13.2 would have three levels, and each level could represent an I/O to the database.

TIP

If the tables being accessed by indexes contain gigabytes of data, you might want to consider using a larger default block size when creating the database. The larger the block size, the more of these index pointers can be read into the SGA with a single read operation. The more quickly these index pointers are read into memory, the more quickly the row(s) can be located for the application.

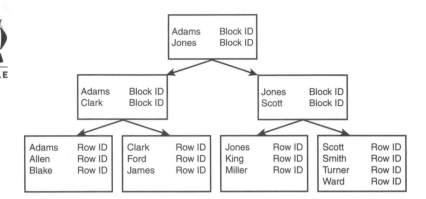

Figure 13.2: *B-tree index illustration on the EMP.ENAME column.*

Oracle always traverses the index from left to right. A branch block will always point to the left-most leaf (or next level of branch blocks) block that contains the key value. This allows for Oracle to easily range-scan across several blocks with a minimal amount of I/O.

The PCTFREE parameter helps Oracle manage index space by leaving a percentage of space behind when it is known that additional rows may be added in the middle of the index. This helps Oracle because it does not have to split blocks as often, a time-consuming process for Oracle that can attribute to wasted space and Oracle having to add another level to maintain the balance. This is discussed later in this chapter in the "Tips and Techniques" section.

B-tree indexes can be based on a single column of a table or on multiple columns of a table. A key comprised of multiple columns of a table is a composite key. If the data requirements for a SQL statement are satisfied from information in an associated index, the table structure is not accessed. This is where the idea of an index-organized table (IOT) originated.

IOT Overview

An *index-organized table* is a b-tree index structure that acts like a table. All the data is stored within the b-tree structure or in an overflow tablespace. Listing 13.1 illustrates the basic syntax for an IOT. Notice everything is pretty much the same, down to the organization index clause. This tells Oracle that this is an IOT. The pctthreshold tells Oracle to store the remainder of the row in the defined overflow tablespace if a row is larger than this percentage of the block size. This ensures that multiple key values exist in each index block. If the b-tree index block contains only a few rows, it would be more efficient not to have an index, defeating the purpose of an index—fast access to rows.

The advantage, in regards to storage, is that the key values are not stored twice, once in the underlying table and again in the index. As mentioned in the previous section, sometimes the underlying table is never accessed if the results of the SQL statement can be achieved with information stored in the index. This is the main reason for the development of the IOT.

EXAMPLE

Listing 13.1: IOT Syntax

```
create table <TABLE NAME>
(field descriptions
    .
    .
    .
<FIELD NAME>
primary key (<KEY FIELDS>))
organization index tablespace <TABLESPACE NAME>
pctthreshold 20
overflow tablespace <TABLESPACE NAME>ok PM
```

NOTE

In Oracle8, IOTs had no ROWID, so it was not possible to add more indexes. Oracle8i supports a logical ROWID so that additional columns in an IOT can have their own indexes as well.

Oracle9i Indexing Options

Oracle9i supports several indexing options that improve on the traditional b-tree indexes. Oracle7.3 introduced bitmap indexes, star queries, histograms, and hash joins. Oracle8 introduced index-organized tables and reverse-key indexes. Oracle8i introduced the function-based index. Oracle9i introduces the bitmap join index.

BITMAP INDEXES

Bitmap indexes were introduced with Oracle v7.3. Each bit location in a bitmap index relates to a ROWID within the table object. If a row contains the key value, a 1 is stored in the index row for that value. Bitmap indexes can be very fast because all Oracle has to do is search for the presence of a 1 to know it must retrieve this row. Also, this is not a b-tree index structure, so the goal is that the row can be located with a single read of the bitmap index structure. This indexing option is intended for columns with low cardinality of data, such as color, sex, and so on. If too many values are found in a column, additional I/Os are necessary to find the table ROWID, defeating the purpose of this kind of index. Figure 13.3 illustrates how the

EMP table (bitmap index on DEPTNO) object might look in a bitmap index. Listing 13.3 gives a bitmap syntax example.

```
                    Rows
            1 2 3 4 5 6 7 8 9 ...
        10  1 0 0 1 0 1 0 0 0 1 1 0 0 0
        20  0 0 1 0 0 0 1 0 0 0 0 0 1 0
        30  0 1 0 0 1 0 0 1 0 0 0 0 0 1
        40  0 0 0 0 0 0 0 0 1 0 0 1 0 0
```

Figure 13.3: Bitmap index illustration.

Listing 13.2 can help identify table columns for possible bitmap index consideration.

Listing 13.2:   Candidates for Bitmap Indexes

```
select owner "Owner", index_name "Index Name", distinct_keys "Distinct Keys"
from DBA_INDEXES
where distinct_keys < 15
```

EXAMPLE

Listing 13.3:   Bitmap Index Syntax Example

```
CREATE BITMAP INDEX on DEPT (DEPTNO);
```

EXAMPLE

Bitmap Join Indexes

Oracle9i introduces the bitmap join index, expanding upon the technology introduced with bitmap indexes allowing for faster table join conditions in SQL statements to be processed.

A bitmap join index is a good method to save both time and temporary storage space (nested loops, merge-joins, and so on) by tracking the rows in the primary table (the one with the bitmap) that match the criteria of the join condition and the column being indexed.

Listing 13.4 illustrates how the syntax would work. Remember that the bitmap index is actually being created on the ST_VENDOR table but the bits track just those rows that meet the join condition of the WHERE clause. Listing 13.5 shows a SQL example that would use this bitmap join index.

Listing 13.4:   Bitmap Join Index Syntax Example

```
CREATE BITMAP INDEX ST_VENDOR_STATE_BJI on ST_VENDOR (VENDOR_STATE)
FROM ST_INV I, ST_VENDOR V
WHERE I.INV_PURCHASE_VENDOR_ID = V.VENDOR_Id ok pm
```

EXAMPLE

EXAMPLE

Listing 13.5: Bitmap Join Index SQL Example

```
SELECT SUM(INV_SALE_AMT)
FROM ST_INV I, ST_VENDOR V
WHERE I.INV_PURCHASE_VENDOR_ID = V.VENDOR_ID
AND V.VENDOR_STATE = 'IA'; ok pm
```

Reverse-Key Indexes

The *reverse-key* index introduced in Oracle8 reverses the order of the bytes of a numeric key. It therefore provides a good way to help keep all the leaf blocks of a b-tree index structure more evenly populated with values. Candidates for reverse-key indexes are keys with a sequence number or incremental-type keys. Listing 13.6 illustrates how to make regular indexes reversed and changes the reverse key back to a regular key.

NOTE

Reverse-key indexes can only be used to return individual rows. Oracle does not perform range-scans on reverse-key indexes.

EXAMPLE

Listing 13.6: Reverse-Key Index Syntax

```
create index <INDEX NAME> on <TABLE NAME> (<COLUMN NAME(S)>) reverse
alter index <INDEX NAME> rebuild noreverse/reverse
```

FUNCTION-BASED INDEXES

If a function is used in the WHERE clause on an indexed column, Oracle does not use the index. For example, if you were giving all the SCOTT.EMP employees in dept 10 a raise, and an index existed on column DEPTNO, the statement in Listing 13.7 would result in reading all the rows from the SCOTT.EMP table. By creating a *function-based* index with the WHERE clause calculation, the index is used and only the rows meeting the where criteria are returned (see Listing 13.8). Function-based indexes can also be created as bitmap indexes.

EXAMPLE

Listing 13.7: SCOTT.EMP Access Via Function

```
UPDATE scott.emp
SET sal = sal * 1.10
WHERE (sal * 1.10) > 1000; ok pm
```

EXAMPLE

Listing 13.8: Function-Based Index

```
CREATE INDEX emp_raise_idx ON scott.emp (sal * 1.10); ok pm
```

TIP

Oracle will not use a function-based index if a WHERE clause is not specified. For example, in the case of the SCOTT.EMP table, if you wanted to use the index to return the rows in the order of the index using SELECT * FROM EMP ORDER BY UPPER(ename), to ensure that the function-based index created on this same function was used, you would use SELECT * FROM EMP WHERE UPPER(ename) IS NOT NULL ORDER BY UPPER(ename).

Implementing IOTs into Existing Applications

Several of the Sales Tracking table objects are good candidates for IOTs. A good candidate is a table with infrequent updates but frequent use of some of the columns. The ST_VENDOR table (see Listing 13.9), as well as the ST_CUSTOMER table, lends itself well to IOTs. Both tables have frequent read access with just the ID and names fields being frequently accessed. Notice the INCLUDING clause lists the vendor_name field. This field is frequently accessed by the ST_INVENTORY application when the vendor_id field is used to verify the accuracy of information entered onscreen.

Listing 13.9: ST_VENDOR Index-Organized Table

```
CREATE TABLE st_vendor
    (vendor_id              NUMBER(6)     PRIMARY KEY,
     vendor_name            VARCHAR2(30)     NOT NULL,
     vendor_street1       VARCHAR2(30),
     vendor_street2        VARCHAR2(30),
     vendor_city           VARCHAR2(20),
     vendor_state          VARCHAR2(2),
     vendor_zipcode        VARCHAR2(10),
     vendor_tax_id         VARCHAR2(20)     NOT NULL)
    ORGANIZATION INDEX
    TABLESPACE st_data02
    PCTTHRESHOLD 20 INCLUDING vendor_name
    OVERFLOW TABLESPACE st_iot_overflow01
    STORAGE (INITIAL 5K
        NEXT 5
        MINEXTENTS 5
        MAXEXTENTS 100); ok pm
```

Index Tips and Techniques

Here are a series of tips that should help you decide which indexes are best for your application needs. Also listed are some of the restrictions and caveats of using the various indexing methods.

Unique and NON-Unique Index Tips

Unique indexes store the ROWID of the table's data block along with the key value. This makes for a quick retrieval of the individual row from the table's data block. Nonunique indexes are set up with the pairing of ROWID's to assist Oracle with a range-of-values type of a search.

Reverse-Key Index Tips

Reverse-key indexes assist Oracle with a better balance (resulting in much better index space utilization) of data across the b*tree structure but Oracle does not perform range-scans across reverse-key indexes.

If an application is frequently reading and updating the same key value, a lock will be put on the leaf block during the DML operation. In this case it might be best to consider reverse-key indexes to remove this possible locking contention by spreading the row access across many leaf blocks.

Monitoring Index Usage Tips

Unused indexes not only waste disk space but also cause Oracle to perform maintenance on yet another structure during DML operations. Oracle9i supports a monitoring method to help you see if a particular index is being used or not. When these unused indexes are identified, they should be dropped. Listing 13.10 shows the syntax used to initiate monitoring.

Listing 13.10   Index Monitor Example

```
SQL> ALTER INDEX ST_BT_STAFF_ID MONITORING USAGE;
```

EXAMPLE

This command uses the new V$OBJECT_USAGE, which has five columns: index_name, table_name, monitoring (currently being monitored—ON or OFF), start_monitoring, and end_monitoring. This view is based on a data dictionary table so the data will remain visible even after a crash or a system restart.

Index Space Utilization Tips

Oracle does not physically delete unused leaf blocks. A table with considerable amount of deletes could have indexes with quite a number of unused blocks. Because Oracle always starts from the left-most leaf block (low order) when processing a range of keys, having a significant number of empty or near empty blocks will definitely have an affect on a SQL statement's response time.

A high PCTREE used during initial index creation will assist Oracle later by doing most of the block splitting during the initial load of data. A small PCTFREE is useful to maintain some room in the leaf blocks for later updates and inserts to help keep from having to perform split operations. A PCTFREE of 0 might be useful for those indexes with keys (not reverse-key indexes) that are sequence numbers where the index is always growing on one end. Because no keys will be inserted into the middle of the index, there is no need to leave any additional room for this kind of activity.

Oracle8i and 9i can sense the type of index rows being added via a conventional INSERT statement. If the key data is always random in nature, Oracle v8.1.6 recognizes this and loads the blocks 70% full, overriding the PCT-FREE storage clause value. If the key is noticed to be sequential in nature, Oracle v8.1.6 fills the leaf blocks as full as 95%, once again overriding the PCTFREE storage clause.

Index Reorganization Tips

The SQL script illustrated in Figure 13.4 shows a good way to monitor the growth of indexes. The height is the number of levels an index contains. The fewer the levels, the better the index performance is. On larger indexes, a good time to reorganize the index is when the height changes. Indexes can be reorganized by either dropping them and re-creating them or using the alter index <INDEX NAME> rebuild command. To use this command, you must have enough room in the tablespace to hold both indexes. This method guarantees that an index is available for application use while the index is being rebuilt.

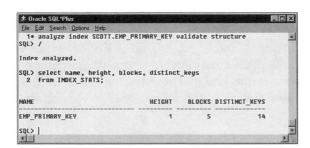

Figure 13.4: *Query to monitor the levels and sizes of indexes.*

IOT Tips

When using IOTs, it is important to keep a certain number of rows per index leaf block. If a leaf block only holds a few rows of data, it defeats the purpose of using an index at all. Conversely, if most of the data being accessed is relatively short in length, the remainder (possibly seldomly accessed data) can be stored in the overflow table by carefully using a mix of 'pctthreshold' and 'including' syntax.

IOT's are ideal for indexing longs, BLOBS, and CLOBS. All the key fields can be stored in the IOT and the long field stored in the overflow area.

The real benefit of using an IOT is that there is no duplication of data between an index and a table structure.

Bitmap Index and Bitmap Join Index Tips

Oracle processes bitmap and bitmap join indexes very efficiently. When two or more bitmap indexes are present on a table object, Oracle can perform Boolean operations (and/or/minus) effectively on the bitmap strings. Count operations are very efficient as well, as all Oracle has to do is count the 1's in the bitmap.

The block structure of a bitmap index is not a b*tree index structure and it does not have any of the Oracle data block header information either. The fewer the unique ids in a column being indexed, the fewer the rows, the fewer the leaf blocks. In other words, the fewer unique values, the faster bitmap indexes perform.

On the other hand, because Oracle has to shuffle the ROWID's when inserting rows into the underlying table, DML operations on bitmap indexes are very slow, as compared to DML operations on the standard b*tree index.

The other thing to note is that there is NO row-level locking. There is no interested-transaction list or other header information that tracks undo/redo information for Oracle in the event of a read-consistent view or a rollback. When DML is being performed on any bitmap index, an exclusive lock is placed on the table object.

Bitmap indexes are only supported by the cost-based optimizer. The rule-based optimizer simply ignores them.

Bitmap indexes are very good for decision-support applications, data warehouse applications with large volumes of rows (and columns with just a few values), and so on.

Reviewing It

REVIEW

1. What would be the advantage of a partitioned index?
2. What is the advantage of an IOT over that of a HEAP Table?
3. Why does IOTs have the pseudo column 'ROWID'?
4. What is a b*tree level telling you?

5. Show the syntax to make a SQL statement use an existing index when a calculation on the indexed column is desired.

6. List some of the benefits and penalties of using bitmapped indexes.

Checking It

1. A Reverse-Key index is useful for what following situation:

    a) The index key value is based on an Oracle Sequence.

    b) The typical access will be via a range of values.

    c) The index key value is always something unique.

2. When might Oracle NOT use a Reverse-Key index?

    a) The WHERE clause is using a < predicate.

    b) The WHERE clause is using a > predicate.

    c) The WHERE clause is using a BETWEEN function.

    d) All of the above

3. A Unique Index is the fastest way to access an individual row in a table.

    True/False

4. What is the IOT overflow tablespace used for?

    a) To store additional indexed rows for the IOT

    b) To store statistics about the IOT

    c) To store additional IOT columns

    d) All of the above

5. A bitmap index is good for large, dynamic tables.

    True/False

6. What is the purpose of a function-based index?

    a) To provide indexing on columns with any mathematical function

b) To provide indexing on columns with any Oracle function

c) To provide indexing on columns with specific functions

7. Bitmap Join Indexes are useful

a) In about any join situation

b) Where the primary table has a primary key constraint

c) Where the primary table has a primary key constraint and the joining table(s) have unique key constraints

d) Where the joining table(s) have primary or unique key constraints

8. In a Bitmap Join Index, what exactly is getting indexed?

a) The primary table's column

b) The join table(s) column

c) Both the primary table and the join table column

Applying It

APPLY

Independent Exercise 1:

- Create a composite index on EMP using the EMPNO and DEPTNO columns.

Independent Exercise 2:

- Convert the DEPT table to an IOT.

What's Next?

This chapter discussed various Oracle indexing features. It is important to understand the various indexing options and how they work before proceeding to the next chapter on application tuning. Chapter 16, "Using TOAD in the Development Arena," discusses the ins and outs of both the Rule-based optimizer and the Cost-based optimizer, how each make their index selections, and so on.

This chapter introduced you to the various Oracle9i indexing features. These examples were highlighted with example usage in the Sales Tracking Application. This chapter also discussed all the Oracle8i partitioning features, examples of good uses of each, and illustrations using these partitioning features in the Sales Tracking Application.

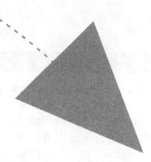

14

Oracle9i Application SQL Tuning

In this chapter, we will discuss how to monitor SQL statements, add indexes, and make the changes necessary to produce top-performing Oracle-based applications. Oracle uses one of two available optimizers to arrive at a plan, the Explain Plan, of how it will retrieve data and what, if any, indexes will be used. Understanding the contents of this explain plan is essential as well as the Oracle startup parameters that help control SQL performance.

This chapter teaches you the following:

- What Is the SQL Explain Plan?
- The Oracle Optimizers
- Tuning SQL Statements
- Helpful INIT.ORA Parameters
- SQL Coding Guidelines

What Is the SQL Explain Plan?

The *explain plan* illustrates the *execution plan* for any SQL statement. It shows the tables and indexes Oracle will use when processing an SQL statement, as well as the order in which the tables and indexes will be used. The execution plan is the order of events that Oracle will follow to access data and process the SQL statement. The explain plan and execution plan are determined when SQL is presented to Oracle for execution. If an SQL statement's actual code does not change and the SQL statement is still in the library cache, Oracle will simply reuse the original execution plan.

Oracle9i enables you to store and reuse this execution plan, which is known as *stored outlines*, this feature was introduced in Oracle8i. If you develop and tune a SQL statement in a test environment to use a very specific execution plan in the production environment, stored outlines enable you to guarantee that a particular SQL statement used a certain execution plan.

The Oracle Optimizers

Oracle9i supports two optimizers, a rule-based optimizer and a cost-based optimizer. The optimizer determines which explain plan is best for any SQL statement. It is possible that the same explain plan will be generated differently with subsequent submissions of an SQL statement not previously found in the library cache. The stored outlines come in handy, therefore, if the same execution plan is desired.

The rule-based optimizer is the original Oracle optimizer and makes decisions based on how the SQL statement is physically coded and the existence of indexes. The cost-based optimizer, on the other hand, was introduced with Oracle6 and makes its decisions based on statistics gathered by the ANALYZE command.

THE RULE-BASED OPTIMIZER

The rule-based optimizer uses 19 rules to determine the execution path for a SQL statement (see Listing 14.1). The lower the rank (the rules are ranked from 1–19, with 1 being the best), the better the SQL statement should perform. Changing the execution plan (*tuning*) is accomplished by forcing the rule-based optimizer to make different selections. For example, adding an index to a column in the WHERE clause would alter the rank. If you don't want to use an index, you can add a function to an indexed field in a WHERE clause, which changes the rank and effectively disables the use of the index for this particular SQL statement. How the SQL statement is physically coded, particularly the order of the tables listed in the FROM clause, has a dramatic effect on the rule-based optimizer.

For example, consider the concept of a driving table, or the table that is compared to the others in a join SQL statement (multiple tables listed in the FROM clause). Because Oracle parses SQL statements from back to front, the driving table in a rule-based optimized SQL statement is the last one listed in the SQL statement. A few other dependencies can affect this decision, but for the most part, substantial performance gains can be gotten just by changing the order of the tables in the FROM clause.

TIP

The *driving table* is the table that is accessed first and then used to look up information in the other tables in the join condition. The driving table always should be the smaller table or the table with the greatest degree of selectivity in the WHERE clause. The join columns in the other non-driving tables should have a unique index to ensure optimal performance.

NOTE

Oracle offers no guarantee that between releases these rules will remain the same or that the rule-based optimizer will make the same decisions as in prior releases. Therefore, testing applications when moving to newer versions of Oracle software is important.

Listing 14.1:   Rule-Based Optimizer Rules

Rank	Where Clause Rule
1	ROWID = constant
2	unique indexed column = constant
3	entire unique concatenated index = constant
4	entire cluster key = cluster key of object in same cluster
5	entire cluster key = constant
6	entire nonunique concatenated index = constant
7	nonunique index = constant
8	entire noncompressed concatenated index >= constant
9	entire compressed concatenated index >= constant
10	partial but leading columns of noncompressed concatenated index
11	partial but leading columns of compressed concatenated index
12	unique indexed column using the SQL statement BETWEEN or LIKE options
13	nonunique indexed column using the SQL statement BETWEEN or LIKE options
14	unique indexed column < or > constant
15	nonunique indexed column < or > constant
16	sort/merge
17	MAX or MIN SQL statement functions on indexed column
18	ORDER BY entire index
19	full table scans

NOTE

Sort/merge—An execution plan function that can be used when joining two or more tables together in a SQL statement. A *full table scan* is when all the rows are returned from a table by processing the table from beginning to end.

TIP

The bitmap join index discussed in the previous chapter might eliminate the need for Oracle to perform a sort_merge function.

THE COST-BASED OPTIMIZER

The cost-based optimizer makes its decisions based on a cost factor derived from statistics for the objects in the SQL statement. The ANALYZE SQL statement is used to collect these statistics. Oracle9i introduces a new method of collecting statistics. The DBMS_STATS package has quite a bit more power over the existing ANALYZE command, particularly when it comes to large objects and the need to estimate the number of rows to gather statistics. DBMS_STATS is able to do a sampling of data across the object, when the object is large. This is much better than the ESTIMATED rows of the ANALYZE command where the ANALYZE command simply used the first percentage of rows in the object. The cost-based optimizer bases its execution-path decisions strictly on these collected statistics, so it is important to keep the statistics fresh, particularly with objects that have many DML-type SQL statements.

TIP

This command has been around since version 7.0 and is only supported by Oracle9I for backwards compatibility. Expect Oracle Corp to drop support of this command in the future. Begin using the new DBMS_STATS package to collect statistics.

NOTE

The rule-based optimizer has not supported new Oracle features such as bitmapped indexing, partitioning, or performance features since Oracle version 7.3. Options such as partitioned tables, index-only tables, reverse indexes, histograms, hash joins, parallel query, and bit-mapped indexes are supported only by the cost-based optimizer.

You can enable the cost-based optimizer by collecting statistics. The INIT. ORA parameter OPTIMIZER_MODE must be set to CHOOSE or COST or FIRST_ ROWS_n, or it can be set at the user-session level with the ALTER SESSION command. You can disable the cost-based optimizer easily by either resetting the INIT.ORA parameter OPTOMIZER_MODE or deleting the statistics. If the shared pool has any current SQL statements that have execution plans based on newer statistics, Oracle will invalidate the SQL in the shared pool, allowing it to be re-prepared using the new statistics the next time the SQL statement is executed.

NOTE

The database must be shut down and restarted for any INIT.ORA parameter file changes to take effect. The ALTER SESSION command takes effect immediately.

Oracle9i has several new cost-based statistics considerations it can use. Like prior versions of Oracle, Oracle9i will use statistics gathered on particular objects. Along with these statistics, Oracle9i is also able to collect, save, and reset system statistics, information that is important to the cost-based optimizer to help it make better decisions.

Object level statistics are now gathered with the DBMS_STATS package GATHER_SCHEMA_STATS. This functionally replaces the ANALYZE command with the improvement that it gathers statistics for all the objects owned by a particular schema. This new method has the ability to auto sample the data across the object, based on the size of the object and the workspace available to Oracle9i. When using the cost-based optimizer, it makes its best decisions when all objects involved have statistics.

The GATHER_SCHEMA_STATS command has a couple of options when it comes to histograms. If the size option is set to SKEWONLY, then a histogram will be created no matter how the application is using the particular column. In the method_opt option, if the size option is set to AUTO, then the histogram will reflect how the application is using the particular column. It is recommended that when the first time statistics are gathered, that the SKEWONLY option is used and subsequent statistic gatherings should use the AUTO setting. It is also recommended that the option estimate_percent be set to DBMS_STATS.AUTOSAMPLE_SIZE (for example: estimate_*percent* => *DBMS_STATS.AUTOSAMPLE_SIZE*).

NOTE

As of this writing, the author did not have access to the exact syntax of the GATHER_SCHEMA_STATS command. Please check your Oracle9i documentation for the exact syntax and options of this new feature.

NOTE

Histogram—Part of the cost-based optimizer used to manage uneven data distribution in table objects.

TIP

You may want to gather these statistics at off-peak application usage times as the gathering of statistics for particular objects invalidates any pre-parsed SQL statements in the library cache. This is so that when Oracle re-executes the SQL statement again, it will use the fresh statistics. This could have undesirable results if done while the application is being actively used.

System statistics are gathered and used using the DBMS_STATS package options: GATHER_SYSTEM_STATS, SET_SYSTEM_STATS, and GET_SYSTEM_STATS, and IMPORT_SYSTEM_STATS.

System statistics can differ greatly at different parts of the day and based on the types of applications being run at these various times of the day. GATHER_SYSTEM_STATS has a time element involved with it as well as the ability to give the collection a name. This name allows for different pre-collected statistics to be used at different times of the processing day. Listing 14.2 illustrates how this might be used on the first shift and second shift versus subsequent first and second shifts.

EXAMPLE

Listing 14.2: GATHER_SYSTEM_STATS Example

```
First Shift/First Day   EXECUTE DBMS_STATS.GATHER_SYSTEM_STATS (
                            Interval => 90,
                            Stattab => 'System A Stats',
                            Statid => 'shift1');
Second Shift/First Day   EXECUTE DBMS_STATS.GATHER_SYSTEM_STATS (
                            Interval => 90,
                            Stattab => 'System A Stats',

            Statid => 'shift2');

First Shift/Next Day   EXECUTE_DBMS_STATS.IMPORT_SYSTEM_STATS (
                            Stattab => 'System A Stats',
                            Statid => 'shift1');
Second Shift/Next Day   EXECUTE_DBMS_STATS.IMPORT_SYSTEM_STATS (
                            Stattab => 'System A Stats',
                            Statid => 'shift2');
```

SET_SYSTEM_STATS is used to explicitly set the system statistics and GET_SYSTEM_STATS is used to verify system statistics.

NOTE

If statistics have not been collected and the Oracle optimizer mode is set to COST or a cost-based hint is added to a SQL statement when there are no statistics collected, Oracle will use the cost-based optimizer anyway and simply make assumptions about the number of rows in each table, the number of connected users, the distribution of data, and the buffer-hit cache ratio. These assumptions change between releases of Oracle.

Hints are used to influence the cost-based optimizer and can be used to control the optimizer's goal, access methods, join conditions, parallel option, and partitioning option. Hints are specified in the SQL statement syntax. Listing 14.3 illustrates an ALL_ROWS hint in the SCOTT.EMP table.

EXAMPLE

Listing 14.3: Hints in SQL Statements

```
select /*+ ALL_ROWS */ ename, sal from EMP where SAL > 1000
```

Listing 14.4 shows most of the hints for controlling the execution plan available in Oracle9i. The cost-based optimizer also has the driving-table mechanism in join conditions. The ORDERED hint causes the driving table to be the first table in the FROM clause of the SQL statement.

TIP

The optimizer goal hint controls one of three modes: RULE forces the rule-based optimizer; FIRST_ROWS is the quickest at returning initial rows; and ALL_ROWS, which is the best overall, uses the cost-based optimizer and forces the optimizer to the desired goal.

TIP

Oracle9i has introduced a new variation of the FIRST ROWS hint or optimizer mode setting. Now you can tell the cost-based optimizer about how many rows you would like for it to consider. The syntax looks something like this where you can supply the number: FIRST_ROWS=10 or FIRST_ROWS=100. The hint looks like this: /*+ FIRST_ROWS(n) */, where n is the number of rows you would like the cost-based optimizer to consider.

EXAMPLE

Listing 14.4: Access Control Hints

```
Hint              Description
AND_EQUAL         Use the AND_EQUAL hint when more than one equality criterion
                  exists on a single table.
CACHE             Use the CACHE hint to place the entire table in the buffer
                  cache. The table is placed at the most recently used end of
                  the buffer cache. This hint is good for small tables that
                  are accessed often.
CLUSTER           Use the CLUSTER hint to access a table in a cluster without
                  the use of an index.
FULL              Use the FULL hint to perform a full table scan on a table.
HASH              Use the HASH hint to access a table in a hashed cluster
                  without the use of an index.
INDEX             Use an INDEX hint to instruct ORACLE to use one of the indexes
                  specified as a parameter.
INDEX_COMBINE     The INDEX_COMBINE forces the use of bitmap indexes.
NOCACHE           Use the NOCACHE hint to place the blocks of the table at the
                  beginning of the buffer cache so as not to age any  blocks out.
NOPARALLEL        Use the NOPARALLEL hint to not use multiple-server processes to
                  service the operations on the specified table.
```

Listing 14.4:   continued

ORDERED	Use the ORDERED hint to access the tables in the FROM clause in the order they appear.
PARALLEL	Use the PARALLEL hint to request multiple server processes to simultaneously service the operations on the specified table.
PUSH_SUBQ	The PUSH_SUBQ evaluates subqueries earlier, rather than as a filter operation.
ROWID	Use the ROWID hint to access the table by ROWID.
STAR	STAR hint invokes the STAR query feature.
USE_HASH	Use the USE_HASH hint to perform a hash join rather than a merge join or a nested loop join.
USE_MERE	Use the USE_MERGE hint to perform a merge join rather than a nested loop join or a hash join.

Say you have a table full of names, with an index on the last name. Let's also say that this table has proportionately more occurrences of Jones and Smith than most of the other rows. A *histogram* would be useful in this example because data won't be evenly distributed throughout the table object. Prior to histograms, the Oracle optimizer assumed even distribution of values throughout the object.

TIP

Oracle uses a histogram, if it exists, as part of creating an explain plan. To use histograms, Oracle needs a value in the where clause, NOT a bind variable. Oracle needs to see what is being selected to determine whether the data selectivity is good or not based on the histogram. Unfortunately, bind variables are resolved by Oracle after the execution plan phase of processing and will ignore the existence of a histogram if the index being considered is being compared with a bind variable instead of a constant.

Figure 14.1 illustrates a histogram as a series of buckets. Two kinds of histograms are available, width balanced and height balanced. *Width-balanced* histograms have values that are divided up into an even number of buckets, enabling the optimizer to easily determine which buckets have higher counts. In *height-balanced* histograms, however, each bucket has the same number of column values, but a column value can span more than one bucket. Figure 14.1 illustrates what the EMP table might look like in each of these types of histograms.

When two or more tables are joined together, Oracle must pull the columns from each table, creating a *result set*, which is a temporary table of sorts. This result set is created in the TEMPORARY tablespace and contains the combination of rows. The Oracle optimizer chooses one of five methods to perform this join: a nested-loop join, a sort-merge join, a hash join, a cluster join, and (new with Oracle8i) an index join. The most common joins are the first three listed here.

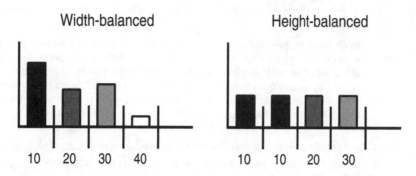

Figure 14.1: The EMP table in a histogram.

A *nested-loop* join reads the first row from the driving table, or outer table, and checks the other table, called the inner table, for the value. If the value is found then the rows are placed into the result set. Nested-loops work best when the driving table is rather small and a unique index is defined on the inner table's joined column.

A *sort-merge* join sorts both of the joined tables by the join column and then matches the output from these sorts. Any matches are subsequently placed into the result set. The big difference between this join and the nested-loop is that in the sort-merge, no rows are returned until after this matching process completes, whereas the nested-loop returns rows almost immediately. Nested-loops are a good choice when the first few rows need to be returned almost immediately. In contrast, sort-merge joins work better with larger amounts of data, or situations in which the two joining tables are roughly the same size and most of the rows will be returned. In practice, there seems to be no good reason to use a sort-merge join.

Hash joins can dramatically increase the performance of two joined tables in situations in which one table is significantly larger than the other. The hash join works by splitting two tables into partitions and creating a memory-based *hash table*. This hash table is then used to map join columns from the other table, eliminating the need for a sort-merge. In the hash join method, all tables are scanned only once. Hash joins are implemented by the INIT.ORA parameters HASH_JOIN_ENABLED, HASH_MULTIBLOCK_IO_COUNT, and HASH_AREA_SIZE. A star query involves a single table object being joined with several smaller table objects, where the driving table object has a concatenated index key and each of the smaller table objects is referenced by part of that concatenated key. The Oracle cost-based optimizer recognizes this arrangement and builds a memory-based cluster of the smaller tables.

NOTE

Hash table or hash index—Results when the column being indexed is applied to a calculation and a unique address is returned. A hash table has a predetermined number of slots allocated for these hash keys. The advantage of using hash tables is that the data can be accessed quickly with one or two I/Os to the database. The downside is that the amount of data must be predetermined. In the previously mentioned hash join, the statistics have the row counts for the tables and the hash table can be built quickly.

Cluster joins are used instead of nested-loops when the join condition is making reference to tables that are physically clustered together. The Oracle cost-based optimizer recognizes this condition and uses the cluster join when the tables being joined are in the same cluster. Tables are candidates for clustering when they are joined together and no other queries are typically run against one or the other. Clustering physically aligns the joined column rows together in the same data block, which is why cluster joins are so efficient—the data is already being accessed with a single I/O to the database.

Index joins work on the concept that if all the information required for the SQL statement is found in the index, the underlying table structure is not accessed or referenced in the execution plan.

Figure 14.2 illustrates the differences in the times of the three main kinds of join conditions. Notice that the nested-loop starts out very fast, but the more rows processed, the slower it becomes. The sort-merge join starts off the slowest because it must sort and merge the columns before returning any rows; however, its overall performance is pretty consistent. The hash join, on the other hand, starts out quickly and has the overall best performance because all the columns in the join conditions have a hash key in the hash table, enabling very quick access to the data.

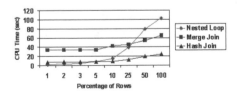

CPU Time (sec) - Parse & Execute

Percentage	Nested Loop	Merge Join	Hash Join
100	103.26	65.63	25.06
50	79.26	54.34	19.16
25	39.01	45.85	12.40
10	15.22	42.26	8.99
5	8.10	34.33	8.50
3	4.54	34.25	7.95
2	3.15	33.47	7.63
1	1.74	33.59	7.60

Figure 14.2: CPU time comparisons between nested-loop, sort-merge, and hash joins.

Which method is best? Once again, it depends on the application, the amount of data being joined, and so on.

Tuning SQL Statements

When we tune SQL statements at the application level, it is important that we are able to monitor and capture long-running, or very I/O-intensive, SQL statements. The old 80/20 rule generally applies here: 20% of the SQL statements are consuming 80% of the system resources. Being able to identify and tune the 20% is critical.

Oracle supplies a product called TKPROF, which is a character-mode tool used to interpret the contents of trace files. *Trace files* contain all the SQL statements and statistics for a particular trace session. Traces can be created by an INIT.ORA parameter or more importantly, by setting the trace function to on at the application level. For example, one of the options when starting an Oracle form is to trace the form. Traces also can be created by setting a session-level trace to on with a SQL statement, such as ALTER SESSION SET SQL_TRACE TRUE;.

TIP

If the optimization parameter CHOOSE is issued, Oracle will look to see if statistics has been run. If there are statistics, Oracle will use the cost-based FIRST ROWS setting, otherwise it will use the rule-based optimizer.

The Oracle trace facility captures all the SQL statements, but TKPROF is not a tool for the novice, and finding specific poorly performing SQL statements might be difficult. Oracle also provides an explain plan facility, activated by running the script <ORACLE_HOME>/rdbms/admin/utlxplan.sql, for each user wanting to visualize explain plans (see Listing 14.5). A single explain plan table can be created and given public access, but if several people are performing SQL statement tuning, it is more convenient for them to simply create their own explain tables. Figure 14.3 illustrates using Quest Software SQLab Xpert to submit a SQL statement and the resulting explain plan. SQLab Xpert is very good at monitoring and finding poorly performing SQL statements across the system or for a particular session but also is an excellent SQL tuning environment. Notice that the resulting explain plans are very similar, but the SQLab, being a GUI environment, has many more features for actually tuning the SQL statement.

TIP

Oracle9i has introduced three new columns into the PLAN_TABLE: cpu_cost (the cpu cost estimate per operation, io_cost (the I/O cost estimate per operation), and the temp_space (approximate amount of space needed to perform this step). If you are using the rule-based optimizer, these columns will be null.

EXAMPLE

Listing 14.5: Oracle Explain Plan Using PLAN_TABLE

```
SQL> l
  1  EXPLAIN PLAN INTO plan_table FOR
  2  select sum(bt_time * staff_billing_rate)
  3  from st_bill_time, st_staff
  4  where st_bill_time.bt_inv_id = 14
  5* and st_bill_time.bt_staff_id = st_staff.staff_id
SQL> /

Explained.

SQL> SELECT cost, operation, options, object_name
  2  FROM plan_table;
```

COST	OPERATION	OPTIONS	OBJECT_NAME
3	SELECT STATEMENT		
	SORT	AGGREGATE	
3	HASH JOIN		
1	TABLE ACCESS	FULL	ST_STAFF
1	TABLE ACCESS	FULL	ST_BILL_TIME

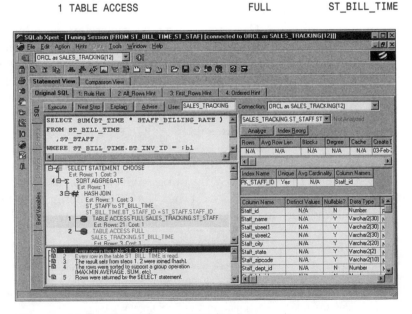

Figure 14.3: SQLab Xpert SQL tuning session.

Understanding the explain plan is a necessity for tuning SQL statements for both the rule-based and cost-based optimizers. Explain plans can be difficult to interpret, but indenting the explain steps greatly aids in understanding the order of the explain steps. The more common explain steps are discussed in Listing 14.6.

Listing 14.6:   Common Explain Plan Symbols

Explain Symbol	Description
AND-EQUAL	Index values will be used to join rows.
CONCATENATION	SQL statement UNION command.
FILTER	FILTERs apply 'other criteria' in the query to further qualify the matching rows. The 'other criteria' include correlated subqueries, and HAVING clause.
FIRST ROW	SQL statement will be processed via a cursor.
FOR UPDATE	SQL statement clause 'for update of' placed row level locks on affected rows.
INDEX (UNIQUE)	SQL statement utilized a unique index to search for a specific value.
INDEX (RANGE SCAN)	SQL statement contains a nonequality or BETWEEN condition.
HASH JOIN	SQL statement initiated a hash-join operation.
MERGE JOIN	SQL statement references two or more tables, sorting the two result sets being joined over the join columns and then merging the results via the join columns.
NESTED LOOPS	This operation is one form of joining tables. One row is retrieved from the row source identified by the first (inner) operation, and then joined to all matching rows in the other table (outer).
NONUNIQUE INDEX (RANGE SCAN)	The RANGE SCAN option indicates that ORACLE expects to return multiple matches (ROWIDs) from the index search.
PARTITION (CONCATENATED)	SQL statement will access a partitioned object and merge the retrieved rows from the accessed partitions.
PARTITION (SINGLE)	SQL statement will access a single partition.
PARTITION (EMPTY)	The SQL statement makes reference to an empty partition.
SORT (ORDER BY)	SQL statement contains an ORDER BY SQL command.
SORT (AGGREGATE)	SQL statement initiated a sort to resolve a MIN or MAX function.
SORT (GROUP BY)	SQL statement contains a GROUP BY SQL command.
TABLE ACCESS (FULL)	All rows are retrieved from the table without using an index.

Listing 14.6: continued

TABLE ACCESS (BY ROWID)	A row is retrieved based on ROWID
TABLE ACCESS (CLUSTER)	A row is retrieved from a table that is part of a cluster.
UNION	SQL statement contains a DISTINCT SQL command.

Oracle version 8 has introduced three new columns: PARTITION_START, PARTITION_STOP, and PARTITION_ID. These three new fields will help in the tuning of SQL statements that access partitioned objects. PARTITION_START and PARTITION_STOP show the range of partitions affected by this explain step, and the PARTITION_ID is the identification number for that particular explain step.

The largest performance gains can be obtained by tuning the top four or five steps of the explain plan. Figure 14.4 illustrates one of the sales tracking SQL statements (from the Profit/Loss Calculation button in the ST_INVENTORY form). SQLab Xpert provides quite a bit of information—notice the indexes listed on the right side and all the column attributes listed as well. This particular SQL statement was captured via monitoring, which is discussed in Chapter 5, "Building Oracle Forms." Notice that SQLab set up five scenarios using hints:

- Original SQL
- Rule Hint
- All_Rows Hint
- First_Rows Hint
- Ordered Hint

SQLab also has the capability to compare each of these scenarios.

In the SQL explain plan, SQLab indents and highlights each of the explain steps (see Figure 14.4). For the novice, SQLab also provides a meaningful explanation—in the box under the explain plan—of what each step really means. On the highlighted explain plan line, notice the Table Access Full, or a full table scan. Also notice the statistics, primarily the number of rows affected. Normally, a full table scan is a bad thing, but when only 21 rows are being affected, a full table scan is actually a good thing. Having an index would only increase the number of I/Os to retrieve this data, which is probably all in the same data block. In addition, notice the hash join in step 3 of the explain plan.

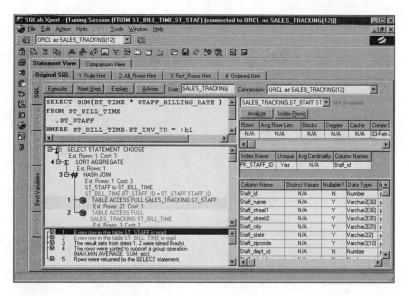

Figure 14.4: *SQLab Xpert SQL tuning session.*

The example in Figure 14.5 is the same tuning session as in Figure 14.4, except the Rule Hint tab is the current tab. Using the rule-based optimizer, the optimizer picked a nested-loop join operation in step 5 of the explain plan because the rule-based optimizer does not support hash joins.

TIP

Sometimes SQL statement performance is better with the rule-based optimizer. Do not automatically rule it out.

NOTE

I would like to see people start using the cost-based optimizer. Use a tool that will compare both the rule-based optimizer and the cost-based optimizer. There are so many more cost-based features in Oracle9i that the Oracle community should start using them.

SQLab can actually give advice on how to rewrite the SQL statement. In Figure 14.6, the Advice tab on the left side of the screen shows that SQLab is recommending to drop the indexes. This recommendation comes because, in this case, the indexes will probably slow down the processing of this SQL statement due to the extra I/Os required to access the indexes. Notice that it is also advising either to analyze all the tables or to have none of them analyzed. Finally, this SQL statement recommends creating indexes on the foreign keys. The Generate SQL button will generate a SQL script to implement any of the recommendations selected.

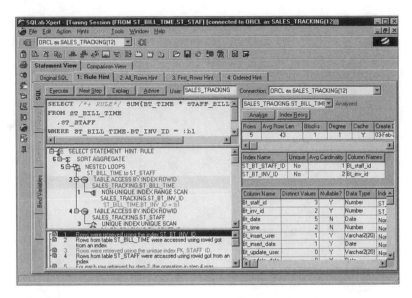

Figure 14.5: *SQLab Xpert SQL tuning session Rule Hint tab.*

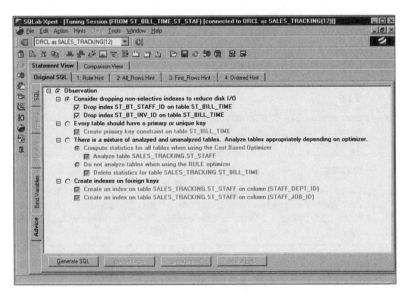

Figure 14.6: *SQLab Xpert SQL tuning session expert advice tab.*

The final SQLab example in Figure 14.7 illustrates another way of viewing the explain plan, in a flowchart mode. SQLab enables the user to toggle between the regular explain display mode and the flowchart mode, which provides a nice way to view the relationships in the explain plan.

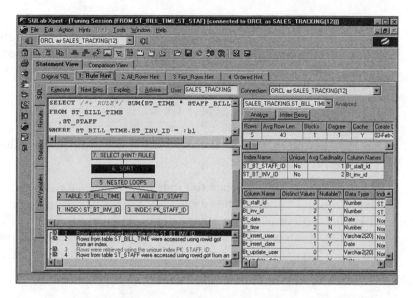

Figure 14.7: *SQLab Xpert SQL tuning session in flowchart mode.*

NOTE

Any change to the SQL statements in any tuning session must be copied back into the program, function, or procedure where it originated.

TIP

In the event of a tie for index usage, Oracle will use the one with the highest Object ID.

The cost-based optimizer uses various statistics to make its decisions. One of the more important statistics is the concept of clustering factor.

Clustering factor is a relationship between the number of data blocks being referenced by each index leaf block. The better this relationship, that is, the fewer different data blocks referenced in each index leaf block, the better the clustering factor. This means for each read of the index leaf block, Oracle will have to do fewer data block reads to satisfy what is found in the index. This is very important when doing any kind of range-scan across the index. A lower clustering factor can be accomplished by sorting the table in the order of the main index that is to be used, prior to loading the table into Oracle.

TIP

The cost-based optimizer uses clustering factor as a part of its decision process. The rule-based optimizer does not, however, a lower clustering factor will greatly increase the indexes ability to find the underlying rows being selected.

Oracle9i can efficiently use concatenated key indexes where the WHERE clause does not contain the leading column of the concatenated key. Oracle9I has implemented a new index-search method called skip scanning. Skip scanning allows Oracle to scan the branch blocks looking for the non-leading key values and ignore the other index blocks.

There are four basic kinds of index scans that can be seen in the explain plan and set using a hint: unique index scan, range scan, full scan (shows up in the explain plan as INDEX_FULL), and fast full scan (shows up in the explain plan as INDEX_FSS).

A *unique index* scan probes the index tree structure for an individual row, using a unique index. The *range scan* probes the index tree structure for the first occurrence of the range, then reads leaf-to-leaf until the range is satisfied. A *full scan* scans leaf blocks using a single-block read and a *fast full scan* uses the multi-block read ahead method, skipping branch blocks and processing the leaf blocks.

Using Stored Outlines

Stored outlines were introduced in Oracle8i as a means to guarantee that a certain execution plan would be used for a particular SQL statement. This is useful for those tuning efforts that want to guarantee a certain index will or will not be used. It is also useful for when tuning takes place on a different system or the tuning effort on one SQL statement is desired to be automatically repeated on other systems where the application resides.

To save a SQL statement in a stored outline, use the syntax CREATE OR REPLACE <outline name> FOR CATEGORY <category name> ON <SQL statement>. You must have the CREATE ANY OUTLINE permission granted to perform this task. The system or session parameter CREATE_STORED_ OUTLINES must be set to true. Categories are used for multiple SQL statements for the same application, for example.

Oracle will use the stored outline if there is an exact match of the SQL text, including any HINT syntax that might be present.

Oracle uses two tables, OL$ and OL$HINTS, to store the stored outline reference and SQL text. The stored outlines will be stored in these tables and used indefinitely unless explicitly removed.

These stored outlines can easily be moved to other systems using Oracle Export/Import: EXP OUTLN/OUTLN FILE = <file name> TABLES = 'OL$' 'OL$HINTS' SILENT=Y [WHERE CATEGORY=<category>] and IMP OUTLN/OUTLN FILE=<file name> TABLES = 'OL$' 'OL$HINT' IGNORE=Y SILENT=Y.

Oracle9i has enhanced the stored outline environment by allowing you to make a private copy of any stored outline into your own schema, and making changes to it in this private, or offline stored outline. Oracle9I supports the OUTLN_PKG.CREATE_EDIT_TABLES package, which will create the private stored outline tables in your schema.

Listing 14.7 shows an example stored outline edit session.

Listing 14.7:   Stored Outline Edit Session

```
SQL> ALTER SESSION SET USE_PRIVATE_OUTLINES = TRUE;
System Altered
SQL> CREATE PRIVATE OUTLINE mysql FROM mysql;
Outline Created
SQL> UPDATE OL$HINTS
2> SET HINT_TEXT = 'INDEX(T1 I1)'
3> WHERE HINT# = 6;
Record Updated
```

NOTE

The Oracle9i V$SQL view now has the outline_sid column so the user can see which stored outline is being from which session.

Helpful INIT.ORA Parameters

The following paragraphs contain some helpful init.ora parameter settings.

OPTIMIZER_PERMENTATIONS = 79,000—This setting defaults to 80,000 and controls the number of various cost factors Oracle will consider before calling it quits and looking at what it has for cost estimates. For some reason, Oracle seems to make slightly better decisions with the cost-based optimizer if this is set slightly lower than its default value.

OPTIMIZER_INDEX_CACHING = 90—The range for this parameter is 0 to 99, where 0 assumes that logical I/O is the same as physical I/O (equivalent of a 0% buffer hit cache ratio). It is recommended to set this to 90 to give the cost-based optimizer the thought that the index might already be in the buffer pool.

OPTIMIZER_INDEX_COST_ADJ = 10 through 50—This parameter is similar to the prior mentioned optimizer_index_caching except that this setting (default setting is 100) assumes the service time on I/O requests is the same for indexed scans as full-table scans. 10 seems to be a good setting for OLTP type applications and 50 seems to be a good setting for decision support type applications. If you have the init.ora parameter timed_statistics set to true, the SQL statement in Listing 14.8 should help come up with a more accurate setting for this parameter for your particular system and applications. Set this parameter to the result of index scans divided by full table scans.

EXAMPLE

Listing 14.8: OPTIMIZER_INDEX_COST_ADJ Settings

```
SELECT event, average_wait
FROM v$system_event
WHERE event like 'db file s%';


EVENT          AVERAGE_WAIT
..........     ........................
db file scattered read    1.12365      (full table scans)
db file sequential read   .13254       (index scan)
```

HASH_JOIN = Enabled   Default setting is 'Disabled'

HASH_AREA_SIZE   This parameter should be twice SORT_AREA_SIZE.

SORT_AREA_SIZE   This parameter benefits both merge-joins and hash joins. Listing 14.9 shows a SQL query that will show if your sort operations are going out to the operating-system for additional space. This setting should be large enough so that this does not happen very frequently.

EXAMPLE

Listing 14.9: Sort Area Size Monitoring

```
select value "Disk Sorts" from v$sysstat
where name = 'sorts(disk)'
```

SQL Coding Guidelines

Finally, we'll discuss some good and poor ways to code SQL statements. The following are some guidelines for SQL statement coding that will help both the rule-based and cost-based optimizers:

- **Do** use the IN operator instead of NOT. Try to avoid using the NOT command by using >=, <=, and so on.

- **Do** use array processing whenever possible (Export, and Pro*C applications).

- **Do** use hints to ensure the desired execution plan results.

- **Don't** use HAVING without a WHERE clause.

- **Don't** use calculations in the WHERE clause on indexed columns. Unless the intended behavior is to disable index use, any function on indexed columns will ignore the index.

- **Don't** use an index if more than 20% of the rows will be returned by the query.

- **Don't** use subqueries if other solutions exist (PL/SQL loop, for example).

- **Don't** write applications that use SQL execution plan defaults. Oracle Corporation makes no guarantees that default behavior will be maintained in future releases, or even between different hardware platforms.

NOTE

Array processing—A method in a C program to select groups of rows into the program over SQL Net; it's much faster than processing one row at a time.

Summary

This chapter concentrated on understanding the explain plan, a key ingredient to tuning the SQL statements found in our Sales Tracking application. We discussed the two Oracle optimizers, how to control both, and how to interpret the output explain plans from both. The author gave some key information on how to help interpret what the cost-based optimizer is doing and some key `init.ora` parameters to assist the cost-based optimizer in its decisions.

REVIEW

Reviewing It

1. What is an explain plan?

2. What is the main difference between the cost-based optimizer and the rule-based optimizer?

3. What is a driving table?

4. What might a histogram be useful for? What SQL syntax does Oracle require to use a histogram?

5. What are the three kinds of join conditions?

6. Is a full-table scan necessarily always bad?

7. What is clustering factor?

8. Describe a good use for a Stored Outline.

Checking It

1. Stored Outlines became available with this release of the database:

    a) V8.0.4

    b) V8.1.5

    c) V8.1.7

    d) V9.0.1

2. Which one of these helps control the rule-based optimizer?

    a) Existence of an index

    b) Use of functions in the WHERE clause

    c) Coding techniques

    d) All of the above

3. The rule-based optimizer uses a list of 18 different rules to make its decision.

    True/False

4. Both the rule and cost-based optimizers supports bitmapped indexes.

    True/False

5. Which of the following commands collects statistics for the cost-based optimizer?

    a) `Analyze <object name> computer statistics`

    b) `Estimate Statistics <object name>`

    c) `Alter System compute statistics <object name>`

    d) Oracle9i supports each of these options

6. If statistics have not been gathered and the OPTIMIZATION MODE is set to CHOOSE, Oracle will use the rule-based optimizer.

    True/False

7. If statistics have not been gathered and the OPTIMIZATION MODE is set to COST, Oracle will still use the rule-based optimizer.

   True/False

8. The init.ora parameter OPTIMIZER_INDEX_CACHING set to 0 says:

   a) The index cache will not be used

   b) Tells Oracle to do full-table scans

   c) Tells Oracle to rely upon indexes more

   d) Assumes a 0 buffer-hit cache ratio

9. Oracle8i allowed you to edit stored outlines.

   True/False

Applying It

APPLY

Independent Exercise 1:

- Install the explain plan table.

- Start SQL*Plus and run the query in Listing 14.4.

- Examine the output.

Independent Exercise 2:

- Add a hint to use the rule-based optimizer.

- Re-run the query in Listing 14.4 and compare the results with those from Exercise 1.

Independent Exercise 3:

- Alter the query in Listing 14.4 to invalid the use of an index.

- For both the cost-based optimizer (use a hint) and the rule-based optimizer (add 0 to a numeric field).

- Re-run the query using the explain table and check the result table.

What's Next?

Chapter 15 discusses Oracle Partitioning. Partitioning is useful to break very large objects into smaller, more manageable pieces. Oracle8 introduced partitioning and Oracle9i enhances it. This chapter also discusses the various partitioned index options as well.

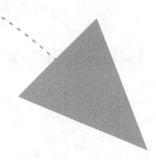

Oracle9i Partitioning Features

Some applications have tremendous amounts of data stored in tables. The larger the table, the longer it takes to perform certain administrative functions, such as backup and recovery. In addition, the larger the index associated with a table, the longer it takes to read through the leaf blocks to locate the row ID of the row or rows being accessed.

This chapter teaches you the following:

- What is partitioning?
- Oracle9i partitioning options
- Range partitioning
- Hash partitioning
- Composite partitioning
- List partitioning
- Oracle9i index partitioning options

What Is Partitioning?

Partitioning is a way of spreading tables and indexes physically, by keys, across two or more tablespaces. The Oracle cost-based optimizer is smart enough to recognize partitions and identify the best way to return rows. Partitioning also aids in backups and recovery by being capable of performing these functions on significantly less data, which means it takes far less time to back up a tablespace as well as recover it (should the need arise).

TIP

It has been my experience that the more one can divide up the disk I/O across disk drives, the better Oracle will perform. The best reason for partitioning Oracle tables and indexes is to break an otherwise large object into smaller, more manageable pieces, both from a data-access point of view and from an availability point of view.

Oracle9i Partitioning Options

Oracle8 introduced table partitioning with a feature known as *range partitioning*. Range partitioning means separating the rows from a table into various predefined tablespaces by a key, known as the *partition key*. The table can be accessed like any other table by its table name, or each partition can be accessed individually. An example of this is a quarterly report on a particular quarter in which the table is partitioned by date so that a quarter's worth of data resides in each tablespace. This report, knowing that it was going to use only data from this one "quarterly" tablespace, could just access this one tablespace, saving the optimizer and Oracle some work.

Each tablespace can be backed up and restored independently from the others.

Oracle8i built on this partitioning feature by offering hash partitioning and composite partitioning. *Hash* partitioning is an alternative to range partitioning when no predictable data pattern, such as a date field, exists. Hash partitioning evenly distributes the rows, based on a hash key, across the defined tablespaces.

Composite partitioning, on the other hand, is a combination of range and hash partitioning. In this process, the table is first distributed across tablespaces based on a range of keys, and then each of these range partitions is further subdivided across subpartitions (where the partition is actually divided a predetermined number of times). Then, rows are evenly allocated across these subpartitions by a hash key.

Oracle9i introduces *LIST partitioning*. This gives Oracle the ability to separate data across partitions based on a character string. List partitioning does not support any kind of order, it simply goes by a list of items that is to go in one partition or another.

Range Partitioning

Range partitioning organizes rows in the various assigned tablespaces based on a column(s). As illustrated in Figure 15.1, a partitioned table is a logical table physically stored across many tablespaces.

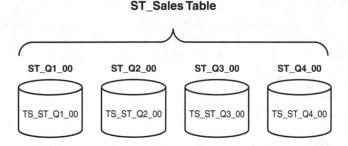

ST_Sales Table

Figure 15.1: *ST_SALES range partitioned table.*

Listing 15.1 illustrates the CREATE TABLE syntax that creates the ST_SALES table shown in Figure 15.1. Notice the PARTITION BY RANGE with the key field on which the partitioning will be based. More than one column can be listed with this clause. Each partition then has a LESS THAN clause that tells Oracle which rows to place in which tablespaces. It is good practice to always use the MAXVALUE clause, as illustrated in the last PARTITION statement in Listing 15.1.

EXAMPLE

Listing 15.1: Sales Tracking ST_SALES Range Partition Table Example

```
CREATE TABLE st_sales
    (sales_customer_id          NUMBER(6),
    sales_sale_amt          NUMBER(9,2),
    sales_sale_date          DATE)
    PARTITION BY RANGE(sales_sale_date)
        (PARTITION st_q1_00 VALUES LESS THAN ('01-APR-2000')
            TABLESPACE ts_st_q1_00,
         PARTITION st_q2_00 VALUES LESS THAN ('01-JUL-2000')
            TABLESPACE ts_st_q2_00,
         PARTITION st_q3_00 VALUES LESS THAN ('01-OCT-2000')
            TABLESPACE ts_st_q3_00,
         PARTITION st_q4_00 VALUES LESS THAN (MAXVALUE)
            TABLESPACE ts_st_q4_00
        ); ok pm
```

TIP

This table easily can be created by first creating the tablespaces, then following the example in Listing 15.1, and finally adding a postupdate and/or a postinsert trigger to execute from the ST_INVENTORY table when the Inv_sale date field is not null.

NOTE

Each partition can have its own defined storage clause.

Each partition can be accessed independently from the others. The SQL statement SELECT sales_customer_id, sales_sale_amt from ST_SALES PARTITION (st_q2_00) would only access the rows in the st-q2-00 table-space.

As new quarters are encountered, the DBA can simply add new partitions. Because the ST_SALES quarterly data is no longer needed, the tablespace can be backed up and then dropped, easily dropping all the rows. However, the rows can be easily re-established if business needs require it. Listing 15.2 shows the valid partitioning tablespace syntax options.

TIP

It is advised that you do not use the keyword MAXVALUE on the last partition of data-sensitive partitioning, such as the date field used in this example. It is easier to use the date for the partitioning and add another partition when the business requires it rather than to have to split, rename, and so on the last partition to accommodate a new range of dates.

EXAMPLE

Listing 15.2: Sales Tracking ST_SALES Partitioned Table Example

```
ALTER TABLE ADD PARTITION
ALTER TABLE DROP PARTITION
ALTER TABLE MOVE PARTITION
ALTER TABLE SPLIT PARTITION
ALTER TABLE TRUNCATE PARTITION
ALTER TABLE MODIFY PARTITION ADD VALUES
ALTER TABLE MODIFY PARTITION DROP VALUES
ALTER TABLE EXCHANGE PARTITION
```

NOTE

Notice in Figure 15.1 that the partitions have meaningful names. Accessing the data by partition might be necessary for good reason. However, with hash partitioning, no real reason exists to access the data by partition, although the Oracle syntax does allow for this.

Hash Partitioning

Hash partitioning is similar to range partitioning except that the partition key is hashed and the rows spread evenly across the assigned tablespaces. This kind of partitioning is convenient when the distribution of the rows might not be even, or no well-defined grouping of the key fields exists (as in the situation of the date field in the range partitioning example). Figure 15.2 illustrates how the tablespaces might appear for a hash-partitioned table, and Listing 15.3 shows the syntax needed to support the example in Figure 15.2. Notice no MAXVALUE clause exists with hash partitioning.

NOTE

Hashing algorithm—Takes a key field and applies a calculation to it that always equals a real number. This number then becomes the position in the table or index for the row or key value. In any kind of hash organization, you almost always need to know about how big the object will be so that Oracle can allocate enough hash positions to hold all the possible key values.

ST_Sales Table

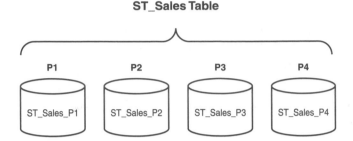

| P1 | P2 | P3 | P4 |

ST_Sales_P1   ST_Sales_P2   ST_Sales_P3   ST_Sales_P4

Figure 15.2: ST_SALES *hash partitioned table.*

EXAMPLE

Listing 15.3:   Sales Tracking ST_SALES Hash Partition Table Example

```
CREATE TABLE st_sales
    (sales_customer_id         NUMBER(6),
    sales_sale_date           DATE,
    sales_sale_amt            NUMBER(9,2))
    PARTITION BY HASH(sales_customer_id)
        (PARTITION p1 TABLESPACE ST_SALES_p1,
         PARTITION p2 TABLESPACE ST_SALES_p2,
         PARTITION p3 TABLESPACE ST_SALES_p3,
         PARTITION p4 TABLESPACE ST_SALES_p4
        ); ok pm
```

Composite Partitioning

Composite partitioning is a combination of range and hash partitioning. Notice in Figure 15.3 that each partition is now subdivided into four additional subpartitions. Listing 15.4 is the syntax used to support Figure 15.3. Each partition named P1, P2, P3, and P4 would contain the range of dates as defined by the STORE IN clause. The SUB PARTITIONS 4 clause subdivides each of these partitions into four logical units. The SUBPARTITION BY HASH clause, on the other hand, equally divides the rows that meet the range criteria, using the ST_CUSTOMER_ID as the hash key to evenly distribute the rows throughout these four subpartitions.

This example gives the ST_SALES object a total of 16 partitions for even row distribution.

ST_Sales Table

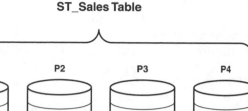

P1	P2	P3	P4
ST_Sales_P1	ST_Sales_P2	ST_Sales_P3	ST_Sales_P4

Figure 15.3: ST_SALES *composite partitioned table.*

EXAMPLE

Listing 15.4:   Sales Tracking ST_SALES Composite Partition Table Example

```
CREATE TABLE st_sales
    (sales_customer_id         NUMBER(6),
    sales_sale_date        DATE,
    sales_sale_amt       NUMBER(9,2))
    PARTITION BY RANGE(sales_sale_date)
    SUB PARTITION BY HASH (sales_customer_id)
    SUB PARTITIONS 4
    STORE IN (ST_SALES_p1, ST_SALES_p2, ST_SALES_p3, ST_SALES_p4)
        (PARTITION p1 VALUES LESS THAN ('01-APR-2000'),
         PARTITION p2 VALUES LESS THAN ('01-JUL-2000'),
         PARTITION p3 VALUES LESS THAN ('01-OCT-2000'),
         PARTITION p4 VALUES LESS THAN (MAXVALUE)
        ); ok pm
```

List Partitioning

List partitioning organizes rows in the various assigned tablespaces based on a list of literals. Listing 15.5 illustrates how list partitioning might be implemented across four partitions named East, South, West, and North.

Listing 15.5 illustrates the CREATE TABLE syntax that creates the ST_SALES table based on a list of characters, in no particular order, and so on. If a value is submitted that does not meet the criteria of any of the partitions, an error will be returned to the user or the application. There is no concept of MAXVALUE in list partitioning.

EXAMPLE

Listing 15.5:   Sales Tracking ST_SALES List Partition Table Example

```
CREATE TABLE st_sales
    (sales_customer_id         NUMBER(6),
     sales_sale_amt        NUMBER(9,2),
```

Listing 15.5: continued

```
sales_state                    VARCHAR(2))
PARTITION BY LIST(sales_state)
    (PARTITION st_east VALUES ('ME','VT','NH','MA','NY','PA')
        TABLESPACE ts_st_east,
    PARTITION st_south VALUES ('FL','TX','SC','NC','TN','KY')
        TABLESPACE ts_st_south,
     PARTITION st_west VALUES ('CA','UT','MT','OR','WA','AK')
        TABLESPACE ts_st_west,
     PARTITION st_north VALUES ('IA','MN','IL','MO','NE')
        TABLESPACE ts_st_north
); ok pm
```

Oracle9i does not support list partitioning for more than one column. The listed values must be unique, NULL can be specified, each partition must have at least one literal, and local/global indexes are supported (index partitioning is covered next).

Oracle9i Index Partitioning Options

Similar to table partitioning, *index* partitioning is a method of intelligently breaking larger indexes into smaller pieces across many tablespaces. The two types of index partitioning are local and global. *Local-partitioned* indexes have the same partitioning key values, number of tablespaces, and partitioning rules as the underlying table, whereas *global-partitioned* indexes have a PARTITION BY RANGE or PARTITION BY LIST clause that enables the partitioning values, number of partitions, and tablespaces themselves to all be defined and vary from the underlying table partitioning structure. These indexes can either be *prefixed* (meaning they contain a leading part of the index key) or *nonprefixed* (meaning they're index partitioned on a value different from the indexing column).

NOTE

Indexes can be partitioned even if the table being indexed is not partitioned. By default, this would be a global index because you would have to define the PARTITION BY RANGE or PARTITION BY LIST clause.

NOTE

Oracle9i does not support a nonprefixed, global-partitioned index. An error is returned if the partition range value is different from the leading column defined in the INDEX clause.

Types of Index Partitioning

A local index is one in which a single index partition's key values reference table rows in a single table partition. Listing 15.6 is an index example based on the ST_SALES table range partitioning example from Listing 15.1. The range partition key on the underlying table, ST_SALES, is sales_sale_date. A locally defined index is said to be *equi-partitioned*, meaning it has the same number of partitions with the same rules of partitioning. All local indexes are equi-partitioned by default. Notice that the locally defined index in Listing 15.6 has no PARTITION BY RANGE or PARTITION BY LIST clause because Oracle automatically uses the same number of partitions, as well as the same partitioning rules. In addition, the PARTITION clause is used in Listing 15.6 to enable you to control the names of the index partitions.

NOTE

If the PARTITION clause is omitted, Oracle creates system-generated partition names. If the TABLESPACE clause is omitted, Oracle places the index partition in the same table-spaces as the underlying table.

EXAMPLE

Listing 15.6:   Sales Tracking ST_SALES Local Partition Index Example

```
CREATE INDEX st_sales_Date_Idx on st_sales (sales_sale_date)
    LOCAL
    (PARTITION st_i_q1_00 TABLESPACE ts_st_i_q1_00,
     PARTITION st_i_q2_00 TABLESPACE ts_st_i_q2_00,
     PARTITION st_i_q3_00 TABLESPACE ts_st_i_q3_00,
     PARTITION st_i_q4_00 TABLESPACE ts_st_i_q4_00
    ); ok pm
```

A global-partitioned index has a partitioning structure (and probably partitioning keys) that differ from the table being indexed. Listing 15.7 illustrates the syntax for a global-partitioned index on the ST_SALES table, as previously discussed in Listing 15.1. Notice that the indexed column and the PARTITION BY RANGE columns are the same. Also notice that having the same number of partitions as the underlying table is unnecessary.

EXAMPLE

Listing 15.7:   Sales Tracking ST_SALES Global Prefixed Partition Index Example

```
CREATE INDEX st_sales_Customer_ID_Idx on st_sales (customer_id)
    GLOBAL
    PARTITION BY RANGE(customer_id)
        (PARTITION st_i_p1 VALUES LESS THAN 1000
            TABLESPACE ts_st_i_p1,
         PARTITION st_i_p2 VALUES LESS THAN 2000
            TABLESPACE ts_st_i_p2,
         PARTITION st_i_p3 VALUES LESS THAN (MAXVALUE)
            TABLESPACE ts_st_i_p3
        );
```

Prefixed Versus Non-prefixed Partitioned Indexes

A local-partitioned index can be created on a column other than the partitioning key of the underlying table. Listing 15.8 shows a nonprefixed index being created on the CUSTOMER_ID column. A local index cannot have a PARTITION BY RANGE clause (because it would not be a local-partitioned index), so the same partitioning rules from the underlying table apply here. The index will be created based on the Customer ID field, but the index values will be partitioned by sales_salp date as defined in the underlying table.

EXAMPLE

Listing 15.8:   Sales Tracking ST_SALES Local, Nonprefixed Partition Index Example

```
CREATE INDEX st_sales_Customer_ID_Idx on st_sales (customer_id)
    LOCAL
    (PARTITION st_i_q1_00 TABLESPACE ts_st_i_q1_00,
     PARTITION st_i_q2_00 TABLESPACE ts_st_i_q2_00,
     PARTITION st_i_q3_00 TABLESPACE ts_st_i_q3_00,
     PARTITION st_i_q4_00 TABLESPACE ts_st_i_q4_00
    );
```

NOTE

If the underlying table is hash-partitioned and the STORE IN clause is not specified on the CREATE INDEX clause, Oracle uses the same tablespaces as the underlying tables. If the underlying table is composite-partitioned, the same holds true. This default can be overridden by specifying STORE IN and new SUBPARTITION definitions in the CREATE INDEX clause.

TIP

Oracle8i and 9i support bitmap-partitioned indexes.

Evaluating the Index Partitioning Options

A local, prefix-partitioned index relationship to the base table is illustrated in Figure 15.4. Notice that a local partition is equi-partitioned and the index has the same partitioning structure and rules as the underlying table.

Local, prefixed-partitioned indexes are the most efficient of the partitioned indexes because the optimizer knows that the rows in the underlying table will be indexed in a single partition. Oracle therefore does not have to scan all the partitions to satisfy the SQL statement request.

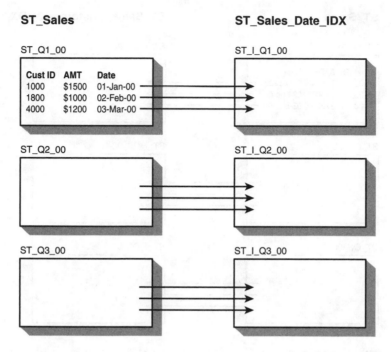

Figure 15.4: *Local prefix-partitioned index relationship illustration.*

A local, nonprefix-partitioned index is more work for Oracle because it must scan each of the partitions looking for values. In Figure 15.5, the index is created on the CUSTOMER_ID column, but the index leaves are still organized by the date field as defined by the underlying ST_SALES table. The CUS-TOMER_ ID leaves can be in any of the partitions. This type of index is best suited for parallel-processing Oracle environments in which each processor working on the SQL statement can search a partition.

Global, prefix-partitioned indexes are best for any kind of range-scan–type processing. This kind of an index groups the rows together in the same partition, and the cost-based optimizer knows in which partition to look for the range of values being requested. Figure 15.6 illustrates the relationship of a global index to its underlying table.

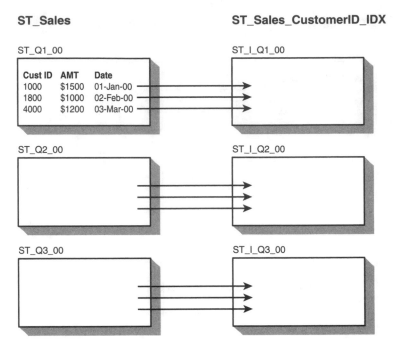

Figure 15.5: *Local, nonprefixed-partitioned index relationship illustration.*

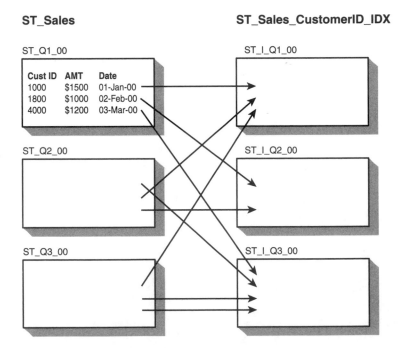

Figure 15.6: *ST_SALES composite-partitioned table relationship illustration.*

Summary

This chapter introduced you to all the Oracle9i partitioning features, examples of good uses of each, and illustrations using these partitioning features in the Sales Tracking application.

Reviewing It

1. What is the difference between a range partition and a list partition?

2. Briefly explain the difference between a hash partition and a composite partition.

3. What is the difference between a local-partitioned index and a global-partitioned index?

Checking It

1. You can perform a partition split operation on a list partition.

   True/False

2. Hash Partitioning

   a) Automatically spreads the rows across partitions

   b) Uses a RANGE clause

   c) Allows for MAXVALUES

   d) All of the above

3. If you have a partitioned index, the table MUST be partitioned as well.

   True/False

4. Which of these options is the easiest for the cost-based optimizer?

   a) Local prefixed index

   b) Local nonprefixed index

   c) Global index

5. Which of these options is the easiest for parallel processing?

   a) Local prefixed index

   b) Local nonprefixed index

   c) Global index

What's Next?

The next chapter begins the next section of this book: Working with Oracle9i Tools and Utilities. Chapter 16 covers the popular TOAD Oracle development tool, Chapter 17 covers loading and moving data, and Chapter 18 illustrates Log Miner.

Part IV

Working with Oracle9i Tools and Utilities

Working with Oracle9i Tools and Utilities

Using TOAD in the Development Arena

Using SQL*Loader, External Tables, and Export/Import

Using Log Miner

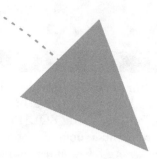

Using TOAD in the Development Arena

This chapter begins the tools and utilities part of the book with a thorough review of the popular Oracle development tool: TOAD.

This chapter teaches you the following:

- The History of Toad
- Using the Main Interface
- Building SQL and PL/SQL with TOAD
- Using the PL/SQL Debugger
- Using other TOAD Utilities

The History of TOAD

TOAD began with one window, the SQL Editor. Jim McDaniel developed it to improve the efficiency of developing and testing code (see Figure 16.1). The alternative at the time was using SQL*Plus only, or using SQL*Plus in conjunction with a text editor. Both methods were cumbersome. So, the SQL Editor was developed. It is still the window where developers spend most of their time.

TOAD developed a following. As the product expanded into multiple windows loyal followers of TOAD offered requests for additional features and options. As a result, the features, options, and even windows expanded.

Quest Software purchased TOAD in November of 1998. TOAD was already a full-featured product. Additional developers were added to the project. TOAD continues to evolve, and the customer base continues to grow. TOAD has evolved into an all-around full-featured Oracle development tool, which includes Procedure Editor, a symbolic debugger, Schema Browser, SQL Modeler, and Object Browser.

Figure 16.1: *TOAD splash screen.*

Figure 16.2 shows the main TOAD interface screen. The various tabs enable you to create, browse, or alter objects (tables, views, indexes, and so on) including abstract data types; graphically build, execute, and tune queries as well as edit, debug, and profile stored procedures—including procedures, functions, packages, and triggers. TOAD also allows you to search for objects and fix database problems with constraints, triggers, extents, indexes, and grants.

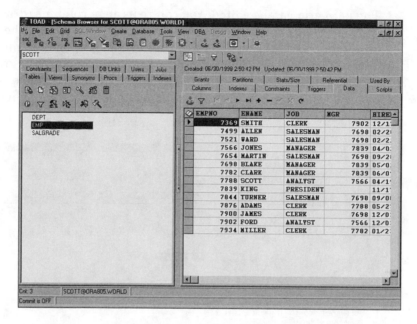

Figure 16.2: *TOAD main interface screen.*

Using the Main TOAD Interface

When TOAD starts up, it puts you in the SQL Editor window. The SQL Editor is the heart of TOAD, and it lets you type, edit, recall, execute, and tune. The window contains an editor to compose SQL statements or scripts and a results grid to display the results from SELECT SQL statements. A horizontal splitter between the editor and the results grid lets you size each panel accordingly. The *Show Tables* window (see Figure 16.2) button invokes the *Table Names Select* window, which lets you select tables from a dropdown list.

TIP

Many windows in TOAD contain an additional menu of useful options, accessed by a right mouse click. In the Editor the menu includes the ability to comment/uncomment highlighted statements as well as formatting options for the entire context of the editor.

The data grid on the right has several features, such as the ability to change the font, record selectivity, column size, number of rows displayed, row height, and the display of row ids.

The data grid can be edited. You can rearrange columns (drag and drop) without having to re-execute your queries. TOAD retains the column layout (order and widths) from query to query as long as the column list in the query remains the same. You can sort columns in the data grid in ascending or descending order. If a column has a lot of text, the memo editor can be used. The Memo editor is invoked by double-clicking on a cell; see Figure 16.3.

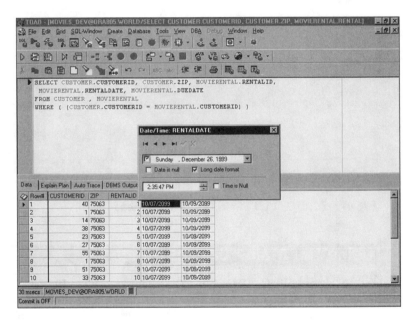

Figure 16.3: *Memo editor.*

Notice the (red) box at the bottom of the screen—this indicates that the selected field is not editable. A red or green box displays in the status panel at the bottom of the SQL Edit window indicating whether the recordset is editable (green) or not editable (red). If the indicator is red, while the data can't be edited, it can still be selected and copied.

The Single Record View button is present throughout TOAD data windows and results grids. It is located on the top left of the table. The *Single Record View* window is for displaying, editing, and inserting records of selected items. You can advance forward and backward through the records by clicking the arrow buttons, and you can post edits, as shown in Figure 16.4.

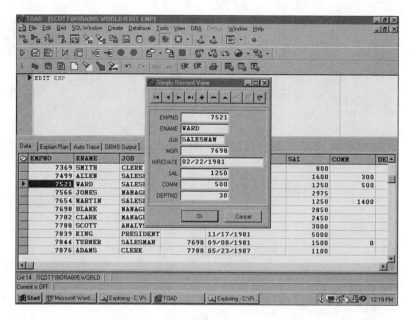

Figure 16.4: *Single Record Viewer.*

TOAD enables you to visually explain plans in a number of ways, as illustrated in Figure 16.5. You can see the steps in a tree diagram and click expand buttons to see the explain plan step details.

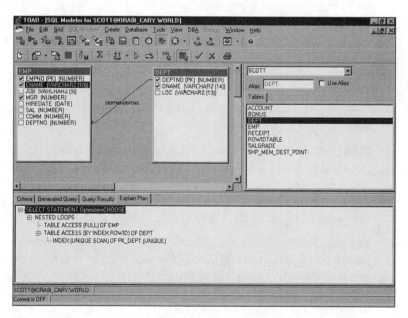

Figure 16.5: *Explain Plan Viewer.*

Auto Trace tab displays the results of every statement issued while in Auto Trace mode. It helps with the tuning of SQL statements. When you run a query you can find out some performance statistics related to that query.

When you execute a DBMS Output statement, the DBMS Output will automatically display in the DBMS Output tab of the results grid; see Figure 16.6.

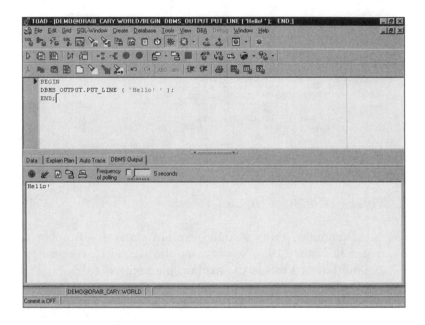

Figure 16.6: *DBMS output example.*

TOAD also interfaces with other code development tools such as VB, Java, C++, or Delphi, allowing the code to be copied to and from TOAD to these other coding environments.

TOAD allows you to create and edit scripts without being connected to an Oracle database. This can be useful in numerous situations, such as when using a laptop computer on a trip, when an Oracle database goes down, or when working with a language such as HTML. The file language types supported are PL/SQL, HTML, INI, JAVA, and TEXT.

You can choose the Commit button from the main toolbar or from the Database, Commit menu item. You can turn "Commit automatically after every statement" on or off through the Oracle options menu (see Figure 16.7). The status panel shows the status of Commit. You can also set TOAD to prompt for commit before closing.

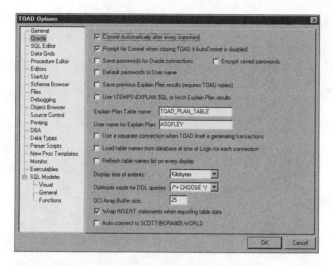

Figure 16.7: *Commit status panel.*

Building SQL and PL/SQL Using TOAD

TOAD enables you to create and modify SQL and PL/SQL. This code can be entered in a blank SQL Edit window, load SQL in from a file (menu bar File, Open File, see Figure 16.8), recall a previously edited SQL statement, or be recalled from a previously created work session. A SQL edit window can also be launched from the object browser, the schema browser, or the SGA trace window.

Working with SQL

TOAD allows you to view available columns while working on a SQL query.

1. After you type the table name (or view name) and the period, press CTRL+T or wait a few seconds.

2. A list of columns displays, see Figure 16.9.

3. Click the column you want to select. (Hold the CTRL key to select multiple columns.)

4. Press Enter and TOAD places the selected column(s) into the SQL Editor in your query.

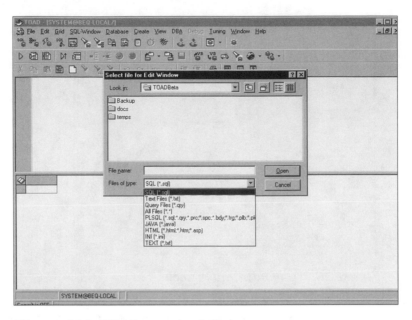

Figure 16.8: *TOAD supported file types.*

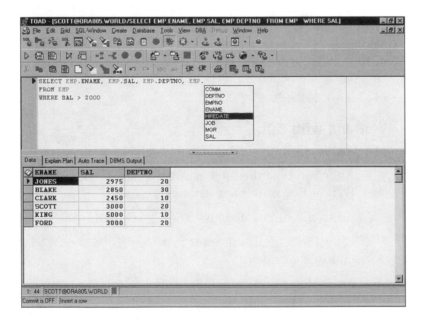

Figure 16.9: *Column Display / Column Insert while working on SQL.*

After a query populates the SQL Results Grid, you can press CTRL+T to display a list of the columns from the SQL Results Grid.

The View, Options displays a series of tabs that control virtually every aspect of TOAD. The SQL Editor tab contains numerous options for the SQL Editor; see Figure 16.10.

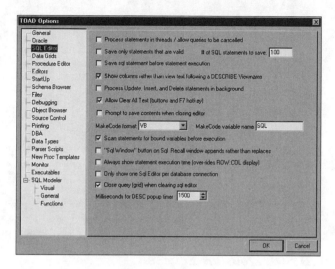

Figure 16.10: SQL Editor options page.

Working with PL/SQL

The Procedure Editor lets you create or modify procedures, functions, packages, triggers, types, and type bodies. If you have the optional PL/SQL Debugger, the debugger buttons will display enabled to the right of the Procedure Editor toolbar.

The Procedure Edit window has two panels. The left panel contains the Package Navigator List, which is a list of objects or package contents. The right panel contains the Procedure Editor, which shows the code for the selected object.

Packages are composed of a SPEC and a BODY. Functions in the navigator list are indicated with an *F( )* and procedures are indicated with a *P( )*. A sort button lets you sort the navigator list in the source code order or in an alphabetized Spec and Body list. You can synchronize the navigator list to your new code edits. Each object being edited will have its own tab in the right window.

With TOAD you can create stored procedures (such as functions and procedures), test them, grant privileges on them, and create public synonyms to them.

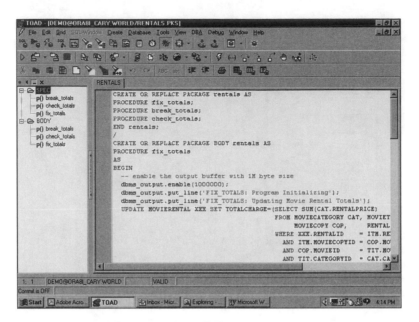

Figure 16.11 SQL Procedure Editor.

You run a selected procedure by clicking the Execute button in the Schema Browser, or right-click the "Execute without debugging" menu item in the Procedure Editor.

There are two main ways to get code into the Procedure Editor: read from a file or load from the database (as illustrated in Figure 16.12).

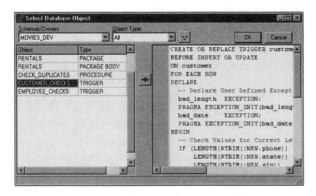

Figure 16.12: TOAD accessing database objects.

To Load Source from an existing object:

1. Click the Load Source from an existing object button.

2. The Select Database Object window will display, see Figure 16.12.

3. Select the desired schema from the schema drop-down list.

4. You can filter using the object types drop-down list, which defaults to All.

5. You can further filter by clicking the filter button (funnel icon next to object types), which shows/hides widgets that let you set up a starts with, includes, or ends with filter.

6. To preview the source for an object, select the object from the object list and click the right arrow. (You can double-click an object name to load it directly into the Procedure Edit window.)

7. The selected object's SQL script is displayed in the right panel of the Select Database Object window.

8. Click OK. The code is opened in the Procedure Editor, and the Select Database Object window closes automatically.

CREATING A NEW PROCEDURE

The Create a New Procedure button invokes the New Procedure Create Options window (see Figure 16.13). You select the Object Type from the drop-down list and enter the New Object Name. You also select the Object Template from a drop-down list. If the object type is a trigger, the trigger options panel is enabled. A template script (appropriate to the object type you selected) with your object name is pulled into the editor. TOAD automatically substitutes values for keywords in the template such as object name, user name, and time.

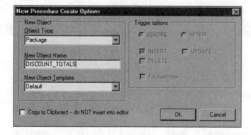

Figure 16.13: *TOAD Creating New database objects.*

Using the PL/SQL Debugger

TOAD has an optional symbolic debugger, a procedure that allows you to watch the execution of the code, set variables on the fly, see contents of variables, and set break points and conditions (when the debugger is to start). The debugger is toggled on or off in the Procedure Edit window by pressing the icon that looks like a bug or by accessing the Debug option on the menu bar (see Figure 16.14). The debugger lets you step through the code as it executes line-by-line. You can add and delete breakpoints (using the Debug menu item or key strokes Ctrl+Alt+B and even set conditional breakpoints. You can also check for dependencies and loops.

The PL/SQL Debugger has numerous options, including colors for the breakpoints, allowing watches on package variables, and choosing whether or not you want dependencies to be compiled. You can even choose to have a prompt for compiling dependencies.

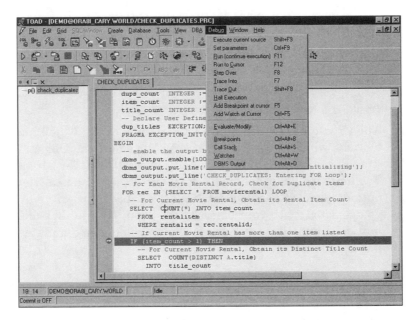

Figure 16.14: *TOAD Debug options.*

To Start the Debugger:

1. Open the Procedure Edit window from either the Database, Procedure Editor menu item, or Click the Open a New Procedure Edit window button on the main toolbar.

2. Load a PL/SQL procedure into the editor or write a new procedure. You can load a procedure from a file on disk or you can load a procedure from an existing object in the database.

3. Compile the procedure by pressing F9 OR by clicking the Compile button on the Procedure Editor toolbar.

4. Press F7 (Trace Into) to step through the code. TOAD generates the symbol table required to obtain debug information for this procedure.

If you want to step into other procedures and view debug information, you'll need to click the Compile Dependencies with Debug toolbar button before beginning the debug process.

Using Other TOAD Utilities

TOAD contains many other useful utilities. These modules are covered in the next few sections: the schema browser, SQL Modeler, the DBA Module, SQL*Loader assistance, a NT scheduler, and source-code control.

The Schema Browser

The Schema Browser separates database objects in a selected schema by type, using tabs (or with a drop-down list that you can select through the options menu). The left panel lists the objects and the right panel displays the details (see Figure 16.15 and 16.16). To see the tables in a schema, click the Tables tab and a list of the tables displays in the objects panel. Object details are displayed in tabs in the Details panel. To see a table's columns, simply click the Columns tab in the Details panel. To see a table's data, click the Data tab. To manually edit, add, or delete data in the Schema Browser, simply double-click on the cell.

You can change the options and appearance of the schema browser via the menu bar View, Options and clicking the Schema Browser section or by right-mouse clicking on the Schema Browser itself.

The Status panel shows what session you have currently selected. The CNT on the Status panel shows how many objects are in the object list for the object tab that has been selected.

Some objects have object name and other filtering capability. On the Schema Browser page, Tables, Data tab and Views, Data tab, a four-way filter button displays a dialog box where you can sort and/or filter. The filter can display four states: empty (default), filtered (only display certain objects, ascending/descending filtered (only display certain objects in a particular order), ascending/descending empty (display all objects in a particular order).

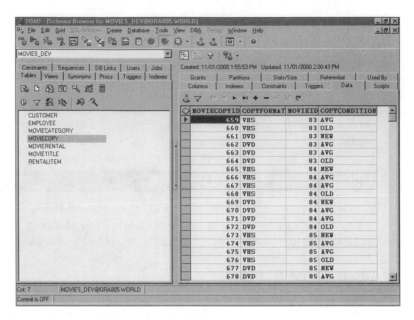

Figure 16.15: *TOAD Schema Browser.*

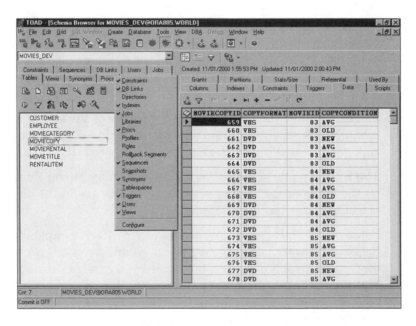

Figure 16.16: *TOAD Schema Browser configuration.*

TOAD can create scripts (through the Create Script buttons on the object tabs), for most objects that are displayed in the Schema Browser. You can copy object names and column data from the Schema Browser panels to a clipboard or another application.

TIP

Creating scripts from the database is a good practice, as scripts stored on the computer might not accurately reflect what is in the database.

The View, Options, Schema Browser page provides numerous options for the Schema Browser.

To Create a User using the Schema Browser:

1. Open the Schema Browser window.

2. Click the User tab on the object panel.

3. Click the Create New User button on the User object panel.

4. The Create User window will display. (You can also access the window through the Create, User menu item.)

5. Fill in the user information on each tab: User, Tablespace, Roles, System Privileges, and Grants.

6. When you are done, click OK.

This procedure copies column names from the list on the Tables/Columns tab or the Views/Columns tab via multi-select list and copy.

From Tables, Columns

1. Click the Column you want to copy. To select more than one column, press CTRL while clicking the columns you want to select. To select a continuous block of columns, select the starting point, press SHIFT, and click the ending part of the blocked selection.

2. Press CTRL+C or select Edit, Copy from the menu.

The selection is copied to the clipboard. In this example, the following selection is copied to the clipboard.

MOVIECOPYID, COPYFORMAT, COPYCONDITION

SQL Modeler

The SQL Modeler dialog box lets you quickly create the framework of a SELECT, INSERT, UPDATE, or DELETE statement allowing you to view the generated code, execute, and view the results.

The Table Model Area lets you graphically lay out a query, as shown in Figure 16.17. Drag-and-drop columns from one table to another to create joins between the tables. Click the Generated Query tab to view the generated SQL query. Click the Execute button, and the results will display in the Query Results tab near the bottom. Notice that there are various tabs to show the various outputs such as the explain plan, the data output, and so on.

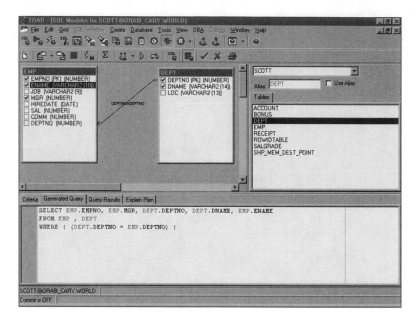

Figure 16.17: *TOAD SQL modeler.*

To perform a join, drag-and-drop a column from one table to another table column. A line between the related tables is automatically drawn showing the relationship. Double-click the line to adjust the properties (inner join, outer join, and so on). See Figure 16.18.

TOAD DBA

The optional DBA module is designed to make common DBA tasks easy. It offers security, storage, and database object management (see Figure 16.19). You can compare and synchronize schemas. It has Oracle Import, Export, and SQL*Loader interfaces. The DBA module adds extra features to the Create menu, the Schema Browser, and the DBA menu. A TOAD Monitor feature lets you view database performance, (see Figure 16.20) and TOAD also contains a proportional spacemap showing you how objects appear in the tablespaces (see Figure 16.21).

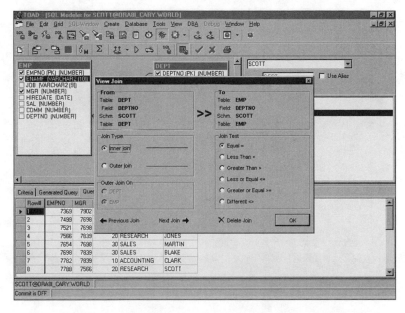

Figure 16.18: *TOAD SQL Modeler entity relationships.*

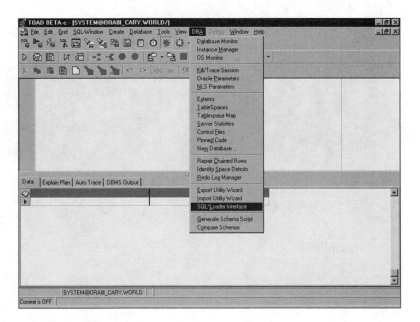

Figure 16.19: *TOAD DBA.*

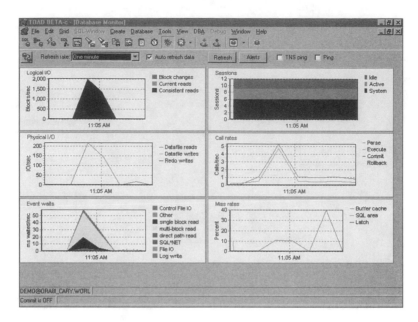

Figure 16.20: *TOAD DBA monitoring.*

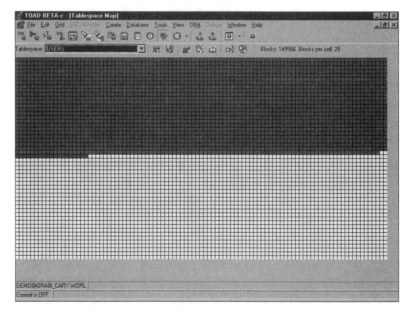

Figure 16.21: *TOAD DBA spacemap.*

You can create entire databases, alter libraries, profiles, roles, rollback segments, snapshots, tablespaces, and more.

SQL*Loader Wizard

The TOAD SQL*Loader is a utility that lets you graphically build a control file for use with the Oracle SQL*Loader, a database server application (see Figure 16.22). You configure the location of the utility in the View, Options, Executables page.

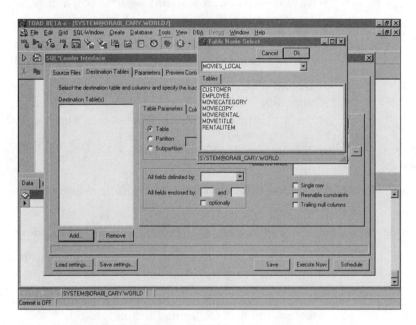

Figure 16.22: *TOAD DBA SQL*Loader utility.*

Throughout the SQL*Loader Interface, you can move your mouse pointer over a field to display microhelp for that field.

To Load a Data File:

1. Click the DBA, SQL*Loader Interface menu item. The SQL*Loader Interface window displays with the Source File tab selected.

2. In the Source File tab type click the Add button.

3. The Add Input File window displays. Click the drill down next to the Input filename box to choose the data file. The Bad file and Discard file textboxes are automatically entered with their default extensions.

4. Enter the rest of the data for the Source File.

   The Bad File box lists a file in which to place rejected records.

   The Discard box lists a file in which to place records that weren't inserted during the load, because they didn't match any of the selection criteria.

- **Stream Format**—the default. Lines are read until an end-of-record marker is found (end-of-line character, by default).

- **Fixed Record Format**—each record must be a fixed number of bytes in length.

- **Variable Record Format**—each record may be a different length as specified by a special field, the first field in each record.

- **End of Record Box**—If you leave this field empty, the end-of-line character will be the end-of-record by default.

- **Discard Up to ___ Records Box**—This field indicates the maximum number of records to put into the discard file. If you leave this box empty, it indicates that you want all records.

5. Once you have entered all the data, click OK. The filename appears in the window under Input File.

6. Click the Destination Tables tab. This is where you select the destination table(s).

7. Click the Add button. The Table Name Select window displays.

8. Select a schema from the drop-down list and click on a table and click OK to select a table from the list.

9. Specify the parameters for your destination table(s) in the Table Parameters tab and Columns Parameters tab.

10. Click the Parameters tab. Here, you can name the control file whatever you want. Fill in the desired options. Remember, move the mouse over a field to display the microhelp.

11. When you are finished, click the Execute Now button. This will execute your control file.

TIP

Save Button

Click Save at any time to save the control file. The control file is also automatically saved whenever you click Execute Now.

Execute Now Button

This executes your control file.

TOAD Job Scheduler

The SQL*Loader has a scheduler that lets you schedule the load as a windows task. Clicking the Schedule button opens the NT Job Scheduler window. You can set the time for it to run and the frequency. Once you click OK, your job is added.

TOAD Source Code Control

TOAD supports Source Code Control through most major source control vendors (see Figure 16.23). Source Control is run through the Procedure Editor. The toolbar on the Procedure Editor contains the check-in and check-out buttons.

NOTE

You must set the Source Control options including the Source Control provider from the View, Options, Source Control page. Source Control does not work with database objects; it only works with files.

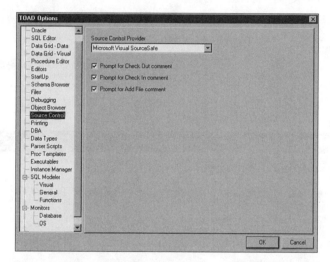

Figure 16.23: TOAD DBA Source Code utility.

Summary

This chapter covered some of TOAD's basic windows and functions. The TOAD software comes with a tutorial as well as extensive online documentation on all of its features including the following list of topics and optional modules:

- TOAD Reports
- Master/Detail Record Browser
- Privileges

- Rebuild Table
- TOAD Security
- SGA Trace Optimization
- Estimate Table Size
- Estimate Index Size
- Profiler Analysis
- Object Browser
- Server Statistics
- Repair Chained Rows
- Identify Space Deficits
- Object Search
- Oracle Parameters
- Kill/Trace
- SGA Trace

REVIEW

Reviewing It

1. What does TOAD stand for?
2. Where can I download the current version of TOAD?
3. Where do you access the single record viewer?
4. What is the Schema Browser useful for?

CHECK

Checking It

1. Is TOAD strictly a development tool?

   Yes/No
2. When TOAD starts up, this window comes up first:

   a) SQL Modeler

   b) SQL Editor

  c) SQL Procedure Builder

  d) SQL Schema Browser

3. TOAD only works with SQL and PL/SQL.

 True/False

4. How many different ways are there to get code into the Procedure Editor?

  a) 1

  b) 2

  c) 4

  d) 6

APPLY

Applying It

Independent Exercise 1:

- Build a simple SQL query, logged in as SCOTT, using the EMP and DEPT tables.

  - Display the results.

  - Model the SQL relationships.

  - Show an explain plan.

  - Change some salaries one row at a time.

Independent Exercise 2:

- Add a new user.

- Grant this new user the same privileges as SCOTT.

Independent Exercise 3:

- Build a POST-INSERT trigger on the EMP table.

  - Have it make sure the DEPTNO code is in the DEPT table.

  - Have it loop 10 times, updating a variable by 10 with each loop.

- Set a break point just inside the loop.
    - Check the value of the variable with each loop.

Independent Exercise 4:

- Using the Schema Browser, see if EMP has any procedures.

What's Next?

Chapter 17, "Using SQL*Loader, External Tables, and Export/Import," covers some of the various Oracle data-handling facilities, such as SQL*Loader, Export and Import, and External Tables.

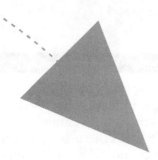

Using SQL*Loader, External Tables, and Export/Import

This chapter introduces the reader to the Oracle data loading and data movement utilities: SQL*Loader, External Tables, and Export and Import. SQL*Loader, Export, and Import have been with the Oracle product in one form or another since version 4 where the External Tables are new with Oracle9i. This chapter will cover usage of all of these utilities. This chapter teaches you the following:

- What Is SQL*Loader
- What Are External Tables
- Using Export and Import

What Is SQL*Loader

Oracle Databases today are ever increasing in complexity and size. Gigabyte-sized databases are common, and data warehouses are often reaching the terabyte-sized range. With the growth of these databases, the need to populate them with external data quickly and efficiently is of paramount importance. To handle this challenge, Oracle provides a tool called SQL*Loader that loads data from external data files into an Oracle database.

SQL*Loader has many functions that include the following capabilities:

- Data can be loaded from multiple input data files of differing file types.

- Input records can be of fixed and variable lengths.

- Multiple tables can be loaded in the same run. SQL*Loader can also logically load selected records into each respective table.

- SQL functions can be used against input data before being loaded into tables.

- Multiple physical records can be combined into a single logical record. Likewise, SQL can take a single physical record and load it as multiple logical records.

SQL*Loader is a flexible tool as well. SQL*loader can load data from specifically formatted files (files with data fields in fixed locations), files where the fields have some kind of field separator (such as a '.'), data that is in its own definition file, or it can even load data via the Unix pipe command. SQL*Loader can also take advantage of Oracle Parallel Server, is one of the tools covered by Oracle9i resumable features, and can perform direct-path loads to the database. This method using the direct-path option skips the traditional logging of data to Oracle's recovery mechanisms and simply loads data blocks in the tablespaces, it is much faster than the conventional load previously described here.

SQL*Loader works in conjunction with a control file (see Figure 17.1). This control file contains syntax defining what format and field separation is in the input data file, what table and table columns are to be populated, and can contain many of the command-line options such as the reject file (rejected records), commit point (how many records to insert prior to doing a database commit), degree of parallelism, and so on.

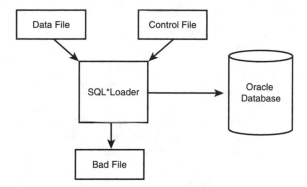

Figure 17.1: *SQL*Loader configuration.*

SQL*Loader Syntax

SQL*Loader has many options that can be defined both in a control file or on the command line when executing SQL*Loader. Listing 17.1 shows the SQL*Loader help text. As you can see, SQL*Loader has many options. This section covers the basics and provides useful examples that comprise some typical data-loading exercises.

Notice near the end of Listing 17.1, the command line syntax: `'sqlldr scott/tiger control=foo logfile=log'`. SQL*Loader needs a valid userid and password and it needs a control file. The control file will be covered shortly. You can use the keyword syntax `userid=scott/tiger` or the userid and password can be the first syntax after the command `sqlldr`. In other words, some of these options are positional on the command line, others are not.

TIP

The author recommends using keywords on the command line, which helps for readability when used inside command scripts, and it ensures that the options desired are the options specified.

EXAMPLE

Listing 17.1:   SQL*Loader Help Text

```
SQL*Loader: Release 9.0.1.0.0 - Production on Sun Aug 12 14:36:04 2001

Copyright 2001 Oracle Corporation.  All rights reserved.


Usage: SQLLOAD keyword=value [,keyword=value,...]

Valid Keywords:
```

Listing 17.1: continued

```
      userid -- ORACLE username/password
     control -- Control file name
         log -- Log file name
         bad -- Bad file name
        data -- Data file name
     discard -- Discard file name
  discardmax -- Number of discards to allow        (Default all)
        skip -- Number of logical records to skip  (Default 0)
        load -- Number of logical records to load  (Default all)
      errors -- Number of errors to allow          (Default 50)
        rows -- Number of rows in conventional path bind array or
      between direct path data saves
                  (Default: Conventional path 64, Direct path all)
    bindsize -- Size of conventional path bind array in bytes  (Default 256000)
      silent -- Suppress messages during run (header,feedback,errors,discards,
      partitions)
      direct -- use direct path                    (Default FALSE)
     parfile -- parameter file: name of file that contains parameter specifications
    parallel -- do parallel load                   (Default FALSE)
        file -- File to allocate extents from
skip_unusable_indexes -- disallow/allow unusable indexes or index partitions
        (Default FALSE)
skip_index_maintenance -- do not maintain indexes, mark affected indexes as
      unusable  (Default FALSE)
commit_discontinued -- commit loaded rows when load is discontinued
      (Default FALSE)
    readsize -- Size of Read buffer                (Default 1048576)
external_table -- use external table for load; NOT_USED, GENERATE_ONLY,
      EXECUTE  (Default NOT_USED)
columnarrayrows -- Number of rows for direct path column array  (Default 5000)
streamsize -- Size of direct path stream buffer in bytes  (Default 256000)
multithreading -- use multithreading in direct path
  resumable -- enable or disable resumable for current session  (Default FALSE)
resumable_name -- text string to help identify resumable statement
resumable_timeout -- wait time (in seconds) for RESUMABLE  (Default 7200)
PLEASE NOTE: Command-line parameters may be specified either by
position or by keywords.  An example of the former case is 'sqlldr
scott/tiger foo'; an example of the latter is 'sqlldr control=foo
userid=scott/tiger'.  One may specify parameters by position before
but not after parameters specified by keywords.  For example,
'sqlldr scott/tiger control=foo logfile=log' is allowed, but
'sqlldr scott/tiger control=foo log' is not, even though the
position of the parameter 'log' is correct.
```

The control file is used to tell SQL*Loader what format the data to be loaded is in and it also tells SQL*Loader where to load the data. Many of the command-line options can also be specified in the control file. The control file typically has a suffix of .ctl.

In Listing 17.1, with CONTROL=FOO, it would be assumed that there is a control file named FOO.CTL in the computer directory where the SQL*Loader was executed from. The logfile can be specified either on the command line or in the control file. This is the journal of how the loader session went, what time it was initiated, and how many records were loaded into what object from what data source. Any errors that might occur will also appear in this log file. If a suffix is not given to the log file name, a .log suffix will be added to it. Another file, refer to Figure 17.1, is the .bad file. This file will be created even if it is not defined. If not defined, it will have the same filename as the control file but with a .bad suffix. This file will contain any records not loaded by SQL*Loader. This gives the user the ability to load most of the records that are not problematic and deal specifically with those records that are.

Another key syntax in Listing 17.1 is SKIP, the number of records to skip at the beginning of the load; LOAD, the number of records to load then stop the load process; and ERRORS, the number of bad records to encounter before stopping the load process. The remainder of the syntax listed in Listing 17.1 is useful but beyond the scope of this chapter.

The control file syntax is as follows. It must start with LOAD DATA or with the recoverable or unrecoverable option set as in UNRECOVERABLE LOAD DATA. The default is recoverable. Unrecoverable is like a direct-path load, it bypasses the Oracle recovery and read-consistency mechanisms giving a faster load but with data loss if something happened during the load. Listing 17.2 shows the control file syntax (defaults are underlined, syntax in [ ] are optional) and Listing 17.3 shows a simple example with its data file.

The INSERT mode requires that the table being loaded is empty. An error will result if the table has rows in it and SQL*Loader will stop. APPEND simply does inserts to the table whether there are any rows or not. REPLACE will do a DELETE of any rows in the table and then insert the data, and TRUNCATE will truncate the table the insert the data. The BEGINDATA section is needed if the data being loaded is actually in the control file. Notice that you can specify more than one INFILE.

Listing 17.2: Control File Syntax

```
[UNRECOVERABLE | RECOVERABLE] LOAD DATA
[INFILE <computer file name> [INFILE <computer name>]…]
[INSERT | APPEND | REPLACE | TRUNCATE] [Options] INTO TABLE <table name> …)]
    [FIELDS TERMINATED BY] [( <column name column data type and field
    location or delimiter, [ …]
[BEGINDATA and data in control file]
```

The columns that the data is associated with are named. These columns can have a data type, they should have either the infile location by location start and location end position or have a field delimiter specified. Files being loaded where the fields are in fixed locations use the location start and end position, as shown in Listing 17.3. The position is the number of positions from the beginning of the record.

Listing 17.3: Control File Column Definition Syntax

```
( EMPNO     POSITION(01:04) INTEGER EXTERNAL,
  ENAME     POSITION(06:15) CHAR,
  JOB       POSITION(17:25) CHAR,
  MGR       POSITION(27:30) INTEGER EXTERNAL,
  SAL       POSITION(32:39) DECIMAL EXTERNAL,
  COMM      POSITION(41:48) DECIMAL EXTERNAL,
  DEPTNO    POSITION(50:51) INTEGER EXTERNAL)
```

Notice the CHAR, INTEGER EXTERNAL, and other commands in Listing 17.3. This is defining the type of field in the data file. INTEGER EXTERNAL is commonly used for numbers with no decimal positions. DECIMAL EXTERNAL is used for numbers with decimal locations, CHAR is used for character fields, and so on. There are many kinds of field types but these are the common ones. An Oracle date mask (HIRE_DATE DATE 'mm/dd/yy') follows the DATE column type.

SQL*Loader Examples

Notice how the control file in Listing 17.4 follows the column format rules of Listing 17.3. This control file uses a delimited file to separate the fields. Notice the INFILE syntax, the REPLACE syntax is used causing any rows that were in the table TEST_PWD to be deleted. When loading a delimited file, the first field in the data file will be loaded into the column login_id, the second field (determined by the delimiter ':' in this example) will be loaded into the column xfield, and so on.

Listing 17.4: Simple Control File Example

```
load data
infile 'passwd.dat'
replace into table test_pwd
fields terminated by ':'
```

Listing 17.4: continued

```
(
    login_id      char,
    xfield        char,
    user_id       integer external,
    group_id      integer external,
    full_name     char,
    full_path     char,
    start_shell   char)

passwd.dat data file

skanathu:x:1030:10:Swamy Kanathur:/home/skanathu:/bin/ksh
pmcgrath:x:1100:10:Patrick McGrath:/export/home/pmcgrath:/bin/ksh
rvanderz:x:1101:10:Ryan Vanderzanden:/export/home/rvanderz:/bin/ksh
jgreenle:x:1102:10:Jerry Greenlee:/export/home/jgreenle:/bin/ksh
amohamed:x:1103:10:Azeem Mohamed:/export/home/amohamed:/bin/ksh
cspacko:x:1107:10:Chris Spacko:/export/home/cspacko:/bin/ksh
mkurtz:x:1108:10:Mark Kurtz:/export/home/mkurtz:/bin/ksh
solson:x:1109:10:Scott Olson:/export/home/solson:/bin/ksh
shealy:x:1110:10:Steve Healy:/export/home/shealy:/bin/ksh
imnadm:x:1111:2504:NetQuestion:/opt/IMNSearch:/bin/sh
jsteffan:x:1034:102:Joshua Steffan:/export/home/jsteffan:/bin/ksh
rbuglio:x:1001:102:Rick Buglio:/export/home/rbuglio:/bin/ksh
djenson:x:1007:102:Deb Jenson:/export/home/djenson:/bin/ksh
mfriel:x:1009:102:Mike Friel:/export/home/mfriel:/bin/ksh
```

After the load is complete, Listing 17.5 illustrates the data in the table.

EXAMPLE

Listing 17.5: SQL Query Showing Data Loaded by Listing 17.4

```
SQL> select login_id, user_id
  2  from test_pwd;

LOGIN_ID                 USER_ID
-------------------- ----------
skanathu                    1030
pmcgrath                    1100
rvanderz                    1101
jgreenle                    1102
amohamed                    1103
cspacko                     1107
mkurtz                      1108
solson                      1109
shealy                      1110
imnadm                      1111
jsteffan                    1034
```

Listing 17.5: continued

```
rbuglio                 1001
djenson                 1007
mfriel                  1009
```

Listing 17.6 shows the SQL*Plus help system control file. Notice the INFILE is a *, which means that the data will be supplied (see the BEGINDATA syntax). This control file is using the APPEND feature and loads a table called HELP.

EXAMPLE

Listing 17.6: SQL*Plus HELP Table Control File

```
--
-- Copyright  1997 by Oracle Corporation. All Rights Reserved.
--
load data
infile *
preserve blanks
into table help append
fields terminated by '^'
TRAILING NULLCOLS
(
    topic, seq, info
)
BEGINDATA
Assignment Statement^1^
Assignment Statement^2^ Assignment Statement
  .
  .
  .
```

Listing 17.7 shows the familiar EMP table being loaded with SQL*Loader. Notice the INFILE has fixed position fields. Because there is no MODE specified, INSERT is assumed and the EMP table being loaded must not have any rows in it.

EXAMPLE

Listing 17.7: EMP Table Control File

```
LOAD DATA
INFILE 'employees.dat'
INTO TABLE EMP

( EMPNO     POSITION(01:04) INTEGER EXTERNAL,
  ENAME     POSITION(06:15) CHAR,
  JOB       POSITION(17:25) CHAR,
  MGR       POSITION(27:30) INTEGER EXTERNAL,
  SAL       POSITION(32:39) DECIMAL EXTERNAL,
  COMM      POSITION(41:48) DECIMAL EXTERNAL,
  DEPTNO    POSITION(50:51) INTEGER EXTERNAL)
```

Listing 17.8 illustrates the log file generated from the load of the table in Listing 17.4. If there were any errors, they too would have appeared in this file. Notice all the options and any default options taken are specified. This was a successful load because all 14 records loaded with no errors or rejects. Be sure to look at the time stamp at the end of the listing.

EXAMPLE

Listing 17.8: TEST_PWD Table Load Log File

```
SQL*Loader: Release 9.0.1.0.0 - Production on Sat Aug 11 17:10:13 2001

Copyright 2001 Oracle Corporation.  All rights reserved.

Control File:   passwd.ctl
Data File:      passwd.dat
  Bad File:     passwd.bad
  Discard File: none specified

 (Allow all discards)

Number to load: ALL
Number to skip: 0
Errors allowed: 50
Bind array:     64 rows, maximum of 256000 bytes
Continuation:   none specified
Path used:      Conventional

Table TEST_PWD, loaded from every logical record.
Insert option in effect for this table: REPLACE


   Column Name              Position  Len Term Encl Datatype
-----------------------     --------- ----- ---- ---- -----------------------
LOGIN_ID                    FIRST      *    :         CHARACTER
XFIELD                      NEXT       *    :         CHARACTER
USER_ID                     NEXT       *    :         CHARACTER
GROUP_ID                    NEXT       *    :         CHARACTER
FULL_NAME                   NEXT       *    :         CHARACTER
FULL_PATH                   NEXT       *    :         CHARACTER
START_SHELL                 NEXT       *    :         CHARACTER


Table TEST_PWD_EXT:
  14 Rows successfully loaded.
  0 Rows not loaded due to data errors.
  0 Rows not loaded because all WHEN clauses were failed.
  0 Rows not loaded because all fields were null.
```

Listing 17.8: continued

```
Space allocated for bind array:                    115584 bytes(64 rows)
Read   buffer bytes: 1048576

Total logical records skipped:        0
Total logical records read:          14
Total logical records rejected:       0
Total logical records discarded:      0

Run began on Sat Aug 11 17:10:13 2001
Run ended on Sat Aug 11 17:10:20 2001

Elapsed time was:      00:00:07.50
CPU time was:          00:00:00.07
```

What Are External Tables

External tables are new to Oracle9i. This feature enables computer files to be accessed while still outside the Oracle database. These files that become relational tables are read-only, cannot have indexes (no ROWID), and are designed for data loading, allowing the load process to take full advantage of the SQL language. For example, when loading, it might be desirable to make changes to it upon the load (such as using a DECODE function to change data values or concatenating fields together). Using SQL*Loader, you would have to load a table then use SQL syntax to perform the desirable changes. Using external tables, this is accomplished in a single step.

External Table Syntax

External table definitions resemble SQL*Loader control files and both have similar information such as delimiters (see line 14 of Listing 17.9), log and bad files (lines 15 and 16), as well as other similarities. Listing 17.9 creates the EXTERNAL_PWD file, an external file version of Listing 17.4. Notice that this is a pretty standard CREATE TABLE until line 9, where instead of a storage clause, there is the syntax ORGANIZATION EXTERNAL. The remainder of this script contains information that would be found in a SQL*Loader control file.

Notice the default directory in line 11. This is an Oracle directory that must be set up ahead of the external table. Oracle directories were introduced in Oracle8i and simply give a name to a computer directory location. This location is then appended to any file reference, including the file being accessed as an external table at line 18. Listing 17.10 shows the syntax necessary to create the Oracle Directory.

Listing 17.9: External Table Syntax

```
1:    create table EXTERNAL_PWD (
2:          login_id    char(20),
3:          xfield      char(1),
4:          user_id     number,
5:          group_id    number,
6:          full_name   char(30),
7:          full_path   char(30),
8:          start_shell char(20))
9:    organization external (
10:       type oracle_loader
11:       default directory hotka
12:       access parameters (
13:            records delimited by newline
14:            fields terminated by ':'
15:            badfile 'passwd_bad_ext'
16:            logfile 'passwd_log_ext'
17:            missing fields are null)
18:       location ('passwd.dat'))
19:    reject limit unlimited;
```

Listing 17.10: Oracle Directory Setup

```
SQL> connect scott/tiger
Connected.
SQL> create directory hotka as '/disk10/o901ut01/hotka';

Directory created.

SQL>
```

Using SQL with External Tables

After the external table has been created, it acts pretty much like any other Oracle table. Listing 17.11 shows a description of the newly created table from Listing 17.9, and Listing 17.12 shows a simple query being run against the external table. Statistics on the options used to create the external table are stored in DBA_EXTERNAL_TABLES.

Listing 17.11: External Table Describe

```
SQL> desc EXTERNAL_PWD
```

Name	Null?	Type
LOGIN_ID		CHAR(20)
XFIELD		CHAR(1)
USER_ID		NUMBER
GROUP_ID		NUMBER

Listing 17.11:   continued

FULL_NAME	CHAR(30)
FULL_PATH	CHAR(30)
START_SHELL	CHAR(20)

EXAMPLE

Listing 17.12:   Simple SQL Query

```
SQL> select login_id, full_name
  2  from test_pwd_ext;

LOGIN_ID                   FULL_NAME
-------------------        ------------------------------
skanathu                   Swamy Kanathur
pmcgrath                   Patrick McGrath
rvanderz                   Ryan Vanderzanden
jgreenle                   Jerry Greenlee
amohamed                   Azeem Mohamed
cspacko                    Chris Spacko
mkurtz                     Mark Kurtz
solson                     Scott Olson
shealy                     Steve Healy
imnadm                     NetQuestion
jsteffan                   Joshua Steffan
rbuglio                    Rick Buglio
djenson                    Deb Jenson
mfriel                     Mike Friel

14 rows selected.
```

Converting SQL*Loader Control Files

Existing SQL*Loader scripts can be converted to external tables easily with SQL*Loader. Use this command line script used against the employee.ctl (refer to Listing 17.7): Unix> sqlldr user_id=scott/tiger external_file= generate_only . This command then prompts you for the control file. Listing 17.13 illustrates the employee.log file that was generated. The external table definition as well as the file location information are in this log file. Notice that it uses generated names for the table name and the Oracle directory.

EXAMPLE

Listing 17.13:   External Table Conversion

```
SQL*Loader: Release 9.0.1.0.0 - Production on Tue Aug 21 23:14:35 2001

Copyright 2001 Oracle Corporation.  All rights reserved.

Control File:   employee.ctl
Data File:      employees.dat
```

Listing 17.13: continued

```
  Bad File:     employees.bad
  Discard File: none specified

 (Allow all discards)

Number to load: ALL
Number to skip: 0
Errors allowed: 50
Continuation:   none specified
Path used:      External Table


Table EMP, loaded from every logical record.
Insert option in effect for this table: INSERT

     Column Name                Position  Len  Term Encl Datatype
----------------------------- ---------- ----- ---- ---- --------------------
EMPNO                               1:4    4             CHARACTER
ENAME                              6:15   10             CHARACTER
JOB                               17:25    9             CHARACTER
MGR                               27:30    4             CHARACTER
SAL                               32:39    8             CHARACTER
COMM                              41:48    8             CHARACTER
DEPTNO                            50:51    2             CHARACTER



CREATE DIRECTORY statements needed for files
---------------------------------------------------------------------
CREATE DIRECTORY SYS_SQLLDR_XT_TMPDIR_00000 AS '/disk10/o901ut01/hotka'


CREATE TABLE statement for external table:
---------------------------------------------------------------------
CREATE TABLE "SYS_SQLLDR_X_EXT_EMP"
(
  EMPNO NUMBER(4),
  ENAME VARCHAR2(10),
  JOB VARCHAR2(9),
  MGR NUMBER(4),
  SAL NUMBER(7,2),
  COMM NUMBER(7,2),
  DEPTNO NUMBER(2)
)
ORGANIZATION external
(
```

Listing 17.13: continued

```
TYPE oracle_loader
DEFAULT DIRECTORY SYS_SQLLDR_XT_TMPDIR_00000
ACCESS PARAMETERS
(
  RECORDS DELIMITED BY NEWLINE CHARACTERSET US7ASCII
  BADFILE 'SYS_SQLLDR_XT_TMPDIR_00000':'employees.bad'
  LOGFILE 'employee.log_xt'
  FIELDS LDRTRIM
  (
    EMPNO (1:4) INTEGER EXTERNAL(4),
    ENAME (6:15) CHAR(10),
    JOB (17:25) CHAR(9),
    MGR (27:30) INTEGER EXTERNAL(4),
    SAL (32:39) INTEGER EXTERNAL(8),
    COMM (41:48) INTEGER EXTERNAL(8),
    DEPTNO (50:51) INTEGER EXTERNAL(2)
  )
)
location
(
  'employees.dat'
)
)REJECT LIMIT UNLIMITED


INSERT statements used to load internal tables:
---------------------------------------------------------------------
INSERT /*+ append */ INTO EMP
(
  EMPNO,
  ENAME,
  JOB,
  MGR,
  SAL,
  COMM,
  DEPTNO
)
SELECT
  EMPNO,
  ENAME,
  JOB,
  MGR,
  SAL,
  COMM,
```

Listing 17.13:   continued

```
  DEPTNO
FROM "SYS_SQLLDR_X_EXT_EMP"


statements to cleanup objects created by previous statements:
----------------------------------------------------------------
DROP TABLE "SYS_SQLLDR_X_EXT_EMP"
DROP DIRECTORY SYS_SQLLDR_XT_TMPDIR_00000



Run began on Tue Aug 21 23:14:35 2001
Run ended on Tue Aug 21 23:14:41 2001

Elapsed time was:     00:00:05.58
CPU time was:         00:00:00.07
```

Using Export and Import

Export and Import are two character-mode utilities supplied by Oracle Corporation as early as Oracle4. The utilities perform a function that their name implies: export creates operating-system files of data from Oracle tables and import reads these operating-system files and creates the tables and loads the data back into the tables. The two utilities are used together primarily to back up and restore data, move data to other Oracle databases, and migrate data from earlier releases of Oracle to newer releases.

The common utilities Export and Import also have some serious enhancements. Export and Import now support all objects in a particular tablespace as well as wild-card selections when table objects are selected for export.

Export and Import can perform many important tasks in the Oracle9i environment. Export can be used to store data in archives, removing rows that are not being used but can easily be added with Import if the need exists.

Export and Import can play an important backup and recovery role that will be discussed later in this section. Export and Import can be used to create test environments; they have the ability to capture all of a particular user's tables, indexes, and data and re-create these objects in another Oracle instance.

Export/Import Syntax

The operation of the Import and Export utilities is quite straightforward. Export writes the DDL (table definitions, index definitions, privileges, and so on) as well as the data itself. There are many options available to both Export and Import, such as just capturing the DDL information and not the data. Export then saves this information to named operating system files. The operating system files that Export creates are known as *dump files*. The dump files, which are in an Oracle proprietary format, are only useful to the Import utility. These dump files can be given specific names (operating-system dependent) or allowed to default to a preassigned name of EXPDAT.DMP.

Listing 17.14 shows the various parameters available for Export, and Listing 17.15 shows the various parameters available for Import.

NOTE

Export creates files that only Import can read and process. Be careful when using Export and Import to move data between different versions of Oracle. Older releases of Import will not necessarily read operating-system files created by newer versions of Export.

EXAMPLE

Listing 17.14:   Export Help Information

```
Invoking SQL*Export:
$ exp help=y

Export: Release 9.0.1.0.0 - Production on Sat Aug 11 15:38:22 2001

 Copyright 2001 Oracle Corporation.  All rights reserved.



You can let Export prompt you for parameters by entering the EXP
command followed by your username/password:

    Example: EXP SCOTT/TIGER

Or, you can control how Export runs by entering the EXP command followed
by various arguments. To specify parameters, you use keywords:

    Format:  EXP KEYWORD=value or KEYWORD=(value1,value2,...,valueN)
    Example: EXP SCOTT/TIGER GRANTS=Y TABLES=(EMP,DEPT,MGR)
             or TABLES=(T1:P1,T1:P2), if T1 is partitioned table

USERID must be the first parameter on the command line.

Keyword     Description (Default)       Keyword     Description (Default)
--------------------------------------------------------------------------
USERID      username/password           FULL        export entire file (N)
BUFFER      size of data buffer         OWNER       list of owner usernames
```

Listing 17.14:   continued

FILE	output files (EXPDAT.DMP)	TABLES	list of table names
COMPRESS	import into one extent (Y)	RECORDLENGTH	length of IO record
GRANTS	export grants (Y)	INCTYPE	incremental export type
INDEXES	export indexes (Y)	RECORD	track incr. export (Y)
DIRECT	direct path (N)	TRIGGERS	export triggers (Y)
LOG	log file of screen output	STATISTICS	analyze objects (ESTIMATE)
ROWS	export data rows (Y)	PARFILE	parameter filename
CONSISTENT	cross-table consistency	CONSTRAINTS	export constraints (Y)

FEEDBACK	display progress every x rows (0)
FILESIZE	maximum size of each dump file
FLASHBACK_SCN	SCN used to set session snapshot back to
FLASHBACK_TIME	time used to get the SCN closest to the specified time
QUERY	select clause used to export a subset of a table
RESUMABLE	suspend when a space related error is encountered(N)
RESUMABLE_NAME	text string used to identify resumable statement
RESUMABLE_TIMEOUT	wait time for RESUMABLE
TTS_FULL_CHECK	perform full or partial dependency check for TTS
VOLSIZE	number of bytes to write to each tape volume
TABLESPACES	list of tablespaces to export
TRANSPORT_TABLESPACE	export transportable tablespace metadata (N)
TEMPLATE	template name which invokes iAS mode export

Export terminated successfully without warnings.

EXAMPLE

Listing 17.15:   Import Help Information

Invoking SQL*Import:

$ imp help=y

Import: Release 9.0.1.0.0 - Production on Sat Aug 11 15:38:44 2001

Copyright 2001 Oracle Corporation. All rights reserved.

You can let Import prompt you for parameters by entering the IMP
command followed by your username/password:

   Example: IMP SCOTT/TIGER

Or, you can control how Import runs by entering the IMP command followed
by various arguments. To specify parameters, you use keywords:

   Format: IMP KEYWORD=value or KEYWORD=(value1,value2,...,valueN)

Listing 17.15:   continued

```
     Example: IMP SCOTT/TIGER IGNORE=Y TABLES=(EMP,DEPT) FULL=N
              or TABLES=(T1:P1,T1:P2), if T1 is partitioned table
```

USERID must be the first parameter on the command line.

```
Keyword  Description (Default)       Keyword       Description (Default)
-----------------------------------------------------------------------
USERID   username/password          FULL          import entire file (N)
BUFFER   size of data buffer        FROMUSER      list of owner usernames
FILE     input files (EXPDAT.DMP)   TOUSER        list of usernames
SHOW     just list file contents (N) TABLES       list of table names
IGNORE   ignore create errors (N)   RECORDLENGTH  length of IO record
GRANTS   import grants (Y)          INCTYPE       incremental import type
INDEXES  import indexes (Y)         COMMIT        commit array insert (N)
ROWS     import data rows (Y)       PARFILE       parameter filename
LOG      log file of screen output  CONSTRAINTS   import constraints (Y)
DESTROY                 overwrite tablespace data file (N)
INDEXFILE               write table/index info to specified file
SKIP_UNUSABLE_INDEXES   skip maintenance of unusable indexes (N)
FEEDBACK                display progress every x rows(0)
TOID_NOVALIDATE         skip validation of specified type ids
FILESIZE                maximum size of each dump file
STATISTICS              import precomputed statistics (always)
RESUMABLE               suspend when a space related error is encountered(N)
RESUMABLE_NAME          text string used to identify resumable statement
RESUMABLE_TIMEOUT       wait time for RESUMABLE
COMPILE                 compile procedures, packages, and functions (Y)
VOLSIZE                 number of bytes in file on each volume of a file on tape
```

```
The following keywords only apply to transportable tablespaces
TRANSPORT_TABLESPACE import transportable tablespace metadata (N)
TABLESPACES tablespaces to be transported into database
DATAFILES datafiles to be transported into database
TTS_OWNERS users that own data in the transportable tablespace set
```

Import terminated successfully without warnings.

Export Example

Export and Import are easily initiated with the EXP or IMP syntax. All the options can be specified on the command line, redirected from a file, or both Export and Import will prompt you for the options if no options appear on the command line. Figure 17.2 illustrates this dialog box for Import.

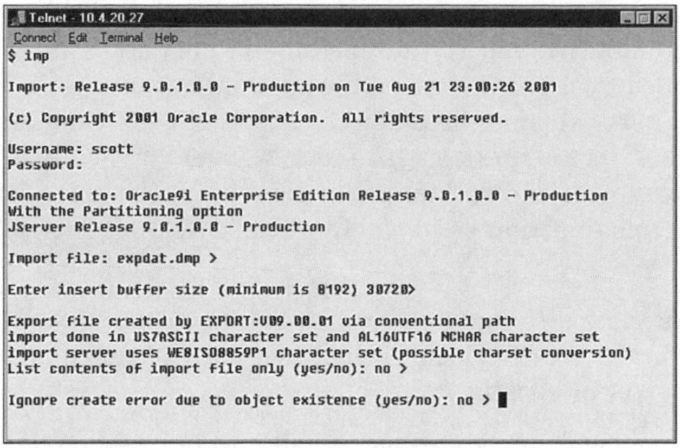

Figure 17.2: Import dialog box example.

TIP

The option Ignore Errors due to Object Existence should be set to YES. I highly advise creating the objects, with the proper storage parameters, prior to doing an Import. Export, especially if the compress option is used, will arrive at its own extent sizes based on the amount of data in the table object. I find it convenient to create the objects prior to running Import so that the DBA has complete control over the storage parameters.

Using Export/Import for Backup and Recovery

Oracle9i has many backup and recovery features, including cold backups (database down and all files backed up), hot backups (occurs at the tablespace level with the database fully operational), and using RMAN (covers a variety of recovery scenarios).

Oracle's Export and Import utilities provide a different method of backing up and recovering database objects. The Oracle utilities Export and Import provide many functions to the Oracle RDBMS environment. Both are useful in moving individual objects or entire groups of objects owned by a single user from one Oracle RDBMS to another. These same utilities provide the Oracle9i environment with a way of incrementally backing up only those objects that have changed since the prior incremental backup. The hot and cold backup methods concentrate on copying the database files assigned to the tablespaces. This incremental backup method utilizing Export and Import concentrates on copying the objects out of the tablespace and has nothing to do with the database files assigned to the tablespaces.

There are three levels of Export for object backup and recovery: complete export, cumulative export, and incremental export. The level of the export is controlled by a parameter on the command line or in the export parameter file. There are also three objects that track the time and type of export backup: SYS.INCEXP, SYS.INCFIL, and SYS.INCVID, which are optionally created by the CATEXP.SQL file at database install time. Consult with your DBA if there is some question as to whether this CATEXP.SQL script was installed or not.

There are some different settings for the export to support this incremental backup mode. These options are FULL=Y and INCTYPE=COMPLETE (or CUMULATIVE or INCREMENTAL).

These three levels of export backup all build on one another. Incremental backups only have changes made to objects from the most recent incremental or cumulative export, in this order. Cumulative exports have all changes made to objects from the most recent cumulative or complete export backup. Complete export backups have all changes to objects from the next previous complete export. The three levels of export supersede each other, in that, when a complete export is done, all prior complete, cumulative, and incremental exports become obsolete. Similarly, when a cumulative export is done, all incremental exports to the next-most-recent cumulative export become obsolete. Incremental exports are the lowest level of export in this backup scenario.

Figure 17.3 illustrates a typical incremental backup scenario utilizing the Export process. Point A on the time line is the complete backup. Point B is the first incremental backup and contains all the changed objects from Point A to Point B. Point C is the first cumulative backup. At this point, the cumulative file contains all the changed objects to the database from Point A, including those changed objects captured in the incremental backup of Point B. At Point C, the incremental backup from Point B is no longer of any value. The same is true of the relationship of Point C to Point F. Point F will contain all the changed objects to the database from Point C, the last most-previous-incremental backup at the same level. Each level (Complete, Cumulative, or Incremental) will contain the changed objects from the last incremental export of the same level.

The reason for all these levels is time. It takes longer to do the complete export than to do the cumulative and/or incremental exports. This system was designed to work best with the following scenario: perform complete exports once a month, perform cumulative exports on each of the following weekends, and perform incremental exports daily. Each cumulative export will contain all the changes to the database from either the previous cumulative or the complete export. The incremental exports will contain the changes made on that particular day. This incremental backup scenario is best used in a development or an environment with many end users doing their own object manipulation. This method of export/import gives the DBA great flexibility to restore single objects or data that was inadvertently dropped or deleted.

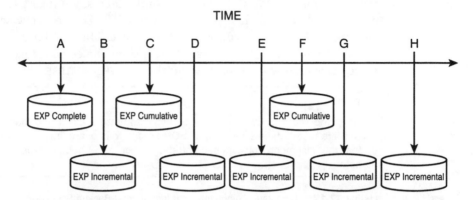

Figure 17.3: Incremental backup scenario.

Listing 17.16 illustrates two weeks' worth of backups. This scenario performs a complete export (begins with an F) on the first of the month and cumulative backups on the weekends. An incremental backup is performed daily. Each of the incrementals only contains changes from the prior complete (F) or cumulative. The cumulative contains all the changes from the last cumulative or the last complete.

EXAMPLE

Listing 17.16: Complete, Cumulative, and Incremental Backup Scenario

```
F_day1.exp
I_day2.exp
I_day3.exp
I_day4.exp
I_day5.exp
I_day6.exp
C_day7.exp
I_day8.exp
I_day9.exp
I_day10.exp
  .
  .
  .
```

When restoring a series of exported files, it is important to do the last export first with the INCTYPE=SYSTEM to restore the Oracle9i data dictionary.

This parameter needs to be done first to restore any changes to objects owned by SYS. An INCTYPE=RESTORE will restore all other objects except those owned by SYS. Run these non-SYS restores in the order that they were created.

The recovery scenario in Listing 17.17 is based on the same backups illustrated in Listing 17.16. For the example, let's say a user's table got dropped on the 11th and was last updated on the 7th. The recovery scenario in Listing 17.17 would recover that lost object. The last backup needs to be run first with the INCTYPE=SYSTEM first, then the series of export files needs to be recovered with import using the INCTYPE=RESTORE.

TIP

When the INCTYPE=SYSTEM, only those objects that have changed that are owned by SYS are restored, thus restoring the Oracle data dictionary first. This is important so that the incremental objects can find the correct object settings when they run and load data.

EXAMPLE

Listing 17.17: Complete, Cumulative, and Incremental Backup Scenario

```
IMP system/manager FULL=Y INCTYPE=SYSTEM FILE=I_day10.exp
IMP system/manager FULL=Y INCTYPE=RESTORE FILE=C_day7.exp
IMP system/manager FULL=Y INCTYPE=RESTORE FILE=I_day8.exp
IMP system/manager FULL=Y INCTYPE=RESTORE FILE=I_day9.exp
IMP system/manager FULL=Y INCTYPE=RESTORE FILE=I_day10.exp
```

Summary

This chapter introduced you to the Oracle data handling utilities: SQL*Loader, External Tables, and Export/Import. Each has its own place in the Oracle9i database and application environment and the examples used here are both simple and real-world.

REVIEW

Reviewing It

1. What is the purpose of SQL*Loader?

2. Why would someone use External Tables instead of SQL*Loader?

3. Why would you want SQL*Loader to skip records?

4. What are Export/Import used for?

Checking It

1. Which of the following is proper SQL*Loader command line syntax:

   a) `Sqlldr userid=scott/tiger control=foo.ctl`

   b) `Sqlldr scott/tiger foo`

   c) `Sqlldr`

   d) All of the above

2. Data will be inserted and any data in the table will remain with which mode:

   a) INSERT

   b) APPEND

   c) REPLACE

   d) TRUNCATE

3. The table is expected to be empty with which mode:

   a) INSERT

   b) APPEND

   c) REPLACE

   d) TRUNCATE

4. `INTEGER EXTERNAL` is used to define numbers with decimal points?

   True/False

5. A converted SQL*Loader control file to an External file puts the `CREATE TABLE` in a separate file with a `.SQL` suffix.

   True/False

6. Which of the following is NOT valid `EXPORT` syntax:

   a) `EXP SCOTT/TIGER GRANTS=Y TABLES=(EMP,DEPT,MGR)`

   b) `EXP`

   c) `EXP USERID=SCOTT/TIGER`

   d) All are valid syntax

Applying It

Independent Exercise 1:

- Export the SCOTT schema.
- Drop the SCOTT.EMP table.
- Import just the SCOTT.EMP table.

Independent Exercise 2:

- Create a SQL*Loader control file for EMP.
- Delete all the rows in EMP.
- Use SQL*Loader to put data into the SCOTT.EMP table.

Independent Exercise 3:

- Create a simple data file using ':' as field delimiters.
- Create an External Table based on this simple data file.
- Query your simple data using the External Table.

What's Next?

The next chapter focuses on using Log Miner, a utility useful in reviewing Oracle online and archiving log files. You will learn how to recover transactions using Log Miner as well as perform various user audit functions.

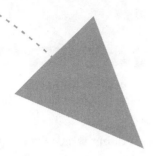

Using Log Miner

This chapter teaches you the following:

- What Is Log Miner?
- Using the Log Miner Interface
- Practical Uses for Log Miner
- Oracle9i enhancements

What Is Log Miner

Log Miner is used to view into the Oracle online or archive redo logs. This is useful in creating 'undo' SQL, and is useful to back out committed transactions.

This information is also useful to see who has been doing what; for example, some uses for auditing.

Log Miner first appeared with Oracle8.1.7 and is a free utility that comes with the database and examines and extracts information from Oracle Redo logs. This log information can be used to undo committed transactions, such as erroneous DELETEs, and this same information can be used to audit database activity such as table access, who is making DML changes to sensitive objects, and how often certain objects are being accessed.

When re-doing a transaction, there might be a complicated fix that needs to be replicated on many servers. The DBA can manually fix one server and use Log Miner to create a script of the changes that can then be easily applied to the other servers via SQL*Plus. An undo example might be where a user deleted some information but either forgot the where clause (deleting all of the rows), or put the wrong information in the where clause (deleting the wrong rows).

Log Miner requires an Oracle 8.1 or 9.0 database but can read log files belonging to Oracle8.0 databases. The 8i version of Log Miner does not support IOTs, clustered tables, advanced data types, or row chaining (a type of database fragmentation) whereas 9i covers many of these things.

Using the Log Miner Interface

Log Miner uses the DBMS_LOGMNR package through the SQL*Plus interface to the database. One of the new Oracle9i enhancements is a GUI interface.

NOTE

As of this writing, the Oracle9i Log Miner GUI Interface was not available. The examples in this chapter will work with an Oracle9i database.

There are some items that need to be set up prior to using Log Miner. You need an operating-system directory (such as c:\LogMinerOutput) to hold the log miner output files and you need to create a dictionary file that will contain the redo logs being examined. The init.ora parameter UTL_FILE_DIR = <this new directory> will need to be set as well. Make sure to stop and start your database instance so that Oracle will use this new parameter setting.

Create the log miner dictionary file by using the commands shown in Listing 18.1.

Listing 18.1:   Create the Log Miner Dictionary File

```
SQL> execute dbms_logmnr_d.build(dictionary_filename=>'logminerdictionary.ora',
        dictionary_location=>'c:\LogMinerOutput');
```

EXAMPLE

TIP

On my NT 4.0 PC, using Oracle8.1.7, I was logged into SQL*Plus as INTERNAL to get these dbms_logmnr packages to work. The Oracle9i equivalent is to be connected as SYSDBA or SYSOPER.

Now you will need to know which redo logs you wish to examine. Use the SQL*Plus command in Listing 18.2 to add the log file or files to the dictionary file created in Listing 18.1.

Listing 18.2:   Add Logs to the Dictionary File

```
SQL> execute dbms_logmnr.add_logfile(
        LogFileName => 'd:\orant\database\log1orcl.ora',
        Options => dbms_logmnr.NEW);
```

EXAMPLE

The syntax NEW creates a new output file. To add more log files to the dictionary file use ADDFILE, and to remove any unwanted log files, use REMOVEFILE.

To begin log mining, use the command in Listing 18.3 to load the V$LOGMNR_CONTENTS virtual table with information from the assigned redo logs. This command loads the entire contents of the log into the virtual table. Listing 18.4 shows how to limit the search by either SCN (Oracle change number, Oracle's internal time stamp of any transaction) or by date and time.

Listing 18.3:   Starting the Log Miner Process

```
SQL> execute dbms_logmnr.start_logmnr(
        DictFileName => 'logminerdictionary.ora');
```

EXAMPLE

Listing 18.4:   Limiting the Log Miner Search

```
SQL> execute dbms_logmnr.start_logmnr(
        DictFileName => 'logminerdictionary.ora',
        StartTime => to_date(`23-Nov-2000 20:00:00', 'DD-MON-YYYY HH:MI:SS')
        EndTime => to_date('23-Nov-2000 20:30:00', 'DD-MON-YYYY HH:MI:SS'));
```

EXAMPLE

```
SQL> execute dbms_logmnr.start_logmnr(
        DictFileName => 'logminerdictionary.ora',
        StartScn => 1200,
        EndScn => 1500);
```

The following are the fields available in the Oracle9i V$LOGMNR_CONTENTS table. Using standard SQL, you can now look for particular transactions and easily create a REDO or an UNDO script from the SQL_REDO or SQL_UNDO columns; see Listing 18.5 for the entire list of available columns in v$logmnr_contents. You can use the OPERATION and USERNAME columns to search for specific user activity or types of transactions.

EXAMPLE

Listing 18.5: V$LOGMNR_CONTENTS Listing

```
SQL> desc V_$LOGMNR_CONTENTS;
 Name                                      Null?    Type
 ----------------------------------------- -------- ----------------------------
 SCN                                                NUMBER
 CSCN                                               NUMBER
 TIMESTAMP                                          DATE
 COMMIT_TIMESTAMP                                   DATE
 THREAD#                                            NUMBER
 LOG_ID                                             NUMBER
 XIDUSN                                             NUMBER
 XIDSLT                                             NUMBER
 XIDSQN                                             NUMBER
 RBASQN                                             NUMBER
 RBABLK                                             NUMBER
 RBABYTE                                            NUMBER
 UBAFIL                                             NUMBER
 UBABLK                                             NUMBER
 UBAREC                                             NUMBER
 UBASQN                                             NUMBER
 ABS_FILE#                                          NUMBER
 REL_FILE#                                          NUMBER
 DATA_BLK#                                          NUMBER
 DATA_OBJ#                                          NUMBER
 DATA_OBJD#                                         NUMBER
 SEG_OWNER                                          VARCHAR2(32)
 SEG_NAME                                           VARCHAR2(256)
 SEG_TYPE                                           NUMBER
 SEG_TYPE_NAME                                      VARCHAR2(32)
 TABLE_SPACE                                        VARCHAR2(32)
 ROW_ID                                             VARCHAR2(19)
 SESSION#                                           NUMBER
 SERIAL#                                            NUMBER
 USERNAME                                           VARCHAR2(30)
 SESSION_INFO                                       VARCHAR2(4000)
 TX_NAME                                            VARCHAR2(256)
 ROLLBACK                                           NUMBER
 OPERATION                                          VARCHAR2(32)
 OPERATION_CODE                                     NUMBER
```

Listing 18.5:   continued

SQL_REDO	VARCHAR2(4000)
SQL_UNDO	VARCHAR2(4000)
RS_ID	VARCHAR2(32)
SEQUENCE#	NUMBER
SSN	NUMBER
CSF	NUMBER
INFO	VARCHAR2(32)
STATUS	NUMBER
REDO_VALUE	RAW(4)
UNDO_VALUE	RAW(4)
SQL_COLUMN_TYPE	VARCHAR2(32)
SQL_COLUMN_NAME	VARCHAR2(32)
REDO_LENGTH	NUMBER
REDO_OFFSET	NUMBER
UNDO_LENGTH	NUMBER
UNDO_OFFSET	NUMBER

Practical Uses for Log Miner

This example uses the famous SCOTT schema tables EMP and DEPT. Rows were deleted from the EMP table. To create an undo SQL file for this transaction, the DBA should do an ALTER SYSTEM SWITCH LOGFILE as SYSDBA then assign the newly created archive log file to the log miner dictionary file. Listing 18.6 shows the syntax necessary to create an undo SQL script that can then be ran using SQL*Plus to reapply the 10 dropped records. Make sure to capture the output by using the spool command.

EXAMPLE

Listing 18.6:   Creating UNDO SQL

```
SQL> set heading off
SQL> set feedback off
SQL> set verify off
SQL> set pagesize 0
SQL> spool undo_sql.sql
SQL> SELECT sql_undo
SQL> FROM v$logmnr_contents
SQL> WHERE username = 'SCOTT' and operation = 'DELETE';

SQL_UNDO
----------------------------------------------------------------------
insert into SCOTT.EMP(EMPNO,ENAME,JOB,MGR,HIREDATE,SAL,COMM,DEPTNO) values (7839
,'KING','PRESIDENT',NULL,TO_DATE('17-NOV-1981 00:00:00', 'DD-MON-YYYY
HH24:MI:SS')
    ,5000,NULL,10);

insert into SCOTT.EMP(EMPNO,ENAME,JOB,MGR,HIREDATE,SAL,COMM,DEPTNO) values (7782
,'CLARK','MANAGER',7839,TO_DATE('09-JUN-1981 00:00:00', 'DD-MON-YYYY HH24:MI:SS')
```

Listing 18.6: continued

```
    ,2450,NULL,10);

insert into SCOTT.EMP(EMPNO,ENAME,JOB,MGR,HIREDATE,SAL,COMM,DEPTNO) values (7934
,'MILLER','CLERK',7782,TO_DATE('23-JAN-1982 00:00:00', 'DD-MON-YYYY HH24:MI:SS')
    ,1300,NULL,10);
```

3 rows selected.

You can also do some analysis with this same log information. The listing in 18.7 shows how easy it is to see the objects with the most activity. Listing 18.8 shows a report by user and operation they performed. If you desire to see the exact SQL the users have been running, this is stored in the SQL_REDO column.

Listing 18.7: Audit Trail Listing

```
SQL> select seg_owner Owner, seg_name Object, username, 'Accessed By', count(*)
2  from v$logmnr_contents
3  where seg_owner not in ('SYS')
4  group by seg_owner, seg_name, username;
```

PM note: SQL Plus inserts the line numbers "2","3","4" so this display is accurate

OWNER	OBJECT	Accessed By	COUNT(*)
SCOTT	CUSTOMER	SCOTT	9
SCOTT	CUSTOMER_PRIMARY_KEY	SCOTT	9
SCOTT	DEPT	SCOTT	4
SCOTT	DEPT_PRIMARY_KEY	SCOTT	4
SCOTT	DUMMY	SCOTT	1
SCOTT	EMP	SCOTT	17
SCOTT	EMP_PRIMARY_KEY	SCOTT	17

Listing 18.8: Audit Trail Listing by Access Type

```
SQL> select seg_name Object,  username ,'Accessed By', operation 'Access Type',
count(*)
 2  from v$logmnr_contents
 3 where seg_owner not in ('SYS')
  4  group by seg_name, username, operation;
```

OBJECT	Accessed By	Access Type	COUNT(*)
CUSTOMER	SCOTT	INSERT	9

Listing 18.8:   continued

```
CUSTOMER_PRIMARY_KEY        SCOTT        INTERNAL        9
DEPT                        SCOTT        INSERT          4
DEPT_PRIMARY_KEY            SCOTT        INTERNAL        4
DUMMY                       SCOTT        INSERT          1
EMP                         SCOTT        DELETE          3
EMP_PRIMARY_KEY             SCOTT        INSERT          14
EMP_PRIMARY_KEY             SCOTT        INTERNAL        17
```

Oracle9i Enhancements

Oracle9i Log Miner now supports objects with chained and migrated rows, and data types such as longs, lobs, and even CREATE TABLE and CREATE INDEX commands.

The Oracle8i version used ROWID in the REDO and UNDO SQL. This made it rather difficult to use this script on other Oracle databases. The Oracle9i version uses primary key values instead of ROWID. This should make it easier to apply a desired transaction to multiple Oracle databases. The Oracle9i version of V$LOGMNR_CONTENTS also includes 2 new columns: redo_value and undo_value. This has a number of uses including seeing exactly what the user changed.

Oracle9i Log Miner has added 4 new PL/SQL functions to the DBMS_LOGMNR package: COLUMN_PRESENT, MINE_VARCHAR, MINE_NUMBER, and MINE_DATE. The four commands will allow you to compare logs the user to access and compare values in the logs. The column_present function allows the user to interrogate the log for specific columns in the SQL. For example, this would allow for the DBA to audit for specific updates to specific columns of specific tables, all without any overhead on the Oracle database itself.

There are some new features for setting up LogMiner before mining into the logs. The ADD_FILE and DROP_FILE features still exist as they did in the 8i version. New options such as COMMITTED_DATA_ONLY should improve performance by only gathering the log information of interest to the LogMiner user. Also, LogMiner can be directed to use the Oracle data dictionary information with the USE_ONLINE_CATALOG. The Oracle data dictionary can also be captured into the redo logs via USE_DICT_REDO_LOG.

LogMiner also comes with a new GUI that is available through Oracle Enterprise Manager.

LogMiner in Oracle9i also has a persistent mode, so that logs can be continuously monitored as new information is added. This feature acts much like the Unix tail -f in that only new items appearing in the log will be processed. As of this writing, it is not clear to me how new log files will be added, old or not used log files be dropped, and so on. This feature will be used to support new Standby-database features.

Summary

Log Miner is a useful tool to both reverse erroneous transactions, create scripts to reapply the same transaction, and to see who has been doing what in the database.

Reviewing It

REVIEW

1. What is the purpose of the dictionary file?

2. Briefly describe how you would reverse a database table delete.

3. What is persistent mode?

Checking It

CHECK

1. Log Miner can read Oracle v7.3 log files.

   True/False

2. Which of the following is NOT valid syntax?

   a) ADDFILE

   b) DELETEFILE

   c) REPLACEFILE

   d) All of the above

3. Log Miner can be used as an audit trail.

   True/False

Applying It

Independent Exercise 1:

- Make sure your database is in Archive Log mode
- Delete all the records from the SCOTT.EMP table.
- Use Log Miner, find the records, and make an UNDO script
- Apply the UNDO Script
- Query the SCOTT.EMP table

Independent Exercise 2:

- Check to see what activity the user SCOTT has been doing to the database
- Check to see who has done what kind of activity to the SCOTT.EMP table

What's Next?

In this chapter, you learned how to use the new Log Miner tool from Oracle Corp. The next chapter wraps up all of these topics into an Auto Sales Tracking application.

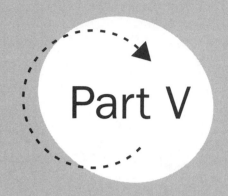

Part V

Putting It All Together

Putting It All Together

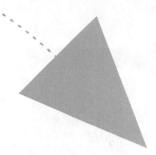

Putting It All Together: A Sales Tracking Application

The final section of this book attempts to bring together all of the topics and examples used throughout this book into a single application. The reader will see how the author uses the knowledge in this book to build an actual application.

This chapter teaches you the following:

- Application concepts
- The Sales Tracking application

Application Concepts

The Auto Sales Tracking application is based on a hypothetical car dealership that repairs used cars and then resells these cars to the public. The sale price of the completed car is based on the original cost of the car plus all the time and repairs. This application tracks all the information necessary: where the car came from, where the parts came from, who the car was sold to, and all the costs associated with each individual car.

NOTE

I got the idea for this hypothetical car dealership from a good friend, Tom Bickel, who makes a business of repairing and reselling mostly insurance-claimed vehicles. The automobiles that have appeared in the book illustrations belong to me and were purchased from Bickel Motors.

The Sales Tracking Application

I have used a naming convention so that the relational objects associated with this application can be easily identified when looking at any data-dictionary view such as DBA_Tables, or even TAB. Because this is a Sales Tracking application, I chose ST to depict the initial prefix to every table, index, or object (tables, indexes, triggers, and so on) that is part of this application. I also like to use part of the table as a prefix to each column name. This really assists the programmer or end user when working with the SQL language because a column name directly refers to one table or another. You will notice that I have prefixed all the application objects with ST_; all the column attributes have part or all of the table name in them, such as the ST_Inventory table; and all the entities begin with INV_. Your data center may have its own standards. Please consult your database administrator if you need assistance in the naming of application objects and/or programs.

The Database Layout

The Sales Tracking database consists of 11 relational tables (see Figure 19.1), 3 sequence generators, and 5 database triggers. Three major tables that track the inventory (used automobiles in this case) support the application: ST_Inventory, ST_Parts, and ST_Bill_Time. Three minor tables are related to the major tables: ST_Vendor, ST_Customer, and ST_Staff. Finally, there are five reference tables that contain consistent data used to ensure that valid data is being stored in the five major and minor tables as well as give descriptions to this same data when displaying information on a screen or in a report. These reference tables are ST_Departments, ST_Job_Code, ST_Model, ST_Make, and ST_Type.

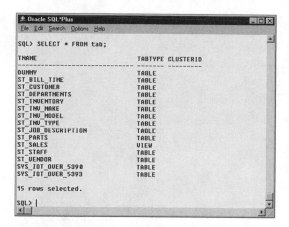

Figure 19.1: Select from tab to show the Sales Tracking objects.

The Entity Relationship Diagram (ERD) in Figure 19.2 shows the major and minor tables of the Sales Tracking application. The central table is the ST_Inventory table, the central repository for the main business focus; the inventory of the automobiles that have been purchased, are in various stages of repair, are ready for sale, or have been sold.

The two other major tables are the ST_Parts and the ST_Bill_Tie tables. These tables are used in conjunction with ST_Inventory to provide such useful information as what the car originally cost, total cost of repairing the car, as well as the profit/loss of each automobile sold. Notice the many-to-one relationship from ST_Parts to ST_Inventory. This indicates from this picture that there can be one or more parts associated with each car in the ST_Inventory table. A part can be a fender, a tire, or a complete motor. Likewise, with ST_Bill_Time, there can be one or more mechanics working on each car, especially through several stages of repairs. There is the welder, who might fix any physical damage, a mechanic, who might have installed a new motor or transmission, and the painter if the car required painting.

NOTE

A crow's foot depicts that there is a many relationship between the object that this is pointing to and the object at the other end. Let's look at ST_Customer and ST_Inventory. There is just one record in the ST_Customer table for just one record in the ST_Inventory table, a one-to-on relationship. This makes sense to the application, because only one person will be purchasing each individual car. The ST_Parts table has a many-to-one relationship to the ST_Inventory table because there can be many parts (ST_Parts) for each car (ST_Inventory) being processed.

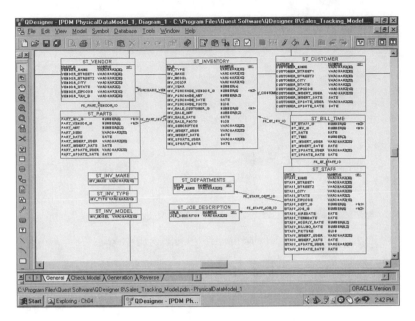

Figure 19.2: *Entity Relationship Diagram (ERD) of the Sales Tracking application database objects.*

Notice that ST_Inventory and ST_Parts share a table used for reference, the ST_Vendor table. This table contains information about who is supplying the dealership with both cars and parts. A salvage yard, for example, could be supplying repairable cars as well as fenders and motors.

The ST_Inventory table has three supporting reference (look up/editing) tables associated with it that are not illustrated here, but are included in the installation scripts (see appendix B). These tables are ST_Type, or the type of automobile such as a SUV, sedan, and so on; the ST_Make, or name of the car such as Intrepid, Camry, Corolla, and so on; and the ST_Model, 4-door, hatchback, automatic, and so on. Each of these tables will be used by the forms programs to ensure only valid information is entered into the ST_Inventory table. The ST_Customer table records the buyers of automobiles. The one-to-one relationship indicates that there is only one record in the ST_Inventory that is associated with a single record in the ST_Customer table. For simplicity's sake, this application will make the assumption that only one person can purchase a single automobile from this dealership.

The ST_Bill_Time table has a many-to-one relationship to the ST_Inventory table. Several staff members could be involved in the various stages of preparation of a single automobile for final sale. The ST_Bill_Time and the ST_Staff table have a many-to-many relationship in that staff members would be working on more than one automobile and possibly even more than one automobile in a single day.

The ST_Staff table is supported by ST_Departments and ST_Job_ Description. Each staff member is associated with different departments, such as collision repair, mechanic, detailing (cleanup), painting, sales, or management. This information could be useful to see what percentage of an automobile is handled by each type of process required. The ST_Job_ Description is a reference table to the ST_Staff (note the one-to-one relationship) to ensure the correct job code is assigned to each staff member recorded in ST_Staff. The ST_Departments is another reference table to the ST_Staff (note the one-to-one relationship) to ensure the correct department code is assigned to each staff member recorded in ST_Staff.

The ST_Inventory table contains the necessary entities or columns to store a unique identifier for each automobile, in other words, the ST_INV entity. This field is associated with one of the Oracle sequence generators, ST_INV_SEQ. This sequence is used to ensure that a unique number is associated with each automobile, no matter how many people may be entering cars into the ST_Inventory table. This field is also the primary key so that referential integrity constraints can be established, enforcing the relationships between the tables (as shown in Figure 19.3).

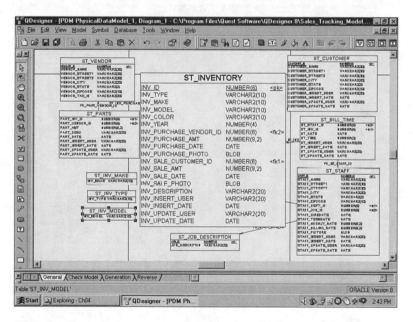

Figure 19.3: *Sales Tracking application ERD diagram focusing on the* ST_Inventory *entities.*

There are several foreign keys, or fields that will have relationships to other tables as well. These fields include Inv_Purchase_Vendor_Id and Inv_Sale_Customer_Id. These fields will be respectively related to ST_Vendor and ST_Customer. The referential integrity rule will ensure that there is a valid record in ST_Vendor and ST_Customer before the ST_Inv record will be recorded (or committed in relational terms) to the database. The Inv_Model, Inv_Type, and Inv_Make will be enforced by the ST_MAIN program used to maintain the ST_Inv table. The remainder of the fields are used to store pertinent information that relates to a particular car.

NOTE

Entity in relational terms is another name for fields or columns in a table.

The ST_Parts table (see Figure 19.4) contains the information necessary to track parts purchased for the cars in ST_Inventory. There is the price of the part, the date it was purchased, and a brief description as well as two foreign keys PARTS_INV_ID and PARTS_VENDOR_ID. PARTS_Inv_Id is related to ST_Inventory INV_Id to ensure that all parts acquired are associated with a particular automobile. The PARTS_Vendor_Id is associated with the ST_Vendors table to ensure that all parts purchased can be traced back to their origin.

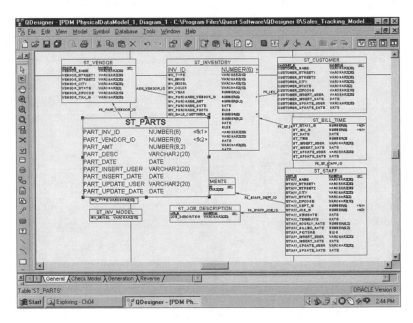

Figure 19.4: *Sales Tracking application ERD diagram focusing on the* ST_Parts *entities.*

There are four fields that do not appear in this list. These fields are Inv_Insert_User, Inv_Insert_Date, Inv_Update_User, and Inv_Update_Date. These same fields appear in all the major and minor tables of this application (ST_Parts, ST_Vendor, ST_Bill_Time, and ST_Staff). These four fields track which user inserted the record to the table and which user was the last to update the table. This information could be useful if the wrong information was entered to see who might need additional training on how to use the application.

These fields are automatically maintained by database triggers (Figure 19.5 maintains the proper data in the `ST_Inventory` maintenance fields: INSERT_USER, INSERT_DATE, and so on) or some code that executes each time a record is inserted or updated in these tables.

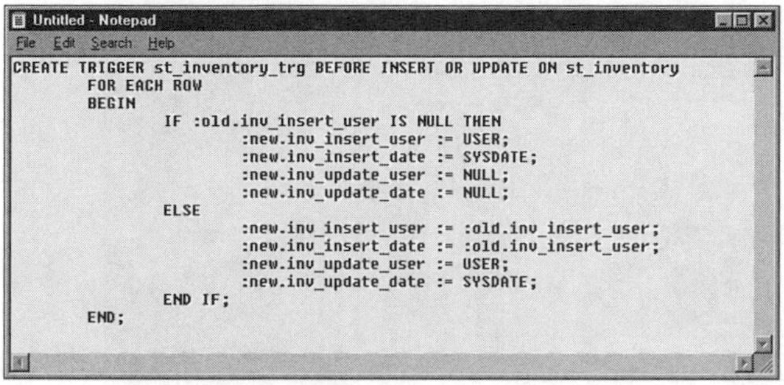


```
CREATE TRIGGER st_inventory_trg BEFORE INSERT OR UPDATE ON st_inventory
        FOR EACH ROW
        BEGIN
                IF :old.inv_insert_user IS NULL THEN
                        :new.inv_insert_user := USER;
                        :new.inv_insert_date := SYSDATE;
                        :new.inv_update_user := NULL;
                        :new.inv_update_date := NULL;
                ELSE
                        :new.inv_insert_user := :old.inv_insert_user;
                        :new.inv_insert_date := :old.inv_insert_user;
                        :new.inv_update_user := USER;
                        :new.inv_update_date := SYSDATE;
                END IF;
        END;
```

Figure 19.5: *`ST_Inventory`'s database trigger.*

The Programs

The Sales Tracking application consists of 9 screen-based programs that add or maintain the data in the 11 database tables. Each of these programs will have an icon that will start the program. `ST_Inventory` is the main program used to enter and track important information as it relates to a particular vehicle. Figure 19.6 shows the main entry screen. Each of these tabs represents a different part of the process of a vehicle. The final tab (see Figure 19.7) shows the profitability of the vehicle, allowing the sales person to see how much the firm has invested in this particular vehicle.

Figure 19.8 shows the main icons where the Sales Tracking programs can be easily accessed. Clicking the icon buttons will access the most important programs. These programs include `ST_TIME_CLOCK`, `ST_PARTS`, `ST_INVENTORY`, `ST_SALES`, `ST_PROFIT/LOSS`, and `ST_STAFF_UTILIZATION`. These are the programs used to enter and maintain data in the underlying relational tables.

NOTE

An icon is a term given to a small picture or graphical representation of a task. An icon is typically associated with a button or an object on a GUI screen that can be clicked with the mouse to run the underlying program or perform the assigned computer task.

The name implies the table associated with each program—for instance, `ST_TIME_CLOCK` will add records to the `ST_BILL_TIME` table. Likewise, `ST_INVENTORY` will add and maintain records in the `ST_INVENTORY` table (refer to Figure 19.6). This program will also make use of the three look-up type tables: ST_TYPE, ST_MAKE, and ST_MODEL. These three tables will appear in this application as a pull-down menu that is easily accessed with the mouse.

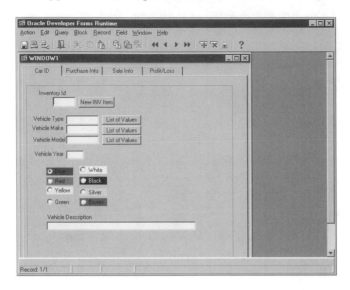

Figure 19.6: *Sales Tracking inventory program.*

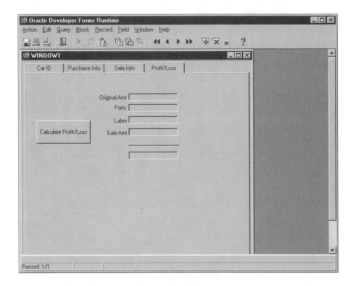

Figure 19.7: *Sales Tracking inventory profitability tab.*

ST_PROFIT/LOSS and ST_STAFF_UTILIZATION are screen-based programs that display or report on data from one or more tables. ST_PROFIT/LOSS displays the profit or loss on each vehicle in ST_INVENTORY. This calculation will include information from ST_PARTS and ST_BILL_TIME as well as

ST_INVENTORY. As the name implies, ST_PROFIT/LOSS will help management charge appropriately for each automobile. This screen can be consulted prior to a sale or in a sales situation to permit the salesperson to easily see the total investment in any particular car at any time. ST_STAFF_ UTILIZATION will display summary information, by week, for all employees or just selected employees. In an auto sales environment, it is important for overall profitability to keep all the mechanics, painters, and body-repair people busy. This program will help management track who has plenty to do and who might need more work.

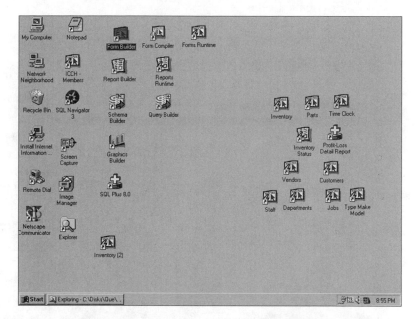

Figure 19.8: *Sales Tracking application icons.*

There will be a series of reports associated with this application as well. Reports are needed to display data from the underlying relational tables in a meaningful manner. Some of these reports will be GUI-based and some will be character-mode based. There is no reason why reports cannot be all one environment or the other. Typically, character-mode printers are much less expensive (inkjet printers) than printers that can handle images, such as laser printers.

Each item on this report menu will also be a separate program or SQL*Plus script. Each program may access individual or multiple Sales Tracking relational tables. Each SQL*Plus script will be handled with a batch file on the Windows NT environment and by a Unix shell script in a Unix environment. This batch file or shell script is useful to run the actual SQL*Plus syntax as well as print and/or delete the output from the script.

There are also icons for the two reports (Inventory Status Report, see Figure 19.9, and Profit/Loss Detail, see Figure 19.10), icons for Vendor and Customer entry and maintenance, and icons for Staff, Departments, Jobs, and Type/Make/Model entry and maintenance. Each of these entry programs relates directly to one of the relational table objects, as the name would imply. Notice that the icon picture depicts the type of program that is being assigned to the icon: the Oracle Forms-based icon is used for the Oracle Developer forms-based programs, the Oracle Reports for the Oracle Developer reports-based programs, and the SQL*Plus icon for the SQL*Plus-based reports.

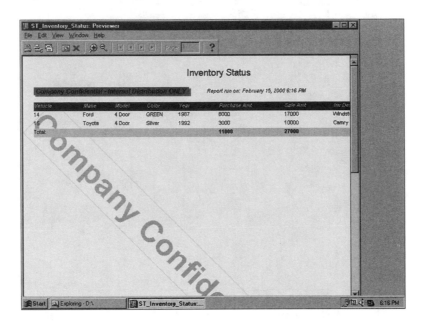

Figure 19.9: *Sales Tracking application inventory status report.*

Reports are needed to display data from the underlying relational tables in a meaningful manner. One of these reports will be GUI-based and the other will be character-mode based. There is no reason why they cannot be all one environment or the other, but for learning purposes, we will create both kinds. Figure 19.9 shows the Oracle Developer-based report and Figure 19.10 shows the character-mode SQL*Plus-based report.

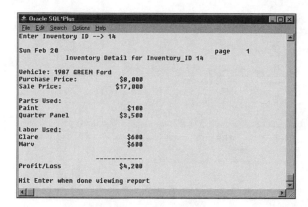

Figure 19.10: *Sales Tracking application profit/loss detail report.*

This book also built a Web site based on this application. Figure 19.11 shows the main Web page used to purchase one of these vehicles over the Web and Figure 19.12 shows a SQL*Plus Web-based report shown in Figure 19.10.

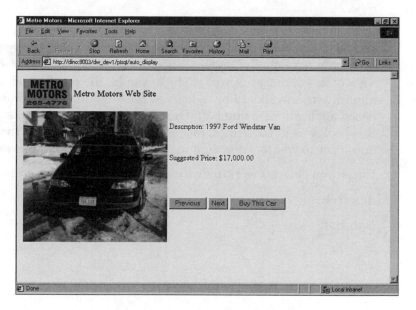

Figure 19.11: *Sales Tracking application web application.*

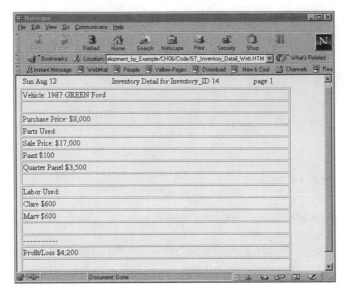

Figure 19.12: *Sales Tracking application web-based profit/loss detail report.*

Book Summary

This book walked you through, by example, the creation of an integrated application. You should have learned how to build both windows and Web-based applications using both Oracle tools and generic tools. My idea for this book was to cover all Oracle9i features necessary for the application developer to create, tune, and maintain Oracle-based programs and reports.

I hope you enjoyed working with this book as I have in creating it.

Sincerely,

Dan Hotka

Part VI

Appendixes

Answers to Quizzes

Oracle9i Architecture and Complete Sales Tracking Installation Scripts

Web Sites and Product Codes

Appendix A

Answers to Quizzes

Answers to Chapter 1

Reviewing It

1. What is a relational database?

2. What is the difference between a primary key and a unique key?

3. Who is considered the father of relational databases? What was the first SQL language called? What company produced the first working relational database?

4. The type of SQL used to update data, delete rows, and so on is known as what? The type of SQL used to create objects is known as what?

5. What is Deja-view?

6. List-partitioning is useful for what?

7. How does Data Pump work?

8. What would be a good use of having multiple buffer pools?

9. What is the old name for Net8?

10. Describe the basic role of DBA Studio.

11. Describe Log Miner and what it might be useful for.

Answers: 1=The relational database supports a single, "logical" structure called a relation, a two-dimensional data structure commonly called a table in the database; 2=Unlike primary keys, unique keys can contain null values; 3=Dr. E. F. Codd, SEQUEL, Relational Systems, Inc (later became Oracle Corp); 4=DML and DDL; 5=The ability to produce a result set based on a particular time (utilizing Oracle's read-consistent view mechanism); 6=partition data based on character data; 7=treat operating-system files as Oracle tables for the purposes of data loading; 8=Gives the DBA the ability to further separate various types of object access from other types of object access; 9=SQL*Net; 10=Oracle click 'n shoot administrative tool; 11= Displays information from the Oracle online and archive log files, creates UNDO and REDO SQL, and can audit a variety of user activities.

Checking It

1. Oracle is (mark all that apply)

    a) A hierarchical database

    b) A network database

    c) A relational database

    d) An Object-oriented database

2. ISAM and VSAM are examples of a network database.

  True/False

3. Referential integrity is

    a) A relationship enforced at the database level by PL/SQL

    b) A relationship enforced at the database level based on primary and foreign keys

    c) A relationship enforced at the application level by PL/SQL, Java, or XML

    d) A relationship enforced by using concatenated keys

4. Which of the following statements is true?

    a) COBOL works with groups of records

    b) SQL processes data row at a time

    c) SQL lets you work with data at the logical level

    d) It matters to Oracle the order of the data in the database

5. SQL is a procedural language in that it processes sets of records at a time rather than single records at a time.

  True/False

6. Object-oriented support in the Oracle RDBMS was first introduced with which version:

    a) 7.3

    b) 8.0

    c) 8.1

    d) 9.0

7. Resumable SQL allows some Oracle processes/tools to pickup where it left off in the event of space-oriented errors.

  True/False

8. A compiler

    a) Makes machine language from source code

    b) Makes source code from machine language

c) Makes runtime interpreters that then read the source code

d) Makes machine code for runtime interpreters

9. SQL*Plus can

   a) Process any SQL statement

   b) Handle administrative functions in the database

   c) Can format SQL output into reports

   d) Can take input from a file

   e) All of the above

Answers: 1=b and d; 2=False; 3=b; 4=c; 5=False (non-procedural language); 6=b; 7=True; 8=a; 9=e.

Answers to Chapter 2

Reviewing It

REVIEW

1. What is Oracle's main character-mode interface?

2. What is the syntax of the CHANGE command to change text in the SQL buffer?

3. The DESCRIBE command is useful for what?

4. What will the command SELECT * FROM EMP do?

5. In the table EMP, give the ORDER BY clause that will return the rows in the order of DEPTNO ascending and within DEPTNO, SAL descending.

6. What is the difference between a NULL and a 0 field?

7. When using substitution characters (say in an INSERT statement), what is the difference between & and &&?

8. What is the difference between the DELETE command and the TRUNCATE command?

9. Tablespaces are used for what?

10. Show the syntax to create an index on ename for the table EMP.

11. What is an EXTENT?

Answers: 1=SQL*Plus; 2=C/<source string>/<new string>; 3=Displaying Object column names and attributes; 4=This will show all the rows in the table EMP; 5=ORDER BY DEPTNO, SAL desc; 6=NULL contains no value at all; 7=& prompts the user for a value with each execution of the SQL statement, && only prompts the user to provide a value on the first SQL statement; 8=DELETE can selectively delete rows and this command can be undone with a ROLLBACK statement. The TRUNCATE drops all the rows, no selectivity, and the command cannot be reversed; 9=Tablespaces are storage areas in Oracle, much like a directory structure of a computer. Tablespaces have physical disk drives assigned; 10=CREATE INDEX <some name> ON EMP (ENAME); 11=One or more Oracle datablocks assigned in a contiguous manor to a particular object.

CHECK

Checking It

1. SQL*Plus can

    a) Display data from the Oracle database

    b) Format data into reports

    c) Perform database administrative functions

    d) All of the above

2. In the SQL Buffer, the command I is short for INSERT.

    True/False

3. The default behavior of the ORDER BY clause is ascending.

    True/False

4. Which of the following LIKE commands will return the rows with a name like HOTKA?

    a) WHERE ename LIKE '_HOT%'

    b) WHERE ename LIKE 'H_T%'

    c) WHERE ename LIKE '%TKA_'

    d) WHERE ename LIKE '%TOK%'

5. Which is the valid UPDATE statement?

    a) UPDATE emp SET SAL = SAL * 1.05

    b) UPDATE emp WHERE SAL = 20000

    c) UPDATE emp SET ENAME = 1234 WHERE DEPTNO = 10

    d) UPDATE emp WHERE DEPTNO = 10 SET ENAME = 'HOTKA'

6. Which of the following is NOT a valid data type?

    a) BLOB

    b) CHAR

    c) VARCHAR

    d) INTEGER

7. CREATE TABLE <table name> AS SELECT can create a duplicate object.

    True/False

8. You change your mind on a DROP COLUMN command and return the column to the original object.

    True/False

9. Selecting which field causes a SEQUENCE generator to increment?

    a) CURRVAL

    b) NEXTVAL

    c) LASTNUMBER

    d) PREVAL

10. Constraints are useful for

    a) Ensuring parent/child table relationships

    b) Ensuring only certain kinds of data is in a field

    c) Ensuring uniqueness of column data

    d) All of the above

Answers: 1=d; 2=False (stands for INPUT); 3=True; 4=b; 5=a; 6=d; 7=True, the rows and columns depends on the SELECT statement; 8=False, DROP COLUMN is unrecoverable; 9=b; 10=d.

APPLY

Applying It

Independent Exercise 1:

- Create a Table called people with columns of dept (numeric 4 positions), last_name (character 10 positions), start_date (date field), and salary (numeric 5 positions with 2 decimal positions).

Independent Exercise 2:

- Insert the following data into the table, try out the & substitution character:

- Dept 10, SMITH, SYSDATE, 10000
- Dept 10, JONES, SYSDATE, 20000
- Dept 20, KING, SYSDATE, 15000
- Dept 20, JONES, SYSDATE, 18000
- Dept 20, FOUNTAIN, SYSDATE, 12000

Independent Exercise 3:

- Select those rows from Dept 20.

- Select name and start_date with the start_date in the format of MM/DD/YYYY.

- Give everyone in dept 10 a 10% increase in salary.

- Set AUTOCOMMIT off, drop all the rows, and issue a ROLLBACK. Make sure all the rows are put back.

Independent Exercise 4:

- Create a sequence that increments by 10 and begins at 10 over the current DEPT in the PEOPLE table.

  - INSERT <sequence name>.NEXTVAL, GARN, SYSDATE, 5000.

  - Create a primary key constraint on the DEPT column.

  - INSERT <sequence name>.CURRVAL, HACKETT, SYSDATE, 4500.

  - Why did you get this error?

NOTE

The next chapter uses this PEOPLE table for its Exercise examples as well.

Answers to Chapter 3

Reviewing It

REVIEW

1. What does PL/SQL stand for?

2. What exactly is a stored procedure?

3. What is the difference between a Named PL/SQL block and an Un-named PL/SQL block?

4. What are the three syntax basics of any PL/SQL block?

5. The special datatype %TYPE is useful for what?

6. PL/SQL uses the DBMS_OUTPUT.PRINT_LINE. What needs to be set in SQL*Plus to see this output?

7. What are the three kinds of loops?

8. What are the two variables available to PL/SQL when Oracle errors occur?

Answers: 1=Procedural Language SQL; 2= A stored procedure is a code module that does some processing and returns a code stating that the procedure was successful or not; 3=Named PL/SQL blocks can be called in the form of procedures or functions, un-named PL/SQL are imbedded in applications; 4= Begin, Exceptions, End; 5 = %TYPE is useful to guarantee that the datatype and length of the variable matches that of a column in the database; 6= use of SQL*Plus environment setting SET SERVEROUTPUT ON is set when the PL/SQL feature DBMS_OUTPUT.PRINT_LINE is used; 7= Basic, For, and While; 8= SQLCODE and SQLERRM.

CHECK

Checking It

1. Triggers, Functions, and Procedures can also be coded in JAVA.

   True/False

2. Cursors are

   a) Temporary storage area for PL/SQL

   b) Work area for SQL returning more than 1 row

   c) Work/storage space for PL/SQL

   d) Executable code modules

3. Procedures differ from Functions in that

   a) Procedures takes no input variables but output variables

   b) Procedures take input variables but Functions cannot

   c) Functions have an output variable where Procedures do not

   d) Functions can have input variables but Procedures cannot

4. The PL/SQL variable name must be unique to the PL/SQL block.

   True/False

5. What is the difference between implicit cursors and explicit cursors?

   a) Explicit processes only 1 row, implicit processes many rows

   b) Explicit cursors are only for DML statements

    c) Implicit cursors are only for DML statements

    d) Implicit cursors can only handle 1 row returned, explicit can handle multiple rows

6. An IF statement really doesn't need an ENDIF.

True/False

7. If an error condition is not handled by the PL/SQL block

    a) It is ignored.

    b) It is propagated to the calling program.

    c) It causes an error inside the PL/SQL.

    d) It is handled by PL/SQL default behavior.

8. The WHEN_OTHERS error condition can appear *where* in the EXCEPTIONS area:

    a) It must be the first condition

    b) It must be the last condition

    c) It can appear anywhere, the order of conditions does not matter

Answers: 1=True; 2=b; 3=c; 4=T; 5=d; 6=False; 7=b.

APPLY

Applying It

Independent Exercise 1:

- Create a PL/SQL Procedure that displays the total employee count and the total salary by department.

Independent Exercise 2:

- Create a PL/SQL Procedure that gives the DEPT 10 people a 10% increase in salary and the DEPT 20 people a 20% increase in salary.

Independent Exercise 3:

- Create a Function that outputs the total amount of salary only after the last row has been processed.

- Drop the PEOPLE table.

Answers to Chapter 4

Reviewing It

1. Why does the author recommend using a prefix on all the application database objects?

2. Why does the author use a database trigger to maintain the data in the INSERT_USER, INSERT_DATE, UPDATE_USER, and UPDATE_DATE?

3. Why does the author spool a .log file out of the INSTALL scripts?

4. What is the ST_INV_SEQ useful for?

5. What is the difference between an inline and an out-of-line constraint.

Answers: 1=To quickly identify related application objects when querying DBA_OBJECTS; 2=To automatically maintain the data in these fields no matter what tool is used to insert or update these objects; 3=To capture any error and/or warning statements issued during the execution of the script; 4=To help insure a unique ST_INV_ID in the ST_INVENTORY table; 5=An inline constraint is one that is defined where the field that it applies to is defined. An out-of-line constraint is one that is added with separate syntax at a later time.

Checking It

1. An ERD crows foot pointing towards an object means

   a) The table with the crows foot is a subset of the table at the other end

   b) The table with the crows foot has a 1-to-many relationship with the other object

   c) The table with the crows foot has more rows than the other object

2. A straight line in an ERD diagram indicates a one-to-one row relationship between the two objects.

   True/False

3. Creating multiple tablespaces is useful for

   a) Tuning the application via distribution

   b) Aid in moving the application to larger computer systems

c) Allows for different storage parameter defaults

d) All of the above

4. SQL*Plus is the only tool useful in creating database objects.

True/False

5. What is the purpose of `:new.inv_insert_user := :old.inv_insert_user;` in the Listing 4.3?

a) To insure the contents of the `INV_INSERT_FIELD` does not change

b) To force the `INV_INSERT_FIELD` to a new value

c) To allow for other processes to change the `INV_INSERT_FIELD`

Answers: 1=b; 2=True; 3=d; 4=False 5=a.

Applying It

APPLY

Independent Exercise 1:

- Download both INSTALL scripts from www.quepublishing.com.

- Review the Oracle9i directory structure on your computer.

- Edit `INSTALL_Sales_Tracking_Database.sql` and validate/change the file locations on the various `CREATE TABLESPACE` statements

- Execute the edited `INSTALL_Sales_Tracking_Database.sql` to create the book example Tablespaces.

- Review the `LOG` file for any errors.

Independent Exercise 2:

- Review the `INSTALL_Sales_Trackng_Objects.sql`.

- Execute the `INSTALL_Sales_Tracking_Object.sql` to create the book example objects.

- Review the `LOG` file for any errors.

Independent Exercise 3:

- Download the `EXPORT_Sales_Tracking.dmp` file from www.quepublishing.com.

- IMPORT the `EXPORT_Sales_Tracking.dmp` file.

Answers to Chapter 5

Reviewing It

1. What is the Data Block Wizard useful for?

2. What is the difference between a content canvas and a stacked canvas?

3. Does Oracle Developer come with online help?

4. What is the role of the Item Property Palette?

5. In the following example, explain what this code is doing and explain the column with the ':'

   begin

   select st_vendor_seq.nextval

   into :st_vendor.vendor_id

   from sys.dual;

   end;

6. What is a LOV and what is it useful for?

7. How should a LOV be accessed?

8. Describe Query mode and what it is useful for.

9. What is a control block and how does it differ from a data block?

10. In Web-based forms, what triggers may be undesirable?

Answers: 1= This section will build applications that are always based on tables or views; 2= A *content canvas* is the canvas that appears when the application first starts up. Each form must have a content canvas. A *stacked canvas*, on the other hand, has the capability to overlay or appear on top of other canvases to hide information or to show parts of information when other information is being accessed; 3=Yes, All the Oracle manuals are available by clicking the Help button at the right end of the toolbar; 4= This palette controls all the aspects of each item, including its visual attributes, how text is entered, and whether the field is even enterable, as well as its associated help text and its list-of-values (LOVs); 5=This code would be used to populate the variable 'vendor_id' in the block 'st_vendor' with the next value of the sequence; 6= List Of Values and is useful to display items in a popup-like pick list with the contents of another table; 7= add a button with WHEN-MOUSE_CLICK trigger assigned and the only contents of this trigger is to call the LIST_VALUES key built-in; 8=Query Mode allows the forms user to see all rows of the assigned table or only certain rows depending on the data entered into the form columns. If data is entered, the data becomes the 'where' clause; 9=A control block has no underlying table. It is useful for hidden work fields, fields that allow data entry for use elsewhere in the form, and so on; 10='WHEN-MOUSE-' type triggers, they may not work and/or they may create quite a bit of additional network traffic.

CHECK

Checking It

1. What are Forms Builder program units called?

    a) Program Units

    b) Modules

    c) .FMB files

    d) .FMX files

2. Data blocks can be based on tables, views, or stored procedures.
True/False

3. What forms naming standard should be adhered to?

    a) An 8-character name

    b) A name relative to the table being accessed

    c) Ask your database administrator

    d) Forms enforces no naming standards

4. A property palette is associated with

    a) Items

    b) Data Blocks

    c) Canvases

    d) All of the above

5. How do you change the 'Edge Pattern'?

    a) Frame Property Palette

    b) Item Property Palette

    c) Data Block Property Palette

    d) Canvas Property Palette

6. What block-level trigger should be used for sequence generators?

   a) Post-Update

   b) Pre-Update

   c) Pre-Insert

   d) Pre-Commit

7. The purpose of a tabular form is to display more than 1 row of data at a time.

   True/False

8. By default, LOVs can be accessed in a form via

   a) Simply navigating to the field

   b) Using the 'Display List' from the menu bar

   c) Right-mouse clicking the item with the assigned LOV

   d) Left-mouse clicking the item with the assigned LOV

9. How are radio-buttons added to a data item?

   a) By the radio-button property palette

   b) By the canvas property palette

   c) By the item property palette

   d) By highlighting the item then adding the radio buttons

10. In a Web-based form: where does the form actually run?

   a) Java code at the Web browser

   b) .FMX file at the Web browser

   c) On the apps server via an applet on the Web browser

   d) .FMB file at the Web browser

Answers: 1=b; 2=True; 3=d; 4=d; 5=a; 6=b; 7=False, Have items appear on different tabs but on one canvas; 8=b; 9=d; 10=c.

Applying It

Independent Exercise 1:

APPLY

- Create a simple form from the SCOT.DEPT table. Display 4 rows and all columns.

- Query just Dept 10.

- Add Enter Query/Execute Query buttons

Independent Exercise 2:

- Create a sequence generator that starts at 60 and increments by 10.

- Add this new sequence to the deptno item in the form created in example 1 when adding rows to the table.

Independent Exercise 3:

- Create a form on the SCOT.EMP table. Display 1 row.

- Add a radio group for job title.

- Add a LOV for deptno.

Answers to Chapter 6

REVIEW

Reviewing It

1. What is the difference between a tabular report and a form-like report?

2. Using Oracle Reports, what are the two ways of putting in a SELECT statement for data selection?

3. What is the spool command useful for in SQL*Plus style reports?

4. Where is the best place to put the SRW procedures when enhancing HTML reports?

5. Does Oracle Reports support Java? If so, where does it go?

Answers: 1=The Tabular report is the typical style with rows and columns, whereas Form-like can print a row of data per page; 2=Query Builder or a pre-written SQL statement; 3=To capture the report output image in an operating system file; 4=The BEFORE REPORT trigger; 5=Yes, Boilerplate Text Item with "Contains HTML tags" property item set to YES.

CHECK

Checking It

1. How many different report style sheets are there?

   a) 4

   b) 6

   c) 8

   d) 10

2. SQL*Plus is useful for making HTML style reports.

   True/False

3. SQL*Plus Column headings are controlled by

   a) TTTLE

   b) BREAK

   c) COLUMN

   d) None of these

4. SQL*Plus can make a master/detail report.

   True/False

5. HTML can easily be added to SQL*Plus reports.

   True/False

6. Oracle Reports can easily generate HTML from a command-line command.

   True/False

Answers: 1=c; 2=False; 3=c; 4=True; 5=False, HTML can easily be added to Oracle reports; 6=True.

Applying It

APPLY

Independent Exercise 1:

- Build a master/detail report using Emp and DEPT, showing each department (deptno and dname) followed by an ordered list of employee name, title, and salary, with a subtotal by department on salary and a report total of all salaries.

Independent Exercise 2:

- Build the same report as Exercise 1 using SQL*Plus.

Independent Exercise 3:

- Create HTML output from Exercise 1 and add the Metro Motors Logo to the top of each report, add "Contact us" with an e-mail hyperlink to the bottom of each report.

Answers to Chapter 7

Reviewing It

REVIEW

1. What is the purpose of SQL functions?
2. What is the DUAL table useful for?
3. Explain SQL concatenation.
4. The DECODE statement is what?
5. When might you use the HAVING clause?
6. Briefly describe what a JOIN is.
7. What is 'qualification' and why is it important to a self-join?
8. Name the four types of sub-queries.
9 What is an IN-LINE view?

Answers: 1=SQL functions perform a variety of tasks such as date compares, date formatting, a host of character functions, as well as several numerical functions; 2=The DUAL table contains one column and one row and is useful when wanting to run a function once; 3=Concatenation is when two or more columns are merged together, many times merged with some text items, to form a single column of outout; 4=The DECODE function is the IF-THEN-ELSE logic to SQL; 5=to limit the rows returned from a GROUP BY clause; 6=A join is when two or more tables are required to be used in the same SQL statement; 7=A self-join is where you are joining the same table to itself and you will need to qualify the columns in the where clause so Oracle knows which table a column belongs to; 8=those that return a single row; those that return multiple rows; those that return multiple columns in a single row; and those that return multiple columns in multiple rows; 9=Oracle9i supports a subquery in the FROM clause. This type of SQL statement is also known as an 'INLINE View.'

Checking It

CHECK

1. SQL functions falls into

    a) 1 Category
    b) 2 Categories
    c) 3 Categories
    d) Does not have categories

2. A single-row function can only return one row.

   True/False

3. In a DATE mask, the RR means

   a) Current century if the year tested is between 00 and 49 and the current year is between 50 and 99

   b) Current century if the year tested is between 00 and 49 and the current year is between 00 and 49

   c) Next century if the year tested is 00 through 49 and the current year is 50 through 99

   d) Current century if the year tested is 50 and 99 and the current year is between 00 and 49

4. When might a group function return more than one row?

   a) When used with a WHERE clause

   b) When used with an ORDER BY clause

   c) When used with a GROUP BY clause

   d) Cannot have more than one row returned

5. Cartesian Joins have a valid use.

   True/False

6. Oracle9i supports a subquery in the FROM clause.

   True/False

7. SQL*Plus can

   a) Take input from the command line

   b) Format column output

   c) Sum the contents of a column

   d) All of the above

8. SQL*Plus can be used to create GUI reports.

   True/False

Answers: 1=2: single-row functions and multiple-row functions; 2=True; 3=b; 4=c; 5=False, usually occurs when the WHERE clause is accidentally left off of a join condition; 6=True; 7=d; 8=False, Character mode only.

APPLY

Applying It

Independent Exercise 1:

- SELECT the departments with a count of the rows for each department.

Independent Exercise 2:

- Build a Master/Detail report using DEPT and EMP.
- Show just the Department Name on the master record.
- Show the employees name and salary in the Detail.
- Create a Cross-matrix report using EMP, showing the salaries summed by JOB and by DEPTNO.

Independent Exercise 3:

- UPDATE the EMP table, give everyone a 10% increase in salary.
- Show the values of ENAME and SAL prior to the UPDATE.

Answers to Chapter 8

REVIEW

Reviewing It

1. What kind of networks do Web browsers support?
2. Explain what a CGI is.
3. What is the difference between an Applet and a Servlet?
4. What is the difference between thin and thick JDBC Drivers?
5. What is a virtual address?
6. Briefly describe why one might use PL/SQL or Java or Portal (and vice versa).

Answers: 1=TCP/IP; 2=Usually a program being accessed instead of a computer file; 3=*Applets* are Java programs that are parts of Web pages. They are downloaded through the listener to a compliant Web browser and are executed on the client machine. *Servlets* are host-based Java programs that build dynamic Web pages that are then passed back to the Web browser; 4=*Thin* JDBC is used by applets and provides database connectivity for a particular client session. *Thick* JDBC is used to maintain connectivity for the duration of the servlet process; 5=What follows the first / of a URL is the virtual address, which relates to a physical location on the particular computer; 6=Programmers are already familiar with PL/SQL but features might be limited, Java has a steep learning curve, Portals appearance is not that flexible.

Checking It

1. HTTP is

   a) The Internet

   b) The protocol between the Web browser and the Web server

   c) The language used to build Web pages

   d) The CGI program

2. HTML is

   a) The Internet

   b) The protocol between the Web browser and the Web server

   c) The language used to build Web pages

   d) The CGI program

3. A URL is a Universal Resource Locator.

   True/False

4. Oracle9iAS is

   a) Oracle's latest database engine

   b) Oracle's latest Web server

   c) Oracle's latest forms server

   d) Oracle's latest clustered database technology

5. Oracle Corp refers to Oracle9iAS as a

   a) 1-Tier environment

   b) 2-Tier environment

   c) 3-Tier environment

   d) 4+-Tier environment

6. PL/SQL is

   a) Runtime interpreted

   b) Full-featured open language

   c) Wizard-based Web development

7. Java is

    a) Runtime interpreted

    b) Full-featured open language

    c) Wizard-based Web development

8. Portal V3.0 is

    a) Runtime interpreted

    b) Full-featured open language

    c) Wizard-based Web development

Answers: 1=b; 2=c; 3=False, Uniform Resource Locator; 4=b; 5=c; 6=a; 7=b; 8=c.

Applying It

APPLY

Independent Exercise 1:

- Web browse www.quepublishing.com.

- On your browser tool bar (Netscape), select View, Page Source, (Internet Explorer) select View,Source.

- Review the various HTML tags and commands that make up this Web page.

- Notice the tags around any pictures or objects that downloaded.

Answers to Chapter 9

Reviewing It

REVIEW

1. Explain the difference between the HTP package and the HTF package.

2. What is htp.p used for?

3. Why would you want to call another PL/SQL procedure in a Web environment?

4. In Listing 9.9, line 4, why is the p_inv_id variable set to null?

5. In Listing 9.10, what error message will be displayed if the car requested cannot be found?

Answers: 1=The *HTP* package contains PL/SQL procedures that generate HTML output, whereas the *HTF* package contains PL/SQL functions that return HTML code as the return value; 2=htp.p can be used to pass the text <HTML> to the HTML output; 3=This called pl/sql is a way of giving a consistent look with appearances and error messages across the Web site; 4=To provide the procedure with a default value in the case that no value was passed, the Web page displays with the lowest inv_id record in the database; 5=42:p_text => 'The auto selected could not be found'.

Checking It

CHECK

1. If you have an htp.bodyopen command you need an

   a) Htp.htlmopen

   b) Htp.htlmclose

   c) Htp.bodyclose

   d) Htp.textopen

2. What happens if an input parameter does not have a default value and none is passed?

   a) Nothing happens, the Web page displays as programmed

   b) An error is returned to the user complaining about a missing mandatory parameter

   c) The results may be unpredictable as the Web page will try to display the variable

   d) The Web server will crash

3. When using PL/SQL, you do not need a virtual path at all.

   True/False

Answers: 1=c; 2=b; 3=False, the virtual path tells the Web server that this is a PL/SQL.

Applying It

APPLY

Independent Exercise 1:

- Start your favorite editor and put the few HTML commands in to simply display your name.

- Name this file Ch9_ex1.htm.

- Access this file with your favorite Web browser.

Independent Exercise 2:

- Start your favorite editor and build and compile a simple PL/SQL procedure that performs the same task as Exercise 1 except use the PL/SQL htp package to create the HTML.

Independent Exercise 3:

- Create a small table object with one character field.

- Build a simple PL/SQL Web-based procedure that

    - Prompts the user for a variable.

    - Checks to make sure something was entered.

    - Inserts into your table object the contents of this variable.

    - Displays what has been inserted.

    - Clears the entry field so that additional information can be entered.

Answers to Chapter 10

REVIEW

Reviewing It

1. Explain the purpose of a JAR file.

2. Why does the JDeveloper software create a HTML file when saving the Java program?

3. Why does the JDBC thin client software prompt for userid and password?

4. What is a DAD and why is it important?

5. What does the java function out.println() do.

Answers: 1=To put all associated pieces of code together in a single downloadable file; 2=The HTML file will be accessed by the Web browser. This file contains the necessary HTML code to access the java program; 3=Because the thin drivers maintain connectivity between the client and the database where the thick drivers maintain connectivity between the servlet and the database; 4=This database descriptor is used by servlets to make automatic connections to the database when the DAD name is referenced in the URL; 5=Creates output in the HTML file.

CHECK

Checking It

1. What does JAR stand for?

    a) Java Archive Resource

    b) Java Archive File

      c) Java Active Repository

      d) Java Archive Repository

2. The DB Servlet runs on

      a) The client

      b) The database server

      c) The Web server

      d) Any of the above

3. You have to FTP the servlet code created to its intended target.

   True/False

Answers: 1=b; 2=c; 3=False, the JDeveloper software can do the deployment.

APPLY

Applying It

Independent Exercise 1:

- Build the 'Hello World' example in Listing 10.1.

- Deploy it and run it.

Independent Exercise 2:

- Build a master/detail servlet that displays department information then displays the employees and their managers underneath.

- Deploy and run the servlet.

Independent Exercise 3:

- Build an applet and a servlet that prompts the user for a valid EMPNO in the EMP table, then displays the correct row from the EMP table.

- Deploy and run the code.

Answers to Chapter 11

REVIEW

Reviewing It

1. What is a PL/SQL Page?

2. Why would you want to use PL/SQL procedures in a JSP?

3. What are Apache Virtual Directories useful for?

4. What does DAD stand for and what is it useful for?

5. What is the purpose of JSP and PSP?

6. What is a Java Bean?

7. What functions are used in JSPs to pass parameters?

8. What is the purpose of a stylesheet?

Answers: 1=PL/SQL Pages are a way of imbedding PL/SQL into existing HTML Web applications; 2=PL/SQL is excellent for Oracle database interaction; 3=They are aliases and will allow for more Web-environment-neutral access to files (such as pictures, code, and so on); 4=Database Access Descriptor and it essentially hides the login process from the Web user; 5=To easily allow static HTML pages to become dynamic via database interaction; 6=A Java class used to do something specific; 7=Post and get; 8=Used to format XML into HTML or the target language such as WML.

Checking It

CHECK

1. JSP stands for

    a) Java Servlet Pages

    b) Java Server Procedures

    c) Java Servlet Procedures

    d) Java Server Pages

2. XML can only create HTML pages.

    True/False

3. The following syntax, `Alias /icons/ "C:\oracle\ora81\Apache\Apache\icons/"` is from which Apache configuration file:

    a) `ojsp.conf`

    b) Httpd.conf

    c) Page1.xsl

    d) Xml.conf

4. The `<% %>` tags are found in what syntax:

    a) PSP

    b) JSP

    c) XSP

    d) WML

5. What does XSQL produce?

    a) HTML

    b) JSP

    c) XML

    d) WML

6. The <?   ?> tags are found in what syntax:

    a) PSP

    b) JSP

    c) XSP

    d) XML

7. XML stylesheets read XML data pages.

True/False

Answers: 1=d; 2=False; 3=b; 4=a; 5=c; 6=d; 7=True.

APPLY

Applying It

Independent Exercise 1:

- Download the Chapter 11 examples from www.quepublishing.com.

- Build the PL/SQL procedures getcar and makeoffer.

- Build a simple PSP that gets the first record from getcar.

Independent Exercise 2:

- Download the java bean programs from www.quepublishing.com.

- Compile the java bean programs.

- Build a simple JSP that gets the first record from getcar.

Independent Exercise 3:

- Download the cell phone emulator from www.phone.com.

- Build a simple XML application using the following query:

```
Select DNAME, SUM(SAL)
From EMP, DEPT
Where EMP.DEPTNO = DEPT.DEPTNO
```

Answers to Chapter 12

REVIEW

Reviewing It

1. What is Portal v3.0?

2. What are key differences between Portal v3.0 and its predecessor WebDB?

3. What is a portlet?

Answers: 1=It is Web-based Web-page development software from Oracle Corp; 2=WebDB had its own listener and was basically independent of the Web server where Portal v3.0 is integrated with Oracle9iAS; 3=A small application, Web URL, and so on, that can be included in a Portal page.

CHECK

Checking It

1. What URL starts the Portal environment:

    a) `http://<host-name>/portal30`

    b) `http://10.4.50.100/pls/portal30`

    c) `http://<host-name>/portal30/portal30`

    d) All of the above

2. Portal is only a Web-development tool.

    True/False

3. Portal can build which of these:

    a) Form

    b) Report

    c) XML

    d) Menu

    e) List of Values

    f) All of the above

4. On the base tabular form, there are four buttons by default.

    True/False

Answers: 1=b; 2=False, it monitors and administrates the database as well; 3=False; 4=False, three buttons.

APPLY

Applying It

Independent Exercise 1:

- Build a simple Portal Application Form based on the EMP table.
- Query KING.
- Query all those making more than $2,000.

Independent Exercise 2:

- Build a Portal Application Report based on

  SELECT DNAME, SUM(SAL)

  FROM DEPT, EMP

  WHERE DEPT.DEPTNO = EMP.DEPTNO

Independent Exercise 3:

- Build a portal page with three columns.
- Populate these columns with various portlets.
- Run this newly created page.

Answers to Chapter 13

REVIEW

Reviewing It

1. What would be the advantage of a partitioned index?
2. What is the advantage of an IOT over that of a HEAP Table?
3. Why does IOTs have the pseudo column 'ROWID'?
4. What is a b*tree level telling you?
5. Show the syntax to make a SQL statement use an existing index when a calculation on the indexed column is desired.
6. List some of the benefits and penalties of using bitmapped indexes.

Answers: 1=To make less b*tree levels when indexing very large tables; 2=No underlying table structure is required; 3=So that indexes can be created on IOTs; 4=The number of levels in the index, the fewest number of reads required to find a table ROWID; 5=WHERE sal > 1000/1.10; 6=Advantages: Speed Disadvantages: Causes exclusive lock on table during DML, very slow at DML.

CHECK

Checking It

1. A Reverse-Key index is useful for what following situation:

   a) The index key value is based on an Oracle Sequence.

   b) The typical access will be via a range of values.

   c) The index key value is always something unique.

2. When might Oracle NOT use a Reverse-Key index?

   a) The WHERE clause is using a < predicate.

   b) The WHERE clause is using a > predicate.

   c) The WHERE clause is using a BETWEEN function.

   d) All of the above

3. A Unique Index is the fastest way to access an individual row in a table.

   True/False

4. What is the IOT overflow tablespace used for?

   a) To store additional indexed rows for the IOT

   b) To store statistics about the IOT

   c) To store additional IOT columns

   d) All of the above

5. A bitmap index is good for large, dynamic tables.

   True/False

6. What is the purpose of a function-based index:

   a) To provide indexing on columns with any mathematical function

   b) To provide indexing on columns with any Oracle function

   c) To provide indexing on columns with specific functions

7. Bitmap Join Indexes are useful

   a) In about any join situation

   b) Where the primary table has a primary key constraint

   c) Where the primary table has a primary key constraint and the joining table(s) have unique key constraints

   d) Where the joining table(s) have primary or unique key constraints

8. In a Bitmap Join Index, what exactly is getting indexed?

   a) The primary table's column

   b) The join table(s) column

   c) Both the primary table and the join table column

Answers: 1=a; 2=d, any range scan will not use a reverse-key index; 3=False, ROWID is the fastest method of access; 4=c; 5=False, low cardinality and few table changes; 6=c; 7=c; 8=a.

APPLY

Applying It

Independent Exercise 1:

- Create a composite index on EMP using the EMPNO and DEPTNO columns.

Independent Exercise 2:

- Convert the DEPT table to an IOT.

Answers to Chapter 14

REVIEW

Reviewing It

1. What is an explain plan?

2. What is the main difference between the cost-based optimizer and the rule-based optimizer?

3. What is a driving table?

4. What might a histogram be useful for? What SQL syntax does Oracle require to use a histogram?

5. What are the three kinds of join conditions?

6. Is a full-table scan necessarily always bad?

7. What is clustering factor?

8. Describe a good use for a Stored Outline.

Answers: 1=The *explain plan* illustrates the *execution plan* for any SQL statement. It shows the tables and indexes Oracle will use when processing a SQL statement, as well as the order in which the tables and indexes will be used; 2=The Cost-based optimizer makes its decisions based on pre-collected statistics where the rule-based uses a set of 19 rules; 3=The *driving table* is the table that is accessed first and then used to look up information in the other tables in the `join` condition; 4=Histograms are useful to help the cost-based optimizer see the selectivity of data desired to be selected. A value must be given in the `WHERE` clause, not a bind variable, for Oracle to use a histogram; 5=Nested-loops, sort-merge, and hash joins; 6=No, not when either the index selectivity is poor on a range-scan or just a few blocks of data exist in the table; 7= Clustering factor is a relationship between the number of data blocks being referenced by each index leaf block; 8=To insure that a very particular execution plan gets used when ever and/or where ever the SQL statement appears.

CHECK

Checking It

1. Stored Outlines became available with this release of the database:

    a) V8.0.4

    b) V8.1.5

    c) V8.1.7

    d) V9.0.1

2. Which one of these helps control the rule-based optimizer?

    a) Existence of an index

    b) Use of functions in the `WHERE` clause

    c) Coding techniques

    d) All of the above

3. The rule-based optimizer uses a list of 18 different rules to make its decision.

    True/False

4. Both the rule and cost-based optimizers supports bitmapped indexes.

    True/False

5. Which of the following commands collects statistics for the cost-based optimizer?

    a) `Analyze <object name> computer statistics`

    b) `Estimate Statistics <object name>`

    c) `Alter System compute statistics <object name>`

    d) Oracle9i supports each of these options

6. If statistics have not been gathered and the OPTIMIZATION MODE is set to CHOOSE, Oracle will use the rule-based optimizer.

   True/False

7. If statistics have not been gathered and the OPTIMIZATION MODE is set to COST, Oracle will still use the rule-based optimizer.

   True/False

8. The `init.ora` parameter `OPTIMIZER_INDEX_CACHING` set to `0` says:

   a) The index cache will not be used

   b) Tells Oracle to do full-table scans

   c) Tells Oracle to rely upon indexes more

   d) Assumes a 0 buffer-hit cache ratio

9. Oracle8i allowed you to edit stored outlines.

   True/False

Answers: 1=c; 2=d; 3=False, 19 rules; 4=False, just the cost-based optimizer; 5=a; 6=True; 7=False, Oracle will make statistic assumptions; 8=d; 9=False, an Oracle9i feature.

APPLY

Applying It

Independent Exercise 1:

- Install the explain plan table.

- Start SQL*Plus and run the query in Listing 14.4.

- Examine the output.

Independent Exercise 2:

- Add a hint to use the rule-based optimizer.

- Re-run the query in Listing 14.4 and compare the results with those from Exercise 1.

Independent Exercise 3:

- Alter the query in Listing 14.4 to invalid the use of an index.

- For both the cost-based optimizer (use a hint) and the rule-based optimizer (add 0 to a numeric field).

- Re-run the query using the explain table and check the result table.

Answers to Chapter 15

Reviewing It

1. What is the difference between a range partition and a list partition?

2. Briefly explain the difference between a hash partition and a composite partition.

3. What is the difference between a local-partitioned index and a global-partitioned index?

Answers: 1=Range works with numeric values and divides across partitions based on a range of values. List works with literals and simply puts the rows in the proper partitions based on a literal value; 2=*Composite* partitioning is a combination of range and hash partitioning; 3=*Local-partitioned* indexes have the same partitioning key values, number of tablespaces, and partitioning rules as the underlying table, whereas *global-partitioned* indexes have a PARTITION BY RANGE or PARITION BY LIST clause that enables the partitioning values, number of partitions, and tablespaces themselves to all be defined and vary from the underlying table partitioning structure.

Checking It

1. You can perform a partition split operation on a list partition.

    True/False

2. Hash Partitioning

    a) Automatically spreads the rows across partitions

    b) Uses a RANGE clause

    c) Allows for MAXVALUES

    d) All of the above

3. If you have a partitioned index, the table MUST be partitioned as well.

    True/False

4. Which of these options is the easiest for the cost-based optimizer?

    a) Local prefixed index

    b) Local nonprefixed index

    c) Global index

5. Which of these options is the easiest for parallel processing?

   a) Local prefixed index

   b) Local nonprefixed index

   c) Global index

Answers: 1=False, this only applies to range partitioning; 2=a; 3=False; 4=a; 5=b.

Answers to Chapter 16

Reviewing It

REVIEW

1. What does TOAD stand for?

2. Where can I download the current version of TOAD?

3. Where do you access the single record viewer?

4. What is the Schema Browser useful for?

Answers: 1=Tool for Oracle Application Development; 2=www.toadsoft.com; 3=Any window that displays data; 4=Allows you to quickly find and edit various Database objects.

Checking It

CHECK

1. Is TOAD strictly a development tool?

   Yes/No

2. When TOAD starts up, this window comes up first:

   a) SQL Modeler

   b) SQL Editor

   c) SQL Procedure Builder

   d) SQL Schema Browser

3. TOAD only works with SQL and PL/SQL.

   True/False

4. How many different ways are there to get code into the Procedure Editor?

   a) 1

   b) 2

c) 4

d) 6

Answers: 1=No, it does many DBA functions as well; 2=b; 3=False, TOAD also interfaces with other code development tools such as VB, Java, C++, or Delphi; 4=b, read from a file or load from the database.

Applying It

Independent Exercise 1:

APPLY

- Build a simple SQL query, logged in as SCOTT, using the emp and dept tables.

  - Display the results.

  - Model the SQL relationships.

  - Show an explain plan.

  - Change some salaries one row at a time.

Independent Exercise 2:

- Add a new user.

- Grant this new user the same privileges as SCOTT.

Independent Exercise 3:

- Build a POST-INSERT trigger on the EMP table.

  - Have it make sure the DEPTNO code is in the DEPT table.

  - Have it loop 10 times, updating a variable by 10 with each loop.

- Set a break point just inside the loop.

  - Check the value of the variable with each loop.

Independent Exercise 4:

- Using the Schema Browser, see if EMP has any procedures.

Answers to Chapter 17

Reviewing It

1. What is the purpose of SQL*Loader?

REVIEW

2. Why would someone use External Tables instead of SQL*Loader?

3. Why would you want SQL*Loader to skip records?

4. What are Export/Import used for?

Answers: 1= SQL*loader can load data from specifically formatted files (files with data fields in fixed locations), files where the fields have some kind of field separator such as a ':', data that is in its own definition file, or it can even load data via the Unix pipe command; 2=External tables gives the user the ability to run full SQL against the data, performing data conversions with DECODE, concatenations, and so on; 3=Perhaps there is some header information in the data file that is not to be loaded or the user is creating some test data from the middle of a data file; 4=Export and Import can be used to move data from one Oracle instance to another, to backup a particular users data, to create test environments, and to provide incremental backup and recovery.

CHECK

Checking It

1. Which of the following is proper SQL*Loader command line syntax:

    a) `Sqlldr userid=scott/tiger control=foo.ctl`

    b) `Sqlldr scott/tiger foo`

    c) `Sqlldr`

    d) All of the above

2. Data will be inserted and any data in the table will remain with which mode:

    a) INSERT

    b) APPEND

    c) REPLACE

    d) TRUNCATE

3. The table is expected to be empty with which mode:

    a) INSERT

    b) APPEND

    c) REPLACE

    d) TRUNCATE

4. `INTEGER EXTERNAL` is used to define numbers with decimal points?

    True/False

5. A converted SQL*Loader control file to an External file puts the CREATE TABLE in a separate file with a .SQL suffix.

   True/False

6. Which of the following is NOT valid EXPORT syntax:

   a) EXP SCOTT/TIGER GRANTS=Y TABLES=(EMP,DEPT,MGR)

   b) EXP

   c) EXP USERID=SCOTT/TIGER

   d) All are valid syntax

Answers: 1=d; 2=b; 3=a; 4=False; 5=False, it puts it in the log file; 6=c.

Applying It

Independent Exercise 1:

APPLY

* Export the SCOTT schema.

* Drop the SCOTT.EMP table.

* Import just the SCOTT.EMP table.

Independent Exercise 2:

* Create a SQL*Loader control file for EMP.

* Delete all the rows in EMP.

* Use SQL*Loader to put data into the SCOTT.EMP table.

Independent Exercise 3:

* Create a simple data file using ':' as field delimiters.

* Create an External Table based on this simple data file.

* Query your simple data using the External Table.

Answers to Chapter 18

Reviewing It

1. What is the purpose of the dictionary file?

REVIEW

2. Briefly describe how you would reverse a database table delete.

3. What is persistent mode?

Answers: 1=You need to create a 'dictionary file' that will contain the redo logs being examined; 2=Create dictionary file, use ADDFILE, select UNDO_SQL from V$LOGMNR_CONTENTS where USERNAME = <'username'> and OPERATION = 'DELETE'; 3=Allows Log Miner to mine the contents of active logs, creating output files in real-time mode.

CHECK

Checking It

1. Log Miner can read Oracle v7.3 log files.

   True/False

2. Which of the following is NOT valid syntax?

   a) ADDFILE

   b) DELETEFILE

   c) REPLACEFILE

   d) All of the above

3. Log Miner can be used as an audit trail.

   True/False

Answers: 1=False, 8.0 on; 2=c; 3=True.

APPLY

Applying It

Independent Exercise 1:

- Make sure your database is in Archive Log mode

- Delete all the records from the SCOTT.EMP table.

- Use Log Miner, find the records, and make an UNDO script

- Apply the UNDO Script

- Query the SCOTT.EMP table

Independent Exercise 2:

- Check to see what activity the user SCOTT has been doing to the database

- Check to see who has done what kind of activity to the SCOTT.EMP table

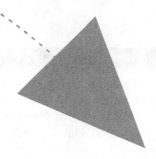

Appendix B

Oracle9i Architecture and Complete Sales Tracking Installation Scripts

This appendix introduces you to the Oracle9i database computer architecture. The first portion discusses the various features of the Oracle9i database. The remainder of the appendix gives complete listings of the scripts used to create the sales tracking sample database.

Oracle9i Architecture

This section describes the base components of the Oracle9i database software across all computers. It describes the various components (including memory, hardware, and network components) that make up the Oracle9i RDBMS environment as well as the interaction between them. In addition, it discusses some of the internal mechanisms to provide a better understanding of how Oracle9i works.

Computer memory is a physical storage device (computer chips) where instructions (programs) and data (data read from the hard disks) are entered and retrieved when needed for processing. It is literally hundreds of thousands times faster to read information from memory rather than directly from disk. It is the job of the computer's operating system to read both programs and data from hard disks and place them in memory. The more physical memory that can be allocated to the Oracle RDBMS, the more data can be stored there from the hard disks and the faster the applications will respond to end-user requests.

For Oracle, the processes are the Oracle system (background) processes that look after the database and performs the actual access to the database for the users of the database.

In today's computing environment, including the Internet, networks, and networking computers together have become a way of life. A network is a system of connections between machines that enable one machine to communicate with another and share resources. As well as the physical wires and components, there needs to be a set of rules for communication; this is known as a protocol.

Oracle can support many different types of networks and protocols. If communication between computers running Oracle software is required, the Oracle Net software must be installed on all the computers participating in this network. The Oracle Net software hides the complexities (and even the type of network) from the end user. The software handles all the issues, the end user does not have to do anything to access Oracle from one network type to another. This networking independence is also what makes Oracle applications very portable across physically different computers.

The Oracle9i architecture described in this section is the generic architecture that applies to all platforms on which Oracle runs. There might be subtle differences in the architecture between different platforms, but the fundamentals are all the same.

A database is nothing more than a collection of related data that is used and retrieved together for one or more computer-based applications. The physical location and implementation of the database is transparent to the application programs and the physical database can be moved without affecting the programs. This is another great feature of the Net*8Oracle Net software. All the user needs is a connect string (a name given to a particular Oracle database) and Oracle Net will know how to find it and connect the user.

Physically, an Oracle database is a set of files somewhere on disk. The physical location of these files is irrelevant to the function of the database. You will learn in this book that the location of these files can have a significant impact on how quickly requests for data can be supplied to the end-user. The files are binary files that you can only access using the Oracle RDBMS.

Schemas and User Accounts

Logically, the Oracle9i database is divided into a set of user accounts known as schemas. Each schema is associated with a user id that was used to create the objects in the schema. It is good practice to create a super-user type account (usually with DBA privileges) that owns all the objects for a particular application and also controls the privileges to those same objects. Without a valid username, password, and access privileges, access to information within the database is not possible, no matter what tool you are using. Typically, the Oracle username and password are different from the operating system username and password, however, Oracle does allow for the same operating system username and password to be used to log in to the Oracle environment. This is known as OPS$ Login and additional information about using this feature can be found in the Oracle9i Database Administrators Guide.

Oracle user accounts provide a method of separating applications. It is common practice to have a single application residing in a single Oracle database. The same table name can coexist in two separate Oracle user accounts or schemas; although the tables might have the same name, they are different tables containing different information. Sometimes, the same database is used for holding different versions of tables for the developers, system testing, or user testing, or the same table name is used in different application systems. In Oracle, the schema name is the same as the Oracle user who created the table.

TIP

It is a good practice to have a single Oracle user account create all the database objects for a single application.

N O T E

It is also a good practice to have an application test and development environment physically on a separate computer from where the users are using the application (the production system).

Figure B.1 shows the basic Oracle9i architecture that will be discussed in the remainder of this section.

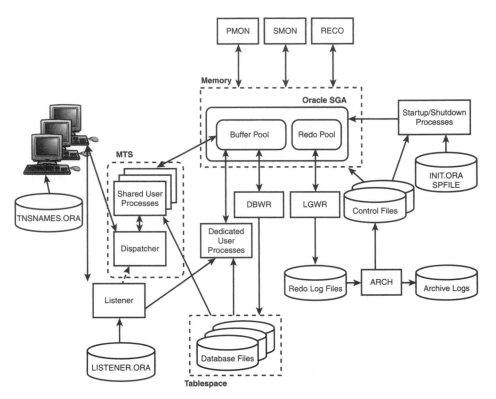

Figure B.1: *Oracle9i architecture.*

Oracle9i Database Files

There are three sets of files that actually store the user data and control the various Oracle9i database functions. These sets (database files, control files, and redo logs) must be present, open, and available to Oracle before any data can be accessed. The most important of these are the database files, in which the actual data resides. The control files and the redo logs support the functioning of the architecture itself.

Oracle9i User Background Processes

For the database to be accessible, the Oracle9i system processes and one or more user processes must be running on the computer. The Oracle system processes, also known as Oracle background processes, provide necessary functions for the user processes to access the database. There are many background processes that are initiated, but as a minimum, only the PMON, SMON, DBWR, and LGWR must be up and running for the database to be useable. There will be more details on these specific processes later in this appendix.

Other background processes support optional additions to the way the database runs. Each logged on user needs a background process, called a *shadow process*, to communicate with the Oracle9i database. There are two methods of assigning these background processes: the default method is that each user is assigned a background process (a dedicated background process) as part of the logon process (see Figure B.2), or users share a pool of background processes via the multi-threaded server (see Figure B.3). In both cases, the listener process routes the user traffic to the proper Oracle database being requested. In the case of dedicated background processes (see Figure B.2), once the background process is established the listener is no longer involved with this particular user. In the case of the multi-threaded server, the users are passed to a dispatcher and the dispatcher interacts with the user programs to share a pool of dedicated background processes.

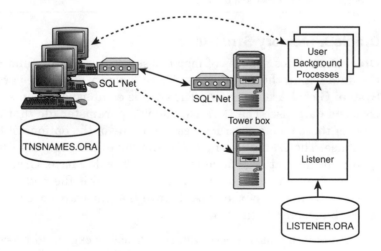

Figure B.2: *User background processes.*

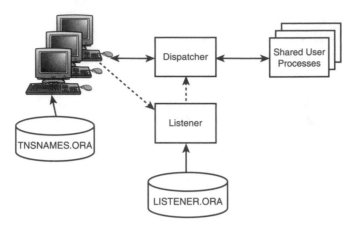

Figure B.3: *Multi-threaded server shared background processes.*

NOTE

User background processes are started when a user logs in to Oracle. These processes are used to pass data to and from the user application (SQL*Plus, forms, a 'c' program perhaps). The multi-threaded server (MTS) is a way of sharing a set number of these background processes as each of these background processes takes computer memory and processing time to manage. When there are a large number of users on a particular computer (such as 500 or more users accessing a single Oracle database), it might be a better use of memory to use MTS. MTS uses a queuing mechanism and works on the assumption that not all users are reading or writing the database at the exact same time.

Oracle9i Memory Structures

Oracle9i requires a series of memory structures to store and manipulate the data within the data blocks. These memory structures are known as the System Global Area, or SGA. The SGA is established upon startup of the Oracle9i database. The INIT.ORA file is a parameter file that defines the sizes of these memory structures and many of the options of the Oracle database. The SPFILE is a new file, similar to the INIT.ORA file, but also maintains any settings done from inside the database. Oracle9i will use the SPFILE, if present. The startup process reads this file and builds the various memory structures of the SGA. Figure B.4 illustrates these memory structures that comprise the SGA.

The combination of the SGA and the Oracle background processes make up an Oracle9i database instance. There are various features and options that affect how many instances can use the same set of database files. An Oracle instance comprises a unique set of Oracle background processes, shared memory, and database files. A single computer may have several Oracle instances running on it.

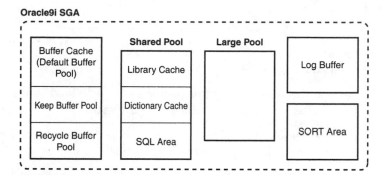

Figure B.4: *The Oracle9i system global area.*

NOTE

An Oracle instance is a common way to refer to unique Oracle database environments, whether they are on the same physical computer or not.

Each Oracle instance has its own SGA. These memory structures are created when the Oracle instance is started up and the memory allocated to these structures is returned to the computer when the Oracle instance is shutdown.

As illustrated by Figure B.4, there are several areas of the SGA.

The buffer cache is the work space for data blocks when user processes make requests for data from the tablespaces. Oracle will always check for the existence of a requested data block before performing a read-operation to retrieve it. The buffer cache hit ratio is a ratio of the number of times that a data block was already in the buffer cache versus the number of times Oracle had to read the requested data block from a tablespace. Listing B.1 shows a SQL statement that can be used to monitor this buffer hit cache ratio. Generally speaking, setting this buffer hit cache ratio correctly can have the greatest impact on performance in any Oracle instance. All applications will have different needs but this buffer cache hit ratio should be generally above 90% the majority of the time.

TIP

Adjustments to the buffer hit cache ratio can be controlled by setting the DB_BLOCK_BUFFERS in the INIT.ORA parameter file. Tuning the Oracle environment is covered in this book.

Listing B.1: Buffer Hit Cache Ratio

```
select round(((sum(decode(name,'db block gets',value))
        + sum(decode(name,'consistent gets',value)))
        - sum(decode(name,'physical reads',value))) /
```

EXAMPLE

Listing B.1: continued

```
              (sum(decode(name,'db block gets',value))
            +  sum(decode(name,'consistent gets',value))) * 100) "Buffer Cache
Hit Ratio"
from v$sysstat;
```

Oracle9i allowed for this buffer pool to be sub-divided into three additional areas to better control the buffer cache hit ratio:

- The keep pool is designed for those objects that may be referenced many times but with few new inserts.

- The recycle pool is for those objects that may have quite a bit of insert and update activity that may not be immediately referenced again.

- The default pool (also known as the buffer pool) is for all other objects.

By monitoring and placing various objects in these different pools, objects with frequent read activity can be separated from those that do not spend much time in memory, thus allowing those with frequent read activity to remain in the SGA longer and not be processed out via the LRU process.

The shared pool contains the library cache, dictionary cache, and the SQL area. The SQL area holds the actual text of the SQL statement. The library cache is for the application SQL statements and the dictionary cache is for the data dictionary SQL statements.

The shared pool size is determined by the init.ora parameter SHARED_POOL_ SIZE.

The large pool was introduced by Oracle8 to help relieve some traffic and contention in the shared pool. The multithreaded server and the Oracle backup processes will use space here rather than in the shared pool. The large pool is defined by setting the LARGE_POOL_SIZE and LARGE_POOL_MIN_ ALLOC parameters in the INIT.ORA parameter file.

Oracle9i Default Tablespaces

During the installation process, Oracle9i will create several default database files. These database files are assigned to various tablespaces. Tables and other objects can be stored together via a tablespace. A tablespace is like a directory or folder on a computer, a point of organization within the Oracle database environment. The database files are created for the tablespaces. Each tablespace must have at least one database file assigned to it. Oracle requires at least two very specific tablespaces: System and TEMP. The System tablespace contains all the objects (tables, indexes, clusters, and so on) that the Oracle9i database uses to keep track of itself. These objects are known as the Data Dictionary. The TEMP tablespace is a work area for may kinds of SQL statements that may be joining data together (multiple tables in the FROM clause) as well as the sorting of data, and so on).

Oracle9i Miscellaneous Files

The control file records the name of the database, the date and time it was created, the location of the various database and redo logs, and information to make sure, at startup time, that all these files are from the same date and time from when this Oracle instance was previously shutdown. This is one way that Oracle can tell that it might be in a recovery situation—the control file is an important part of the recovery process because all the required recovery information is more than likely stored in the control file. As you can see, this is a rather important file. If it is missing, or corrupted, the Oracle instance will not start up. The INIT.ORA or SPFILE parameter file allows for multiple copies of the control file to be automatically maintained.

> **NOTE**
>
> The Oracle9i database must have at least one control file. I highly recommend at least three control files be maintained and that these control files are on separate physical disk drives.

The redo log files (sometimes called the online redo logs) are the master record of all activity going on in the database: the redo logs record all changes to the user objects or system objects. If any type of failure occurs, such as loss of one or more database files, the changes recorded in the redo logs will be used to recover the Oracle database without losing any committed transactions. If the computer was simply experiencing some problems (loss of electricity for example) Oracle applies the information in the redo logs automatically. The SMON background process automatically reapplies the committed changes from the redo logs to the database files.

These redo logs are always in use while the Oracle instance is up and running. Changes made to the Oracle instance are recorded to each of the redo logs in turn. When one is full, the other is written to; when that becomes full, the first is overwritten and the cycle continues. If there is not enough room in the redo logs for a large update, for example, the error Snapshot too old will be returned. This means that the end of the transaction has used all the space in the redo logs and has found the beginning of the transaction in the redo logs.

> **NOTE**
>
> The Oracle9i database must have at least two redo logs. The redo log files are fixed in size and never grow from the size at which they were originally created.

The Oracle RDBMS has the ability to save these redo logs so that the information in them can be applied in the event that recovery is required. The names of these logs are stored in the control file. The process is called Archive Log Mode and can be turned on with a series of manually entered commands or it can be automatically turned on within the INIT.ORA parameter file. These archive logs are exact copies of the online redo logs that have just been filled and are created when Oracle switches to another online redo log.

NOTE

Archive Log Mode is turned off by default at database installation time.

Oracle9i Database Background Processes

There are four main Oracle background processes that must always be running for the database to be accessible by the users. These processes include DBWR (Database Writer), LGWR (Log Writer), SMON (System Monitor), and PMON (Process Monitor).

The DBWR process writes database blocks that have been changed (inserted, updated, or deleted rows) in the SGA to the correct database files. A block that is in the SGA and has a change to it but has not yet been written back to the disk drive is known as a dirty block. The DBWR only writes dirty blocks, starting with the oldest block (or the block longest in the SGA) first.

NOTE

Least-recently used or LRU is used throughout Oracle to describe the process of only dealing with the oldest of anything first, or the least-recently used.

The LGWR process writes the redo information from the SGA's redo log buffer into the online redo log files. When a user or a transaction issues a commit to the Oracle database, it is the LGWR's job to write out the contents of the redo log buffer before acknowledging a successful commit. This will ensure in the event of some kind of computer failure, that all committed transactions can be recovered.

SMON performs a variety of tasks including the monitoring of multiple users trying to change the same object at the same time. This can lead to a dead lock situation. SMON will review each transaction, rollback, and return an error to the transaction with the lessor of processing time. SMON also does some space management in the tablespaces and is used to apply the transactions in the online redo log files in the event that the Oracle database was not shutdown in a normal manor (including shutdowns that did not wait for transactions to complete or some kind of computer failure that stopped the Oracle processes).

NOTE

A *dead lock* is where transactions are trying to make multiple updates to the same objects. One transaction is trying to lock an object that another transaction already has a lock on and that other transaction is trying to get a lock on an object that the first transaction already has a lock on. As you can see, these transactions would wait indefinitely because the locks would never clear.

PMON monitors the user processes as well as the dispatcher and shared background processes of the multi-threaded server. If any failure occurs with these background user processes (either shared or dedicated), PMON automatically rolls back the work of the user process since the transaction started (anything since the last COMMIT or ROLLBACK) and releases any locks that the transaction might have been holding.

There are a series of optional background processes that will be started if certain features of the Oracle database are being used. The ARCH process is used in Log Archive Mode to actually create the archive log files from the online redo log files. The RECO process is used if Oracle Replication has been implemented. This process is used with transactions that span two or more Oracle instances. In the event of a failed transaction, RECO will need to either commit or rollback parts of the transaction that failed. The LCK process is used by Oracle Parallel Server.

The listener process is like a traffic cop between the users connecting to an Oracle instance and the Oracle instance. The listener process is not related to any particular Oracle instance and uses the information in the LISTENER.ORA file to know which Oracle instance to route the user traffic. There is a listener process for each type of network being accessed by a particular computer. In a non-MTS environment, the listener actually starts up the background process on the same computer as the requested Oracle instance is running, logs the user in, and returns to listening for new users wanting to connect to Oracle. The users then directly communicate with this background process for the duration of their connection to an Oracle instance. In an MTS environment, the listener hands the user request off to an available dispatcher. This dispatcher then handles the user's requests between existing background processes, allowing many users to share just a few background processes. The users interact with the dispatcher and the dispatcher then routes the requests of users to a free background process (or starts additional background processes if the user demand is high). MTS is very useful when there are hundreds or even thousands of users connecting into a single instance of Oracle. Each user has access to a TNSNAMES.ORA file that contains information about the type of network and the name of the Oracle instance where the connection is desired.

Sales Tracking Database Setup Script

All these scripts and test data are available at www.quepublishing.com. Put 0789726718 in the search field.

```
rem
rem      Sales Tracking Application Oracle9i Initial Database Setup
rem          Oracle9i Development By Example
rem             by Dan Hotka
rem          Que Publications May 2001
rem          All Rights Reserved
rem
spool INSTALL_sales_tracking_database.log

DROP TABLESPACE st_data01              INCLUDING CONTENTS CASCADE CONSTRAINTS;
DROP TABLESPACE st_data02              INCLUDING CONTENTS CASCADE CONSTRAINTS;
DROP TABLESPACE st_index01             INCLUDING CONTENTS CASCADE CONSTRAINTS;
DROP TABLESPACE st_refdata01           INCLUDING CONTENTS CASCADE CONSTRAINTS;
DROP TABLESPACE st_iot_overflow01      INCLUDING CONTENTS CASCADE CONSTRAINTS;
DROP TABLESPACE st_lob01               INCLUDING CONTENTS CASCADE CONSTRAINTS;


CREATE TABLESPACE st_data01
        DATAFILE 'd:\Oracle\Oradata\ORCL\st_data01.dbf' SIZE 10M REUSE
        DEFAULT STORAGE (INITIAL 10K
                        NEXT 10K
                        MINEXTENTS 5
                        MAXEXTENTS 100
                        )
        ONLINE;


CREATE TABLESPACE st_data02
        DATAFILE 'd:\Oracle\Oradata\ORCL\st_data02.dbf' SIZE 10M REUSE
        DEFAULT STORAGE (INITIAL 5K
                        NEXT 5K
                        MINEXTENTS 5
                        MAXEXTENTS 100
                        )
        ONLINE;


CREATE TABLESPACE st_refdata01
        DATAFILE 'd:\Oracle\Oradata\ORCL\st_refdata01.dbf' SIZE 1M REUSE
        DEFAULT STORAGE (INITIAL 1K
                        NEXT 1K
                        MINEXTENTS 1
                        MAXEXTENTS 100
                        )
        ONLINE;
```

```
CREATE TABLESPACE st_index01
        DATAFILE 'd:\Oracle\Oradata\ORCL\st_index01.dbf' SIZE 5M REUSE
        DEFAULT STORAGE (INITIAL 5K
                    NEXT 5K
                    MINEXTENTS 5
                    MAXEXTENTS 100
                    )
        ONLINE;

CREATE TABLESPACE st_iot_overflow01
        DATAFILE 'd:\Oracle\Oradata\ORCL\st_iot_overflow01.dbf' SIZE 10M REUSE
        DEFAULT STORAGE (INITIAL 5K
                    NEXT 5K
                    MINEXTENTS 5
                    MAXEXTENTS 100
                    )
        ONLINE;

CREATE TABLESPACE st_lob01
        DATAFILE 'd:\Oracle\Oradata\ORCL\st_lob01.dbf' SIZE 10M REUSE
        DEFAULT STORAGE (INITIAL 10K
                    NEXT 10K
                    MINEXTENTS 1
                    MAXEXTENTS 100
                    )
        ONLINE;


CREATE USER sales_tracking
        IDENTIFIED BY sales_tracking
        DEFAULT TABLESPACE st_data01
        TEMPORARY TABLESPACE temp;

GRANT CONNECT, DBA TO sales_tracking;

spool off
exit
```

Sales Tracking Object Setup Script

All these scripts and test data are available at www.quepublishing.com. Put 0789726718 in the search field.

```
rem
rem     Sales Tracking Application Oracle9i Objects
rem         Oracle9i Development By Example
rem           by Dan Hotka
```

```
rem         Que Publications May 2001
rem         All Rights Reserved
rem
spool INSTALL_sales_tracking_objects.log

DROP TABLE st_inventory        CASCADE CONSTRAINTS;
DROP SEQUENCE st_inv_seq;

DROP TABLE st_parts            CASCADE CONSTRAINTS;
DROP TABLE st_inv_type               CASCADE CONSTRAINTS;
DROP TABLE st_inv_make               CASCADE CONSTRAINTS;
DROP TABLE st_inv_model        CASCADE CONSTRAINTS;
DROP TABLE st_vendor           CASCADE CONSTRAINTS;
DROP SEQUENCE st_vendor_seq;
DROP TABLE st_customer               CASCADE CONSTRAINTS;
DROP TABLE st_staff            CASCADE CONSTRAINTS;
DROP SEQUENCE st_staff_seq;
DROP TABLE st_bill_time        CASCADE CONSTRAINTS;
DROP TABLE st_departments      CASCADE CONSTRAINTS;
DROP TABLE st_job_description    CASCADE CONSTRAINTS;




CREATE TABLE st_inventory
        (inv_id                 NUMBER(6)    CONSTRAINT pk_inv_id PRIMARY KEY
                                             USING INDEX TABLESPACE st_index01,

        inv_type               VARCHAR2(10),
        inv_make               VARCHAR2(10),
        inv_model              VARCHAR2(10),
        inv_color              VARCHAR(10),
        inv_year               NUMBER(4),
        inv_purchase_vendor_id NUMBER(6),
        inv_purchase_amt       NUMBER(9,2)   NOT NULL,
        inv_purchase_date      DATE          NOT NULL,
        inv_purchase_photo     BLOB,
        inv_sale_customer_id   NUMBER(6),
        inv_sale_amt           NUMBER(9,2),
        inv_sale_date          DATE,
        inv_sale_photo         BLOB,
        inv_description        VARCHAR2(20),
        inv_insert_user        VARCHAR2(20),
        inv_insert_date        DATE,
        inv_update_user        VARCHAR2(20),
        inv_update_date        DATE)
        TABLESPACE st_data01
        PCTFREE 30
```

```
            PCTUSED  50
            STORAGE (INITIAL 10K
                    NEXT 10K
                    MINEXTENTS 5
                    MAXEXTENTS 10)
            LOB (inv_purchase_photo, inv_sale_photo) STORE AS
                    (TABLESPACE st_lob01
                    STORAGE (INITIAL 10K
                            NEXT 10K
                            MINEXTENTS 5
                            MAXEXTENTS 100)
                    CHUNK 500
                    NOCACHE
                    NOLOGGING);


CREATE SEQUENCE st_inv_seq
        START WITH 1
        INCREMENT BY 1
        CACHE 10;

CREATE TRIGGER st_inventory_trg BEFORE INSERT OR UPDATE ON st_inventory
        FOR EACH ROW
        BEGIN
                IF :old.inv_insert_user IS NULL THEN
                        :new.inv_insert_user := USER;
                        :new.inv_insert_date := SYSDATE;
                        :new.inv_update_user := NULL;
                        :new.inv_update_date := NULL;
                ELSE
                        :new.inv_insert_user := :old.inv_insert_user;
                        :new.inv_insert_date := :old.inv_insert_date;
                        :new.inv_update_user := USER;
                        :new.inv_update_date := SYSDATE;
                END IF;
          END;
/

CREATE TABLE st_inv_type
        (inv_type           VARCHAR(10))
        TABLESPACE st_refdata01
        CACHE
        PCTFREE 1
        PCTUSED 90
        STORAGE (INITIAL 1K
                NEXT 1K
                MINEXTENTS 1
```

```
                          MAXEXTENTS 100);

         CREATE TABLE st_inv_make
             (inv_make              VARCHAR(10))
             TABLESPACE st_refdata01
             CACHE
             PCTFREE 1
             PCTUSED 90
             STORAGE (INITIAL 1K
                     NEXT 1K
                     MINEXTENTS 1
                     MAXEXTENTS 100);

         CREATE TABLE st_inv_model
             (inv_model             VARCHAR2(10))
             TABLESPACE st_refdata01
             CACHE
             PCTFREE 1
             PCTUSED 90
             STORAGE (INITIAL 1K
                     NEXT 1K
                     MINEXTENTS 1
                     MAXEXTENTS 100);


         CREATE TABLE st_vendor
             (vendor_id             NUMBER(6)       PRIMARY KEY,
              vendor_name           VARCHAR2(30)    NOT NULL,
              vendor_street1        VARCHAR2(30),
              vendor_street2        VARCHAR2(30),
              vendor_city           VARCHAR2(20),
              vendor_state          VARCHAR2(2),
              vendor_zipcode        VARCHAR2(10),
              vendor_tax_id         VARCHAR2(20)    NOT NULL)
             ORGANIZATION INDEX
             TABLESPACE st_data02
             PCTTHRESHOLD 20 INCLUDING vendor_id
             OVERFLOW TABLESPACE st_iot_overflow01
             STORAGE (INITIAL 5K
                     NEXT 5
                     MINEXTENTS 5
                     MAXEXTENTS 100);

         CREATE SEQUENCE st_vendor_seq
             START WITH 1
             INCREMENT BY 1
             CACHE 10;
```

```
ALTER TABLE st_inventory       ADD CONSTRAINT fk_inv_purchase_vendor_id
     FOREIGN KEY (inv_purchase_vendor_id)
                               REFERENCES sales_tracking.st_vendor(vendor_id);

CREATE TABLE st_customer
       (customer_id            NUMBER(6) PRIMARY KEY,
        customer_name          VARCHAR2(30) NOT NULL,
        customer_street1       VARCHAR2(30),
        customer_street2       VARCHAR2(30),
        customer_city          VARCHAR2(20),
        customer_state         VARCHAR2(2),
        customer_zipcode       VARCHAR2(10),
        customer_insert_user   VARCHAR2(20),
        customer_insert_date   DATE,
        customer_update_user   VARCHAR2(20),
        customer_update_date   DATE)
       ORGANIZATION INDEX
       TABLESPACE st_data02
       PCTTHRESHOLD 20 INCLUDING customer_id
       OVERFLOW TABLESPACE st_iot_overflow01
       STORAGE (INITIAL 5K
               NEXT 5
               MINEXTENTS 5
               MAXEXTENTS 100);


CREATE TRIGGER st_customer_trg BEFORE INSERT OR UPDATE ON st_customer
       FOR EACH ROW
       BEGIN
               IF :old.customer_insert_user IS NULL THEN
                       :new.customer_insert_user := USER;
                       :new.customer_insert_date := SYSDATE;
                       :new.customer_update_user := NULL;
                       :new.customer_update_date := NULL;
               ELSE
                       :new.customer_insert_user := :old.customer_insert_user;
                       :new.customer_insert_date := :old.customer_insert_date;
                       :new.customer_update_user := USER;
                       :new.customer_update_date := SYSDATE;
               END IF;
       END;
/

ALTER TABLE st_inventory       ADD CONSTRAINT fk_inv_customer_id FOREIGN KEY
     (inv_sale_customer_id)

                               REFERENCES sales_tracking.st_customer(customer_id);
```

```
CREATE TABLE st_parts
      (part_inv_id              NUMBER(6)     CONSTRAINT fk_part_inv_id
                                              REFERENCES st_inventory (inv_id),
       part_vendor_id            NUMBER(6)     CONSTRAINT fk_part_vendor_id
                                              REFERENCES st_vendor (vendor_id),
       part_amt                 NUMBER(8,2)   NOT NULL,
       part_desc                VARCHAR2(20),
       part_date                DATE,
       part_insert_user         VARCHAR2(20),
       part_insert_date         DATE,
       part_update_user          VARCHAR2(20),
       part_update_date          DATE)
      TABLESPACE st_data02
      STORAGE (INITIAL 5K
            NEXT 5
            MINEXTENTS 5
            MAXEXTENTS 100);

CREATE TRIGGER st_parts_trg BEFORE INSERT OR UPDATE ON st_parts
      FOR EACH ROW
      BEGIN
            IF :old.part_insert_user IS NULL THEN
                  :new.part_insert_user := USER;
                  :new.part_insert_date := SYSDATE;
                  :new.part_update_user := NULL;
                  :new.part_update_date := NULL;
            ELSE
                  :new.part_insert_user := :old.part_insert_user;
                  :new.part_insert_date := :old.part_insert_date;
                  :new.part_update_user := USER;
                  :new.part_update_date := SYSDATE;
            END IF;
      END;
  /


CREATE TABLE st_departments
      (dept_id              NUMBER(6),
       dept_name            VARCHAR2(20))
      TABLESPACE st_refdata01
      CACHE
      PCTFREE 1
      PCTUSED 90
      STORAGE (INITIAL 1K
            NEXT 1K
            MINEXTENTS 1
            MAXEXTENTS 100);
```

```
ALTER TABLE st_departments ADD CONSTRAINT pk_dept_id PRIMARY KEY (dept_id)
      USING INDEX TABLESPACE st_index01;


CREATE TABLE st_job_description
      (job_id                 NUMBER(6),
      Job_descrition           VARCHAR2(20))
      TABLESPACE st_refdata01
      CACHE
      PCTFREE 1
      PCTUSED 90
      STORAGE (INITIAL 1K
            NEXT 1K
            MINEXTENTS 1
            MAXEXTENTS 100);

ALTER TABLE st_job_description ADD CONSTRAINT pk_job_id PRIMARY KEY (job_id)
      USING INDEX TABLESPACE st_index01;



CREATE TABLE st_staff
      (staff_id               NUMBER(6),
       staff_name             VARCHAR2(30),
       staff_street1          VARCHAR2(30),
       staff_street2          VARCHAR2(30),
       staff_city             VARCHAR2(20),
       staff_state            VARCHAR2(2),
       staff_zipcode          VARCHAR2(10),
       staff_dept_id          NUMBER(6)      NOT NULL,
       staff_job_id           NUMBER(6)      NOT NULL,
       staff_hiredate         DATE           NOT NULL,
       staff_termdate                  DATE,
       staff_hourly_rate      NUMBER(6,2)    NOT NULL,
       staff_billing_rate      NUMBER(6,2)    NOT NULL,
       staff_picture          BLOB,
       staff_insert_user      VARCHAR2(20),
       staff_insert_date      DATE,
       staff_update_user      VARCHAR2(20),
       staff_update_date      DATE,
       CONSTRAINT pk_staff_id PRIMARY KEY (staff_id)
       USING INDEX TABLESPACE st_index01,
       CONSTRAINT fk_staff_dept_id FOREIGN KEY (staff_dept_id)
       REFERENCES sales_tracking.st_departments (dept_id),
       CONSTRAINT fk_staff_job_id FOREIGN KEY (staff_job_id)
       REFERENCES sales_tracking.st_job_description (job_id))
```

```
                TABLESPACE st_data01
                PCTFREE 30
                PCTUSED 50
                STORAGE (INITIAL 10K
                        NEXT 10K
                        MINEXTENTS 5
                        MAXEXTENTS 100)
                LOB (staff_picture) STORE AS
                        (TABLESPACE st_lob01
                        STORAGE (INITIAL 10K
                                NEXT 10K
                                MINEXTENTS 5
                                MAXEXTENTS 100)
                        CHUNK 500
                        NOCACHE
                        NOLOGGING);


        CREATE SEQUENCE st_staff_seq
                START WITH 1
                INCREMENT BY 1
                CACHE 10;

        CREATE TRIGGER st_staff_trg BEFORE INSERT OR UPDATE ON st_staff
                FOR EACH ROW
                BEGIN
                        IF :old.staff_insert_user IS NULL THEN
                                :new.staff_insert_user := USER;
                                :new.staff_insert_date := SYSDATE;
                                :new.staff_update_user := NULL;
                                :new.staff_update_date := NULL;
                        ELSE
                                :new.staff_insert_user := :old.staff_insert_user;
                                :new.staff_insert_date := :old.staff_insert_date;
                                :new.staff_update_user := USER;
                                :new.staff_update_date := SYSDATE;
                        END IF;
                END;
        /

        CREATE TABLE st_bill_time
                (bt_staff_id            NUMBER(6),
                bt_inv_id               NUMBER(6),
                bt_date                 DATE            NOT NULL,
                bt_time                 NUMBER(3)       NOT NULL,
                bt_insert_user          VARCHAR2(20),
                bt_insert_date          DATE,
```

```
                bt_update_user                    VARCHAR2(20),
                bt_update_date         DATE,
                CONSTRAINT fk_bt_staff_id FOREIGN KEY (bt_staff_id)
                REFERENCES sales_tracking.st_staff(staff_id),
                CONSTRAINT fk_bt_inv_id FOREIGN KEY (bt_inv_id)
                REFERENCES sales_tracking.st_inventory(inv_id))
                TABLESPACE st_data01
                PCTFREE 1
                PCTUSED 80
                STORAGE (INITIAL 10K
                        NEXT 10
                        MINEXTENTS 5
                        MAXEXTENTS 100);

CREATE INDEX st_bt_staff_id ON st_bill_time (bt_staff_id)
        TABLESPACE st_index01
        STORAGE (INITIAL 5K
                NEXT 5K
                MINEXTENTS 5
                MAXEXTENTS 100);

CREATE INDEX st_bt_inv_id ON st_bill_time (bt_inv_id)
         TABLESPACE st_index01
         STORAGE (INITIAL 5K
                NEXT 5K
                MINEXTENTS 5
                MAXEXTENTS 100);


CREATE TRIGGER st_bill_time_trg BEFORE INSERT OR UPDATE ON st_bill_time
        FOR EACH ROW
        BEGIN
                IF :old.bt_insert_user IS NULL THEN
                        :new.bt_insert_user := USER;
                        :new.bt_insert_date := SYSDATE;
                        :new.bt_update_user := NULL;
                        :new.bt_update_date := NULL;
                ELSE
                        :new.bt_insert_user := :old.bt_insert_user;
                        :new.bt_insert_date := :old.bt_insert_date;
                        :new.bt_update_user := USER;
                        :new.bt_update_date := SYSDATE;
                END IF;
        END;
/
```

```
spool off
exit
```

Chapter 11 Objects Setup Script

All these scripts and test data are available at www.quepublishing.com. Put
0789726718 in the search field.

```
rem
rem    Sales Tracking Application Oracle9i Objects
rem        Oracle9i Development By Example
rem             by Dan Hotka
rem          Que Publications August 2001
rem          All Rights Reserved
rem
drop table st_cars_for_sale;
create table st_cars_for_sale
(
   inv_id    Number
,  auto_description VARCHAR2(60)
,  sale_amt number
,  sale_photo_location VARCHAR2(50)
,  buyer_name   VARCHAR2(20)
,  buyer_phone VARCHAR2(10)
,  buyer_offer number
,  buyer_date date
);


insert into st_cars_for_sale values
(1,'2000 Austin Martin DB7 Coupe',
142000,'/austinmartin.jpg',null,null,null,null);

insert into st_cars_for_sale values
(2,'1999 Lexus ES300', 29000,'/lexuses300.jpg',null,null,null,null);

insert into st_cars_for_sale values
(3,'1965 Ford Galaxie V8 Automatic', 3000,'/galaxie.jpg',null,null,null,null);


CREATE OR REPLACE PROCEDURE get_car_xml (
    p_id           IN st_cars_for_sale.inv_id%TYPE DEFAULT NULL
) IS
   l_id          st_cars_for_sale.inv_id%TYPE := p_id;
   l_description st_cars_for_sale.auto_description%TYPE;
   l_image       st_cars_for_sale.sale_photo_location%TYPE;
   l_amount      VARCHAR2(20);
```

```
BEGIN
    IF l_id IS NULL THEN
        l_id := 1;
    END IF; — l_id IS NULL
    get_car
    (
        px_id           => l_id
    ,   x_description   => l_description
    ,   x_image         => l_image
    ,   x_amount        => l_amount
    );
    htp.p('<CAR>');
    htp.p('<ID>'||TO_CHAR(l_id)||'</ID>');
    htp.p('<DESCRIPTION>'||l_description||'</DESCRIPTION>');
    htp.p('<IMAGE>'||l_image||'</IMAGE>');
    htp.p('<AMOUNT>'||LTRIM(l_amount)||'</AMOUNT>');
    htp.p('</CAR>');
END get_car_xml;
/

show errors

CREATE OR REPLACE PROCEDURE get_car (
    px_id           IN OUT   st_cars_for_sale.inv_id%TYPE,
    x_description   OUT      st_cars_for_sale.auto_description%TYPE,
    x_image         OUT      st_cars_for_sale.sale_photo_location%TYPE,
    x_amount        OUT      VARCHAR2
)
IS
    TYPE cartyp IS REF CURSOR;

    car_cur         cartyp;
    l_description   st_cars_for_sale.auto_description%TYPE;
    l_image         st_cars_for_sale.sale_photo_location%TYPE;
    l_id            st_cars_for_sale.inv_id%TYPE                := px_id;
    l_amount        VARCHAR2 (15);
BEGIN
    IF l_id < 1
    THEN
        l_id := 1;
    END IF; — l_id < 1

    OPEN car_cur FOR     'SELECT NVL(auto_description,''NO CARS FOUND'')'
        || ', NVL(sale_photo_location,''/no_photo_available.gif'')'
        || ', NVL(TO_CHAR(sale_amt,''$999,990.00''),''Name Your Price!'')'
        || ', inv_id'
```

```
                    || ' FROM st_cars_for_sale WHERE inv_id>=:id ORDER BY inv_id'
                USING l_id;
        FETCH car_cur INTO l_description, l_image, l_amount, l_id;


        IF car_cur%NOTFOUND
        THEN
            CLOSE car_cur;
            OPEN car_cur FOR    'SELECT NVL(auto_description,''NO CARS FOUND'')'
                || ', NVL(sale_photo_location,''/no_photo_available.gif'')'
                || ', NVL(TO_CHAR(sale_amt,''$999,990.00''),''Name Your Price!'')'
                || ', inv_id'
                || ' FROM st_cars_for_sale WHERE inv_id<=:id ORDER BY INV_ID DESC'
                USING l_id;
            FETCH car_cur INTO l_description, l_image, l_amount, l_id;

        END IF; — car_cur%NOTFOUND

        CLOSE car_cur;
        x_description := l_description;
        x_image := l_image;
        x_amount := l_amount;
        px_id := l_id;
    END get_car;
    /

    show errors

    CREATE OR REPLACE PROCEDURE make_offer_xml(
        p_id        IN      st_cars_for_sale.inv_id%TYPE,
        p_buyer     IN      st_cars_for_sale.buyer_name%TYPE,
        p_phone     IN      st_cars_for_sale.buyer_phone%TYPE,
        p_offer     IN      VARCHAR2
    ) IS
    l_success BOOLEAN;
    l_result VARCHAR2(500);
    BEGIN
        IF p_offer IS NOT NULL THEN
            make_offer
            (
                p_id        =>  p_id
            ,   p_buyer     =>  p_buyer
            ,   p_phone     =>  p_phone
            ,   p_offer     =>  p_offer
            ,   x_success   =>  l_success
            ,   x_result    =>  l_result
            );
            htp.p('<OFFER>'||l_result||'</OFFER>');
```

```
    ELSE
        htp.p('<OFFER/>');
    END IF; — p_offer IS NOT NULL
END make_offer_xml;
/



CREATE OR REPLACE PROCEDURE make_offer (
   p_id        IN       st_cars_for_sale.inv_id%TYPE,
   p_buyer     IN       st_cars_for_sale.buyer_name%TYPE,
   p_phone     IN       st_cars_for_sale.buyer_phone%TYPE,
   p_offer     IN       VARCHAR2,
   x_success   OUT      BOOLEAN,
   x_result    OUT      VARCHAR2
)
IS
   l_success   BOOLEAN          := TRUE;
   l_result    VARCHAR2 (500);
   l_offer     NUMBER;
BEGIN
   IF p_id IS NULL
   THEN
       l_success := FALSE;
       l_result := 'Missing Inventory ID';
   END IF; — p_id IS NULL

   IF l_success
   THEN
       IF (p_buyer IS NULL)
       THEN
           l_success := FALSE;
           l_result := 'Missing Buyer Name';
       END IF; — p_buyer IS NULL
   END IF; — l_success

   IF l_success
   THEN
       IF (p_phone IS NULL)
       THEN
           l_success := FALSE;
           l_result := 'Missing Phone Number';
       END IF; — p_phone IS NULL
   END IF; — l_success

   IF l_success
   THEN
       IF (p_offer IS NULL)
       THEN
```

```
                    l_success := FALSE;
                    l_result := 'Missing Offer Amount';
              END IF;  — p_offer IS NULL
       END IF;  — l_success


       IF l_success
       THEN
              BEGIN
                    l_offer := TO_NUMBER (p_offer);
              EXCEPTION
                    WHEN OTHERS
                    THEN
                          l_success := FALSE;
                          l_result := 'Invalid Offer Amount';

              END;
       END IF;  — l_success


       IF l_success
       THEN
              IF (l_offer <= 0)
              THEN
                    l_success := FALSE;
                    l_result := 'Cannot have negative offers.';
              END IF;
       END IF;  — l_success


       IF l_success
       THEN
              UPDATE st_cars_for_sale
                    SET buyer_name = p_buyer,
                          buyer_phone = p_phone,
                          buyer_offer = l_offer,
                          buyer_date = SYSDATE
              WHERE inv_id = p_id;

              IF SQL%ROWCOUNT < 1
              THEN
                    l_success := FALSE;
                    l_result :=    'Could not find car id number '
                                || TO_CHAR (p_id);
              ELSE
                    l_success := TRUE;
                    l_result :=    TO_CHAR (l_offer, '999,990.00')
                                || ' offer tendered for '
                                || p_buyer;
              END IF;  — SQL%ROWCOUNT < 1
       END IF;  — l_success
```

```
   x_success := l_success;
   x_result := l_result;
END make_offer;
/

show errors




set serveroutput on size 999999
DECLARE
l_id NUMBER:=-2;
l_sale_photo_location st_cars_for_sale.sale_photo_location%TYPE;
l_auto_description st_cars_for_sale.auto_description%TYPE;
l_amount VARCHAR2(15);
BEGIN
get_car
(
    px_id          => l_id
,   x_description  => l_auto_description
,   x_image        => l_sale_photo_location
,   x_amount       => l_amount
);
dbms_output.put_line('desc='||l_auto_description);
dbms_output.put_line('img='||l_sale_photo_location);
dbms_output.put_line('amt='||l_amount);
dbms_output.put_line('id='||TO_CHAR(l_id));
END;
/
```

Chapter 11 Java Beans Programs

All these scripts and test data are available at www.quepublishing.com. Put
0789726718 in the search field.

```
package beans;
import java.sql.*;
import oracle.jdbc.driver.*;
import java.io.*;

public class CarConnection {

  public static Connection getConnection() throws Exception {
    String driverClass = "oracle.jdbc.driver.OracleDriver";
    String username = "scott";
    String password = "tiger";
```

```
      String dburl = "jdbc:oracle:thin:@localhost:1521:dto";
      Driver d = (Driver)Class.forName(driverClass).newInstance();
      return DriverManager.getConnection(dburl,username,password);
  }
}


package beans;
import java.sql.*;
import oracle.jdbc.driver.*;
import java.io.*;

public class CarGetCar extends Object {

  private int id = 0;
  private String description ="";
  private String image ="";
  private String amount ="";

  public void setId(int id) {
    this.id = id;
    getCar();
  }

  public int getId() {
    return id;
  }

  public String getDescription() {
    return description;
  }

  public String getImage() {
    return image;
  }

  public String getAmount() {
    return amount;
  }

  public void getCar() {
    try {
      Connection conn = CarConnection.getConnection();
      CallableStatement cs = conn.prepareCall("begin get_car(?,?,?,?); end;");
      cs.setInt(1,id);
      cs.registerOutParameter(1,Types.INTEGER);
      cs.registerOutParameter(2,Types.VARCHAR);
      cs.registerOutParameter(3,Types.VARCHAR);
```

```java
        cs.registerOutParameter(4,Types.VARCHAR);
        cs.execute();

        id = cs.getInt(1);
        description = cs.getString(2);
        image = cs.getString(3);
        amount = cs.getString(4);

        cs.close();
    } catch (SQLException e) {
      id = 0;
      description = "Error";
      image = "/Error.gif";
      amount = "Error";
    }
    catch (Exception e) {
      id = 0;
      description = "Error";
      image = "/Error.gif";
      amount = "Error";
    }

  }

}


package beans;
import java.sql.*;
import oracle.jdbc.driver.*;
import java.io.*;

public class MakeOffer extends Object {

  private int id = 0;
  private String buyer ="";
  private String phone ="";
  private String offer = null;
  private String result ="";

  public void setId(int id) {
    this.id = id;
  }

  public int getId() {
    return id;
  }
```

```java
public void setBuyer(String buyer) {
  this.buyer = buyer;
}

public String getBuyer() {
  return (buyer==null) ? "" : buyer;
}

public void setPhone(String phone) {
  this.phone = phone;
}

public String getPhone() {
  return (phone==null) ? "" : phone;
}

public void setOffer(String offer) {
  this.offer = offer;
}

public String getOffer() {
  return (offer==null) ? "" : offer;
}

public String getResult() {
  makeOffer();
  return result;
}

public void makeOffer() {
  if (offer != null) {
    try {
      Connection conn = CarConnection.getConnection();
      CallableStatement cs =
        conn.prepareCall("declare x boolean; begin make_offer(?,?,?,?,x,?);
end;");
      cs.setInt(1,id);
      cs.setString(2,buyer);
      cs.setString(3,phone);
      cs.setString(4,offer);
      cs.registerOutParameter(5,Types.VARCHAR);
      cs.execute();

      result = cs.getString(5);
      cs.close();
    } catch (SQLException e) {
      result = "Error: "+e;
```

```
            }
        catch (Exception e) {
          result = "Error: "+e;
        }
      }
    }

    }
```

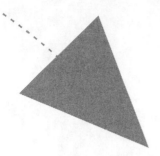

Appendix C

Software Web Sites

This appendix directs you to the Web sites where the book examples can be found as well as the software used throughout the book.

All book examples: www.quepublishing.com

Oracle software: http://otn.oracle.com

Quest software: www.quest.com

TOAD software: www.toadsoft.com or www.Quest.com

A 30-day trial license key will be forwarded to your e-mail address when you download the Quest Software Inc. products.

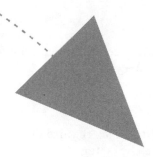

Glossary

boolean variable—A single computer bit that holds a true or false condition. Booleans are useful for holding the success or failure of a procedure, IF statement, and so on.

clusters—A way of physically organizing two or more tables together that have common key fields and are commonly referenced together in the same SQL statement.

COBOL—Short for COmmon Business Oriented Language. Popular for years in the mainframe-computing environment, this programming language handles the transfer of information between terminals and data storage, creates reports from data storage, and manipulates data in the data storage.

compiler—A name for the interpreter that converts the program source code into something else, either p-code or machine language.

composite key—One or more columns, placed at the beginning of the table, in the order of importance, and the group becomes the key value.

Concatenation—When two or more columns are merged together, many times merged with some text items, to form a single column of output.

constraints—Rules that are applied to the data in tables to ensure the accuracy of the data, the accuracy of the data in relation to other tables, and so on. An in-line constraint is one that is defined where the field that it applies to is defined. An out-of-line constraint is one that is added with separate syntax at a later time.

crow's foot—Depicts that there is a many relationship between the object that this is pointing to and the object at the other end.

cursors—Oracle's way of processing SQL statements and storing the records returned from a query, allowing for the PL/SQL block to easily handle individual rows from a query that returns multiple rows. A cursor is a work area in memory for PL/SQL.

data entry operator—Anyone who is working with the application and entering data into it. This data entry is usually done via a screen-based form. The term comes from the days of punched cards when these folks were known as key punch operators.

data warehouse—A large volume of rather undefined data, available for the end-user to query and process with various query tools.

database object—In Oracle9i terms, is something that exists within the database that users interact with.

double-byte characters—Chinese/Japanese languages require double-byte or two bytes of storage to represent a single character.

DUAL table—Contains one column and one row and is useful when wanting to run a function once. Because the dual table only has one row, whatever function is run in the SELECT statement will run once.

entity—In relational terms, is another name for tables or for fields or columns in a table.

extent—A database block or series of contiguous database blocks assigned to the table or index to store rows in.

Gigabyte—A trillion bytes. A byte is a single unit of storage that can represent, for example, a character.

indexes—Allow for quick access to data within tables. Index-organized tables are both a table and an index combined.

object-oriented databases—Can store the data, information about the data, and methods for accessing the data. Oracle has implemented most of the object-oriented features in Oracle9i.

parent table or parent row—Refers to the primary key table or row of data in the primary key table. The child row or children records refers to the foreign key table and foreign key data.

partitions—Allow data-oriented objects to be split across tablespaces.

PL/SQL (pronounced 'P – L – S – Q – L')—A procedural language with SQL imbedded in it. This gives the user the ability to perform various tasks based on row-at-a-time or result set processing of the SQL. PL/SQL is useful for performing looping functions and in-depth calculations based on a variety of variables and other tables.

pseudo column—A table column that is not explicitly defined; that is, one comes with each table such as the ROWID column.

qualification in relational terms—Stating a table's full name including the owner when the same table name might occur in more than one schema. The emp table's fully qualified name is: scott.emp.

RDBMS—Stands for Relational Database Management System.

Referential Integrity—SQL code that enforces the relationship between two or more tables, based on primary and foreign keys.

reverse-key indexes—Used to return individual rows and are not well suited for range searches, where the keys may be spread out across many index leaves.

ROWID—A pseudo column that is really an exact physical location of that particular row.

ROWNUM—A pseudo column associated with the order in which the result set of a query is returned.

schema—A term used to describe all database objects created by a particular user. Oracle9i creates a schema automatically when creating a user.

sequences—A convenient method of generating sequential numbers. These numbers can be used to ensure uniqueness of rows, or any time an application needs some kind of sequential number.

server-side code—Any code that runs where the Oracle9i RDBMS is installed. The database engine actually executes the code and returns just the results such as a few columns or maybe just the output of a calculation.

storage clause—Tells Oracle9i how big to make the extents (how many Oracle data blocks to reserve at a time for data storage), how full to fill the blocks, and so on. The storage clause gives you incredible flexibility in the various data storage requirements for various tables and indexes.

synonyms—Provide an easy way to give a table a different or easier name. Synonyms can hide qualification and database links from end users.

SYSDATE—An Oracle value that always contains the current computer system date and time.

tables—Relational data storage unit in Oracle9i.

tablespaces—A logical name for the physical operating-system files assigned to Oracle9i.

Terabyte—A trillion bytes of information.

user-defined data types—Definable column attributes, other than the ones that Oracle9i supplies (number, date, character, and so on.). These definable data types are convenient for recurring columns such as a series of address fields. They are part of Oracle9i's object-oriented features.

views—Logical table in that they act like tables but are really a SQL query themselves. Views are useful in a number of ways from security (hiding columns/data from certain types of users) to hiding complex SQL access methods from users. A view is accessed with SQL as if it were just a single table.

WYSIWYG—Stands for What You See Is What You Get.

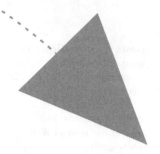

Index